Islamic Development Policy

Islamic Development Policy

The Agrarian Question in Iran

Asghar Schirazi

translated by
P. J. Ziess-Lawrence

Lynne Rienner Publishers ■ Boulder & London

Publication supported by the Volkswagen Foundation

Published in the United States of America in 1993 by
Lynne Rienner Publishers, Inc.
1800 30th Street, Boulder, Colorado 80301

and in the United Kingdom by
Lynne Rienner Publishers, Inc.
3 Henrietta Street, Covent Garden, London WC2E 8LU

© 1993 by Lynne Rienner Publishers, Inc. All rights reserved

Library of Congress Cataloging-in-Publication Data
Schirazi, Asghar, 1937-
　Islamic development policy : the agrarian question in Iran / by Asghar Schirazi; translated by P. J. Ziess-Lawrence.
　　p. cm.
　Includes bibliographical references and index.
　ISBN 1-55587-426-6 (alk. paper)
　1. Agriculture and state—Iran. 2. Agriculture—Economic aspects—Iran. 3. Land reform—Iran. 4. Agricultural laws and legislation (Islamic law). I. Title.
HD2065.2.Z8S35   1993
338.1'855—dc20　　　　　　　　　　　　　　　　　　　92-42208
　　　　　　　　　　　　　　　　　　　　　　　　　　　　CIP

British Cataloguing in Publication Data
A Cataloguing in Publication record for this book
is available from the British Library.

Printed and bound in the United States of America

The paper used in this publication meets the requirements
of the American National Standard for Permanence of
Paper for Printed Library Materials Z39.48-1984.

To Ramin

Contents

List of Tables	viii
Editor's Note	ix
Chronologies	x

Introduction   1

Part I The Agrarian Question Prior to the 1979 Revolution

1 The Agricultural Dilemma   7

2 Theories of Agriculture and Agrarian Policy in the Prerevolutionary Era   31

Part II Agricultural Policy in the Islamic Republic of Iran

3 The Development Dilemma in Iran   73

4 The Objectives of Agricultural Policy   87

5 The Position of Agriculture in Economic and Social Policy   95

6 Planning Agriculture   103

7 Reforming Agricultural Administration   135

8 The Reform of Land Tenure   169

9 The Debate About Land Reform in Islamic Law   201

10 Problems of Agricultural Management   233

11 The Question of Participation   261

12 Financial and Technical Measures to Maximize Production   275

13 The Urban-Rural Divide and Rural Depopulation   303

Conclusions   315

Bibliography	325
Index	337
About the Book and Author	348

Tables

1.1	Agricultural Holdings by Size, 1960 and 1974	12
1.2	Agricultural Holdings by Ownership and Labor Used, 1974	13
3.1	Social Infrastructure of Selected Provinces, 1975	76
3.2	Iranian Oil Exports and Revenues, 1976–1988	77
6.1	Projected and Actual Funding to Complete Projects	121
6.2	Deadlines for Implementation, DPA and SP	124
8.1	Land Transfers by Sevener Commissions, to 1984	184
8.2	Land Transfers by Sevener Commissions, to 1990	194
10.1	Structure of Holdings Before and After the Revolution	253
12.1	Government Fixed Investment by Economic Sectors	276
12.2	Gross Domestic Capital Formation	278
12.3	Bank of Agriculture Loans to Peasants and Farmers	279
12.4	Arable Land Area	281
12.5	Groundwater Used	283
12.6	Yield for Selected Agricultural Products	285
12.7	Sales of Tractors and Other Inputs	287
12.8	Government Investment in Agricultural Research	288
12.9	Wheat Price	290
12.10	Crop Production	294
12.11	Per Capita Crop Production	297
12.12	Food Imports	298
13.1	Net Value Added by Sector	307
13.2	Rural and Urban Income and Consumer Expenditure	308
13.3	Government Expenditure on Improvement	309

Note to the Reader

We hope that the following information and short chronologies will be helpful for the reader.

As of mid-1993, in the Islamic Republic there are ministries of Agriculture and Rural Questions, Heavy Industry, Interior, Water and Energy, Science and Higher Education, Justice, Transport, Jahad-e Sazandegi (after 1983), and Planning and Budget, among others. The Council of Ministers, comprising the heads of all the ministries, operates like a cabinet. The Council of Guardians is the keeper of Islamic law, reviewing legislation to see that it conforms to religious law; this council can declare laws "unconstitutional," rather like a religious version of the U.S. Supreme Court. The Revolutionary Council was the forerunner of parliament from 1979–May 1980.

In the text, the following abbreviations are used:

AB	Agribusiness
CL	Compendium of Laws
DP	1983 Development Plan
DPA	1983 Development Plan, Agriculture Section
FC	Farm Corporation
IP	Izadi's Draft Program
PP	Parliamentary Protocol
RC	Rural Cooperative
RPC	Rural Producer Cooperative
RS	Report of the Organization of Planning and Budget to the September 1979 Seminar
SP	Self-sufficiency Plan

Chronologies

Short History of the Islamic Republic

February 1979	Shah overthrown; Bazargan government takes power; legislative body is called the Revolutionary Council; Dr. Izadi is the minister of agriculture
November 1979	Bazargan government falls; extremist Islamists take over
May 1980	First meeting of parliament (replaces Revolutionary Council as legislative body)
September 1980	Iran-Iraq war begins; Salamati becomes minister of agriculture
November 1983	Organization for Jahad-e Sazandegi becomes Ministry of Jahad-e Sazandegi; Dr. Zali takes over as minister of agriculture
August 1988	UN Resolution 598 accepted, ending Iran-Iraq war
September 1988	Zali out as agriculture minister; Kalantari in
June 1989	Khomeini dies; Khamene'i becomes leader
July 1989	Rafsanjani becomes president
August 1989	Islamic Republic constitution revised
January 1990	First five-year plan approved

Short History of Land Reform in the Islamic Republic

September 17, 1979	Bazargan/Izadi land reform bill approved by Revolutionary Council
February 27, 1980	Esfahani's radical land reform bill approved by Revolutionary Council
March 19, 1980	Esfahani bill amended
April 15, 1980	Esfahani bill approved
October 1980	Implementation of Esfahani's bill stopped
December 1982	New land reform bill passes parliament
January 18, 1983	Council of Guardians rejects December 1982 bill
May 1985	Revised land reform passes in parliament
June 1985	Council of Guardians rejects May 1985 bill

October 30, 1986	Bill legalizing squats passes, is approved by Council of Guardians
August 1988	Determination Council issues decree placing uncultivated land under state administration

Short History of Development Planning in the Islamic Republic

August 1983	First development plan submitted, rejected by committee
January 1986	Development plan resubmitted; approved by parliament on first reading; plan indefinitely shelved
October 11, 1988	New development plan sent to parliament
October 9, 1989	Council of Ministers approves the completed plan
December 10, 1989	Parliament debates plan
January 31, 1990	First five-year plan passes in parliament

Short History of Agricultural Planning in the Islamic Republic

May 1979	Agriculture Minister Izadi drafts agricultural plan (12 points)
September 1980	Agriculture Minister Salamati drafts agricultural plan (14 points; later amended to 19 points)
December 1982	Agriculture plan from Ministry of Agriculture
December 1985	Bill on self-sufficiency in strategic agricultural products introduced in parliament
April 1986	Self-sufficiency bill approved in parliament
May 1987	Self-suffiency plan completed
June 1987	Self-suffiency plan goes to Council of Ministers, drops out of sight, and is forgotten

Introduction

Using the example of agricultural policy in the Islamic Republic of Iran, this book assesses the complications and consequences arising from the Islamization of development policy in the country, which has been ruled by Islamists since February 1979. These complications and consequences are examined both in terms of developmental and agricultural policy and for their impact on Islamism and its changing relationship to Islam.

The analytical point of departure for this assessment is the Iranian Islamists' claim that their interpretations of Islam provide the best possible solutions for all development questions, not only in Iran and the other Islamic countries but throughout the world. The claim is that Islam represents a superior alternative to all other development strategies or social systems in Iran and elsewhere. On the basis of this claim, the Islamists criticized the prerevolutionary regime, including its development policy, and justified the establishment of the Islamic Republic.

The Islamist Republic has now been in existence in Iran for more than thirteen years. The scientific world can examine how Islamists in power have tackled development, the problems that have arisen, the effectiveness of Islamist solutions, and the country's state of development after having been subjected to the Islamist experiment for so long.

A sound scientific answer to these questions can only be given through analysis of the processes in the individual spheres of development policy and the state leadership. This is the task I have set myself, and I shall attempt to answer these questions by investigating agricultural policy in the Islamic Republic.

Agricultural policy is particularly well suited to this inquiry for a number of reasons. Agriculture is still an important factor in Iran's economy and society and thus is the principal element in the state leadership's wider Islamist development alternative. It provides an opportunity to ask questions whose relevance goes beyond agricultural policy. And because Islamic law (with whose help the legalist Islamists in particular hope to resolve development questions) evolved in an agrarian society, it deals at considerable length with agriculture and related matters. This sector, then, provides us with an opportunity to assess whether and how traditional Islamic regulations can be effective in development policy today.

As there are a number of Islamist factions, this work deals with Islamist agricultural policy in all its diversity, but only for the periods in which the various factions were coresponsible for determining policy. Since the fall of the Bazargan government in November 1979, only the legalist faction has made decisions at the state level, and so this work deals largely with their policies.

Part 1 of this book, comprising Chapters 1 and 2, provides a description of the state of Iranian agriculture on the eve of the revolution. The legacy of the shah's regime and of its agricultural policy have significantly influenced policy in the postrevolutionary era. The state of the agrarian economy and the thinking of various scientific and political groups constitute the essence of the agrarian question. This section thus includes not only the objective facts but also subjective reactions to them. The examination of the thinking on Iranian agricultural problems aims to assess the various groups' degrees of awareness and focuses on the Islamists; descriptions of the thinking of other groups are included primarily for comparison with that of the Islamists. The discussion includes both knowledge about agricultural problems and concepts for how to overcome them. These expositions permit conclusions to be drawn about how prepared the Islamists were to solve the problems they were confronted with after they came to power.

Part 2 begins with a brief survey of the economic, social, and political legacies of the shah's reign. This chapter acquaints the reader with the frame in which the Islamists had to implement their agricultural policy and the factors that made solving the agrarian problems more difficult. These factors include fluctuating revenues from oil exports, the war with Iraq, and the leadership of the Islamist state in general. In this connection special attention is given to the Islamist state's war policy.

The other chapters in Part 2 deal with various aspects of the Islamic Republic's agricultural policy, with particular emphasis on the issues that appeared to be substantial before the revolution. The relative importance of the individual aspects is reflected in the amount of space allocated to them, as determined by their significance in terms of the aims of this study and by the attention given to them in the Islamic Republic.

The work concludes with a fairly detailed summary of the results of the study conducted along the line of questioning outlined above. The conclusions drawn however, are based not only on the results of this study but also on systematic observation of the processes at other levels of state leadership in the Islamic Republic.

Much of this work is devoted to legislation pertaining to agricultural policy. This subject clearly illustrates the dilemma of a state ruled by legalistic Islamists who base their claim to welayat-e faqih (absolute power for Islamic jurists such as themselves) on their knowledge of Islamic law, which in their opinion provides unlimited potential for solving all the problems of the individual and society. The basis of their legitimacy is shaken to the core if they encounter obstacles they cannot overcome solely by virtue of their understanding of Islamic law. Agricultural legislation is a prime example.

This work is thus largely based on primary sources: parliamentary protocols, statute books, statements by the Council of Guardians, fatwas (legal opinions), court verdicts, the constitution of the Islamic Republic, and so on. In addition, the literature dealing with an "Islamic economy" reflects Islamist thinking on questions related to agricultural policy. The law books, which are still written and published in the traditional form, deserve to be mentioned here. Other sources are studies and fieldwork on specific agricultural questions done by scientists or experts. Most of them have been mimeographed by ministries, other state agencies, or universities and, like the statistical material, can be obtained only with difficulty. Specialist journals are a further source, as are both the daily newspapers and the organs of various political parties. Secondary literature is largely restricted to the description of the state of agriculture prior to the revolution, with a conscious emphasis on material published by Iranian authors. Scientific studies of postrevolutionary agrarian policy are still rare, and so this work is also based on information from semistructured interviews with politicians, scientists, experts, and state functionaries.

This study deals with agriculture in the narrow sense—i.e., arable farming. A study of agriculture in general (i.e., including forestry, fishery, animal husbandry, etc.) would not be all that much more productive in terms of the line of questioning and would exceed the scope of a single study. Arable farming is the predominant element in Iranian agriculture.

The book covers the period up to the Islamic Republic's adoption of its first development plan at the beginning of 1990. It contains not only a great deal of information about this particular plan but also about the Rafsanjani government's overall agricultural policy, whether connected with this development plan or not.

Quantitative evaluation of the results of agricultural policy in the Islamic Republic is hampered by inaccuracies in the statistical data and the unreliability of other official figures so familiar to experts in this field. I have nonetheless attempted to deduce a reasonably presentable overview from the confusion of contradictory data, though not always with any great success.

The present work is a followup of two other studies, the results of which were published as a smaller study on "The Problem of the Land Reform in the Islamic Republic of Iran" (Schirazi 1987) and as a more substantial work annotated by the author, "Texts on the Agrarian Legislation in the Islamic Republic of Iran" (in German: Schirazi 1988). It will in turn be followed by a study of the constitution of the Islamic Republic that will investigate its problematic evolution as the—supposedly—Islamic path to development. The present study and the three mentioned above are part of the project group "Religion, State and Cultural Integration in the Development Process" within the interdisciplinary research program "Ethnicity and Society: the Problems of Ethnic Boundaries in Societies of the Near and Middle East" at the Free University of Berlin.

Funding by the Volkswagen Foundation made it possible to carry out this work, which I gratefully acknowledge. Professors Friedemann Büttner and Baber Johansen contributed to my work by agreeing to supervise and by making valuable suggestions, for which I express my sincere thanks. I also wish to thank the Department of Political Science at the Free University of Berlin, in particular the Center for Middle East Studies, which provided not only the institutional framework that enabled me to do this work but also the fellowship of the staff and my colleagues. I also wish to thank all those who helped me with interviews, information, and assessments, or by procuring material in Iran, as well as those outside Iran who provided me with source material or gave interviews. I am grateful to the first president of the Islamic Republic, Abolhasan Bani Sadr; its first minister of agriculture, Ali Mohammad Izadi; my fellow sociologists Siawash Amini, Ahmad Ashraf, Hushang Keshawarz, and Hosein Malek; the Islamologist Professor Jawad Falatury; and the geographer Professor Eckart Ehlers. And last but not least, I am grateful to Fritz Rosskopf for his extremely careful edit of the text and the numerous constructive suggestions he made for improving it, to Guenter Lobmeyer for helping me solve many of the problems that turned up during the completion of this work, and to Philip John Ziess-Lawrence for his translation of it.

Part I
The Agrarian Question Prior to the 1979 Revolution

1
The Agricultural Dilemma

In the period immediately prior to the revolution, Iranian agriculture was in a deep crisis caused by the shah's failure to reform the country's traditional agriculture in a comprehensive but circumspect manner. Such reform was necessary for Iranian agriculture to fully develop its potential and satisfy the growing and changing demand for produce. At the least, agriculture's relationship with other sectors of the economy should have been redefined in such a way as to make the overall situation acceptable. The crisis primarily manifested itself in the following ways.

1.1 Inadequate Production

Long before the revolution, Iranian agriculture was unable to meet domestic demand, above all for staple foods, which increasingly had to be imported. Imports of cereals (wheat, barley, rice, and maize) rose from 956,000 to 2,176,000 tons (t) between 1973/4 and 1978/9[1] and grew by 257 percent for sugar, 420 percent for meat, and 70 percent for animal and vegetable oils and fats.[2] More and more of the dollars Iran earned by exporting oil, amounting to $6.6 billion (bn) during the fifth five-year plan (1973/4–1977/8),[3] thus had to be spent on food imports. The increase in food imports was in stark contrast to the past—not only was Iran self-sufficient in the 1950s, it actually exported large quantities of animal products and cereals.[4] The increase in imports was a consequence of rising demand, which in turn was caused by the growth in population from 25.7 to 33.7 million (m) between 1966 and 1976. Other reasons for increased demand were industrialization, which had proceeded apace in the 1970s, and the growth in purchasing power resulting from the general economic boom at that time. Furthermore, the abolition of the tithe in the wake of the land reform enabled peasants to put aside a larger part of the harvest for their own needs, reducing market supplies.[5]

The growth of imports coincided with increases in domestic output. Total agricultural production increased from 7.3m tons to 19m tons between 1960/1 and 1975/6, and arable land grew by some 5m hectares (ha) over the same period. The growth rates for various products differed widely: Whereas cereal production rose by 140 percent, industrial and feed crops rose by 480 percent and 580 percent, respectively, over the same period in conjunction with changes in the use of arable land for the latter crops.[6] Overall production rose 2.6 percent, 4 percent, and 4.6 percent per annum during implementation of the third (which in fact became a five and one-half year plan), fourth, and fifth development plans (1962/3–1977/8).[7] However, these growth rates always lagged behind the goals set by the government as necessary to meet demand. The target for the third development plan was an annual growth rate of 4 percent, and the fourth and fifth plans aimed to achieve 5 percent and 7 percent, respectively.[8] The degree of failure to achieve the targets and thus to reduce import requirements varied from product to product.

There were many reasons for the inadequate growth in production. Generally speaking, they were to be found in the regime's approach to the country's economic, social, and political questions and in the development strategy it pursued. The state was primarily concerned with maintaining and expanding its authoritarian and centralistic power. As such it failed to take full advantage of productive human resources, which can only be mobilized through participation. Its development strategy was modernistic—i.e., it disregarded traditional values unless they served the regime or were part of it. It was also urban oriented and placed great store on prestige, splendor, and displays of power. Thus, it mainly promoted those areas of the economy the shah thought would best demonstrate the progress achieved. Agriculture was apparently not one of them. Oil revenue made the regime largely independent of income from the other sectors of the economy, which could be ignored, particularly if the regime considered them not to be modern. As the shah's regime was largely based on coercion, it seldom concerned itself with social stability or worried about the interests of the poorer classes, foremost among them the rural population.

In short, the inadequate development of agrarian production resulted from the shah's agricultural policy as conceived and implemented since the 1970s. This policy can best be described as neglect.

1.2 The Neglect of Agriculture

The data on government funding of this sector make the state's relative neglect of agriculture clear. Although it still amounted to 28 percent and 30 percent of the total during the first and second five-year plans, the figures dropped to 20 percent and 7.5 percent, respectively, in the fourth and fifth five-year plans—and this despite the fact that the rural population represented 52.2 percent of the total and 32.1 percent of the working-age population in 1976. In addition, 38 percent of the government investment in the sector in the last three development plans was allocated to projects that had little to do with agriculture—for instance, the construction of dams to provide the towns with drinking water and electricity. Insofar as they were used for agricultural purposes, they benefited large agribusiness organizations whose establishment had to prove a failure, as will be shown below.[9]

In practice, the funds and technology intended to step up production were used inappropriately and inconsistently. A large part of the money was used to make interest-free loans to agrarian enterprises, mainly the unsuccessful and ineffective Agribusinesses (ABs). Only 10 to 15 percent was granted to peasants during the fifth development plan, even though they were tilling 90 percent of the arable land.[10] Whereas the ABs were overcapitalized (as Mehner wrote) thanks to loans, grants, subsidies, and other benefits, the peasants used the loans granted them primarily to bring their standard of living somewhat closer to the subsistence level.[11] A further large part of the state's investment was spent on the agricultural administration, which was concentrated in the capital.[12]

The investments that were supposed to provide water for agrarian purposes were largely misdirected and characterized by (1) neglect of the traditional irrigation systems, in particular the qanat (subterranean canals), even though in the opinion of many experts it would have been cheaper and more effective to maintain and expand them;[13] (2) a preference for drilling new wells equipped with motor pumps, even though this practice often caused existing qanats to dry up; and (3) construction of dams that were badly sited, poorly built, and not operational prior to the revolution.[14] Therefore, investments in the water economy did not appreciably expand the area of artificially irrigated arable land and thus did little to improve the yield.[15] While arable land expanded from 11.1m hectares in 1960 to 15.4m hectares in 1977, artificially irrigated land increased by a mere 1.0m hectares. The expansion was thus largely achieved by exploiting naturally irrigated (i.e., not artificially irrigated—also called dry) land—mainly by turning woodland and pasture into farmland—and led the share of less fertile, dry arable land to increase from 59 percent to 64 percent.[16]

Investing in the mechanization of agriculture did not produce the expected results. Iran remained far behind its neighbor Turkey in terms of quantity of equipment,[17] despite a greater use of modern, mechanized equipment.[18] The resultant demand for agricultural products was not as decisive as the desire of the regime to portray itself as modern and progressive. The manufacturers' and dealers' economic interests were significant, but they were not based on developments in the labor market and were not an integral part of a well-conceived development strategy. The regime did not plan for how the national economy was to replace traditional production techniques by modern ones in an organic and harmonious manner. So mechanization followed the same rules as the rest of the regime's modernization policy: Traditional structures, capabilities, and techniques were ignored, with no thought being given to the possibility of improving them by using appropriate technology. Modernization was to be achieved by copying the foreign example, with technocrats from home and abroad brought in to impose it. Machinery was imported assembled without the soil being taken into consideration, maintenance was routinely neglected, and there was hardly any training for the operators.[19] As a consequence, mechanization did not contribute to increasing the yield. This failure is particularly true of cereals, which accounted for 80 percent of arable land: At 810 kilograms per hectare (kg/ha), the yield for wheat in 1974 was only 10kg/ha more than in 1961, and at 670kg/ha it was actually 120kg/ha lower for barley.[20] The yield per hectare for cereals and many other agrarian products in Iran was far below the average in Asia and in the developing countries.[21]

The shah's regime denied the agrarian sector a reasonable pricing policy and helped keep prices low. The government bought the country's main product, wheat, at a fixed price that was below what it paid for imported wheat but was the same as the subsidized price at which it supplied the bakeries in the towns with flour—in effect, it subsidized urban consumers at the expense of the peasants.[22] The government took neither the production costs nor their development into account when fixing its price,[23] and resolutions to correct the practice, such as the one in the fifth development plan, were not implemented.[24]

1.3 The Problems of Land Reform

The agricultural dilemma was still apparent in spite of the land reforms the prerevolutionary regime carried out, mainly in the 1960s. It had officially been expected that the program would boost production by freeing Iranian agriculture from the fetters of the "feudal" land structure, ending the "medieval" relationships prevailing in the countryside to the benefit of the "great mass of needy" peasants[25] and facilitating reform of the antiquated agricultural management system. It was anticipated that this policy would help prevent social tension and anti-shah sentiment from building in rural areas. The regime hoped to create additional social support that could be activated if needed. In short, the government anticipated that land reform would make a decisive contribution toward overcoming the far-reaching crisis in which Iran found itself when it initiated the measure.[26]

The shah's land reform program mirrored the principal characteristics of his modernization policy. It failed to take sufficient account of the actual factors and specific structures of land tenure that were hindering development[27] and failed to recognize the potential for development in the traditional structure of the Iranian village, instead pursuing an extreme reform course that was inconsistent and contradictory.

Land reform was to have changed the structure of land tenure to benefit those peasants with usufructuary rights.[28] Between 1962 and 1974, the number of peasants who became landowners as a consequence of it was 1,766,625, with another 172,103 to whom foundation land was leased long-term (i.e., for ninety-nine years). Thus peasant landowners increased from one-third to two-thirds of the total, and their land leaped from one-third to three-fourths of the total arable land under cultivation at the beginning of the reform.[29] But despite its relatively wide scope, this redistribution of property proved unable to solve all the problems involved in the structure of land tenure for various reasons.

A large number of peasants received no land at all. They numbered some 1.1 to 1.7m in 1976, depending on whether the 550,000 who were employed without pay on family farms are included.[30] Most of them were former sharecroppers without usufructuary rights and were increasingly reduced to being agricultural laborers. Their number grew constantly, largely because of two factors: population growth and the slippage of peasants without much land into the landless group. The latter lived at the lowest level of poverty in the village, working the land for some wealthy peasant or modern farmer for money or a small part of the harvest. They did casual work in the urban centers, too, commuting between their villages and the towns until perhaps finally settling in a town. They formed the bulk of those who fled their villages and were the first victims of land reform, which was not carried out according to social and economic criteria.

Sharecroppers with usufructuary rights who became landowners as a result of the reform but whose plot of land was too small to ensure their livelihoods did not fare much better. Kazeruni puts the number of such peasant families at 1.6m. As they were unable to earn a living by farming, they were compelled to take paid work (sometimes in town), and increasingly the inadequacy of their plot forced them to give up their land—i.e., to sell it, lease it, or leave it fallow—as paid labor was more remunerative. Hence, land reform did not provide a solution to the economic and other problems of these peasants: They became landowners, only to lose their land not long afterwards.

Land reform was not even a success for those peasants whose land sufficed to provide a living, inasmuch as it had been intended that, in addition to satisfying their own needs, they were to help supply the market. These "medium peasants" were scarcely in a position to do so; they only put part of their produce on the market in order to repay some of their huge debts or to pay for the use of a tractor. This class worked almost exclusively in farming and seldom hired workers, as labor requirements could usually be met within the family. Rural sociologists consider peasants with 5 to 10ha of land as belonging to this class, which numbers some 400,000 families.[31]

The land reform clearly benefited the "wealthy peasants" and was beneficial with respect to production for the agromarket, too. But by favoring them, it widened the gap between the various peasant classes and created even more social tension in the countryside. These wealthy peasants owned farms of between 10ha and 50ha (up to 100ha according to Planck 1980 p. 163). But some of the holdings in this category belonged to owners who cannot be considered peasants in the traditional sense of the word. They were actually modern farmers. Much of the arable land belonged to them (see Table 1.1), and most of them had owned land even before the reform. Some were rural moneylenders and traders who had used their money to acquire land. As a rule these wealthy peasants lived on the land, managed their farms themselves, employed hired labor, and produced mostly for the market. They also had other rural sources of income (moneylending, commerce, transport, leasing of tractors and draught animals). The amount of arable land they owned shows how unequally the land was distributed among the peasants. It was no different when it came to enjoyment of the other privileges that are up for grabs in the countryside: All of the social and political positions in the villages were held by members of this class. The wealthy peasants benefited from the land reform in the expectation that they would then prop up the regime in the rural areas, but the shah received no help at all from them during the 1979 revolution.

Table 1.1 Agricultural Holdings by Size, 1960 and 1974

Size in Hectares	Number (in thousands)				Total Area (in thousands of hectares)				Average Area (in hectares)	
	1960	Percent	1974	Percent	1960	Percent	1974	Percent	1960	1974
<1	493	26.2	734	29.6	119	1.7	260	1.6	0.4	0.4
1–2	256	13.6	322	13.0	372	3.2	444	2.7	1.4	1.4
2–5	474	25.2	542	21.8	1,554	13.7	1,743	10.6	3.2	3.2
5–10	340	18.1	428	17.3	2,413	21.2	2,953	18.0	7.0	6.9
10–50	302	16.1	428	17.3	5,264	46.4	7,501	45.7	17.4	17.5
50–100	8	0.4	16	0.7	546	4.9	1,073	6.5	70.5	66.0
100+	4	0.1	10	0.4	991	8.7	2,454	14.9	247.7	256.8

Sources: Markaz-e Amar-e Iran 1974; Ketab-e Agah 1982, p. 180; and A. Malekaniyan 1986, p. 59.

Table 1.2 Agricultural Holdings by Ownership and Labor Used, 1974 (percentage of holdings)

Size in Hectares	Operator-owned	Family Farm	Family Work	Hired Labor
<1	91.3	74.4	20.8	4.7
1–2	90.6	61.1	34.6	4.3
2–5	91.4	61.2	34.1	4.7
5–10	93.3	55.0	40.8	4.2
10–50	92.3	44.2	48.5	7.3
50–100	87.7	17.9	45.4	36.7
100+	83.0	8.9	27.1	64.0

Sources: Markaz-e Amar-e Iran 1974; Ketab-e Agah 1982, p. 180.
Notes: Operator-owned: The farmer owns the farmland
Family Farm: Work is wholly done by family members
Family Work: Most of the work is done by family members
Hired Labor: Work is done mainly by hired labor

A considerable part of the arable land, some 2.7m hectares belonging to over 25,000 families, remained unaffected by this land reform.[32] They apparently managed to keep their land by mechanizing it[33] in accordance with the regulations. Much more than 2m hectares of this belonged to 9,553 families, mainly "absentees"—i.e., landowners who lived in town and had a steward manage the estate; 350 families with a total of 250,000ha topped this group,[34] which included the shah's family. More than any other indicator, the existence of this class of landowners made it evident that land reform had not been designed to achieve social equality, and the large number of economically unviable miniholdings made it equally apparent that it had not been shooting for any economic target at all.

Land reform did increase the number of peasant landowners, but without substantially altering the structure. The expansion of the area under cultivation by more than 4m hectares enabled the large and medium farms, which were the main beneficiaries, not only to maintain but even to increase their share.[35] The small peasants with usufructuary rights had to be satisfied with plots that, although becoming their property, were smaller than the ones their usufructuary rights had permitted them to till prior to the reform. The average size of plots of less than 2ha fell from 0.76ha in 1960 to 0.66ha in 1974.[36] The opening up of new land also worked to the disadvantage of the small peasants inasmuch as it occasionally affected the area around the villages. Land that had been common land used by all the villagers as pasture for their animals was converted into private miniplots.

This loss clearly had an adverse effect on animal husbandry.[37] Basically, the opening up of new land became a contest to occupy or appropriate existing land, a result of "the greed to acquire landed property" induced by the land reform[38]—and the small peasants were the losers. They took revenge at the outbreak of the revolution: Freed from the fetters of the previous rules, they fell upon the estates of the large and medium landowners and occupied them by the hundreds of thousands of hectares.

1.4 The Operational Organization of Agriculture

The structural problems of land ownership arising from the land reform program turned out to be the same as those of the management organization of agriculture. In part, the negative consequences of land reform only became properly visible as management problems.

Land reform smashed the traditional organizational structure of agrarian production in Iran without replacing it by a new and adequate one. The village system (*deh*), which regulated the relationship of the peasants to the land and the water as well as to one another as cooperating producers, within a tradition that was nonetheless capable of reform, was broken up into a loose arrangement of very small, isolated, and fragmented holdings, a system that had to prove unworkable without help. The regular, central distribution of land among the peasants with usufructuary rights, which ensured a certain equality, was replaced by the definitive division of the land into individual, unequal, and scattered plots devoid of any economic sense. The traditional producer community (*bone*) was replaced by the poor, individual peasant, who, though having become the owner of his land, was unable to profit from it by himself. The traditional credit system (*taqawi*) was replaced by a completely inadequate banking system, and local production management by the landlords and their stewards in conjunction with the village mayor and the heads of the producer cooperatives was replaced by an authoritarian, bureaucratic administration run by government employees.[39] In short, the abolition of possessorial relationships was accompanied by the destruction of the positive aspects of the traditional organization. This destruction could have been entirely avoided.[40]

The effect of land reform was to create a dualistic structure at the level of management organization. It was characterized on the one hand by a few enterprises with modern equipment and state subsidies and on the other by the mass of peasant holdings, which had been deprived of the traditional village system's protection. Among the peasant holdings, those with less than 5ha had the most problems—the median size was between 0.4ha and 3.2ha, of which a part had to lie fallow every year. The reform had increased the number of such holdings from 1.2m in 1960 to 1.6m in 1974, but the amount of land available had not increased to the same extent, so that in the end plots were generally smaller than before (see Table 1.1). The miniholdings were further hurt by the reform because the land was now more fragmented.[41] Although fragmentation had increased everywhere (apart from holdings of over 100ha), it caused the smallholders the most concern because it put operational expenses up, made irrigating, tending, and harvesting the crops more difficult, and severely limited the use of modern means of production.[42]

The shah's policy on smallholdings was very contradictory. The state proclaimed support for them by setting up a network of Rural Cooperatives (RCs) intended to compensate for the loss of the village system and its protective functions,[43] but it provided the RCs with so few resources that they were barely able to fulfill their given task. The regime basically abandoned the smallholdings to a "natural" process of dissolution in accordance with its policy of decimating the rural population. Its policy of integration—aimed at merging the countryside into Farm Corporations (FCs), Rural Producer Cooperatives (RPCs), Agribusinesses (ABs), and Rural Poles—pursued the same goals of smallholding dissolution and population decimation, though the regime did not stick to this policy consistently.

Prior to the revolution there were 2,942 RCs amalgamated into 153 associations with a total of 3,014,000 members. Membership was obligatory for peasants with usufructuary rights who became landowners. According to the statutes, RCs were to provide their members with all the resources they needed to manage their enterprises successfully and with the necessities of everyday life, as well as collect farm products and organize their sale. Such a project required sums of money that could in no way be raised by the members and were not provided by the government: Although it had promised to loan each RC ten times more than the amount its members contributed to the formation of its capital, it did not keep its promise, not even during the oil boom.[44] Government loans to the Rural Cooperatives amounted to 109bn rials from 1968 to 1975, or 7,810 rials/ha and 939 rials/ha per year. In comparison, the Farm Corporations, which the government actually promoted, received 122,383 rials/ha and 15,298 rials/ha per year—80 percent of which was in the form of grants.[45] Their capital, 5,050 rials/ha in 1977, was 4,471 rials higher than that of the RCs, even though the FCs only had 33,663 members and 318,734ha, of which a mere 130,337ha were under cultivation.[46]

The lack of funding for RCs was instrumental in preventing them from fulfilling their statutory tasks. Their activities were perforce reduced to granting loans to their members, and the amounts were very low and on such poor terms that they could do little to facilitate the debtors' productive activity. For example, the average loan between 1962/3 and 1973/4 was 6,000 rials. The amount was increased in later years, but not to the same extent as production costs.[47]

More than 90 percent of the loans provided by the RCs were seasonal, i.e., for six to twelve months. Long-term loans accounted for less than 1 percent.[48] Interest on the short-term loans was between 5 and 6 percent; unlike the FCs, the RCs received no grants. The peasants had to assume joint responsibility for repaying loans arranged by the RCs, meaning that no new loans were made until all of them had settled their debts.[49] Another problem with these loans was that they were usually delayed until after the start of the season. Because of the poverty of the borrowers, the money was usually spent on basic consumption.[50]

In the 1960s and 1970s, the loans arranged by the RCs accounted for only 30 percent of the total borrowed by peasants;[51] they had to procure the rest on the private money market, where interest rates were 60 percent and more.[52] In the final analysis, land reform increased the peasants' need for this market. The setting up of the RCs had a similar effect, because the peasants had to borrow from the private moneylenders in order to be able to repay their debts to the RCs on time.[53]

The RCs also were unable to fulfill their other tasks. Their role as the suppliers of working capital and consumer goods for their members could be considered relatively insignificant, and they were equally unsuccessful as marketing agents: The prices they charged for their members' products were too low and were set by the government.[54] The RCs also became involved in activities that had nothing to do with supporting their members, from recruiting conscripts to gathering data on the rural population. Despite being called cooperatives, they were rather more like government agencies with their headquarters in the capital, coming under the Ministry of Cooperatives and Rural Questions. The Central Organization of Rural Cooperatives, a subsidiary organization of that ministry, determined every little detail of the activities of the cooperative associations and the individual co-ops. According to Hooglund, "rather than helping the peasants in concrete ways, the cooperatives rapidly developed into the principal agencies through which the central government exercised its expanding control over villages after 1962. The way in which the societies were set up, the manner in which they were managed, and the type of activities in which they were permitted to engage were all strictly supervised by the bureaucracy."[55]

The peasants were themselves dissatisfied with the RCs, seeing them for what they really were—government organizations. They wanted to have nothing to do with the RCs unless it was to their advantage. The RCs were foreign bodies in the life of the village that had to be put up with.

The government's neglect of the peasants' holdings was not based on rational economic considerations. Neither was the government able to transform the peasants' smallholdings into efficient corporations or cooperatives on a large scale, nor could much transformation be justified by any record of success on the part of the existing extensive farms; rather, it was rooted in ignorance about peasant farming and disdain for the peasantry.[56]

Comparative studies by various experts had shown both the adaptability of smallholdings to new production techniques and their superior economic performance relative to modern farms—units of under 10ha accounted for some 41 percent of the gross agricultural product in 1973 and 38 percent of the arable land, while the respective figures were 6 percent and 12 percent for units of over 100ha and 36 percent and 50 percent for units of 10–100ha.[57] Hoseini Kazeruni (1981) observed that for certain products (barley and wheat) farms with under 10ha did better than those with 10–50ha and that for rice the former were the most productive (pp. 30ff). Nuri Na'ini (1976) confirmed these findings in his own study, concluding that small and medium units were "sensible" in the prevailing social and technical conditions and that under certain circumstances and given an appropriate policy they would be able meet the demands made on them (pp. 3ff). In yet another study, the authors of a reader titled *Rural and Peasant Problems in Iran* came to the conclusion that "the bigger the enterprise, the smaller the yield."[58] Other experts confirmed these results.[59]

On the basis of these and other studies, there was a call—even under the shah—for the government to acknowledge the advantages of peasant farming, producer cooperatives, and the village system and to support them.[60] There was, however, no great enthusiasm for accepting or implementing such proposals, and after he had caused the dissolution of the traditional systems, the shah staked everything on establishing and supporting modern extensive enterprises, beginning with the fourth five-year plan (1968–73).

The first modern farms brought into being within the framework of this policy were the Farm Corporations (sherkat-e sahami-ye zera'i). According to paragraph 1 of the relevant law, passed in January 1968, they were to "increase the per capita income of the peasants, everywhere create favorable conditions for the mechanization of agriculture, make the peasants familiar with modern methods in agriculture, take full advantage of village labor in the agricultural and industrial spheres of the country, prevent the fragmentation of farmland into uneconomic plots, [and] develop arable land."[61] The law was enacted immediately, and 93 Farm Corporations encompassing 851 villages with 411,114ha of arable land and 35,097 shareholders came into being over the next decade.[62] The shareholders were mainly peasants who had become landowners through land reform and were now forced to exchange their property for shares, plus some well-to-do peasants and landless sharecroppers. A member's shares generally corresponded to the value of the farmland he brought into the corporation. The corporations were headed by a managing director appointed by the Ministry of Cooperatives and assisted by a technical staff, also appointed and paid by the government.

In addition to horticulture, the Farm Corporations engaged in animal husbandry and handicrafts, constructed housing, and provided other services for their members. They were intended to replace the village system and its social functions. The shareholders were entitled to sell their shares, something the government actually encouraged small farmers to do so that the remaining members would have larger blocks of shares (at least 20ha each).[63] The shareholders did the horticultural work either as paid laborers or sharecroppers, and the dividends also contributed to their income.

The government subsidized the FCs fairly heavily, paying the managerial and technical staff and allocating grants or making long-term, low-interest loans at 1 to 6 percent. In many cases the grants came to more than double either the initial capital or the net profits.[64] The government also supported the FCs by exempting them from taxes, making more than enough machinery and equipment available, assigning experts en masse, and providing installations.

Despite these subsidies, the shareholders, especially the smaller ones, were not satisfied with their corporations and longed for them to be liquidated for various reasons. The setting up of the corporations meant a social decline for them, from the landowner status they had so recently acquired to being landless and possessing shares, which had no place in their system of values. In addition, they had to hire themselves out to the corporations as agricultural laborers or sharecroppers, which they also saw as a social decline—having just risen above their status as "subjects of the landlords" (raʿaiyat-e arbab), they had now reverted to being "subjects of the state" or "the director's workers."[65] Neither the reasons for setting up the corporations nor the way they operated had been explained to the peasants, they had no access to management,[66] and because they considered the corporations state agencies they reacted with mistrust and rejection, withholding their cooperation, trying to work as little as possible and accusing the managers of embezzlement, favoritism, and so forth.[67]

With few exceptions, the Farm Corporations did not even provide economic benefits. Mechanization only increased underemployment: In Garmsar, for example, the shareholders only worked thirty-four days a year for the corporation.[68] The corporations were unable to counter this trend by creating new jobs in crafts or animal husbandry, so the shareholders' income from working for them was very low.[69] Even the dividends paid out were not enough to supplement the average shareholder's income by much, and sociologists observed that in most cases the corporation members' total annual income was lower than before the FCs were set up.[70]

The Farm Corporations also had very little success with raising production levels: They registered a slight increase up to 1975, followed by stagnation and in some cases even decline.[71] As there were huge variations in the number of shares held by members,[72] the advantages and disadvantages were not equally weighted among them. The principal shareholders not only were better off when it came to receiving dividends but also were privileged when it came to employment opportunities. This gap increased tension within the corporations and contributed to the great dissatisfaction of the vast majority of members, which accounts for the alacrity with which they got rid of them when the revolution began.

On the initiative of some technocrats, a new type of structure for organizing peasant farming on a large scale was created in 1972 parallel to the Farm Corporations. Known as Rural Producer Cooperatives (ta'awoni-ye toulidi-ye rusta'i), they were supposed to be organized as cooperatives, as the name implies, in order to revive the traditional collective cultivation of the land. The peasants' desire to retain their newly acquired property was to be taken into account: They kept their title deeds but placed their land at the disposal of the RPCs. Each year, management divided this consolidated estate among the members in proportion to the size of their holdings; the members of then organized themselves into groups of five to twenty, each group tilling the land allocated to it. Every group elected a leader (sargruh) to direct and represent it. The management passed the available loans on to the groups and provided them with machinery and services. A member's share of the harvest, which was brought in collectively, was calculated on the basis of the size of his holding, the amount of work he had done, and the quantity of other means of production he had provided. The cost of RPC services he had used was deducted. The government appointed and paid the managers and subsidized the RPCs with soft loans, grants, equity participation, and various infrastructural services; however, it interfered in management affairs to the same degree.

The same social tension prevailed here as in the Farm Corporations because of the unequal sizes of the members' plots on joining the RPCs.[73] The poor members had so little land that they often preferred to earn a living working outside the RPC, in which case their land was tilled by other members of the group, agricultural laborers, or sharecroppers. The peasants' dissatisfaction with the RPCs was neither as widespread nor as intense as with the FCs, which is why relatively few of them were disbanded after the revolution (see Chapter 10.3.3). Even as critical an expert as Malek rated the RPCs "somewhat better" than the corporations, although he also remarked that they were basically no different as both were run by technocrats (1978, vol. 1, p. 85). Prior to the revolution, 35 to 38 RPCs with 11,200 members were set up in 258 villages with 99,546ha, although only 31,000ha were cultivated.[74]

The use of such supposedly modern inputs as machines, wage labor, and technical experts reached its peak with the Agribusinesses (sherkat-e kesht wa san'at). The government decided to set them up in 1968, passed the necessary law the same year, and made the best land available to them—namely, estates in the provinces of Khuzestan, Azerbaijan, and Gilan, which were irrigated by dams, as well as fertile land scattered throughout various other provinces—a total of slightly more than 220,000ha,[75] most of it owned by peasants. The government employed its usual methods to urge the peasants to sell their land, and 67,000ha were taken away from those in the area irrigated by the Dez Dam in the southeast of the country.[76]

Eleven of the ABs were state run. Before the revolution these had from 1,000 to 48,000ha,[77] producing sugar, paper, meat, and fodder. They had been established primarily to encourage private investment in similar businesses but also to supply the army.[78]

The private ABs were located either on private land or on leased land that the government made available for thirty years. The government encouraged the establishment of ABs with incredibly large concessions and privileges: They were exempted from all tax for ten years; the government paid 50 percent of the cost of irrigation plant, roads, and other infrastructure; they were given long-term loans at a favorable 6 percent rate of interest; repatriation of capital was guaranteed for foreign companies; minimum prices were guaranteed for products;[79] the rent was so low that it was termed "almost free";[80] and in the Dez Dam area the state subsidy for every cubic meter of water provided to foreign companies was ten times higher than the fee it charged them for it.[81]

Five foreign companies were established between 1969 and 1974 on 68,000ha of leased public land in the Dez Dam area. These ABs were formed with state and private equity participation and on the foreign side involved such multinational corporations as Hawaiian Agronomics, Dow Chemicals, Shell Oil, and Mitchell Cotts and banks such as the Bank of America, Manhattan Bank, and First National City. A number of ABs were set up on private property, most of them belonging to members of the shah's family or to enterprises they protected for a consideration.[82]

The ABs, especially the foreign ones, were mostly unsuccessful. The specialist literature gives several reasons, including the high costs of overmechanization and overcapitalization, the huge area cultivated, high pay, failure to use appropriate technology, lack of knowledge about local conditions on the part of the management, lack of interest, and corruption.[83] Malek observed that in Khuzestan they could only make a profit by subletting to peasants who planted summer crops (1979, pp. 157ff). Contrary to the government's promises and (possibly) expectations, the ABs had rather more of a negative than a positive effect on the development of Iranian agriculture. Ehlers summarized this effect as follows: destruction of numerous peasant farms, destruction of long-established villages, constriction of rural labor without providing alternative jobs, and the uprooting and social decline of those affected by the aforementioned consequences (1979, p. 448). These consequences affected 55,000 families on 67,000ha in the Dez Dam area. The peasants concerned were either banished or relocated in settlements unsuited to their habits of a lifetime. Some found jobs as paid workers in the ABs; others had to turn to smuggling in the Persian Gulf, theft, or even prostitution.[84]

In addition to the ABs, RPCs, and RCs, there was a wide variety of commercial enterprises, each of over 50ha, totalling more than 2.6m hectares. Most of them had succeeded in having their estates exempted from the land reform by mechanizing them or through various other legal or illegal means. They, too, were encouraged by the government. Most of their owners lived in the towns,[85] and the postrevolutionary efforts at an Islamic land reform concentrated on them.

After land reform, several new types of organization for agricultural production came into being on the initiative of the peasants. These were either modifications of the traditional producer collectives, which were now being run in the absence of the landlord, or new types of sharecropping introduced by enterprising peasants on leased land. Such land was leased by (1) absentee nonpeasant landowners or (2) peasants who were earning a living outside their villages. Modern methods of cultivation were sometimes used in such enterprises. The harvest was split between the landowner, leaseholder, fellow workers, moneylenders, owners of machines, and so forth according to a contract. Paid workers were used, too. Such producer collectives arose in various parts of the country on the initiative of the local peasants and worked together during the different stages of production. The government took no notice of such endeavors, to say nothing of supporting them.[86]

Sharecropping (mozare'e), the traditional relationship between peasants and landlords to combine the productive factors of labor and land, was increasingly replaced but not eliminated by paid work. Its continued existence was ensured not only by the persistence of traditional forms but also by the FCs and the newer types of enterprises set up on the initiative of the peasants. All these forms of sharecropping lacked the landlord element.[87] After taking power in the revolution, the Islamists tried to revive sharecropping, which is enshrined in Islamic law. The results will be shown in Chapter 10.2.

1.5 The Antiparticipatory Character of Agrarian Policy

In keeping with the authoritarian and centralistic nature of the regime, which did not even tolerate independent thinking in the upper ranks of the bureaucracy, the shah's agrarian policy lacked any emancipatory and participatory traits. One consequence of the "White Revolution," which centered on land reform, was state penetration of the rural areas and agriculture to a previously unknown degree and with such forcefulness that some observers consider this to have been its real aim.[88] Even if this interpretation is rightly disputed,[89] there can be no doubt that the White Revolution resulted, among other things, in authoritarian state control over rural life.[90] This consequence was one of the principal causes for the failure of the agrarian reform.

This regime's penetration of rural life began with the way land reform was decided on and carried out (i.e., from the top), which perforce turned the peasants, who until then had been subjects of the landlord, into subjects of the state. This tendency was exacerbated when the government started to consolidate peasant holdings into large farms and thus to bring them under the control of bureaucrats and technocrats, and it was strengthened when a number of government institutions gained access to the regions concerned as part of the rural construction program. Foremost among these agencies was the Army of Knowledge (sepah-e danesh), which was recruited from among school graduates from the mainly urban secondary schools. The Soldier of Knowledge did his military service by attempting to teach the peasants to read and write. He usually did so reluctantly, being constrained to fulfill his state-imposed obligation in an unfamiliar environment and to use teaching material having little to do with rural life. Then there was the Army of Health (sepah-e behdasht), also composed of secondary school graduates who had to do a sort of paramilitary service in rural regions. The third military force of this sort was the Army of Counseling and Construction (sepah-e tarwij wa abadani), whose troops were supposed to teach the rural population agriculture—after acquiring the knowledge they were required to impart themselves in a two-month course in town.

Some of the other new government institutions were nonmilitary. One of the tasks of the House of Rural Culture (khane-ye farhang-e rusta'i) was to encourage the peasants to celebrate the birthdays of the shah, his wife, and their son and other state festivals as splendidly as possible. It also had a library with a hundred books and propaganda material, none of which was read often. The House of Justice (khane-ye ensaf) relieved both the gendarmerie and the courts in the county towns by attempting to settle minor disputes by conciliation or arbitration. Although its five members were elected by the peasants, there was gross interference by government agencies to ensure that members of the wealthy class of the peasantry were elected. The members of the Village Council (anjoman-e deh) were elected in the same manner and from the same circle. The main aim of the Village Council was to mobilize the rural labor force for the projects the government had decided on.

There were further government agencies alongside and above these institutions, both inside and outside the village. The links in the chain went from village headman (kadkhoda) to district village headman (dehyar) to gendarmerie and specialized agricultural banks, right up to departments at the various ministries. According to Farazmand, "the size and functions of the local departments and bureaus of the government grew dramatically during the 1960s and 1970s. What in 1962 was a small office of agriculture with four to five personnel, including the department head, became in the 1970s an office with more than fifty office bureaucrats, not to mention the large number of field officials" (1989, p. 118). The numerous ministries and their departments at the provincial, county, town, district village, and village levels constituted the lines of communication down which the central government passed its decisions about the lives of the rural population. These decisions further disenfranchised the rural population, even though some might have been to their benefit. So the peasants saw these institutions as alien and mistrusted them, which is why they could contribute little to mobilizing the development potential of Iranian agriculture at this level.[91]

1.6 The Urban-Rural Divide and Rural Depopulation

A further indication of the crisis in Iranian agriculture prior to the revolution was the growing social and economic gap between the towns and the countryside and the resultant steady increase in "unchecked" rural migration, which led to the formation of slums in the towns, particularly the capital. This widening urban-rural gap was primarily due to the fact that agriculture's share of GDP was declining while the rural population was increasing and the number of people employed in agriculture was remaining constant. The rural population grew from 13m in 1956 to 17.8m in 1976, and those employed in agriculture were approaching the 3m mark. Meanwhile, the sector's share of GDP (at factor cost and constant prices) fell from 29.3 percent in 1962/3 to 9.6 percent in 1976/7.[92] These developments, despite the absolute increase in agricultural production and the concomitant growth in peasant income, led to a relative decline in income for those employed in agriculture, as shown in the difference between rural and urban personal consumption. The urban population's proportion of total consumption rose from around 54 percent in 1963/4 to 77.5 percent in 1978/9, with a corresponding decline in the rural population's share from 46 percent to 22.5 percent. In absolute figures, per capita urban consumption soared from $210 to $1,442; that of the rural population only increased from $97 to $382. The ratio of rural to national per capita consumption dropped from 0.71:1 to 0.4:1 in the same period, while that of the urban population rose from 1.50:1 to 1.60:1.[93] Income development patterns were parallel: Urban households had 2.7 times the income of rural ones in 1976.[94]

Agriculture's declining share of the GDP and all the consequences for the rural population's standard of living can be considered a direct result of government neglect. The government's allocation of funds increasingly handicapped agriculture, causing a relative decline in capital formation, comparatively low profitability for agricultural investments, and slower growth of the net value added in this sector. This loss of value in agriculture[95] was so marked under the shah that it even caused farmers and wealthy peasants to look out for other employment opportunities.

The upshot of the regime's disdain for agriculture and the rural population was the paucity of government funds allocated to improve rural areas or provide the rural population with social services and infrastructure. Such funds were allocated to the towns in much larger degree.[96] In most respects, rural improvements had no place in the government's development concept; it was aiming to reduce the number of villages, concentrate agricultural production in the so-called poles of agriculture (i.e., in a few relatively fertile regions of the country), and reduce the number of those employed in this sector to 300,000 by the 1980s.[97] The improvements that were nonetheless reluctantly made in some outlying districts were at odds with this aim and proved either that the regime had not made up its mind about its objectives or that it could not ignore the fact that the rural population was not moving in the direction it hoped.[98]

The unfavorable developments in income distribution and living standards were reason enough for the mass migration of the rural population to the towns. The stream of those leaving accelerated at the beginning of the land reform era, growing in breadth and scope again in the 1970s. Around 1.7 percent of the rural population migrated to the towns every year between 1956 and 1966, increasing to 1.9 percent in the following decade. The rural population accounted for 68.6 percent of the total population in 1956/7; the figure fell to 62 percent in 1966/7 and 53 percent in 1976/7.[99] Despite these developments the rural population increased in absolute terms (as stated above), and this increase, together with the fact that agricultural job opportunities were not growing to the same extent, gave yet another reason for migration to the towns. The land reform program contributed to this exodus to the extent that it left in its wake a mass of peasants with little or no land who were unable to earn a living in agriculture. The rise in the price of land in areas near towns, which was caused by the construction boom, encouraged many of them to sell their land; those sales in turn induced even more migration by providing better earnings opportunities. The rising prices for industrial products and equipment that had found acceptance in the villages and the stagnating prices for agrarian products provided another impulse for abandoning agriculture. The breakdown of the village system with its protective functions is just one more of rural depopulation's many causes, which unfortunately cannot be listed in their entirety here.[100]

Rural migration affected all strata of the peasantry. Although the poor ones were motivated primarily by economic considerations, the wealthier ones were motivated more by the cultural attractions in the towns.[101] The towns were incapable of absorbing the migrants and integrating them into the productive sectors. Most of these migrants found jobs in the construction sector, at least while the oil boom lasted. The shah's regime tolerated this migration, even considered it an indication of progress, but was unable to control it, causing experts to talk of an "unchecked" or "unregulated" rural exodus. Attempts to create additional sources of income in rural areas by promoting traditional crafts were doomed to failure, because the regime did not take them seriously and as a result did not fund them adequately.[102] The building of the slums, with their accompanying social anomalies, was the most obvious consequence of this unchecked rural exodus. The social dynamite they contained turned them into powder kegs that exploded during the revolution.

Notes

1. The Islamic year begins on March 21 of the Roman calendar and ends the following March 20. Hence, "1973/4" corresponds to the year beginning on March 21, 1973, and ending on March 20, 1974—in this case, 1352.

2. Bank-e Markazi-ye Jomhuri-ye Eslami-ye Iran (Bank-e Markazi) 1984, p. 23. The annual increase in demand for agricultural produce was 8 percent according to E. 'Ajami 1978, p. 1f. See also H. Katouzian 1981, p. 42. "Nowhere in the economy was the gap between domestic supply and aggregate demand widening more than in farming." Amuzegar 1991, p. 183.

3. M. R. Hoseini Kazeruni 1981, p. 61.

4. U. Planck 1980, p. 165.

5. *Ibid.*, p. 165f. By and large, market supply nevertheless grew as a result of the general increase in production.

6. Ketab-e Agah 1982, pp. 160, 164, and 182f.

7. N. Nattagh 1986, pp. 67 and 81.

8. See the relevant reports from the Organization of Planning and Budget (*Sazman-e Barname wa Budje*), and N. Nattagh 1986.

9. These dams were only used by 100 large holdings, according to M. Azkia 1986, p. 161.

10. *Sazman-e Barname wa Budje* 1973; A. Asharaf 1982, p. 12f; M. Azkia 1986, p. 162; correspondence with H. Keshawarz.

11. S. Amini 1973, p. 189ff; Kh. Khosrawi 1979, p. 156; and U. Planck 1980, p. 166.

12. M. Azkia 1986, p. 166.

13. See H. Malek 1978, section 1, p. 36, section 2, pp. 9ff and 86, and section 3, p. 11f; and K. McLachlan 1989, p. 96.

14. N. Nattagh 1986, p. 32ff; Wezarat-e Keshawarzi [DP] 1983, vol. 1, pp. 5ff.

15. The yield from nonirrigated land is about half that from irrigated land because of the low precipitation in Iran.

16. Ketab-e Agah 1982, p. 179. Artificially irrigated arable land only increased by 300,000ha from the start of the first development plan in 1949 to 1977 (M. Azkia 1986, p. 162). Building the dams led to a further 225,000ha of artificially irrigated arable land being exploited (K. McLachlan 1989, p. 100). Increasing farmland by expanding the naturally irrigated area was termed an "agrocolonialist opening up of new arable land." See E. Ehlers in H. Elsenhaus (ed), *Agrarreform*, 1979, p. 454. More on this point in Chapters 12.2 and 12.3.

17. Turkey already had 155,000 tractors in 1973, according to H. Safari 1977.

18. The number of operational tractors rose from 31,600 to 70,000 between 1973 and 1979. See Markaz-e Amar 1977 and 1982; also see S. W. Fallah 1982.

19. Malek 1978, pp. 8ff and 1979, pp. 69ff; Planck 1980, p. 167; Wezarat-e Keshawarzi 1977, p. 34f; Riyahi 1976, p. 4; and Kadiwaer 1976, pp. 5ff.

20. E. Ehlers 1979, p. 453; see also H. Katouzian 1981, p. 31; and M. Azkia 1986, p. 149.

21. The average for wheat was 1,361kg in Asia and 1,568kg in the developing countries. See M. Azkia 1986, pp. 86, 150.

22. M. Azkia 1986, pp. 165ff.

23. The price of wheat rose by only 4 rials/kg, from 6 rials/kg to 10 rials/kg, between 1959 and 1974, while production costs and the cost of living increased several times over. Hoseini Kazeruni 1981, p. 60f.

24. Wezerat-e Keshawarzi 1977, p. 47f; Sazman-e Barname 1973, pp. 7ff.

25. M. R. Pahlawi 1966.

26. For an account of what the government expected from the land reform, see, inter alia, B. Moumeni 1980, pp. 161ff and 415ff.

27. The reformists had no concept of the principal characteristics of land tenure in Iran, according to H. Malek 1979, p. 36.

28. The peasants with usufructuary rights were those who prior to the reform were entitled to cultivate a plot on the property of the landlord for whom they worked, in contradistinction to the khoshneshins—i.e., peasants without this right.

29. A. Ashraf 1982, p. 11; and E. Hooglund 1982, p. 72.

30. A. Ashraf 1982, p. 22.

31. Planck 1980, p. 163; Azkia 1986, p. 125f; and Khosrawi 1979, p. 171 (the latter includes some peasants with over 2ha in this class).

32. About 670,000 of the some 3.5m hectares that belonged to holdings of over 50ha must be deducted because it was in the hands of the state, cooperatives and farm corporations. See A. Ashraf 1982, p. 44.

33. The mechanization was mostly apparent. See H. Malek 1978, p. 18.

34. K. Khosrawi 1979, p. 179; and M. Azkia 1986, p. 120f. There were more absentees (a total of 200,000) than landowners in this group of greats, at least according to E. Hooglund 1982, p. 78f.

35. Holdings of less than 5ha accounted for only 6 percent of the newly developed land, those between 10ha and 50ha for 44 percent, and those with more than 50ha for 39 percent. See M. Hoseini Kazeruni 1981, p. 13; and A. Ashraf 1982, p. 14.

36. M. Hoseini Kazeruni 1981, pp. 11f and 67.

37. H. Malek 1978, pp. 24ff.

38. *Ibid.*, pp. 19ff.

39. See H. Malek 1978 and 1979; J. Safi Nezhad 1972; S. Amini 1983; E 'Ajami 1978; and E. Ehlers 1985 on these processes.

40. Appropriate proposals were published at the start of the land reform, principally by Khalil Maleki in the magazine *'Elm wa Zendegi,* but were completely ignored by those responsible for the reform. See H. Katouzian 1981, p. 4; and B. Moumeni 1980, pp. 114ff.

41. A holding consisted on average of six parcels of 0.99ha each prior to the reform and in 1971 of 8.5 parcels of only 0.82ha each. See M. Hoseini Kazeruni 1981, p. 24f.

42. *Ibid.,* Wezerat-e Keshawarzi 1977, p. 25; and K. Khosrawi 1979, p. 165.

43. See Sazman-e Barname 1968, pp. 85, 93; and 1973, pp. 68, 72.

44. The maximum credit granted by the government to RCs amounted to four times the capital invested by the members, according to E. Hooglund 1982, p. 109. On the subject of RCs, see S. Amini 1973, pp. 62ff; Sazman-e Markazi-ye Ta'awon-e 1971; and Markaz-e Amar-e Iran 1982.

45. Katouzian 1981, pp. 19ff; and my correspondence with H. Keshawarz.

46. N. Nattagh 1986, p. 52.

47. E. Hooglund 1982, p. 109; S. Amini 1973, p. 72; and Markaz-e Amar 1981.
48. S. Amini 1973, p. 72.
49. E. Hooglund 1982, p. 109.
50. S. Amini 1973, p. 189; H. Malek 1978, p. 39; K. Khosrawi 1979, p. 156; and Wezerat-e Keshawarzi 1977, p. 38.
51. E. Hooglund 1982, p. 110; and B. Moumeni 1980, p. 404.
52. S. Amini 1973, p. 85.
53. E. Hooglund 1982, p. 110; and M. Azkia 1986, p. 130.
54. Amini 1973, p. 74; Malek 1978, Sect. 2, p. 15; and Azkia 1986, p. 177f.
55. E. Hooglund 1982, p. 105. See also S. Amini 1973, p. 68; and M. Azkia 1986, pp. 164 and 180.
56. The ignorance of the bureaucrats and technocrats was pilloried most of all by H. Malek 1978 and 1979.
57. See E. 'Ajami, et al. 1978, p. 8f; 'Ajami 1973, pp. 59ff; and 1976, pp. 193ff.
58. Ketab-e Agah 1982, p. 166.
59. See for instance H. Malek 1978, p. 17; H. Katouzian 1981, p. 21f; and Etemad Moqaddam 1978, p. 355.
60. Two examples are the "third strategy" presented at a May 1978 University of Shiraz seminar and drafted by E. 'Ajami, et al. 1978, as well as the proposals developed by H. Malek 1978 and 1979. Many years later Hushang Nahavandi, a ranking functionary under the shah, reported that a group consisting of 'Ajami, Nader Afshar Naderi, and others had worked at a "study of the problems of Iran" and, inter alia, developed proposals in much the same vein as those presented above. See *Kayhan* (London), May 13, 1990.
61. J. Janzen 1976, p. 168.
62. M. Azkia 1986, p. 228f.
63. H. Elyasiyan 1985, p. 2/4.
64. J. Janzen 1976, p. 113; M. Azkia 1986, p. 239; H. Malek 1979, p. 106f; and A. Nik Kholq 1970, p. 113f.
65. J. Safi Nezhad, et al. 1971, p. 71; E. 'Ajami 1973, p. 177; H. Keshawarz, et al. 1971, p. 201; and J. Janzen 1976, p. 201.
66. J. Safi Nezhad, et al. 1971, p. 71. In one case, 89 percent of interviewees stated that they were not informed about the management of the corporation (D. Kiyani Manesh 1970, p. 175); in a second case, it was 89.9 percent (Qh. Baba'i Hemmati 1971, pp. 231, 238); in a third case, 93 percent (M. Azkia 1970, pp. 240, 251). In another case, communication between the management and the shareholders was impossible because the former spoke no Persian and the latter did not speak the peasants' language (Sazman-e Cherikha-ye Fada'i-ye Khalq, 1973, p. 192).
67. J. Safi Nezhad, et al. 1971, p. 71; Azkia 1970, p. 208; Sazman-e Cherikha 1973, p. 154; and J. Janzen 1976, p. 152.
68. D. Kiyani Manesh 1970, p. 135. The Bagheyn Farm Corporation in the province of Kerman employed 180 workers for three months and only 70 for five to six months every year, but not all of them were shareholders (Sazman-e Cherikha 1973, p. 179).
69. It amounted to 16 percent of total income in Dargazin (M. Azkia 1970, p. 42) and 29 percent at the Farah Corporation in Kurdistan (Qh. Baba'i Hemmati 1971, pp. 212 and 215).
70. See, inter alia, A. Nik Kholq 1970, p. 119; M Azkia 1970, pp. 45 and 103f; H. Keshawarz, et al. 1970 p. 199; and Sazman-e Cherikha 1973, p. 151f.
71. M. Azkia 1986, p. 240.

72. For instance, in Mahabad between 1 and 200 (Mohammadi 1973, p. 36), in Sanandaj 1 and 90 (Qh. Baba'i Hemmati 1971, p. 219). In Dargazin 6 percent of the members held 30 percent of the shares (M. Azkia 1986, p. 236).

73. In the RPC at Marun, for example, the individual members' share of the land varied between 0.87ha and 52.5ha. M. Nouruzi, et al. 1977, pp. 5 and 198.

74. The figures for RPCs are not uniform. See A. Anoushirwani, et al. 1982, p. 35; and M. Azkia 1986, p. 259. It should also be noted that there are fewer reports on RPCs than on Rural Corporations.

75. It was impossible to determine precisely how many hectares. As usual, the figures quoted vary—from 184,645ha (Kadiwar 1976, p. 41) to 238,000ha (Wusuqi 1988, p. 151). If all the ABs (including those involved in animal husbandry and other agricultural activities) are taken into consideration, the total exceeds 600,000ha (Zahedi Mazanderani 1987, p. 29).

76. E. Hooglund 1982, p. 85.

77. Except the "Kashan Aromatic Plant Company," which grew roses for rosewater and perfume on 20ha (Zahedi Mazanderandi 1986, p. 37).

78. *Ibid.*, p. 40; and E. Ehlers 1979, p. 450.

79. Zahedi Mazanderandi 1986, pp. 52ff.

80. R. Dumont 1975, p. 17.

81. *Ibid.*

82. There were twenty-two such companies in the Dez Dam area, according to E. Hooglund 1982, p. 85. The shah's family owned forty-three such companies, according to Zahedi Mazanderandi 1986, p. 69f.

83. See Planck 1980; Ehlers 1979; Mehner 1978; Malek 1978 and 1979; Azkia 1986; and Etemad Moqaddam 1978.

84. Zahedi Mazanderandi 1986, p. 27; and Hooglund 1982, p. 85.

85. See Qahreman 1982; Fallah 1982; Ashraf 1982; and Azkia 1986, pp. 216ff.

86. See Malekaniyan 1986, pp. 34ff; Sa'edlu 1974; Adib Saberi; Azkia 1986, pp. 209ff; 'Ajami 1973, pp. 69ff; Moumeni 1980, p. 335f; and Ashraf 1982, pp. 30ff.

87. On sharecropping, see Lambton 1953; Planck 1962; Alwandi 1982; and Chapter 2.3.1.

88. See the discussion of the various opinions on the motives for the land reform in Moumeni 1980; Najmabadi 1987; Schirazi 1976; and Azkia 1986.

89. For instance, by A. Najmabadi 1987.

90. According to Farazmand 1989, p. 110f: "Nine of the twelve points of the White Revolution created the conditions necessary for the bureaucratization of rural areas." He then lists them.

91. On the subject of government institutions in rural regions, see above all Farazmand 1989; also Planck 1974; Rafipoor 1974; Malek 1979; and Hooglund 1982.

92. Razzaqi 1988, p. 117; and Ketab-e agah 1982, pp. 175ff.

93. Katouzian 1981, p. 24f.

94. Markaz-e Amar 1982.

95. Planck 1980, p. 164. See also Ehlers 1979, p. 456; and Katouzian 1981a, p. 307.

96. Riyahi 1976, p. 9.

97. Katouzian 1981, p. 6.

98. Sa'edlu 1974, p. 22; and Wezerat-e Keshawarzi 1977, pp. 53ff.

99. Hoseini Kazeruni 1982. For more figures on this development, see Taheri 1981, pp. 49ff; and Wusuqi 1987, pp. 36ff.

100. In addition to the works on this subject cited in previous notes, see Farahiyan, et al. 1978; Wezerat-e Keshawarzi 1977; and Riyahi 1976.
101. According to Planck 1980, p. 164.
102. Wezerat-e Keshawarzi 1977, p. 44.

2
Theories of Agriculture and Agrarian Policy in the Prerevolutionary Era

Before the revolution, agrarian policy and the state of agriculture were discussed by various government agencies, scientific institutes, and political organizations, as well as individual scientists and writers. All were motivated by different interests. They often went beyond evaluating the circumstances prevailing at the time to propose ideas for reforms. Some of these reflections came from the state; others came from groups or individuals, including the Islamists, who opposed the regime. The status quo was not without its conservative protectors: This position was taken by the shah's regime before land reform but proved increasingly untenable. However, the scientists and agricultural experts were almost exclusively concerned with reforms, either supporting or criticizing them.

2.1 State and Scientific Thinking

Before the 1960s, the regime was closely allied to the Iranian landowning class, looking after its interests. The shah and his family were the country's largest landowner, being surrounded in the government, in parliament, and in the army by landowners who had their land tilled in the traditional way. However, the steadily worsening economic, social, and political crisis in Iran at the beginning of the 1960s threatened the very existence of the shah's regime and forced modernistic elements to make a decision on agrarian reform (which after 1962 was centered on land reform) and implement it. Making this decision required the regime to assess the state of agriculture, plan the reform, and observe the process of transformation already initiated. Almost all the country's potential was available to the government, which could call on ministries and research or training institutes as well as nongovernmental institutions and independent experts.

The regime actually did activate these resources for the purpose stated, at least in part. Several ministries and other government organizations investigated the problems of agriculture and rural construction. The agencies included:

1. The Organization of Planning and Budget (Sazman-e Barname wa Budje; OPB). Years before the start of agrarian reform, the OPB was concerned with, among other things, introducing modern techniques into Iranian agriculture and collating a wealth of information on the subject. It stepped up its activities at the beginning of the agrarian reform program, extending them to new areas. In so doing, it acquired several research departments specializing in technical, economic, and social matters relating to agriculture. The research results were presented as reports and analyses, up to and including monographs, some being made available to interested parties outside the organization. Azkia's bibliography of literature on agroeconomics and agrosociology lists more than thirty such manuscripts. The Central Statistical Office of Iran (Markaz-e Amar-e Iran), which comes under the OPB, conducted a number of surveys in rural areas, including agricultural censuses. Despite their grave shortcomings these surveys can be seen as an impressive first step toward an assessment of the agrarian economy. Azkia's bibliography lists twenty-nine titles relating to agriculture published by this organization.

2. The Ministry of Agriculture and Rural Construction (Wezerat-e Keshawarzi wa 'Omran-e Rusta'i) was the authority responsible for administering research. Having been split into a number of different organizations, in 1963, it was reconstituted under its old name, Ministry for Agriculture, in 1975,[1] incorporating a number of research units with various tasks. The most important unit from an agricultural point of view was the Center for Rural and Agricultural Surveys (Markaz-e Tahqiqat-e Rusta'i wa Eqtesad-e Keshawarzi). Its mimeographed 1976 bibliography of the results of its surveys contains 126 titles, classified by subject as follows: FCs and RPCs, 47; loans and cooperatives, 26; employment, 15; the rural houses of culture, 14; social insurance for the rural population, 10; the results of land reform, 1; and other, 13. All these studies contributed to a better understanding of the consequences of the reform measures and were available, even if not readily, to interested parties.

3. Ministries other than the Ministry of Agriculture and Rural Construction were concerned with implementing reforms, providing services, and improving the agricultural sector. These included the ministries of Water and Energy, Housing and Town Planning, and Science and Higher Education. They carried out research in their allotted spheres, increasing our knowledge of natural resources, agrarian economics, and rural life. The activities of the Central Bank (Bank-e Markazi), the Central Organization of Rural Cooperatives (Sazman-e Markazi-ye Ta'awon), and the Bank for Agriculture (Bank-e Keshawarzi) also deserve to be mentioned.[2]

4. Iranian universities made important contributions to prerevolutionary studies on rural sociology and agroeconomics. Foremost among the academic contributors was the Institute for Social Research and Studies (Mo'asese-ye Tahqiqat-e Ejtema'i) at the University of Tehran's Faculty of Sociology and Cooperative Systems. Its "List of Field Research and Publications 1337 [1958/9] to 1357 [1978/9]," produced in June 1978, contains eighty-five titles, which were made available to other interested parties as mimeographs. These studies dealt with the results of land reform, social and economic relationships in larger regional areas, farm corporations, rural construction, traditional producer cooperatives, fishery, and the literacy campaign. There were also monographs on complete villages. Furthermore, the institute published the results of independent studies carried out by nonstaff contributors.[3] Institutes attached to the Faculty of Jurisprudence and Politics and the Faculty of Economics at the University of Tehran were engaged in similar research, the results being published in their respective journals.[4] Outside Tehran, the universities of Shiraz, Tabriz, and Hamedan did research on rural sociology and agrarian economics. Particularly important is the research carried out at European and U.S. universities and institutes that has been published in numerous monographs and articles. E. Ehler's 1980 "Bibliographic Research Survey" lists 316 titles under "rural area," 108 dealing with the agrarian reform and changes in rural sociology, 155 with traditional rural areas, settlements, economics, and agrarian social structures, and 45 with overviews of agrarian economics. More than a third (135) are works by Iranian graduates and academics at U.S. and West European universities.

5. The journals published by ministries, universities, banks, and other government organizations also printed numerous articles on the problems of the agricultural system in Iran. The University of Tehran's publications were of great significance, foremost among them the journal of the Faculty of Economics (tahqiqat-e eqtesadi, or Economic Studies), the journal of the Faculty for Jurisprudence and Politics (majalle-ye daneshkade-ye huquq), the journal of the Faculty of Sociology and Cooperative Systems (name-ye 'olum ejtema'i, or Social Sciences' Script), and the journal *Daneshkade* (Place of Science), which was published by the central office of the University of Tehran.

6. The twenty-three agricultural colleges and the research institutes in various provincial capitals also made noteworthy contributions. Several had their own publications.

The extensive literature resulting from the research conducted by government agencies and universities is of varying quality. It includes both theoretically and methodologically sound analyses and works that are purely descriptive, optimistically biased, or journalistic in nature.[5] Whatever reservations there may be about the quality of this literature, it represents the bulk of our systematic knowledge of the agrarian system in Iran and largely contains information gathered on the spot. It is the product of close contact with the matter under investigation, even if it is sometimes spoiled by ideological and other subjective factors. These studies were heavily supported by government funds not freely available to other observers or scientists.

Under the shah, government-funded studies were inhibited from making explicitly negative observations by the dictatorship. Numerous contributions did, nevertheless, express perceptible or even open criticism of the regime's agrarian policy. In those cases where it was officially permitted or even desired, the criticism became known to the public. Three examples—which, characteristically, date from near the end of the regime—can be given here. The first is the report of a seminar on the Investigation of the Reasons for the Migration of the Rural Population into the Towns, held in July 1976 at the University of Hamedan.[6] The participants, among them many opposition experts,[7] sharply censured the regime's agricultural policy, holding it responsible for rural depopulation. The report on the debates at the seminar reflects the breadth of criticism. Hosein Malek's two extremely critical books (1978 and 1979) present the results of research that Prime Minister Amir Abbas Howeyda had practically commissioned from a man whose opposition to the regime was well known and who had found fault with land reform from the very beginning and made counterproposals.[8] Another example is the paper presented by E. 'Ajami, et al. to the Symposium on Agrarian Policy in May 1978. The paper proposed a "Third Strategy for Reconstructing Peasant Agriculture and for Reorganizing Commercial Enterprises" to the government. First it highlighted the regime's failure to reform agribusiness and then outlined a route based on an "autocentric development," which was to be founded on "maintaining the national culture," "love of nature," the "industriousness of the Iranian farmers," and the "variety of native cultures and regional peculiarities." Autocentric development was intended to guide Iranian agriculture between "individual, labor-intensive enterprises" on the one hand and "extensive, capital-intensive farms" on the other. Other critical assessments of agrarian policy at the time contained proposals and projects for reform. These were sometimes adopted in part by the new regime.

2.2 Opposition Thinking

The intensity and quality of opposition thinking on the objective problems of agriculture and how to solve them depended on various factors. First, opposition groups' socioeconomic outlook, as well as their general political and ideological attitudes, determined the positions they took in this particular matter. Their outlook, as well as their attitudes, were a consequence of their being rooted in positions with differing interests on the one hand and, on the other, of their subjective perceptions of these positions. A rough, primarily political classification shows social-liberal or social-democratic, communist, and Islamist trends, each with its own position on the agrarian question. The position of the peasants was the one least independently articulated; peasant movements were almost always part of political movements in the towns and thus indirectly represented by them.

Second, the degree to which opposition groups and individuals had access to the machinery of government played a part. Many well-known experts and scientists cited worked at the universities or the relevant ministries and were opposed to the regime. Their attitude was more or less known, and they were largely responsible for the scientifically worded and officially tolerated criticism from within the state. The knowledge of the agricultural system cited in Chapter 2.1 comes mainly from this source. As far as is known, the authors of these papers are close to the secularist opposition, and only seldom does the name of a clearly identifiable Islamist, such as H. Peyman, crop up.[9] This relationship is borne out by the fact that members of these political trends occupied the relevant government and university posts even after the revolution, in spite of the extensive purges and resignations of non-Islamist experts and scientists. The top posts are an exception inasmuch as they are reserved for those loyal to the regime regardless of their expertise—as indeed was the case under the shah. The opposition groups, in particular the social-liberals, have formed the government in twentieth-century Iran several times and while in power developed the rudiments of an agrarian policy and land reform.

Third, much of the opposition's strength and attention was absorbed by combatting the dictatorship. Opposition groups' exclusion from permitted political life had reached such proportions that they were left with no chance of being able to influence policy. The idea of forming something like a shadow cabinet in the hope of eventually forming the government understandably struck them as absurd. Thus, they were not forced to prepare themselves for the eventuality by dealing with real questions of economic, social, and cultural policy, preferring instead—where they were politically active—to think about how the dictatorship could be toppled, or at least mitigated. This problem had come to dominate the opposition's thinking because of the permanent despotism in the history of Iran. The more radical the opposition, the more it seemed to concentrate on the question of power, and the more its declarations on economic and social policy were either a simplified program or propaganda directed against the regime. Thus, no limits were set on the promises they could or would not keep if they ever did achieve political power. Their criticism was merciless and, as the Persian saying goes, "burned dry and wet wood together."

Fourth, how concrete the reflections by opposition groups were depended on the extent to which the ideas could be based on existing paradigms. The secular opposition was able to build its reform concepts and programmatic declarations into the scientific, empirical, and ideological frameworks provided by capitalism and socialism; the Islamists, however, were compelled to spend a great deal of time working out their systems of social, economic, and political values, leaving them little opportunity to concern themselves with specific questions.

Fifth, the extent to which the opposition could write about the problems of the agrarian economy depended on the latitude of the censor in permitting them to do so. Therefore, most of the papers by the opposition were published abroad, where the exiles' expertise, financial situations, and contacts within Iran determined how they dealt with these questions or whether they could publish their ideas. The Tudeh Party was in a relatively good position, as it had recourse to the opportunities available in the states of the Eastern bloc. The results of some of the work done in Iran were only published after the revolution, when the censorship of such papers was abolished.

Let us now proceed to survey the various trends of thought in the opposition. Presentation of the secularist positions has been kept brief, as it is only intended to provide a basis for comparison with the various trends in Islamist thinking.

2.2.1 Liberal and Social Democratic Thinking

In modern Iran the call by liberal and social democratic writers, political leaders, and parties for land reform and the modernization of agricultural production can be traced back to before the Constitutional Revolution (1906–11). At that time, their demands included the sale of state land to the peasants, the abolition of the "feudal" system (including both the territorial jurisdiction of the landlords and all the services and levies imposed by them on the peasantry), and the reduction of taxes up to and including the confiscation of the estates of the landlords and the clerics. The draft land reform by the writer Talebof proposed that all state and private land be sold to the peasants "so that they [can] become owners themselves and free citizens," that village administration be transferred to a council of trusted locals, and that this, in conjunction with producer and consumer cooperatives, would make feudal control of the village superfluous. The motto of this draft was: "No more landlords in Iran."[10]

The radical democratic newspaper *Sur-e Esrafil,* which was published in the first year of the Constitutional Revolution, drew attention to the need for a peasant revolt throughout the country. The rebellion would start as soon as the peasants were capable of understanding the Islamic saying, "The crop to the peasant, even if he harvests it on squatted land." The paper considered land reform indispensable for developing agriculture but initially favored a much less radical solution—namely, selling one-tenth of existing private property to the peasants. This sale was to be arranged by a National Agricultural Bank, which was to be set up. *Sur-e Esrafil* also criticized the sharecropping enshrined in Islamic law, hoping that the peasants would get rid of it one day.[11]

The Social Democratic Party (hezb-e demokrat-e 'amiyun, founded in 1909) called for the "legally assured abolition of feudalism," to be achieved by declaring illegal on pain of punishment "any and all forms of levy, service or extortion imposed by the landlords on the peasantry." The party thought the best arrangement for horticulture and the development of agriculture would allow everyone who tilled the soil also to derive the benefit from it: "Every peasant should be the owner of as much land as he can till." The landowners were to sell their land to the peasants through a National Agricultural Bank; the government was to be obliged to help the peasants with loans, and the landowners would be advised to invest such money as they received in industry, railways, and trade.[12]

These newspapers pilloried the excesses committed by the landlords and tribal khans against the peasants, printed the rural population's complaints and demands, supported any action they took, and called on them to assist in abolishing despotism and extortion by joining the revolution.[13] Independent peasant action was rare even then, and the residents of villages near towns who joined in revolutionary actions by the townspeople were either called on to do so by the latter or driven to do so by counterrevolutionary excesses.[14]

The liberal and social democratic forces were not strong enough to push through many of their demands against the resistance of the conservative revolutionary forces, or against the counterrevolution (landlords, clergy, court, and bureaucrats) and they did not succeed in making any significant changes to the structure of land ownership apart from the abolition of the tuyul system.[15] They only undertook reforms where they were in a position to form their own local rebel governments, and the programs became ineffective with the dissolution of the latter. For example, in the province of Gilan, the high ratio of peasants in the so-called Jangali movement (1915–20) made reforms to their benefit necessary. Abolition of tuyul levies and services and an increase in the peasants' share of the harvest were among their more moderate demands. The participation of radical democrats and communists in this movement led to more sweeping reforms, such as land being expropriated and divided up among the peasants.[16]

The crushing of the Jangali movement in 1920 ushered in the despotic era of Reza Shah. The liberals and social democrats were first driven into opposition and then suppressed altogether along with the rest of the opposition. Only in 1951–53 did the movement get another chance to form the government, this time under Mohammad Mosaddeq. However, various forces stopped the government from pursuing its socioeconomic reforms energetically and consistently. The resistance to the regime was too strong to let it work on reforms. Furthermore, the circumstances under which the liberals came to power made it imperative to concentrate largely on nationalizing the country's oil industry. The government also had to devote a lot of energy to maintaining democracy;[17] hence, not much was left for social reforms.

In October, 1952, the Mosaddeq government nevertheless decided on a 20 percent reduction in the landlords' share of the harvest, the savings to benefit the peasants and village improvement in equal shares. It also decided to establish councils at the levels of village, district village, district town, and county town, which were to be responsible for the use made of the funds allocated for improvements and other administrative tasks in their respective spheres of operation.

Mosaddeq's approach to land reform differed from the concepts that aimed to divide up the land among the peasants, and the shah took the opportunity to defame him as an "opponent of restricting landed property."[18] When replying to the accusation, Mosaddeq gave the following reasons for being against division: the inordinate length of time required to implement it; the inevitable discrimination against some peasants; the scarcity of irrigated estates, which would make an equitable distribution impossible; the inefficiency of the peasant holdings it would create; and the impossibility of using agricultural machinery on them. He felt that with the cut in the landlords' share of the harvest, the large estates would lose their appeal for landlords; no one would cling to them, and they would gradually disappear.[19]

The accusation by the shah and his followers sounds even less tenable when one realizes that the National Front (of which Mosaddeq was the leader) primarily consisted of parties and individuals that were well disposed to reform in the liberal or even social democratic sense. For Dr. Fatemi, the foreign minister in the Mosaddeq government, radical reforms were the prerequisite for victory in the struggle for the country's independence.[20] The socialist party known as the "Third Force" (niru-ye sewoum), led by Khalil Maleki, spoke out in favor of land reform, as did the social democratically inclined Iran Party (hezb-e Iran).[21] The conservative wing of the National Front withdrew its support for the Mosaddeq government just as it started "to press ahead with social changes."[22]

The liberals' and social democrats' reservations about a reform based on redistributing land to peasants and making them private landowners continued to be a prominent feature of later documents. This perspective is clear in their criticism of the distribution of crown land and the land reform program in the 1960s[23] and in their own programs and plans for land reform. This criticism was clearest in the tracts of the "Third Force" Party (later renamed League of Socialists of Iran). In October 1966 the European branch of this party submitted a proposal to the National Front that criticized the land reform being carried out by the shah's regime and outlined a plan centered on the gratuitous nationalization of land and water—both of which were to be made available to cooperatives set up by peasants. Management of these cooperatives was to be organized in such a way that it was in harmony with the "interests of society," able to promote the independence of the cooperatives and strengthen the democratic spirit among the peasantry, as well as their initiative and sense of responsibility. Later the land reform was to be integrated into a plan that would aspire to solve not only the question of the ownership of both land and water but also the problem of agriculture and of the economy as a whole.[24]

At the time, the League of Socialists and its European branch in particular had come under the influence of the left-wing *etátist* radicalism, which was making itself felt worldwide. It was for this reason that the party largely neglected the emancipatory aspects of the reform, placing great store in the state and its technical and administrative abilities. In Tehran ten years previously, the very same organization had presented a different draft providing for the traditional village system to replace the expropriated landlords, whose estates were to be "nationalized" or "socialized."[25] The League of Socialists was so opposed to reform by distribution that, had it been forced to choose between it and a large capitalist enterprise, it would have decided in favor of the latter.[26] Even long after the 1979 revolution, H. Malek, a leading member of the party, considered it possible to implement a reform based on maintaining the village system.[27]

After the fall of the Mosaddeq government, the Third Force and its successor, the League of Socialists, were—of the parties that had belonged to the National Front—the ones most involved in the questions of agriculture and land reform, working out their own proposals. Others were more inclined to make statements relating to the distribution of crown lands or to land reform. In these declarations they proclaimed their intention of striving for a land reform that would lead to the "removal of feudalism" and the existing structure of land ownership and transfer the land to the peasants.[28]

2.2.2 Communist Thinking

The Communists always took the most radical position concerning the expropriation of large estates, except when they thought it tactically impolitic to articulate such demands. They envisaged realizing their ultimate aims by leading the country through intermediate "democratic" and "socialist" stages. Land should also be transferred in stages, first to the individual peasant, then to state or local authorities. That was the Communists' model at any rate, but in practice there could be deviations from it.

The question of land reform drew the attention of the Communists because it played a central role in their theories on revolution and seizure of power. In the "democratic phase of the revolution" (which they considered Iran to be in), the peasantry had to make a significant contribution to the victory over the "feudal" autocracy and could be encouraged to do so by the prospect of land reform, which is why the Communists concerned themselves with it more than anyone else in the opposition.[29] However, the communist movement in Iran remained an urban phenomenon that tackled the peasants' problems from an urban perspective and cared little about starting an autonomous movement in the countryside.[30]

The earliest Communist statements on land reform in Iran date from the era of the Constitutional Revolution, when the first attempts were undertaken to found social democratic and communist organizations at home and abroad. In their 1906 Mashad program, the Communists set themselves the task "of freeing the peasants and the remainder of the population from the slave-owning yoke of the landlords and their agents." In another program, drawn up in Baku (capital of Azerbaijan) the same year, they raised the demand to make "all the land available to those who tilled it with their own hands, without the help of other peasants and workers."[31] But their main aim at the time was to arouse the peasants' interest in the Constitutional Revolution, and where the latter actually did take part, traces of Communist mobilization campaigns were found, disguised with Islamic slogans to accord with the awareness of the masses.[32]

The Communists played a major part in founding the Social Democratic Party and clearly influenced its demands on the question of land reform.[33] They had a similar effect on the Jangali movement: The Communists were responsible for some of the extremist positions, which were partly to blame for a split in the movement and its defeat by central government troops.

Some of the same Bolsheviks were active in the Communist Party of Iran in the period between the end of the first world war and its suppression by Reza Shah's regime (1925–41). At its first congress in June 1920, the party demanded that the government seize the estates of the great landowners and transfer them to the people, transfer to the peasants medium properties that exceeded the area of farmland to be distributed among peasants, and distribute state land to the peasants if the first two categories of land were insufficient. The second congress a year later made further demands that the state expropriate the shah's water rights; expropriate the pious foundations (waqf land) and transfer the landowners' usufructuary rights to the peasants; cancel debts owed by peasants to the state and moneylenders; and support the peasants by giving them seed corn, livestock, and soft, long-term loans. In addition, the nomads should be assigned enough land to establish a sedentary economy. The Communists also adopted a resolution to the effect that "the agrarian revolution, its preparation and victorious conduct [is] the most important question of all," and that the most important slogan should therefore be: "Final destruction of the remains of feudalism and distribution of the landlords' land among the peasants."[34]

The Tudeh Party succeeded the Communist Party of Iran after Reza Shah's abdication. Founded in 1941, it always devoted some attention to the agrarian question and land reform, although less than the Communists had. The policies it pursued and the demands it made were calculated based on two decisive factors: the power constellation within Iran and the requirements of Soviet foreign policy, including its policy toward Iran. As a satellite party subject to Soviet war policy, Tudeh devoted itself primarily to antifascist aims and organizing the appropriate forces in Iran and so made very modest demands concerning agricultural policy in this initial phase. In 1941 its professed objectives were "necessary improvements in the use of land" and "improving the situation of the peasants." Its programs up to when it was banned in 1949 did not go beyond demanding that state and crown lands and the estates of the great landowners be assigned free of charge to peasants. The government was to pay the purchase price of the land to the former owners. The Tudeh agenda also included demands for financial support for the peasants and changes in the quotas for dividing the harvest. Other demands were made unofficially in the party press and showed that various groups in the movement had been brought together. Broadly speaking the movement was for the abolition of "feudalism" and the "tribal order," which was to be succeeded by a progressive social and economic system that took into account the interests of the majority of the population.

During this phase the Tudeh Party made an attempt to organize the countryside, setting up a Union of Peasants (ettehadiye-ye dehqanan) in 1944. By March 1947 it had branches in villages near towns in more than twelve provinces, and it reputedly succeeded in organizing active resistance to the landlords in many places. The party set up the union in the hope of correcting one of its greatest shortcomings—namely, that only 2 percent of its members at the time were peasants. The attempt was unsuccessful, however, in that it had only managed to enroll several thousand peasants by the time it was banned in 1949.[35]

Between November 1945 and December 1946 the Democratic Party of Azerbaijan (ferqe-ye demokrat-e Azarbaijan), which was ideologically and organizationally close to the Tudeh Party and a provincial power independent of the central government, succeeded in taking some practical steps toward reforming agricultural policy in the area under its control. It formed an autonomous government in the province of Azerbaijan that was propped up by the Soviet occupying power and only lasted as long as the occupation itself. Its aim was autonomy, to which end it was trying to form the Azerbaijanis into a united front against the central government. Therefore, its social and economic policies were far removed from what might otherwise be expected of a communist party—its land reform only encompassed distributing state land, as well as that belonging to non-Azerbaijani landowners and people considered to be traitors or opponents of the autonomy movement, to peasants.[36]

Political liberalization under the Mosaddeq government permitted the Tudeh Party to become quite active in many parts of the country, including many rural regions. It established the Association for the Support of Peasants, published a peasant newspaper called *Ruzname-ye Enteqad,* set up a Cooperative and Promotion Fund for peasants, conducted a literacy campaign, tried to organize the peasants both in the party and in unions, called on them to chase off the great landowners, and involved them in demonstrations in the towns, especially in Tehran, in support of the party's own interests, which went beyond those of the peasants. Over and above these demands and measures, it insisted that all the peasants' debts be waived and that the payments the peasants had had to make to buy the crown lands be reimbursed.[37]

After the successful coup against the Mosaddeq government in August 1953, the Tudeh Party had to go into exile. Operating from Eastern Europe, it was reduced to long-distance observation and analysis of agricultural policy. The resumption of activities coincided with the beginning of the discussion in Iran about the land reform. The party often contradicted itself when assessing the character, significance, and effects of the land reform program. For example, it declared in the summer of 1961 that land reform would be unable to alter the nature of the regime, which had come into being as a result of a combination of feudalism and imperialism.[38] Two years later a presidium member, Kiyanuri, further declared that land reform would not result in any basic change to the semifeudal and semicolonial nature of Iranian society, but that feudal relationships would become somewhat weaker and capitalist ones somewhat stronger (1963, pp. 9ff). By 1973 the party had reversed its estimation of the consequences of the land reform. It now accused "several of the opposition groups operating abroad" of closing their eyes to change by continuing to talk about a regime in Iran characterized by a mixture of feudalism and capitalism and refusing to see that "the land reform, despite all [its] inadequacies, has dealt the feudal order a serious blow and moved Iranian villages forward in the direction of capitalist relationships."[39] The Tudeh Party did not, however, view these changes as sufficient. It thought they would not lead to a solution of the agrarian problem that would be to the benefit of the peasants. They were also at odds with the course of world history, in that they ran counter to the transition from world capitalism to world socialism.[40] They did indicate that the peasants had successfully fought for their rights and effected the collapse of the old fuedal order.[41] In any event, they were still far from being a party that advocated fundamental land reform.

The Tudeh Party's documents and publications in the 1960s and 1970s showed what a fundamental reform ought to look like. True to its Leninist theory of revolution, the party's reform program consisted of three stages. "Until the phase in which the objective and subjective conditions are ripe for the (democratic-national) revolution and for carrying out a democratic land reform, it is the task of all national and progressive forces to support the peasants in their fight for the following urgent demands and mobilize [them] for the realization of these slogans":

1. distribution of the large estates still in the possession of the great landowners
2. transfer of the estates that are below the large dams and in the possession of the U.S., British, French, and Japanese monopolies to peasants with little or no land
3. remission of the payments that the peasants had been committed to vis-à-vis the state, landowners, and court
4. remission of debts that peasants incurred with former landowners, moneylenders, and RCs before and after land reform

These demands were complemented by a number of others that can be summarized as follows: extend, democratize and dynamize the cooperatives; reform the credit system; provide adequate water, agricultural machinery, and other inputs; develop new arable areas; expel monopoly capital from agriculture; discharge indebted peasants from prison; create jobs by expanding rural industry; and use the material and technical help of the socialist countries in horticulture and stock breeding.

If the democratic-national revolution was successful, additional measures would be taken with the intention of solving the agrarian problem. A "radical land reform" would then take place to block the capitalist path to development, open the noncapitalist path to development, and prepare conditions for transition to the "phase of socialist revolutionary land reform under the leadership of the working class." The reform would encompass transferring all areas under cultivation to peasants with little or no land or to their cooperatives free of charge; nationalizing water; founding bigger, more modern enterprises by means of peasant producer cooperatives; nationalizing banks and other credit institutions; improving rural regions; nationalizing the marketing of agricultural produce; establishing agricultural colleges; and so forth.[42]

The Tudeh Party continued to discuss the problems of agricultural policy after the 1979 revolution. Returned from exile, it fought assiduously in its press organs and in universities, government offices, and the provinces for implementation of a land reform as envisaged in its program for the democratic revolution. It propounded its concepts for solving the agrarian problem in the affiliated journal *Masa'el-e Keshawarzi* (Problems of Agriculture), which was written semiscientifically and published in six bulky volumes between 1980 and 1982. In accordance with the party attitude toward the leadership of the Islamic state, it also used some Islamist jargon so as to influence the government's agrarian policy. It succeeded, sometimes fairly directly, as experts who either belonged to or were affiliated with the Tudeh Party were consulted by Islamist functionaries.[43] This influence is plain in many of the measures advocated by the radical Islamists responsible for agricultural policy.

Other Marxist-Leninist or Maoist groups and individuals discussed land reform and its consequences, too. The four tracts by the Organization of People's Fada'iyain (sazman-e cherikha-ye fada'i-ye khalq) published outside Iran in 1973 and 1974 are of interest here, as they contain reports and analyses of the land reform based on independent observations and interviews in eighty villages and farm corporations. Other organizations, most notably the Revolutionary Organization of the Tudeh Party (sazman-e enqelabi-ye hezb-e Tudeh), the Federation of Iranian Communists (etehadiye-e kommounistha-ye Iran), and the Tufan Organization (sazman-e Tufan), also dealt with this issue.[44] Not to be forgotten is the Confederation of Iranian Students in Europe and the United States, which represented a rallying point for almost every left-wing opposition Iranian outside the country and whose organs *Shanzdah-e Azar* and *Name-ye Parsi* expressed its position on land reform.[45] Individuals such as B. Moumeni (also under his pseudonym B. Parsa) and Sodagar conducted investigations, the results of which were only able to be published in the revolutionary years.

The main purpose of these tracts[46] was to determine the degree to which the land reform had changed the social structure of Iran. The opposition hoped for an answer to the question of which phase of the revolution Iran was in and thus which social forces would be the standard bearers of the revolution. The evaluation of the peasantry as a revolutionary force played a central role. Whereas some organizations, such as the People's Fada'iyain, had come around to the view that land reform had changed the country's social structure from a semifeudal and semicolonial one to a capitalist-imperialist one in which only remnants of feudalism could be made out, others, such as the Tufan Organization, insisted that Iran should still be considered both semifeudal and semicolonial. The Revolutionary Organization of the Tudeh Party based the strategic slogan it had borrowed from Mao Tse-Tung—"Long live the path of encircling the towns by villages"—on just this assessment, meaning the peasants would be the standard bearers of the revolution in Iran.[47] The 1979 revolution showed just how far removed from reality such pseudoanalyses were. The leftists' problem was that they relied on ready-made, alien theories to arrive at a predetermined conclusion, of which they were convinced before they got to know reality. This alienation from society was certainly the root cause of the fiasco experienced by the Iranian left in the revolution.

2.3 Islamist Thinking

Islamist and/or Islamic thinking on agricultural problems in the prerevolutionary era is found in four categories of literature: (1) traditional literature on Islamic law; (2) traditional literature on agriculture and the methods employed; (3) new theoretical and ideological tracts on an "Islamic economy"; and (4) literature on current agricultural problems.

2.3.1 Agriculture in the Literature on Islamic Law

The law books written in the traditional law schools during the prerevolutionary era—known as the touzih ol-masa'el (Solution to the Questions),[48] authorized by the marj'a-e taqlid (Instances of Imitation) or more detailed versions of them,[49] contain decrees and *fatwas*[50] on many questions relating either directly or indirectly to agriculture. They deal with such problems as the organization of enterprises, rent, tax, buying and selling land and agricultural produce, foundations, and landed property.

The decrees relevant to the organization of enterprises are those that regulate tenancy (ejare) as well as sharecropping in field-farming (mozare'e) and in horticulture (mosaqat). They belong to the types of contract known as 'oqud,[51] which have been enshrined in the sharia for centuries and mainly define the relationship between the owner of the land or garden and the peasant that cultivates the soil or trees and splits the harvest. The predominant form in Iran before land reform was mozare'e,[52] a system for combining the productive factors in field-farming (land, labor, draft animal, seed corn, and water) and splitting the harvest that dates back to the pre-Islamic era in Iran and the Byzantine Empire.[53] It formed the foundation of peasant-landlord relationships in Iran prior to land reform. Although the relevant decrees in the sharia do not openly sanction all the exploitative practices of Iran's landowners in respect of mozare'e, they do confirm the basic features of the system—even after land reform, which largely ended sharecropping by transforming the sharecroppers into landowners. Mozare'e fixes the shares due to those who provide the various productive factors as a fraction of the harvest, but the law books set no limit on the individual shares, which are to be fixed by contract or in accordance with local custom. Iran's sharecropping practice made it abundantly clear who benefited from the contract or from local custom in the landlord system.[54] The law books contain a number of decrees describing the landowner as the one who determines the terms of the contract. Thus, the landowner was entitled to decide what happened to the peasant's share if the crop did not ripen during the life of the contract.[55]

Mosaqat is similar: The owner of an orchard and a horticulturist agree that the latter will irrigate and tend the fruit trees for a share of the harvest. Ejare covers "the contractually regulated use of an animal, house, field, garment, product and similar things owned by a person" and includes a person's work. It fixes the level of payment—which may not, however, come from the product of the land that has been leased. Any damage that might occur does not exempt the tenant from paying the rent unless otherwise agreed.[56] Like mozare'e, ejare is also found in older Shi'ite law books,[57] and it, too, was displaced by modern types of business[58] unknown to Islamic law books.

The Islamic laws also refer to other forms of contract, such as ja'ale (contract to manufacture) and mozarebe (on commission). These are not normally used to regulate the relationships between those who provide the various productive factors in agriculture, but they were mentioned as possibilities in this respect after the revolution. They do not mention such forms as the mosha' (farms on jointly owned land), which were set up in great numbers after the revolution and proclaimed Islamic.

The chapters of the traditional law books concerned with commerce and trade (makaseb wa matajer) or buying and selling (bai') refer largely to land and agricultural produce (with separate sections on trading in animals, fruit, vegetables, and cereals). They always elaborate the conditions under which the sharia declares exchange of these products to be permitted, prohibited, recommended, or reprehensible. Practices such as preemption (salaf) of agricultural produce are declared right and proper,[59] despite the fact that they put the peasants at a severe disadvantage. Hoarding is prohibited, but (according to the old sources) only for wheat, barley, dates, raisins, olives, and oils.[60]

Appropriately for the venerable Islamic legal system, its decrees on commerce and trade originate in past social orders. This derivation is made clear by the prevalence of agricultural produce in the cases cited, the simplicity of the business relationships, and the fact that currencies such as the derham, which is no longer legal tender and now only to be found in museums, are mentioned as the means of transaction.[61] It is also anachronistic to talk about kharaj (land tax), eqta' (fief), and land that came into the hands of the Muslims in their first wave of conquests.[62] "Anyone is allowed to receive kharaj land from the state against a sum and to use it for himself for farming or planting orchards. . . . What the [unjust] state collects as taxes . . . in cash or kind for date trees or other trees is subject to the same regulation as that which the just sultan [state] collects. The payer is thus exempted from his kharaj liability, which is the same as the fee for the land."[63] "The landowner pays [the] kharaj which the sultan levies on date and other trees on kharaj land."[64]

Land and agricultural produce are also the basis for the khoms (a tithe of one-fifth) and zakat (poor tax), to which individual chapters are devoted in the traditional law books. The poor tax is to be paid from the camels, cattle, sheep, gold, silver, wheat, barley, dates, and raisins possessed, insofar as they attain a certain measure. It is handed directly to poor devout

Shi'ites without state intervention. The tithe is split into six parts. One part should belong to "exalted God, one part to the Prophet, one part to the Imam." These three parts currently fall to the "Supreme Commander," i.e., the hidden twelfth Imam, or his deputies, meaning the ayatollahs. The other three parts belong to the poor, the orphans, and the fighters for God's cause who are descended on their father's side from 'Abd el-Motalleb, Muhammad's great grandfather. The tithe is levied on the spoils of war, mines, pearl diving, treasure, and the profits made in agriculture, trade, and so on.[65]

There is also a separate chapter in the traditional law books on the regulations concerning foundations established for personal fortunes.[66] In practice, land was also endowed, and prior to the land reform it was cultivated like normal landlords' land—i.e., by tenants and sharecroppers—largely to the benefit of the clerics. It accounted for a considerable proportion of the arable land cultivated in Iran.[67] Land reform let the peasants have most of these tracts on ninety-nine-year leases, much to the annoyance of the clerics, who refused to accept the measure—it was rescinded after the revolution (see Chapter 9.7).

Many of the laws mentioned above presuppose that private land ownership is legitimate and that those providing the labor own no property and approach the landowner intending to sign a lease or sharecropper contract. This sanctioning of private land ownership is also implicit in the regulations in the traditional law books on inheritance, reclamation of wasteland, partnerships, loans, sureties, settlements, gifts, mortgages, and so forth.[68] There is no mention of a quantitative limit on private landed property, other than in the regulations stating that part of the land belongs to the state or the Muslim community. The qualitative limitations ensuing from the ban on certain practices and transactions (e.g., usury, games of chance, trade in alcoholic beverages) and from the repudiation of property rights so acquired as well as from the decree laws (such as the inheritance law) are another matter—all restrict the individual's control of his property. In addition, there are in Islamic law rules (qa'ede) that, like the zarar rules, prohibit or restrict the use of private property rights in ways that would be detrimental to other Muslims (see Chapter 9.2).[69]

Ayatollah Khomeini explicitly sanctioned private property when he expressed his opinion on the taslit rule, according to which, in a saying handed down from Muhammad, "people are lords of their fortunes." Khomeini wrote: "The rule, which respects the fortunes of people, belongs to the derivations of the taslit rule, and this rule is a rational one which, in the opinion of the sages, is to be classed with the decrees that refer to property because the owner of a thing is lord of the same in every respect. The holy legislator has certified and asserted this with the hadith handed down from the Prophet: People are lords of their fortunes."[70]

The traditional law books divide up communal and state land according to the manner in which the Islamic Empire acquired it. Enfal—i.e., assets residing in and administered by the office of the ruler (Prophet, Imam, Sultan, etc.) and which can be transferred by him—is land that came into the possession of the Muslims without the use of force. It includes uncultivated and ownerless land, wasteland, coast lines, woodland, oases, deserts, and mountain peaks.[71] Then there is 'anwa land—i.e., land conquered by force in wars against the infidels—which belongs to the community of Muslims, is administered by the ruler, and can be transferred for kharaj to anyone who ensures its cultivation.[72]

It should be emphasized that the traditional law books do not establish any link between the former enfal or 'anwa land and the present forms of landed property and so do not draw any consequences from these categories to justify reforming the existing structure of land ownership, as happened after the revolution. On the contrary, it is assumed that the present private title to the former 'anwa land was acquired legitimately, by reclamation.[73]

There is nothing in the traditional law books that could be seen as contributing to the formulation of a particular agricultural policy in the modern sense. Not even their sanctioning of private landed property could serve this end, as this doctrine exists in the context of the old landlord structures. Such references to traditional land ownership were certainly one reason most of the prominent clerics opposed the shah's land reform. The decrees that permit individuals to acquire private landed property by reclaiming wasteland might be best able to promote agriculture, as it makes cultivation of unproductive acreage palatable to investors. The land available for the purpose is mostly state land, "which while the [twelfth] Imam is in hiding can be reclaimed by anyone and become his property, irrespective of whether he is a Muslim or an infidel." But there are considerable problems if the land concerned belongs to someone, even an unknown owner. If the owner is known, he must waive his right to cultivate the land before it can be released for reclamation. At any rate, property rights take precedence over the benefits of reclamation, even for wasteland. They only lose their blocking function if the owner waives his cultivation rights. Even 'anwa land can be reclaimed if the ruler so permits.[74]

2.3.2 Agriculture in Other Traditional Literature

The sources on which Shi'ite law is based (Quran, tradition, and the *Nahj al-Balagha*)[75] contain many pointers on the significance and value of agriculture, as well as recommendations that Muslims should engage in it. To the extent that they are cited in the present discussion of agricultural problems, these sources form part of the thinking that is of interest here. The fact that these tracts are constantly reprinted and read makes clear their relevance.

In his 1974 book *Islamic Economy,* Ali Tehrani compiled all the Quran verses and ahadith that he considered relevant to the economic discourse of our time. Some have only a general application inasmuch as they are positive appraisals of the natural resources that God is supposed to have created and made available to man for the purpose of shaping a happy life. Consider verse 2/22, which says: "[Serve him] who has made the earth to a carpet for you and the heavens to its roof and who let water come down from heaven and brought forth fruits as sustenance for you."[76] Sheikh Tehrani interprets such passages as encouraging mankind to productive activity by inserting appropriate sentences or parts thereof into the translation. Productive labor is only properly honored in the ahadith. Here are some examples:

The first Imam, Ali, is quoted by the sixth Imam, Ja'far al-Sadeq, as saying: "God banishes from him he who has water and earth to hand but is yet needy." The sixth Imam is quoted as saying: "No one may become remiss in earning his livelihood and in providing his food[stuffs]." The seventh Imam is quoted as saying: "Avoid negligence, sloth and self-abasement, lest the goods of this world and the next forsake you." Muhammad is quoted as saying: "Striving for permitted foodstuffs is like the holy war for God."

Pursuit of wordly goods is sanctioned in the Nahj al-Balagha, as long as it is done to supply one's own food and does not degenerate into collecting riches (pp. 1103, 1165, etc.). However, the book is somewhat inclined to encourage moderation and a disregard for wordly goods if they exceed what is necessary to satisfy the most basic needs.

Directly related to agriculture are ahadith such as the following:

> "Farm, plant trees: God bears witness that man has done nothing better and fairer than this."
> "Agriculture is great alchemy."
> "Farmers are like treasures among men. On the day of the Last Judgment the highest rank and greatest proximity [to God] is accorded them, and people call them blessed."
> "Farmers are God's treasures on earth. No activity is more loved by God than farming."[77]

All these sayings come from the Shi'ites' sixth Imam, Imam Ja'far Sadeq, and many others point the same way. There is a hadith reporting that the Prophet Muhammad, asked what was the best deed, replied: sowing a field, tending the field, and paying the alms for the needy from the harvest.[78]

These and other ahadith are quoted in various works devoted to presenting the "Islamic economy." They report, for instance, how Ali, the first Imam, was himself a farmer; how Muhammad reported that Jesus had advised tree planters so that their trees would not be infested with worms; and how Imam Sadeq reportedly drew the attention of farmer disciples to the benefits of wind for farming.[79] One factor the Nahj al-Balagha often emphasizes as important to agriculture's success is the way state employees deal with the r'aiyat (peasant subjects). It repeatedly admonishes governors and tax collectors to do so carefully and fairly (pp. 861, 878, 976, etc.).

Old sources devoted to agricultural technology (such as geology, pest control, fertilizing, methods of planting trees, irrigation, etc.) ought not to be ignored.[80] Although it is practically impossible to establish a link between them or their subject and Islam, some of the authors, such as Fakhr ad-Din Razi (died 1209), rank among the great Islamic scholars. Such books as the famous and widely read *Holliyat al-Mottaqin* (Credit to the Pious) by M. Majlesi (died 1699), which deals with the moral code, also contain some recommendations in agrarian issues. This type of literature was rarely published in the prerevolutionary era; I am only aware of one such instance—namely, when H. M. Kermani, a scholar from the Sheikhiye sect, made an attempt in the traditional manner. The result was a booklet called "Tract on the Science of Farming," in which, among other things, the author vents his anger at Europeans, who have some dubious views on fertilizing fields. "As the people have turned their backs on the Prophet's sharia," he argues, "they turn to the Europeans. They even call them infallible, praise them in company and find pleasure in their inclinations; it is sheer unbelief if the Prophet's enemy is praised" (pp. 8ff).

2.3.3 An "Islamic Economy"

More than three dozen works elaborating an Islamic economy appeared in Iran in the three decades preceding the revolution. Some dealt only with individual questions related to this theoretical-ideological construction, whereas others had a broader perspective. Not all of them are of equal importance or even reached a broad public. The most significant authors are M. Taleqani (1954), M. B. Sadr (1969), A. Bani Sadr (1978), A. Tehrani (1974), and H. Peyman (1978).[81]

It is characteristic of these works that they do not base their theories on current economic processes but rather on the written sources of Islam (Quran, *Nahj al-Balagha,* and ahadith). The economic and social life of the past, to which they refer, is in consequence the same as the one that is the social basis of the sources.[82] The Islamic economy so created consists of a corpus of socioethical and canonical imperatives that can be traced back to God's word and constructs a normative system whose implementation is to go hand in hand with the realization of the Islamic social order and Islamic man. The way to these aims is through the Islamic state that is to come out of the struggle against taghut (the illegitimate state, embodying polytheism and evil).

Seen in this light, these works contain nothing of importance on Iran's present agricultural problems, which are no more in evidence than production in general, for which the works show only scant interest—despite production being the cornerstone of any economic order. They discuss all the more eagerly capitalism and socialism and their political pendants—i.e., liberalism and Marxism—as distribution systems and compare them to the supposedly superior alternative of the Islamic economic system (or theory), emphasizing the advantages of the Islamic property system. Property is an important part of Islamic economic ideology, second only to the argument with capitalism and socialism or liberalism and Marxism: Ali Shari'ati reportedly considers economics nothing more than the science of property questions.[83]

When these works refer to property, they focus on landed property, because the sources they are based on date from an era when both land and landed property played a dominant role in economic life. The views expressed on the question of landed property differ from those usually taken by the representatives of the traditional sharia (see Chapter 9.2). Although there are differences of interpretation in the works on Islamic economics, there are as many, if not more, points in common, partly because of the fact that most of these ideologues are intellectually oriented and modernistically inclined clerics or laymen who adopt radical social positions. They are at pains, in particular when discussing Marxism, to emphasize that the Islamic social and economic order is more just than the socialist one even though they are themselves influenced by Marxism, from which they have borrowed a great deal of their theoretical and ideological constructions.

The Islamist economic ideologues agree among themselves and with the ulama (Islamic jurists) that landed property is actually reserved for God.[84] The right to own land (or just the right to use the soil, depending on the sociopolitical attitude of the theoretician) is conferred on (1) all mankind (nas) or the Muslim community (umma); (2) individuals; or (3) states (Prophet, Imam, governor). They determine each category's share by referring to decisions supposedly made during the first Muslim conquests: Enfal land belongs to the state, 'anwa land to the community of Muslims or to mankind, with decisions concerning these two categories being incumbent on the Imam or the Islamic state. However, a politically liberal ideologue such as A. Bani Sadr may want to have the Imam absorbed into the community (and thus see state land become communal land),[85] whereas others distinguish clearly between state and communal land.[86]

Greater differences are apparent with respect to the relationship of the individual to the soil. The economic ideologues, contrary to the ulama, only acknowledge conditional usufructuary rights to the state or communal land that the state has ceded.[87] However, M. B. Sadr acknowledges private ownership in at least two cases: for those who voluntarily convert to Islam and for those who have signed a peace treaty with the Muslims (1969, vol. 2, pp. 94ff and 105f). The Muslim leaders reputedly permitted these exceptions for political reasons. Reza Esfahani observes that in a society whose laws do not correspond to the sharia, a Muslim would on the basis of the secondary decrees (see Chapter 9.4) be allowed to buy and sell land as private property (1978, vol. 4, pp. 17ff). Tehrani acknowledges a very restricted form of private property, which the state can declare invalid whenever its interests so demand (1974, pp. 85f and 269). According to Peyman, in the present societies even natural resources cannot be used by individuals and must be subjected to the principle of common property.[88] Both he and others consider the buying and selling of land mentioned in the sharia to refer to the right to *use* it, not to own the land itself.[89]

These authors prefer to restrict property rights to the products of the soil obtained through work.[90] They see usufructuary rights as being primarily acquired through reclamation of wasteland and lasting as long as the land is cultivated. They also understand these rights as priority rights, meaning that whoever reclaims the land has priority in using it.[91] Land reclamation by individuals ought not to cover large areas but should be restricted by the limits of personal needs or personal labor.[92]

Although sharecropping is acknowledged not only by M. B. Sadr but also by Peyman (1978, p. 205), Bani Sadr (1978, pp. 170ff), Taleqani (1954, pp. 252), and others, they approve of it in a restricted form that differs from the way it was actually practiced before land reform and from the form covered in the traditional law books. First and foremost is the restriction that he who possesses the land must also provide the seed corn if he is to be considered for a share of the harvest, according to a principle laid down by the authors that only the owners of the raw materials involved in the production deserve a share of the product. Sharecropping that does not fulfill this condition is called not mozare'e but rather mokhabere, which the Prophet reportedly termed reprehensible.[93] Thus, the possessor of the land has no share of the harvest, as such, only receiving rent in return for the work he has invested in reclaiming the land. The remuneration received by those who provide the other productive factors is also in exchange for the work involved. Esfahani (1978, vol. 4, p. 31f) accepts sharecropping if the one who provides the land also provides other means of production apart from seed corn; for the work required to make these contributions he receives part of the harvest. Basically, these authors award property rights only to whoever provides the labor; whoever provides other productive factors receives a remuneration for them from the one who provides the labor.[94] The exception, as mentioned above, is the proprietor of the seed corn.

The interpretations of Islam's attitude to landed property made by these ideologues were significant in that they were able to make clear, even before the revolution, the divergent positions taken by the Islamists on the subjects and the consequences this dissonance would have for solving such problems. It was only after the revolution that a complete awareness of the scope of these differences dawned, particularly during the debates about the relevant legislation.

2.3.4 Thinking on Current Agricultural Problems

Islamist thinking on current agricultural problems can be split into two parts: opinions about land reform in the 1960s and criticism of the poor state of agriculture, for which land reform was largely held responsible.

A significant number of the clerics, who can be termed socially conservative, rejected land reform from the very beginning, among them no less a person than Grand Ayatollah Brujerdi, the last individual to hold the normally collective position of "instance of imitation" (marja'-e taqlid). He expressed his opposition to the government's project in a letter dated February 13, 1960, to Ayatollah J'afar Behbahani, condemning the first land reform bill as a measure directed against the sharia and the constitution.[95] Behbahani wrote his own letter against the bill and sent them both to the speaker.[96] Encouraged by this eminent support, parliament—which at the time consisted mostly of landlords—watered the bill down so thoroughly by May 1960 that it had lost its purpose.

But this was not the end of the dispute about land reform—a tenacious and widespread fight broke out that finally led to the so-called White Revolution, which focused on land reform. Advocates and detractors of land reform were involved in this struggle within the government. The regime's political opponents—conservative clerics, left-wing organizations, liberals, social democrats, modern Islamists, etc.—used the relaxation of the dictatorship caused by the internecine battle to conduct a campaign aimed at ending the dictatorship and reinstating the constitution and its democratic principles. The regime's rejection of these demands led the opposition groups to draw closer together and become more intransigent. New leaders came to power who were pugnacious in their statements against the regime and popular enough to get the masses behind them. The opposition clerics, in whose camp various social tendencies came together, gained the most power.

The clerics saw the movement for political democratization mainly as a chance to redress the shift in the balance of power that had occurred after the 1953 putsch. The decisiveness and radicalness of the conservatives among them were reinforced by the modernization measures the regime introduced in the hope of overcoming the political and economic crisis at the end of 1962. On October 8, 1962, the regime announced that the laws governing the election of local councils were to be changed. Women were permitted to participate in the elections, and the condition that only Muslims could stand for election was lifted. If a non-Muslim were elected, he would not have to take his oath on the Quran. The clerics viewed these changes as a conspiracy against themselves and Islam, with the aim of enabling the Baha'i religion, whose adherents they particularly hated, to gain access to the decisionmaking centers.[97] The changes in the electoral law were soon followed by other measures to be implemented as part of the White Revolution, including the dissolution of the landlord-peasant relationship, worker participation in business profits, formation of the Army of Knowledge, and so on. Each of these measures represented an encroachment on the structures and value systems for which the conservative clerics felt responsible.

The increase in political pressure accompanying the introduction of these modernization measures as well as the general protest against the dictatorship enabled the conservative clerics not only to conceal their rejection of land reform behind the opposition's democratic demands but also to emerge as opposition spokesmen. They became more vociferous in their protests against the suppression of political freedoms, demanding that the constitution be reinstated and leading the struggle against the influence of the United States, under whose pressure the shah had become an advocate of land reform. The more the regime emphasized that the clerics were hiding their opposition to land reform behind democratic demands,[98] the more strictly the clerics maintained their silence on the subject[99] or rejected such accusations completely. In a leaflet published by the Society of Iranian Clerics (Jam'e-ye Rohaniyat-e Iran) in Khordad in 1342 (June/July 1963), the authors declared:

> [The] ulama, contrary to the ridiculous and thoroughly false propaganda of the government apparatus, reject any property that has come about through illegal possession of the people's property, oppressing the peasants and depriving them of their rights and/or failing to pay the levies determined by the sharia for the poor.... The ulama approve if (under the supervision of the religious authorities) land is taken away without payment from the owners who have deprived the peasants of it by force and extortion; they also approve of the taking away of land corresponding in value to the rights the peasants have been derived of or the value of the retained sharia levies [poor tax and khoms] represented by the claims of the needy on the public purse. Even the wasteland that has been taken into possession contrary to the standards of the sharia must be removed from the control of its possessors. This must take place under the supervision of righteous people and with the permission of the religious authorities, not through those who themselves are among the feudal lords of the first order and whose hand is plunged up to the elbow in the blood of the peasants and working classes.

The leaflet then makes the following basic statement:

> It can basically be asserted, that if the Islamic theses in respect of land ownership or other things were taken into consideration and if the rights of the needy classes established by the sharia were observed, the ownership structure in our country could not have taken on the form which it

has today. . . . That which the ulama with reference to heavenly Islamic teaching oppose and fight with all their might is the fact that everything is treated alike. No distinction is made between the idle and oppressive owners and the hardworking people who use their capital and strength for the construction of the country, for the improvement of the economy and for creating job opportunities (regardless of how small their number is) and in consequence a movement is oppressed which some people have put in motion for the reclamation of uncultivated land.

The authors also discuss the government's accusation that the ulama are against land reform because they fear the loss of benefits derived from administering the foundation estates: "The waqf estates are all in government hands and if they are misused then this happens due to manipulations by the Foundation Authority." The leaflet also attempts to refute the argument that the ulama received payments from the feudal lords and so tended to support their cause. "Come and investigate whether a penny from the feudal lords has reached the city of Qom or whether anyone has caught sight of a single feudal lord at the religious authorities. Everyone knows that the costs of the religious organizations are borne by people who belong to the third and, to a degree, the second class." In the last paragraph, the authors point out that with land reform the government is aiming "to concentrate all [the] Satanic but fragmented forces of the feudal lords in its own hands," and call this concentration of power "far more dangerous and ominous" than the rule of the feudal lords.[100]

Ayatollah Kazem Shari'atmadari made a similar statement the same month,[101] and the editors of the religious journal *Maktab-e Eslam* (Islamic Teaching) published at least two statements emphasizing that the ulama are not against reforms.[102] A declaration signed by the Movement of Islamic Combatants (Nehzat-e Mobarezin-e Eslami) prophesied that the "bogus land reform" would bring misery to the peasants. Another leaflet, written by the Council of United Muslims (Shoura-ye Mosulmanan-e Motahhed), pointed out that land reform would lead to the landlords being replaced by the state and transform the country into a market for foreign products.[103]

These declarations, made on behalf of the clerics by unknown organizations without naming the signatories, cannot disguise the fact that the clerics disagreed among themselves about land reform. Clerics with radical social views definitely favored a reform of the land ownership structure and, like Sheikh Ali Tehrani and Ayatollah Taleqani, implied so in their writings. The others, whose position was firmly within the majority Shi'ite tradition or who were themselves landowners,[104] were unwilling to accept restrictions on private landed property without a fight.[105] Indeed, this position was taken by a large number of clerics, a fact that became evident in the 1980s, when the conservative clerics, who by then were in power, successfully blocked all attempts to restrict private landed property.[106] Despite protestations to the contrary, a conservative concept of land reform is evident in the June/July 1963 leaflet quoted at length above, inasmuch as it limits reform to landed property whose acquisition can be declared illegal by the sharia.

The positions adopted by various Islamists in their writings on Islamic law or Islamic economy provide another way of determining their views on land reform. It should, however, be borne in mind that their opinions on specific reform concepts might well differ from their basic positions because of an insight into the impracticability of the latter or for reasons of opportunism. This variance can be demonstrated clearly if a concrete reform concept has been formulated, as in Taleqani's case.[107] For the rest of the clerics, one must rely on assumptions or on statements they made while criticizing land reform.

Enough of the clerics on land reform. Statements on the question by lay Islamist theoreticians or Islamist organizations, led in the main by such people, are available as well. The documents of the National Resistance Movement (Nehzat-e Moqawemat-e Melli; NRM)—which came into being shortly after the fall of the Mosaddeq government and in which such Islamists as Mehdi Bazargan, Ayatollah Taleqani, and Yadollah Sahabi played a major part[108]—contain some passages clarifying the movement's position on the question of land reform.

The NRM saw the distribution of crown lands[109] as a measure foreign powers had urged upon the shah with the aim of maintaining their influence in Iran.[110] In a leaflet put out on May 2, 1955, the NRM stated its position on the "land question or the demagogic policy of land distribution." Pointing out the complexity of the problem, it objected to the motives with which various political movements tackled the question and said that the advocates of land distribution lacked any logically conceived solution to the problem. It also promised that "the land question [would] . . . be at the head of all internal problems after the imperialist influence in Iran has been checked."[111] The NRM basically undertook to put an end to "feudalism" in Iran.[112]

The Freedom Movement of Iran (Nehzat-e Azadi-ye Iran; FM), founded by Bazargan, Taleqani, and Sahabi (without the non-Islamist groups) in Tehran on May 15, 1961, was a sort of successor to the NRM. Its foundation coincided with the discussions about land reform and the White Revolution, and so it made its opinions on these questions known, going into the most detail in a document put out on January 23, 1963. The Freedom Movement acknowledged the need for revolution, in which it saw the "indispensable means of progress and renewal" and "the prerequisite of life and its laws of development." But the White Revolution did not accord with this definition of revolutions—it did not come from the peasants and workers but rather from the shah. Thus, it was not a revolution.

The document next criticized the belief held by both some opposition groups and the government that the feudal lords and landlords were the ruling force in Iran. Rather, the Freedom Movement argued, the state and the crown ruled the country, and it was impossible for such an unlimited amount of property and other assets to be concentrated in a few hands without state support. If, despite all this, there was now talk of doing away with feudalism, then it was because the United States wanted it done away with so as to protect the despotic monarchy and to safeguard, or even expand, the imperialist powers' interests in Iran. Land reform, which was initiated to this end, did not meet the requirements of a social revolution. The ill-considered measures to expropriate the landowners and the shock to the traditional agricultural order had, along with profit-sharing for the work force, caused all the foundations of the economy and production to crumble. The result was such stagnation that any hope of improvement in the foreseeable future had to be considered futile.

Land reform would also have the following effects: As individual peasants would not be in a position to take over the productive functions of the landlords, as the redistribution of land would rob the country of the opportunity to use modern means of production, and as the peasants were not yet able to counteract these shortcomings by setting up and successfully running producer cooperatives, they would be forced to accept help from the government or from abroad. However, the state would only bring disaster into the villages with its bureaucratism and corruption. So only one solution remained: the assistance of foreign capital and foreign experts. But that would be the wrong solution, one that imperialist policy hoped to impose, one that had been prepared long in advance. Moreover, replacing the local landlords with foreign ones would not solve the problem. It would simply permit a flood of foreign goods to stream into the Iranian villages. The Iranian market would thus fall into the aggressive claws of bloodthirsty international speculators. Agrarian production would drop to such a degree that "we . . . shall soon be forced to pay for our fodder, peas, beans, cucumbers and tomatoes with foreign currencies." A further result of such measures would be that the wave of dissatisfaction set in motion in the student and urban milieu would soon envelop the villages and factories to a large extent and create favorable conditions for the spread of communism. The FM compared this gloomy prospect with the national liberation revolution, whose approach it desired: "Revolution must come from within and not from without."[113]

This quasi–call for revolution was not, however, followed by an FM program for land reform or for reforms in other areas of economic and social life. Although the FM made it clear that it "by no means supports the unhappy and abnormal relationships between the landlords and peasants, nor the ailing system of land ownership, whose origin lies in numerous plunderings," it said nothing about what it wanted to replace this system with. It contented itself with pointing out that Islam had rejected land ownership for fourteen centuries and that in Islamic law "as presented by Mr. Taleqani," even woods, wasteland, and natural resources counted as public property.

There was no program to be found in the FM's other tracts and statements. Its 1960 party program merely stated that it "is for the creation of such relationships between workers and employers and landowners and farmers as are based on justice and peaceableness."[114] The FM understood the revolution to be a political one that would lead to the fall of the shah's regime and the formation of an Islamic state, and it only wanted to devote itself to solving economic and social problems, for which it had not developed any precise concepts in advance, after the political revolution. The draft land reform drawn up by Ayatollah Taleqani in his 1954 book only permits conjecture about the direction the organization might have taken.

In addition to issuing the tracts cited above, the FM spoke out on numerous other occasions on the problem of land reform, though much more briefly, sometimes in just a few sentences or phrases.[115] Another document deserving of mention in this connection is Yazdi's contribution on the "Islamic economy," as he also sees the solution to the questions of land and agriculture in reclaiming wasteland. According to him, 85 to 90 percent of cultivable land in Iran could be reclaimed, but such land should not become the property of those who reclaim it because there is no private landed property in Islam. All the land in Iran belongs to the category of land that was conquered by force and thus belongs to the community, he argues; it was unlawfully given to private individuals by kings. Having the state buy it, as mandated under the shah's land reform, amounted to sanctioning the illegal appropriation of this land. Selling it to peasants would only harm them; it would signify plunder of public assets and could be of no benefit to agriculture (1968/9, vol. 5, p. 34f).

The political group known as the Fada'iyan-e Eslam (Those Sacrificing Themselves for Islam; FE) also saw the reclamation of wasteland as the solution to the land question; in their 1950 program they cited it as a method "for completely reforming public affairs." The FE also stated that 80 percent of the country's cultivable agricultural area was not cultivated and that water resources were left largely unused. It proposed to provide the necessary means to use these resources to expand agriculture and eliminate unemployment and poverty so that all the goods needed to feed and clothe the people could be produced in abundance domestically. It added, "With the help of appropriate technical means the Caspian Sea [sic] should also be used for the purpose of irrigating uncultivated land." The FE proposed setting up elementary schools in all the district villages, where, in addition to receiving standard lessons, the pupils would be instructed in practical agriculture for half the time. A fund was to be set up to help needy peasants by giving interest-free loans. It was also important that a suitable mosque be erected in all the Ministry of Agriculture's offices and factories, in which the public prayers could be said under the leadership of a worker or peasant, using a muezzin with a beautiful voice "so that everyone becomes clean and righteous." A green flag could flutter alongside the national flag at all three prayer times (p. 43f).

The program drafted by Bani Sadr in Paris in 1971/2, which only appeared as the *Manifesto of the Islamic Republic* after the revolution, sounds somewhat more professional. But this document, which deals with the country's economic, political, cultural, and social problems, is too general to contain details about agriculture. The text consists of two parts in which the aberrations characterizing the respective spheres are identified (part I) and solutions to correct them are addressed (part II). By reason of it, Bani Sadr presumed to claim that he was the only one of those in power after the revolution who had a comprehensive program.[116]

His analysis of the economy identifies processes relevant in part to agriculture: distribution of resources among the world powers; the transfer of the productive sector abroad; gearing production and consumption to foreign expectations; the fragmentation of the national economy into disconnected sectors and branches; severing production from the specific character of Iranian nature and culture and from the basic needs of the population; multiplication of imports, whereby the gap between them and exports also increases; the flight of investments into economic branches working toward the export of riches and the import of foreign products; destruction of the bases of economic independence; and increasing social inequality. These and similar processes, Bani Sadr argues, have resulted in there no longer being anything resembling a national economy in Iran today (pp. 18ff).

> In agriculture, all the good soil is under the control of foreign companies. Downstream from the Dez Dam, the peasants have been driven from their villages and their land given over to the multinational companies. The products which the latter manufacture with Iranian money and Iranian labor . . . are out of all proportion to the basic needs of the country. A large part of it is exported directly. A small part is for the consumption of the Westernized groups at home. . . . The central power is engaged today in destroying the possibilities for expanding agriculture. (p. 27)

Bani Sadr's proposals consist of a series of imperatives, but he has no idea either of their practicability or of how to implement them. He, too, adheres to the principle that the details should only be considered once the bastions of political power have been stormed. He states that agriculture "must be freed from obstacles to development and driven forward in harmony with the all-round development of the country" (p. 102). He expresses this wish in a list of imperatives for other sectors of the national economy and other aspects of social life. They are intended to found a society that is free of condominium by domestic and foreign forces and on the path to becoming the illustrious society of unity and assuming its role as a world pioneer. Bani Sadr adds the hope associated with this dream: "There is no reason why we should not be in a position to play the role of a paradigm for the emancipation of man on a global scale" (p. 96).

The 144-page manifesto has nothing more significant to say on the questions relating to agriculture than what has been quoted here, but what distinguishes these notions is that they are embedded in a survey of social problems and the beginnings of a comprehensive program that relates to real processes—even if the reform proposals are not based on real possibilities.

It is striking that the People's Mujahidin, of all the Islamist groups, gave a great deal of attention to land reform and its consequences. Two tracts concerned exclusively with this subject were published abroad by this clandestine organization, a 1972 book entitled *Rural Regions and the White Revolution* and a 1974 report on field work in the villages of the Arya Mehr Farm Corporation. Both works are exceptions among the Islamists. Like the People's Fada'iyan, the People's Mujahidin undertook such studies so as to become familiar with the changed conditions for revolution brought about by the land reform (1972, foreword). Unlike them, the Mujahidin emphasize the political reasons for land reform in these works without losing sight of its economic causes (pp. 1, 14ff, and 36ff).

The Mujahidin identified two major socioeconomic consequences of land reform—the transition from exploitative feudal relationships to capitalist ones (pp. 15 and 30) and the formation of a class of comparatively wealthy peasants whose political power did not match up to the increase in their economic power (pp. 25f, 42ff, etc.) as the socioeconomic consequences of the land reform. Although it had made smallholders of several thousand landless peasants, the Mujahidin pointed out, land reform had also strengthened the mechanisms that would take the land away from them again, turning them into agricultural laborers and causing the revolutionary potential in the countryside to grow (pp. 23f, 28, etc; 1974, p. 17). The Mujahidin saw the state's increasing infiltration of village life as a further consequence of land reform, which paved the way for social and political confrontation between the state and the peasantry, to which the Mujahidin attached great importance (1972, p. 30f). At the same time, they stated that the regime had failed to attain its aims: If the policymakers had been hoping to prevent the radicalization of the peasantry and build solid social support for the regime among the rural population, they had failed. The mass of exploited peasants—impoverished, deprived of their rights, deceived and disappointed by the land reform—continued to be ripe for revolution (pp. 42ff). Land reform had raised the peasants' awareness of their situation, making them deeply suspicious of the regime: "They are alert . . . , rebellious, and more important than all this is that their mutiny has set [a] course for the destruction of the regime."[117]

The Mujahidin followed some processes in the agricultural sector in their other publications, such as the *Newssheet* (Nashriye-ye Khabari),[118] which was published abroad. Moreover, in defense speeches given by Sa'id Mohsen (one of the founders of the organization) before a military tribunal,[119] he briefly listed some of the worst consequences of the land reform. But the Mujahidin were too strongly motivated by their revolutionary interests to leave much room for an independent analysis of Iranian agriculture or land reform. The organization was crushed early on by the regime, even before the revolution, leaving it no time to follow up its studies. The Mujahidin did not have a program of their own for restructuring the society they claimed to be fighting to liberate. However, their textbook *The Economy in Simple Language* permits the assumption that their agenda would have been very similar to the Leninist model of democratic revolutions.[120]

The *Economic Pointers of the Right Reverend Imam Khomeini,* published in 1985, is invaluable for assessing Islamist thinking on economic and agricultural problems before the revolution. It is a collection of excerpts from his communiqués, speeches, and interviews on various occasions, covering a wide range of subjects, among them ones relevant to agriculture. The first note is dated March 30, 1962, and the statements made before November 4, 1977, account for only thirty-one of the book's pages. Most of the statements (120 of 176 pages) were made during his four-month stay in Paris (October 1978–February 1979). Voicing his opinions on current economic problems at a time when the world had just become aware of him and the international press was asking him about these things, Khomeini gave answers influenced by the expectations placed on him, a man on the verge of leading a unique revolution to victory.[121]

Hence, the collection actually does contain a number of passages where Khomeini airs his views on agricultural questions and land reform, plus statements that, taken together, give a rough idea of the concepts on which his agrarian policy program might be based. Concerning land reform, Khomeini emphasized that it was initiated on U.S. orders[122] and was intended to open the Iranian market to U.S. goods as well as to cement Israeli and U.S. control over the Iranian economy.[123] The nationalization of woods, waters, and pastures, he said, had served the same purpose, among others. "One gave all the good places to American, Zionist or British companies." The British queen and her consort, among others, had benefited from it.[124]

One of the statements made most often in this collection concerned the destruction of agriculture as a result of land reform. "Do you believe that Iran still has farming? . . . They have destroyed our farming, our agriculture to such an extent that we are needy in all [agricultural products], have stretched out our hands so that even Israel gives us fruit."[125] Khomeini pointed out time and again that land reform transformed Iran from an exporter of agricultural produce into a country that even had to import eggs.[126] The Khorasan province alone would have been able to supply the entire population for a year; now Iran as a whole could only supply itself for thirty-three days a year.[127] But this situation was only possible as long as Iran exported oil; when it ran out, said Khomeini, the danger of starvation threatened the country.[128]

The rural exodus and the resultant slums in Tehran and other towns was another subject often mentioned. Khomeini held responsible the destruction of farming and stock rearing, the drying up of the subterranean canals (qanat), the pauperization of the peasants, their expulsion from their villages, and the expropriations.[129] He also criticized the erection of dams by foreign companies,[130] the neglect and waste of traditional water installations,[131] and the establishment of cooperative funds and banks that had reputedly harmed the peasants and merchants.[132] At one point he rejected the accusation that the clerics had been out to get the foundations back; at another he stated that the clerics opposed to the shah were not landowners and that land had nothing to do with the reasons for their opposition.[133]

Khomeini was questioned about his program a few times in Paris. Once he was asked whether he had a clear program or was just mouthing slogans. He answered: "There is a program. Islam has a program, more progressive and better than programs that have been implemented by imperialists." Whereupon the interviewer repeated his question: "Do you have a specific economic program?" Khomeini answered: "Yes, we have a specific, clear program. The Islamic program is specific and clear." Question: "Can we hear its main lines?" Answer: "Not yet. You must go and study to find out its basic lines. We shall announce all the political, economic and cultural lines of our [program] in the future."[134] This question-and-answer game took place on November 12, 1978. He gave similar replies in subsequent interviews.[135]

On January 23, 1979, Khomeini was asked about the form of property, especially landed property, in the Islamic state-to-be. His answer: "This will be clarified later." He became more talkative when asked whether his Islamic state would return the estates affected by land reform to their former owners, replying: "Definitely not." The reason? They had acquired their fortunes by ignoring the Islamic regulations on distribution. "If we assume power we shall seize the riches that these owners have taken possession of illegally and redistribute them fairly among the needy according to the law," Khomeini said, repeating this assurance for the umpteenth time.[136] Beyond that, he affirmed that he would nationalize the estates and natural resources that had been given over to foreign companies.[137] Yet he was at pains to emphasize that "property has been approved of in Islam," although on condition that Islamic regulations in respect of property rights and acquisition are observed.[138]

During the interviews, Khomeini stated self-sufficiency to be the aim of agricultural policy: "Our program is that the country's agriculture is put in a position to satisfy all domestic needs by raising the peasants' living standards up to those of the rest of the population."[139] This aim could be achieved quickly.[140] However, he was not always so optimistic, repeatedly acknowledging that "the reconstruction of agriculture" could not be realized forthwith.[141] In one interview he presented other measures he thought necessary for expanding agriculture: "We shall mechanize our agriculture. The Islamic state is obliged to provide everything the peasants need in best form. If agriculture in Iran is conducted properly we shall in future be among the exporters of foodstuffs. . . . For the mechanization of agriculture we shall obtain agricultural machinery from countries whose products are better value [for money] and more hard-wearing."[142]

Khomeini's statements on agricultural problems and ways to solve them permit the conclusion that his knowledge of and ideas on this complex of subjects remained superficial. In a speech on October 12, 1978, he said: "We do not know what they are doing with the country, we have no information. If [the shah] goes, God willing, then those who possess information can talk, those who know the truth about Iran and about the treasonable acts of this man can talk. But we have no information. With this superficial knowledge that we possess, we see that he has destroyed farming in Iran in the name of the land reform."[143]

We can conclude this survey of the Islamists' ponderings on the problems of Iranian agriculture with this acknowledgment of the lack of information about Iranian agriculture. Although it cannot be said with certainty that this overview covers everything the Islamists have uttered since the 1950s on the questions that are of interest here, the quality of what has been included permits the assumption that there would be no significant difference in any other sources still unknown to us. This assumption is justified by the following facts: (1) In economic and social questions the Islamists were concerned (other than with the relevant sections of traditional Islamic jurisprudence) almost exclusively with elaborating their ideologically based concepts of an "Islamic economy"; (2) Like almost all the other opposition groups, the Islamists were distracted from reflecting sufficiently on basic problems of social life by their overemphasis on the dictatorship and the question of overcoming it; (3) The Islamist periodicals had little interest in modern economic problems, and especially not in agricultural ones. I was unable to find a single article dealing solely with this complex of subjects in *Matab-e Mobarez* (Combatant Teaching), the periodical published by the Association of Islamic Students in Europe and the United States from September 1966 until after the revolution.[144] The same is true of *Maktab-e Eslam* (Islamic Teaching)[145] or *B'esat* (Mission),[146] published in Qom, Iran, between 1958 and 1963.

I occasionally find brief comments on various problematic aspects of agriculture and land reform in publications not so far mentioned here.[147] I also can conceive of other religious authorities apart from Khomeini having expressed their views on current questions. I know that Islamists such as Hojjat ol-Eslam Rafsanjani have themselves worked in agriculture,[148] and I am aware of some contributions to the theory of the Islamic economy that were probably written before the revolution but only published after it and that contain something about the state of affairs in agriculture.[149] All these points confirm my statement that the Islamists were poorly informed and gave little thought to the questions that are of interest here.

The conclusion, then, is that the Islamists were not in a position to confront the economic problems they encountered with concrete solutions of their own when they took power. Bani Sadr and Izadi, the first president and first minister of agriculture of the Islamic Republic, respectively, confirmed this conclusion in personal interviews.[150] Comparing the thinking of the Islamists with that of the other opposition groups, one cannot help but notice the more modest character of the former. Comparison with the works of experts is superfluous. What the Islamists in power brought with them in the way of solutions from the prerevolutionary era was nothing more than a series of vague, controversial ideas formulated in loosely worded, normative phrases whose implementation was more suited to bringing about confusion than a solution. The coming part of this work will report on it.

Notes

1. For more information on this ministry, see Farazmand 1989.
2. For details of the results of these studies, see the bibliography by Azkia.
3. *Ibid.*
4. *Ibid.*
5. Ehlers analyzes this literature in his bibliography, as does Azkia in his bibliography and his 1986 book. All three, however, are too short to do the task properly.
6. See F. Riyahi 1976.
7. Including the Islamist Habib ol-Lah Peyman.
8. Malek was one of the leading cadres of a political group with social democrat leanings known initially as the Third Force (niru-ye sewoum) and later as the League of Socialists in Iran (jam'e-ye sosialist ha-ye Iran), which was unable to be very active because of the dictatorship.
9. As far as I know, he has not written a paper on any subject relating to the agrarian question. Some Islamists, such as A. M. Izadi (1975), wrote their dissertations at universities outside Iran, but such cases are exceptions, as talks with former members of the Association of Islamic Students Abroad revealed.
10. 1967, pp. 98 and 209. The first edition appeared in 1905.
11. Taken from B. Moumeni 1980, p. 87f.
12. *Ibid.,* pp. 80 and 89ff; A. Schirazi 1977, p. 353.
13. See, for example, the Azerbaijan Provincial Council's newspaper *Anjoman,* reprinted and annotated by Mansure Rafi'i 1983, pp. 111 and 123ff; and A. A. Dehkhoda's satires in the 1962 reprint of the newspaper *Sur-e Esarafil.*
14. F. Adamiyat 1976, p. 69; A. Schirazi 1977, pp. 74 and 407ff.

15. In the tuyul system, the shah grants the income from certain estates as a salary to individuals who are in his service or as a reward to those who have rendered him particular services.

16. On this movement, see S. Rawasani 1973; on its land reform, see B. Moumeni 1980, pp. 91 and 129; and E. Hooglund 1982, p. 38f.

17. Mosaddeq himself saw these two points as his government's main tasks. See his *Memoirs*, 1986, p. 279.

18. M. R. Pahlawi 1966, p. 41, note. A. Lambton made the accusation on her own (1969, p. 41), as did K. McLachlan (1989, p. 47). Clearly the shah's criticism was intended to justify his attitude toward Mosaddeq, but the other two authors mentioned are either unable to understand Mosaddeq's point of view with respect to land reform or lack information on the subject, which could account for their errors of judgment.

19. M. Mossadeq 1986, pp. 282ff and 353ff.

20. H. Fatemi 1979, pp. 59ff, 128ff, and 154ff.

21. See E. Abrahamian 1983, p. 227. One leader of the Iran Party, Karim Sanjabi, who also played a significant role as a member of the Mosaddeq government, had already demanded in his dissertation (1944) that the country's "feudal and medieval" order be completely changed. He also pointed out that simply dividing the land up would not make it more fertile, nor would it make the peasants happier. He spoke in favor of a reform that would solve the problems of social justice and growth of production while abolishing feudalism; such a reform would have to be tried out on an experimental basis on state land first. Taken from B. Moumeni 1980, pp. 98ff.

22. E. Abrahamian 1983, p. 275.

23. For example, in the writings of the National Resistance Movement, which were published after the August 1953 coup, see Nehzat-e Azadi 1984, vol. 2, pp. 153ff; vol. 5, pp. 129, 143, and 724; and 1984a, vol. 1, pp. 216ff and 275; H. Malek 1978, and 1979; and A. M. Izadi 1958.

24. Jame'e-ye Sosialist ha-ye Irani dar Orupa 1966, pp. 7ff.

25. See the journal *Nabard-e Zendegi* 10 (May 16, 1956), quoted here from B. Moumeni 1980, p. 116. H. Katouzian (1981, p. 4), himself a member of the party, interprets the term "nationalize" as used here to mean "democratize," as opposed to being controlled by the government or owned by the state.

26. *'Elm wa zendegi*, January 1960, quoted from B. Moumeni 1980, pp. 114ff.

27. Personal interview with author.

28. On this point, see K. Sanjabi 1989, p. 444, and Nehzat-e Azadi 1984, vol. 5, p. 4.

29. See *Donya*, the theoretical and political organ of the Tudeh Party, which continually carried contributions on the agrarian question.

30. This is why the Tudeh Party criticized itself in 1976, admittedly to no great effect because most of the party was in exile at the time. See A. Nik A'in 1976, p. 69.

31. Their 1907 program demanded the free transfer of crown lands to the peasants and the distribution of estates belonging to landowners with more land than they required to provide for themselves. It also pointed out that these demands had been formulated mildly for tactical reasons and that they could if necessary be altered. F. Adamiyat 1976, p. 46; A. Schirazi 1977, pp. 352, 421ff; B. Moumeni 1980, p. 87. For more detailed information on the organization and its activities, see F. Adamiyat 1976; and S. Zabih 1966.

32. F. Adamiyat 1976, pp. 69ff.

33. On this point, see M. T. Bahar 1944 and 1984. It should be borne in mind

that at the time it was not always possible to differentiate between Communists and radical democrats.

34. B. Moumeni 1980, p. 93f.
35. E. Abrahamian 1983, p. 375. The information provided here is based in part on this source but also on B. Moumeni 1980, pp. 100ff.
36. E. Hooglund 1982, p. 41; E. Abrahamian 1983, p. 398f; B. Moumeni 1980, p. 130f.
37. B. Moumeni 1980, pp. 105ff.
38. Anushe 1961, pp. 26–31.
39. M. Mohammadi 1973, p. 58.
40. *Ibid.*, p. 56; and Mas'ud 1966, p. 12.
41. P. Khal'atbari 1965, p. 60.
42. M. Mohammadi 1973, p. 61f; and Nik A'in 1976, pp. 76ff.
43. The author is aware of such contacts from his own observations at the University of Tehran and interviewing former cadres of the Tudeh Party.
44. Printed in their organs *Tudeh, Haqiqat,* and *Tufan.* In 1978 the Revolutionary Group of Marxist-Leninists (gruh-e enqelabiyun-e Marxist-Leninist) published a bulky volume devoted to analysis of Iran's social structure, in which the land reform and its consequences were discussed in detail.
45. See, for instance, *Name-ye Parsi* 1 (March 1973), pp. 1–26; and 2 (November 1976), pp. 41–74.
46. For a discussion of some of these tracts, see A. Schirazi 1976, and A. Najmabadi 1987.
47. In 1969 the organization published a booklet listing arguments for the excellence of this slogan.
48. Touzih ol-masa'el are collections of solutions offered by the grand ayatollahs for the believers' legal problems. Each grand ayatollah usually has his own authorized version but they are almost identical in most cases. An ayatollah is considered to be an Instance of Imitation if his solutions are accepted.
49. Including, for instance, Khomeini's four-volume book *Tahrir al-Wasila* (Notes on the Means)—the one principally cited here for opinions found in the traditional law books. It can be considered quite representative.
50. A fatwa is usually the answer based on Islamic law that an authorized scholar gives to questions put to him by believers.
51. They are found in the first collections of Shi'ite decree laws—see, for example, the collection by Al-Koleini (tenth century) known as "*Al-kafi.*"
52. Sharecropping was practiced in 814,000 enterprises on 54.8 percent of Iran's cultivated land in 1960. See A. Malekaniyan 1986, p. 33.
53. See A. Lambton 53; Z. Haque 1977; and B. Johansen 1988.
54. See U. Planck 1962; and A. Lambton 1953.
55. A. R. Khomeini 1989, vol. 2, pp. 605ff.
56. *Ibid.*, pp. 489ff.
57. See, for instance, S. Tusi 1955.
58. Ejare accounted for 10 percent of farmland or 7.4 percent of farms in 1960 (A. Malekaniyan 1986, p. 33), which fell to 3.1 percent and 0.14 percent by 1974 (Markaz-e Amar-e Iran 1977, p. 53).
59. A. R. Khomeini 1989, vol. 2, p. 435.
60. *Ibid.*, p. 359.
61. *Ibid.*, p. 441.
62. On this subject, see H. Modarresi Tabataba'i 1983; B. Johansen 1989; W. Schmucker 1972; and A. Lambton 1953.
63. A. R. Khomeini 1989, vol. 2, p. 361.
64. *Ibid.*, p. 623.

65. The poor tax and the tithe are dealt with by Khomeini 1989, vol. 2, pp. 5ff and 79ff.
66. *Ibid.*, vol. 3, pp. 109ff.
67. Exact data is not available: 10 percent, according to A. Malekaniyan 1986, p. 57; 38,519 agricultural properties plus 417 palm plantations and 524 pasturelands according to S. Akhavi 1980, p. 132f.
68. A. Ahmadi Miyanji (1984) referred to this fact when condoning private property in the Islamic Republic during the argument about it.
69. A. R. Khomeini gives his opinion of this rule in his book *resale-ye nouwin* (1989a, vol. 2, pp. 302ff; trans. and ann. A. Bi Azar Shirazi).
70. *Ibid.*, p. 292. A *hadith* is a deed or saying handed down from the Prophet or the Imams.
71. *Ibid.*, pp. 122ff; and 1989, vol. 2, pp. 108ff.
72. A. R. Khomeini 1989, vol. 2, p. 389.
73. *Ibid.*, p. 389.
74. *Ibid.*, pp. 113, 389, and 615; and vol. 3, pp. 344ff; and 1989a, vol. 2, pp. 179ff.
75. This book is a collection of sermons, letters, sayings, and so forth on various subjects, attributed to Imam Ali and compiled in the eleventh century by Seyyed Razi under the title *Nahj al-Balagha* (Path of Eloquence).
76. See, among many others, verses 2/29f, 6/165, 7/10, and 7/24f.
77. A. Tehrani 1974, pp. 154ff.
78. *Ibid.*, p. 156.
79. See M. Zamani 1969, p. 42f; M. B. Sadr 1969, vol. 2, p. 249f; H. M. Kermani, pp. 4ff.
80. On this subject, see A. R. Yawari 1980; J. Vesel 1989; I. Afshar 1982; and A. Lambton, 1953.
81. In 1969 the Organization of the People's Mujahidin wrote *The Economy in Simple Language* and published it in 1972. Although the book had a "profound influence" on the organization's members and supporters, it barely touched on Islam and its written sources and is a simplified, slightly rewritten presentation of political economy as found in this Leninist organization's textbooks. In comparison to the other contributions mentioned, it benefits from citing examples from everyday life to clarify its theoretical position and is thus more realistic.
82. There are occasional allusions in some of these works to the fact that some of the things these sources approve of are no longer practicable.
83. See H. Tawanayan Fard 1983, p. 12.
84. Taleqani 1954, p. 144; Sazman-e Mojahedin 1972, p. 83; Tehrani 1974, pp. 84 and 89; Peyman 1978, pp. 172 and 176; Bani Sadr 1978, pp. 143 and 194; Etehadiye-ye Anjomanha-ye Eslami-ye Daneshjuyan dar Urupa (hereinafter: Etehadiye) 1975, pp. 11 and 28; E. Yazdi 1967–69, pp. 3/16 and 5/29. The contribution published by Etehadiye consisted of two independent tracts by unnamed authors. In conversation with Hadi Rezazade, I learned that he had written the one entitled "Islamic Ideology and the Problem of the Economy" (pp. 20–71). He named H. Namazi, former minister of economics and finance, as the author of the other tract (pp. 1–19).
85. 1978, pp. 143, 285, and 337. God's property is vested in the community of man and assigned to the masses (Etehadiye 1975, p. 28); the property left to the community is at the disposal of the state, as an authority elected by the people (E. Yazdi 1967–69, pp. 3/18 and 5/29).
86. Peyman 1978, pp. 190ff; R. Esfahani 1978, pp. 6ff; and M. B. Sadr 1969, vol. 2, pp. 68ff and 81ff.
87. Taleqani 1954, pp. 145 and 238; Tehrani 1974, p. 84; Peyman 1978, p.

188; M. B. Sadr 1969, vol. 1, p. 402; and E. Yazdi 1967–69, pp. 3/22 and 5/30. Islam has supposedly banned the concept of private property from economic terminology and has instead awarded it to God (Etehadiye 1975, p. 27f).

88. 1978, p. 212. Peyman and others sometimes take account of the current economic facts in this way.

89. *Ibid.*, p. 196; and Tehrani 1974, pp. 104 and 267f.

90. Taleqani 1954, p. 164; Peyman 1978, p. 207f; M. B. Sadr 1969, vol. 1, pp. 299ff, 341, and 401, and vol. 2, pp. 101 and 147; Etehadiye 1975, pp. 11 and 16; and Tehrani 1974, pp. 216 and 267.

91. Taleqani 1954, p. 238; Peyman 1978, p. 188f; M. B. Sadr 1969, vol. 1, p. 403, and vol. 2, p. 85; Bani Sadr 1978, pp. 190ff and 339f; Esfahani 1978, vol. 3, p. 19; and Tehrani 1974, pp. 84 and 89.

92. Esfahani 1978, vol. 4, p. 28; Bani Sadr 1978, pp. 149 and 339; Peyman 1978, pp. 189 and 205; Tehrani 1974, p. 216; and Taleqani 1954, pp. 223 and 230f.

93. M. B. Sadr 1969, vol. 2, p. 205.

94. *Ibid.*, pp. 187, 190ff, and 221f; Tehrani 1974, pp. 283ff; Peyman 1978, p. 288f; and Bani Sadr 1978, pp. 163ff.

95. The government had put it to parliament on December 5, 1959.

96. On this point, see S. Akhavi 1980, p. 91.

97. The cleric Falsafi stated in a sermon: "This decision is a plot against the exalted Prophet. It represents the precondition for dirty Baha'i elements to smash the power of the exalted Quran and to master the Muslims, who constitute the majority in this country." See A. Dawani, vol. 3, p. 149.

98. See *Ettela'at*, January 9, 23, and 24, May 5 and 8, and June 5, 1963. See also S. H. Rohani 1985 pp. 1/169ff.

99. According to Bani Sadr, the ranking clerics had agreed not to mention land reform in their protests. Ayatollah Khounsari earned a rebuke from his colleagues when he broke this agreement. In general, the clerics must have kept the agreement. There is no indication of the conservative clerics' rejection of land reform in "The Movement of the Clerics" and "The Movement of Imam Khomeini," the two documentations by Dawani and Rohani—not even Brujerdi's letter to Behbahani (quoted above) is mentioned in them. According to Rohani, only two "naive clerics" fell into the trap the regime had set for them. They were to be talked into breaking their silence on the land reform and speaking out against it. The four were told that the shah had made other points of the "White Revolution" public with the object of distracting attention from the land reform and so it was necessary for the clerics to register their protest against it. Two "naive clerics," who were not named, had fallen into this trap (1985, vol. 1, pp. 169ff).

100. A. Dawani, vol. 4, pp. 134ff.

101. *Ibid.*, vol. 4, pp. 104ff.

102. *Maktab-e Eslam* 12 (1963) and 11 (1964).

103. A. Dawani, vol. 3, pp. 238ff and 241ff.

104. See the list of landowners in Isfahan province in S. Akhavi 1980, p. 96f. It includes several clerics. There is no list for the whole country.

105. According to (a personal interview with) H. Keshawarz, Ayatollahs Kamare'i and Borqe'i made a declaration in support of the land reform. In his 1954 book, Ayatollah Taleqani drafted a land reform program. It was, however, much more moderate than the same book's theories on the question of landed property would have led one to expect. His draft provided for (1) uncultivated land and wasteland fit for cultivation, including the other inputs required for cultivation, to be given free to peasants so that they "become the legal owners of the seed corn and the usufructuary rights to land and water"; (2) the existing landed property to be

restricted to its cultivated and surrounding area and for peasants to receive the right to plant on the uncultivated parts, whereby they could become the legal owners of their produce; and (3) the government to stop using its power to support the landlords and thus prevent them from being able to take possession of land illegally and fetter the peasants (p. 239f).

106. See Chapter 9. On July 12, 1984, the Council of Guardians wrote a letter to the Ministry of Agriculture in which it declared all instructions based on the land reform laws from the shah era invalid because they were contrary to the sharia. See J. Madani 1986, vol. 4, p. 444f.

107. See note 105.

108. They are inclined to declare the NRM an Islamist organization although the League of Socialists in Iran was among its members. It is certain that the League influenced the NRM's concepts of land reform. The more extensive and repressive the dictatorship that followed the Mosaddeq government became, the more the NRM retreated from its initial activities. It had virtually ceased to exist when land reform started.

109. Initiated long before actual land reform, it was supposedly to create a model that the other landowners should have followed. These crown lands were appropriated by the founder of the Pahlavi dynasty by force during his short reign (1925–42) and so their sale appeared to the opposition to be a further illegal act, of which they could not approve.

110. Nehzat-e Azadi-ye Iran 1984, vol. 5, p. 144.

111. *Ibid.*, 1984, vol. 2, pp. 153ff.

112. According to its "Manifesto of National Unity" (*ibid.*, vol. 5, p. 4).

113. Nehzat-e Azadi-ye Iran 1982, vol. 1, pp. 203ff.

114. *Ibid.*, p. 54.

115. See the "Documents of the FM," published in several volumes after the revolution.

116. Personal interview. Bani Sadr actually was one of the few Islamists who even before the revolution studied the political economy of Iran, conducted investigations on the subject and published the results. Agriculture was not, however, one of the questions that interested him. He wrote a book, *Oil and Rule*, published abroad in 1977.

117. *Ibid.*, p. 35; see also A. Schirazi 1976.

118. There is, for example, a two-page report in no. 14 (March 7, 1975) about participation by members of the shah's family in various agricultural companies, forcible land seizure by one of the shah's brothers, and migration by impoverished peasants.

119. This was part of Mohsen's summing up of the White Revolution to unmask the regime in court. The text was published abroad in February 1973 by the Confederation of Iranian Students Abroad.

120. For more about the Mujahidin, see E. Abrahamian 1989.

121. In an interview with the author, Bani Sadr said that what Khomeini said from his arrival in Paris to his arrival in Tehran "came from us." "The questions were given to a commission. It wrote the answers down and Khomeini gave them. ... We composed them. We wrote them." See also Bani Sadr 1982, p. 330.

122. pp. 57 and 62.

123. pp. 5, 11, 33f, 41, 55, 57, 62, 80, 117, 120, 169, and 172. The number of pages cited is intended to make clear the importance of the idea in question in Khomeini's thinking. The rough date of the statement can be ascertained by referring to the categorization mentioned above.

124. pp. 19, 27, 31, 45, 55, 114, 116, 119, 121, 126, 136, 171, and 174.

125. pp. 1, 14, 16, 30, 33f, 51, 55, 59, 67, 79, 83, 103, 106, 113, 115, 125f, 130, 134, 140, 154, 256f, 169, 173, and 176.

126. pp. 1, 2, 5, 30, 34ff, 40, 47, 51, 59, 67, 80, 103, 113, 115, 134, 154, 156f, 169, and 176.

127. p. 34. On another occasion (p. 120) the talk is of Azerbaijan province being able to do it; on p. 133 it is an unspecified region; on p. 143 "one or two provinces."

128. pp. 22, 28f, 113, 173ff.

129. pp. 28, 43, 46f, 51, 56, 62, 103, and 176.

130. pp. 1 and 140.

131. pp. 46 and 109.

132. pp. 17 and 132.

133. p. 142f.

134. p. 99f.

135. pp. 104 and 168.

136. pp. 41, 123, 133, 143, 147, and 153.

137. pp. 129 and 133.

138. p. 164.

139. p. 86.

140. p. 94.

141. pp. 154, 167, 169, and 172.

142. p. 143.

143. p. 54f.

144. Apart from a series of ideological and theoretical articles by E. Yazdi on the *Islamic economy*. In 1975 the association also published a slim volume containing two articles by H. Namazi and H. Rezazade (frequently quoted in the preceding section). Rezazade's article devoted two pages to current agricultural problems (i.e., land reform), and, according to him, readers familiar with the classical texts on the Islamic economy could consider them "superfluous and long-winded." They were, however, necessary (p. 37).

145. To be on the safe side, I should mention that I was only able to scrutinize three years thoroughly—not all editions were available for the other years.

146. The secret organ of the theology students at the religious academy in Qom, published 1342–1344 (1963–66) See A-Hojjati Kermani 1989.

147. For example, the documents of the "Jonbesh-e Mosalmanan-e Mobarez" (Movement of Combatant Muslims), pp. 16, 18f, 50, and 71; or the Jami'atha-ye M'otalefe-ye Eslami" (Allied Islamic Societies), pp. 25f, 36, 38, and 44; or in the booklet by M. 'Asgari published in the "Now Rouz" series of tracts in Paris, in which the land reform is criticized.

148. Personal interview with M. 'Alibaba'i.

149. Reference here is mainly to the works by H. Tawanayan-e Fard.

150. Bani Sadr saw himself as an exception, while Izadi had some theoretical and practical knowledge of the problems in Iran's agriculture.

Part II
Agricultural Policy in the Islamic Republic of Iran

3
The Development Dilemma in Iran

In part, agricultural development in the Islamic Republic of Iran has been held back by factors beyond the government's control. First, the new regime inherited from the shah a lopsided economy. Second, it suffered through a period of instability in the international price of oil, Iran's primary export product. Third, the country was attacked by Iraq in September 1980, touching off a costly eight-year-long war that sapped the nation's resources. All of these factors have had a negative impact on the formulation of agricultural policy.

3.1 The Legacies of the Shah's Regime

The crisis in agriculture outlined in Chapter 1 is not the only legacy of the shah's regime. It is merely one aspect of a general developmental crisis, whose total burden is influencing decisions on development policy in the Islamic Republic.

3.1.1 The Economic Legacy

On one hand, the economic legacy of the shah's regime is expressed by a series of indexes, which can be used to diagnose Iran's economic underdevelopment at the end of the prerevolutionary era and to establish the difficulty of the task involved in overcoming it. On the other, it is expressed in a multitude of developmental disparities that will dictate development strategy for some considerable time to come.

The factors affecting misdevelopment and underdevelopment have been detailed in the relevant literature.[1] A few examples are given below to remind the reader of the scope of the economic mess confronting the new regime.

The predominance of revenue from oil exports in both the national economy and the state budget is the most obvious feature of the imbalanced development of the prerevolutionary era. In 1976 oil revenues represented 35 percent of GNP, 77 percent of state income, and 84 percent of foreign currency earnings.[2] As will be shown below, any change in the price of oil or in the exchange rate for the U.S. dollar as well as any limit on Iran's share of the world market had considerable consequences for the Iranian economy. The dependence on oil is even more apparent in foreign trade. Oil accounted for 96.4 percent of Iranian exports in 1976,[3] whereas industrial products only represented 0.45 percent, a figure exceeded even by the carpet industry (0.61 percent). Agriculture made up 1.6 percent of the country's exports of goods.[4]

This hopeless picture of the export structure corresponds to the overall deformity of the Iranian economy. In 1976 a mere 0.7 percent of the country's work force was employed in the oil industry, which accounted for 35 percent of GNP. Conversely, although it employed 34 percent of the work force, agriculture only accounted for about 8 percent of GNP. Industry and mining produced roughly equal shares of GNP with a combined 18 percent of the work force. The service sector accounted for some 40 percent of GNP with 31 percent of the work force. The construction industry accounted for 13.5 percent of the work force and almost 9 percent of GNP.[5] It is not just oil's predominant share of GNP that characterizes the deformation of the economic structure; for whatever reason, revenues from oil exports were primarily administered, distributed, consumed, and wasted in the service sector. A huge effort was needed to stop the hypertrophic growth in this sector.

Despite considerable development in the 1970s, the result of an import substitution development strategy, modern industry has proved itself incapable of replacing oil. It remains in a phase where it would have to shut down to a large extent without support from oil export revenues. On average it is 72 percent dependent on imported raw materials and capital goods.[6] The products are highly uncompetitive and thus extremely difficult to sell on the world market. As in agriculture, the modern factories in the industrial sector lead a marginal existence. They are unable to generate any decisive momentum to spur development of the still largely traditional artisanal enterprises.

This already bleak survey of the economic legacy becomes even more discouraging if data are included on, for example, the totally inadequate infrastructure, the shortfall in energy supplies, the chronic shortage of skilled workers, and the (at times) three-figure inflation rate. In addition, the self-employeds rabidly dislike paying taxes, and consumption patterns for large sections of the urban population are out of all proportion to the country's productive capacity.

3.1.2 The Social Legacy

Social ills parallel the economic grievances and uneven development in the various sectors of the economy, further worsening the shah's legacy. A few examples will suffice to make the point clear.

The population is increasing annually by 3 percent, one of the highest rates of increase in the world. Obviously, only very rapid economic growth would be able to keep pace with it. The population structure is imbalanced, with the proportion of younger age groups being too high. One- to nine-year-olds make up 31.7 percent of the total population, and those fourteen years old and younger constitute 44.5 percent.[7] The discrepancy between those of working age (fifteen to sixty-five) and those employed and seeking work is conspicuously large, the former constituting 52 percent of the population, the latter a mere 29 percent. In fact, this discrepancy is even larger, as more than 635,000 of those employed are in the ten- to fourteen-year-old age group and more than 377,000 of those employed are over sixty-five years old.[8] In 1976 the official unemployment figure was slightly below 1 million.[9] The extent of hidden unemployment is not apparent from official statistical sources, but it is generally considered to be quite large.

Variations in the distribution of the national income are a very serious aspect of the social legacy. In the period immediately preceding the revolution, 0.005 percent of the population disposed of 3.8 percent of the country's total income, whereas a mere 0.8 percent of the total income was available to 17.2 percent of the population. A mere 1 percent of the population claimed 52.3 percent of the national income; only 18.4 percent remained for 90.6 percent of the population.[10]

This disparity in income distribution is repeated in the unequal regional distribution of developmental spoils. Tehran and some of the other cities, along with the provinces of Mazanderan and Gilan on the Caspian Sea, received the lion's share. Table 3.1, which compares several provinces, makes the extent of the gap clear.

This disparity can be seen even more clearly when one compares the absolute figures. In 1975 there were about 12,440 doctors in the whole country, or one doctor for every 2,682 Iranians. But in Kurdistan province there were 121 doctors for a population of 731,000, or one doctor for each 6,041 people. And whereas 3,001 of the 4,310 specialists in the whole country were located in the Central province, seven provinces had less than ten specialists.[11] The basic schools in the table are not even directly comparable as they differ considerably in the number of pupils. The schools in Kohgiluye averaged only 46 pupils, in the Central province 218.

This description of the social and economic legacies could of course be supplemented by statistics about other grievances and disparities, but such analysis would go beyond the scope of this work.

Table 3.1 Social Infrastructure of Selected Provinces, 1975 (in percent)

	Population[1]	Unemployment	Basic Schools	Doctors	New Apartments	Large Industry[1]
Central province	19.0	5.8	25.0	49.0	50.4	53.6
Kurdistan	2.3	19.4	1.6	0.9	2.2	0.4
Luristan	2.7	13.8	2.2	1.1	0.4	0.6
Bushehr	1.3	14.7[2]	0.9	0.8	2.0	0.06[3]
Boyer Ahmadi and Kohgiluye	0.7	13.0	0.7	0.2	0.4	0.0

Source: Markaz-e Amar 1982, pp. 83, 90, 139, 180f, and 442.
Notes: 1. Figures for 1976
2. Including Saheli province
3. Together with Ilam province

3.1.3 The Political Legacy

The political legacy of the shah's regime is evident in systems of values such as the primacy of politics,[12] particularism,[13] absolutist authoritarianism,[14] and gigantism.[15] These are some of the political factors that had the most lasting influence on the development of Iran under the shah's regime and in the preceding centuries. They have lost none of their potency since the fall of the shah. As postrevolutionary political developments show, these factors continue to determine the political climate in the country. The reason a break was not made, despite expectations and hopes, is that the aforementioned value systems determined not just the behavior and concepts of the group in power in prerevolutionary Iran but the country's entire political culture. These factors, in other words, determine the political concepts and behavior of broad segments of the opposition. The only major exception is the liberal movement, which sees the solution to the country's development problems in the democratization of political relations and so favors subordinating politics to interests that can more properly be termed economic and social. Nonetheless, the legacy of the shah's regime can be viewed as a burden on the entire political tradition—even the Islamic tradition, which the Islamists who took power in the revolution believe they are upholding.

The political legacy's burden on the agricultural policy of the postrevolutionary era can best be appreciated in the sections of this work dealing with the political conceptions and practices of the ruling Islamists and the form of government they have established. References to the political and cultural traditions of the country will make clear the Islamists' role as testators.

3.2 Fluctuations in Oil Export Revenues

I have already mentioned the danger for the economic development of Iran posed by fluctuations in the international oil market. The Islamic Republic has indeed been hard hit in this way, particularly in 1986. Three factors in the oil and money markets have had an effect: fluctuations in oil price, fluctuations in oil sales, and fluctuations in the exchange rate for the U.S. dollar. These factors have increased the instability of the postrevolutionary economy.

From 1977 to 1980, Iranian oil production dropped from 5.9m to 1.5m barrels a day. There was a parallel decrease in oil exports, from 5.0m to 0.95m barrels a day, over the same period.[16] Iran's oil exports dropped off even more in 1981 but recovered slowly after 1982, without, however, attaining their 1977 level (see Table 3.2).

Initially, this development was almost counterbalanced by a rapid increase in oil prices. A barrel of crude climbed from $13.34 on January 1, 1979, to $28.50 on January 1, 1980. A year later, Iranian oil cost $37 per barrel. At the beginning of 1983, the Iranian government was still getting $31.20 per barrel on the world market.[17]

Table 3.2 Iranian Oil Exports and Revenues, 1976–1988

	thousands of barrels per day	billions of dollars
1976	5,329	22.9
1977	4,986	23.6
1978	4,574	18.1
1979	2,579	19.3
1980	951	12.1
1981	808	11.9
1982	1,718	17.3
1983	2,045	20.2
1984	1,609	15.7
1985	1,465	13.2
1986	1,251	5.9
1987	1,535	9.1
1988	1,469	9.0

Sources: Markaz-e Amar-e Iran (Statistical Yearbook), various years; Bank-e Markazi 1984; Iran Yearbook 1989/90.

As rapid as the rise in the price of oil was, it was still unable to fully compensate for the loss of income caused by the drop in the quantity exported. The Iranian government earned $22.9bn from oil exports in 1976. The corresponding income in 1981 was $11.9bn. Income rose to $20.2bn in 1983 but fell back again the following year and amounted to a mere $5.9bn in 1986.[18] The net price for Iranian oil fell even further during this period. At times it was nine times lower than the price in 1980, according to the spokesman for the parliamentary budget commission.[19] The aerial warfare between Iran and Iraq over the Gulf, which resulted in Iran having to pay up to $3 per barrel for insurance and shipping costs, was one factor contributing to the reduction in the net price.[20]

The downward trend in the exchange rate for the dollar further worsened the income situation for the Islamic government. Because revenue from oil exports is calculated in dollars, the purchasing power of the Islamic government's income was reduced by the fall of the value of the dollar, in particular after 1985. This trend is apparent when one considers the dollar's exchange rate against the Deutschmark: A dollar was worth DM3.31 in February 1985 and DM1.97 in September 1986. According to a report by the Iranian Central Bank, the dollar's weakness and the high inflation rate on the world market caused the Islamic state to lose purchasing power equivalent to half its 1981 income.[21] It should be pointed out, however, that the general trend with respect to the exchange rate for the dollar was positive from 1979 to 1985. This trend ought to have benefited the Iranian government.[22]

The fluctuations in income from oil exports placed a heavy burden on Iran's economic development in this period and later. This instability began in the phase when the oil price was still rising rapidly. GDP at factor costs (in 1974/5 prices) fell from 3,922bn rials in 1356 (1977/8) to 2,568bn in 1359 (1980/1).[23] This trend continued (with fluctuations, especially after 1985), totaling 3,230bn rials in 1365 (1986/7) and 3,203bn a year later.[24] This decrease in the domestic product cannot, of course, be blamed entirely on the developments in the oil market. The continuation of the instability that began during the revolution on into the postrevolutionary era and the Islamic regime's inability to make social and economic decisions have also had an impact. Declining GDP combined with the rapid rate of population growth has produced an even more rapid decline in domestic product per capita. At 55,400 rials, GDP per capita in 1988/9 is at the same level as in 1968/9—and this after it had reached 111,900 rials in 1977/8 (base year 1974/5).[25] There has been a parallel development in per capita income from oil exports, which dropped from $460 in 1982/3 to $110 in 1986/7.[26]

The fluctuations in revenues from oil exports are also evident in the state budget, particularly so for expenditure on development, which decreased by 38.7 percent from 1977/8 to 1980/1, even at current prices.[27] Only in 1982/3 did the government succeed in achieving at nominal prices the level of development expenditure that prevailed in 1977/8: 926bn rials.[28] However, it dropped to 746bn rials in 1986/7[29] and to 729bn (at current prices) the following year.[30] It has fallen by an average of 10 percent in the years since the revolution. This reduction is even more pronounced at constant prices. The government is only spending 163bn rials at 1974/5 prices on investments for development, even less than its expenditure in the base year.[31]

Each year, the fluctuations in the revenue from oil exports seem to surprise the Islamic government anew. Or maybe the effect they have on the state's total income is so drastic that the government simply refuses to consider them possible. Every year it prepares a budget on the basis of the revenue it believes it will earn from oil exports—it has not been able to put most of them into effect. The budget deficit amounted to 50 percent in 1986/7.[32] This year, income from oil exports will again be reduced by 50 percent.[33]

The Islamic government tries to compensate for losses in oil revenue by taking various contradictory measures that have a negative influence on the national economy, including its efforts (accompanied by a great deal of propaganda) to promote export of both agricultural and nonagricultural products. In view of the decline in almost all branches of production, this measure (which has only recently been taken) unavoidably must fail and result in shortages, because goods that are desperately needed on the domestic market are being exported. The fact that in 1987/8 foreign currency earnings from the export of such products amounted to only $1bn[34] speaks for the failure of the measure. They dropped by 32 percent in the first eight months of 1988/9.[35] According to the daily *Ettela'at,* Iran was only able to export industrial goods to the value of $9m in the first nine months of 1988/9.[36] These statistics underline the point that it is highly improbable that the Islamic government will be able to use this means to offset the reduction in foreign currency earnings from its oil exports.

Tax increases are another way of attempting to offset the loss of revenue from oil, but they only produce negligible results. The national income simply does not provide a very suitable tax base. Revenues can only be increased by taxing sources of income that have not been taxed to date (e.g., self-employeds' income) or by levying higher taxes on wage and salary earners. The government is in fact making use of both measures. As a result, it was able to almost double its tax revenues between 1981/2 and 1986/7.[37] But even with this increased tax revenue, the government is unable to do much more than cushion the loss it must bear because of the much higher rate of inflation. According to official statistics, the cost-of-living index rose from 100 to 300 between 1978 and 1987. In reality, it is rising at more than double this rate.[38]

The third measure taken to try to offset the loss of revenue from oil exports is one of the causes of the rapid increase in the rate of inflation—

namely, the huge debts the government incurs each year at the Central Bank in order to balance the budget. In 1986/7, 40.5 percent of its income was derived from this source.[39] On January 24, 1989, a former minister of labor, Tawwakolli, stated in the daily *Resalat* that the state is in debt to the Central Bank to the tune of 10,000bn rials.[40] In doing so he had only admitted an open "secret," which did not prevent 137 members of parliament from writing to the speaker, Rafsanjani, to demand that Tawwakolli be charged with betraying state secrets.[41]

Until now I have reported the fluctuations in revenue from oil exports and their effects on the government's financial position and on the development of the country's GDP. I have also stated that the loss of revenue was particularly pronounced after 1985. However, comparing the first ten years after the revolution with the last few years before the revolution makes it clear that the Islamic government has done better than the one it ousted vis-à-vis revenue. Total foreign currency earnings in the decade prior to the revolution amounted to $91.54bn, but in the next ten years the Islamic regime earned some $134.55bn.[42] The difference might be more than enough to offset the drop in the dollar's exchange rate. Be that as it may, the recent revenue figure is high enough for the government to be able to invest effectively in development. If it has not done so—or if it has only done so to a small and decreasing extent—other factors are responsible. These will be dealt with, at least in part, in the course of this work. One of them is the war with Iraq, to which I shall turn now.

3.3 The War with Iraq

The war between Iran and Iraq, which began in September 1980 and ended in August 1988 with the acceptance of UN Resolution 598, further reduced the Islamic regime's chances of achieving anything with its development policies. With the invasion of Iran by Iraq, the war became a negative development factor imposed upon the Islamic Republic. However, after the Iraqi army was defeated and driven from Iranian soil in the summer of 1982, the Islamic state could have ended the war. Moreover, as the victor it enjoyed the prospect of demanding and obtaining reparations. It refused to avail itself of the opportunity. The reasons are rooted in the character of the Islamic state, and I shall return to them in my conclusions. However, I also intend to deal with the war's consequences for the Islamic Republic's economic and agricultural policies in the various chapters of this part. A summary will suffice at this point.

Essentially, the war prevented the Islamic Republic from implementing many of its development policies. As will be shown in Chapters 5.2 and 5.4, the war had the highest priority in all the Islamic state's political considerations. Development plans had to be deferred or were doomed to failure from the very outset because the corresponding funds were spent on the war.[43] All of the economy's resources, whether human, organizational, or financial, were devoted to the war effort. The whole system took on the air of a war economy and was thus geared for destruction instead of for construction. It is not surprising that after the end of the war, the talk was not of a construction program—which would only have needed to be continued—but of a *re*construction program, which for years to come will have to be used for the restoration of the values, both economic and other, destroyed in the war.

The extent to which the war placed a financial burden upon the state can be seen from the war costs listed in the government's annual budgets. According to these documents, the costs amounted to 30 to 35 percent of state expenditure each year. Only in the year in which the war started did the government devote as low as 26.6 percent of its expenditure to this purpose.[44] The war costs in the state budget regularly exceeded expenditures on development investments, which amounted to a mere 28.7 percent in their best year and about 22.5 percent in the years from 1981/2 to 1986/7.[45] Not all the costs incurred by the state because of the war are included in the state budget's allocations for war costs—all the ministries and state departments allocated an undisclosed share of their respective budgets, which cannot be accurately determined, to the war. For some years there has been a codicil to the laws on the state budget according to which the organizations named are obliged "to give priority to the projects entrusted to them by the Supreme Defense Council and to put their staff and funds at the disposal of the war effort."[46] The State Budget Act of 1985/6 provided for several ministries to allocate 20 percent of their funds to the war.[47] It has proven impossible to get more precise details about the demands the war made on the executive organs of the state, but they certainly exceed 20 percent. In an interview with the daily *Kayhan,* the minister for planning and budget, Zanjani, declared: "The expenditure allocated for the war in the budget represents only part of the real costs incurred by the state on this account." The real costs, he continued, "are not mentioned in the details and statistics which have been made public."[48] In addition to the costs of the war for the state budget, there are also the huge payments—whether voluntary or not, in cash or in kind—by the population into the war coffers. Some of these payments would doubtless otherwise have been used for construction in the country.[49]

It is difficult to assess the havoc wreaked by the war. A study commissioned in 1985 by Iran's Ministry of Planning and Budget came to the conclusion that the loss amounted to $189bn to the end of 1363 (March 20, 1984). According to the study, the damage to agriculture alone amounted to $31.7bn,[50] equivalent to about 38 percent of the total contribution by the agricultural sector to GDP from the beginning of the war to that date. Total damage was assessed as equivalent to the contribution by the agricultural, industrial, and oil sectors to Iran's economy over the same period. In 1986 the economic damage as a result of the war was put as high as $309bn (24,730bn rials).[51] According to the Japanese Institute for Middle East Economics, war damage on the Iranian side through the end of 1986 came to $188.7bn, excluding losses in the oil industry.[52] There are more precise figures for damage to clearly defined objects. Thus, according to an official reconstruction plan, 750 villages were destroyed or damaged in the war.[53] Damage to the large oil refinery at Abadan is reputed to be some $9bn.[54] Not a few towns (such as Khorramshar, Qasr-e Shirin, and Howeize) were completely destroyed and others (Ahwas, Abadan, and Dezful) badly damaged.[55]

Human loss is even more difficult to assess than the material damage. The Japanese institute mentioned above speaks of almost 1m dead, 650,000 injured, and 2.3m homeless.[56] Controversial as these figures may be, they do give a rough idea of the colossal energies for development that were lost to the country in the eight years of war.

The political and social atmosphere that gained the upper hand in Iran because of the war and the exploitation of the state of war must be characterized as grave. It is an atmosphere of death, in which preparation for the hereafter rather than the shaping of this life is propagated as the decisive value in life. In this atmosphere, war is seen as "God's blessing"[57] and as the "essence of our existence," as Ayatollah Jawadi Amoli once put it.[58] Every other impulse is to be subordinated to it, and any other considerations—such as the problems of agriculture, industry, labor, justice, etc.—are to be deferred. Any appeal against this assignment of priorities is decisively rejected with reference to the state of war.

3.4 Final Observation

The external factors mentioned above are the most important ones having a negative influence on the developmental policies of the Islamic Republic. These factors could be further expounded in a work devoted exclusively to this subject, which in order to be comprehensive would have to include such aspects as the 1979 U.S. trade embargo imposed on Iran, inflationary tendencies in the international markets, and the attitude of the opposition to the new government.

Some of the factors referred to here are without doubt beyond the control of the Islamic regime. They are external and, to varying degrees, make it more difficult for the ruling clerics to take social and economic action. The negative effects of some factors, such as the war against Iraq, could have been decisively ameliorated by the new regime; to that extent, they cannot be viewed as external conditions. Truly external factors do diminish the Islamic government's successes in development policy, but the factors it *can* control determine whether the new rulers and the political system they have established are able to provide a suitable framework for encouraging a successful development policy. I intend to deal with this question in detail below.

But before turning to it, there is another element that ought to be pointed out, if only to avoid leaving the impression that the circumstances are entirely negative. There is at least one extremely positive factor for a development policy that promises success. It is not, however, used to this end but instead is used almost exclusively to maintain and safeguard political power. This favorable factor is the readiness to work actively and collectively toward positive national goals, to suppress egocentric interests, to make sacrifices, and to shun no effort while doing so. The nation had utilized its own combined strength to topple the shah's regime, which it had feared for decades. In so doing it had regained its lost self-confidence and was calling for political, economic, and cultural development, ready to follow any leadership offering positive reform. If the new rulers behaved properly and did not only look to safeguard their own interests, if they governed by consensus and welcomed the participation of the people in the decisionmaking processes instead of monopolizing power for themselves, then the populace was prepared to make any effort required of it. The actions of the new rulers are, however, diametrically opposed to these conditions, as will be frequently shown in the course of this work.

Notes

1. See H. Katouzian 1981; R. Looney 1982; D. Gholamazad 1985; etc.
2. Markaz-e Amar 1982, p. 746.
3. *Ibid.,* p. 666.
4. *Ibid.,* p. 673.
5. *Ibid.,* pp. 94 and 746.
6. Cf. Gholamazad 1985, p. 319.
7. Markaz-e Amar 1982, p. 69.
8. *Ibid.,* pp. 69 and 80f.
9. *Ibid.,* p. 80f.
10. Cf. Gholamazad 1985, pp. 296f and 808.
11. Markaz-e Amar 1977, pp. 34 and 112.
12. I consider this to mean subordinating the interests of society to those of politics or of those in power.
13. Particularism obtains when the decisions affecting society by social or political groups or individuals are guided by their own interests and ignore the welfare and thus the existence of society.
14. This condition is deemed to obtain in Persian if the ruler can dispose of the "life, fortune, and family" of those under his rule at will.
15. A characteristic of Iran's rulers is that even when they are politically weak, they have the feeling that they can rule the world or at least the Middle East. They also believe that they have a mission to save the world.

16. Bank-e Markazi 1984, pp. 545ff.
17. *Ibid.*, p. 552.
18. *Ibid.*, pp. 548ff. See also Dr. F. J. A. Chalibi 1988, p. 23. During the 1366 (1987/8) budget debate, revenue for 1365 was given as 375bn rials; cf. Parliamentary Protocols (hereinafter PP), March 7, 1987, p. 38.
19. PP, March 5, 1987, p. 24. The oil price fell to $6 a barrel in 1966; cf. Chalibi 1988, p. 23.
20. *Le Monde*, December 10, 1988, quoted from *Enqelab-e Eslami*, December 19, 1988. The tanker war begun in April 1984 damaged or destroyed 350 tankers by May 1987.
21. Cf. *Enqelab-e Eslami*, December 19, 1987.
22. H. J. Lotze 1987.
23. Bank-e Markazi 1984, p. 504f.
24. Markaz-e Amar 1988a, p. 462.
25. *Hafte Name* 4 (1989), pp. 3ff.
26. According to Prime Minister Musawi in *Kayhan*, December 30, 1987.
27. Equivalent to 358.7bn rials.
28. Bank-e Markazi 1984, p. 619.
29. Markaz-e Amar 1988a, p. 441; *Kayhan*, June 7, 1966.
30. *Ibid.* The 1989/90 budget proposals earmarked 802.2bn rials, still less than in 1977/8; cf. *Kayhan*, January 1, 1989.
31. As calculated by Gholamhosein Nadi MP; cf. PP, March 7, 1987, p. 39.
32. Figure given by Gholamhosein Nadi MP, cf. PP, March 3, 1987, p. 17.
33. Chalibi 1988, p. 103.
34. Cf. *Middle East Economic Digest* (MEED) loc cit.
35. *Resalat*, December 26, 1988.
36. *Ettela'at*, January 19, 1989.
37. *Kayhan*, August, 29, 1987. Tax revenue in 1987/8 was 1,029bn rials, still double the 554bn rials in 1981/2. Cf. *Resalat*, April 19, 1988.
38. Nehzat-e Azadi-ye Iran 1987, pp. 5ff. According to this study, the price index rose from 100 to 703 points over the same period.
39. *Kayhan*, August 29, 1987.
40. For comparison, total state revenue for 1989/90 was estimated at 3,861bn rials. Cf *Kayhan*, January 1, 1988.
41. *Resalat*, February 1, 1989.
42. *Hafte Name* 4 (1989), pp. 3ff.
43. Dorri Najafabadi, spokesman of the parliamentary commission for budget and planning, stated: "The principal cause of the failure of the development plan was the war." PP, March 8, 1987, p. 24.
44. The minister of planning and budget quoted 18 percent for 1980/1 (PP, March 8, 1987, p. 23). Prime Minister Musawi quoted 26.6 percent *(Kayhan,* November 30, 1985, supplement), as did the minister of agriculture *(Kayhan,* December 15, 1984).
45. Calculated on the basis of absolute figures. *Kayhan*, August 29, 1987.
46. See, for example, the 1364 (1985/6) law in *Wezarat-e Dadgostari: Compendium of Laws* (hereinafter CL) 1985/6, p. 629, and 1984/5, p. 524.
47. CL 1984/5, p. 524.
48. *Kayhan*, March 9, 1987. Speaker Rafsanjani once stated during Friday prayers he was leading that 1,000bn rials from the state budget and $3bn in foreign currency were spent on the war each year. Cf. *Kayhan*, July 18, 1987.
49. Amirahmadi 1988, pp. 134ff, gives an overview based on official figures for war costs and damage to September 1985, according to which the state's current

expenditure between 1981 and 1985 came to $26.6bn, equivalent to $30bn if reconstruction costs are included, but excluding the cost of maintaining the army. A total of 79.6 percent of oil revenues were spent on this purpose in 1981.

50. Wezarat-e Barname wa Budje 1986, pp. 35ff.
51. *Kayhan*, September 21, 1986.
52. See the periodical *Ruzegar-e Nou* 12 (1989), p. 84.
53. *Kayhan*, October 15, 1988. The latest official figures for damage as a result of the war give Iran's direct losses as over 30,811bn rials and indirect losses as over 34,542bn rials. The figures for agriculture are 14,173bn and 17,833bn rials, respectively. The term "indirect losses" refers to development opportunities lost as a result of the war. See H. Mirzazade, deputy president for executive questions, *Kayhan*, January 6, 1991. According to Rafsanjani, total losses amount to $1,000bn (*Kayhan*, January 10, 1991). This figure is calculated on the basis of the official exchange rate of about $1 to 70 rials. According to *Kayhan*, December 28, 1991, the UN report presented that month arrives at a figure of some $97.6bn, supposedly on the basis of an exchange rate of 1:230.
54. *Resalat*, January 29, 1989.
55. According to Amirahmadi 1988, p. 127, 51 towns and 3,891 villages were damaged to varying degrees. Over 5m people lost their homes and jobs, and 2.5m were forced to flee.
56. *Ruzegar-e Nou* 12.
57. Khomeini; cf. *Kayhan*, December 12, 1984.
58. *Resalat*, January 21, 1986.

4
The Objectives of Agricultural Policy

4.1 Self-sufficiency: The Main Objective of Agricultural Policy

By and large, self-sufficiency in agricultural production can be seen as a primary objective of all Islamist factions sharing power in the Islamic Republic of Iran since February 1979. Self-sufficiency is the main declared aim not only of the regime's agricultural policy but equally of every other area of economic policy. All other aims are subordinated to it, at least verbally. In the constitution of Iran, it is expressed as the "aim," "guideline," or "basis" of all economic policy (Articles 3 and 43). Although the constitution says the Islamic Republic should strive for self-sufficiency in both the agricultural and industrial sectors, all other expressions of will, programmatic remarks, and draft plans make it clear that self-sufficiency is to be achieved in agriculture first of all.

The importance of self-sufficiency in agriculture was first expressed during the shah's reign by experts and members of the opposition who were critical of his agricultural policy. It was clearly demonstrated in Chapter 1 that Iran's increasing dependence on imported produce was criticized even by experts employed in the bureaucracy of the shah's regime. This dependency was contrasted with at least partial or relative self-sufficiency, which, in the opinion of the experts, the country ought to be striving for. Before the start of the oil boom in the 1970s, autarky was an aim that even the shah's economic planners pursued. The third economic plan (1962–67) explicitly stated that one of its goals was satisfying the national demand for foodstuffs and agricultural raw products from domestic production.[1]

This criticism of the dependence on imported agricultural produce continued unabated into the postrevolutionary era and formed the prelude to almost all declarations on the new aims. It appeared, for example, as early as May 1979 in a draft program stipulating "the guidelines for objectives in Iranian agricultural policy and organization." First there was a harsh rebuke of the shah's policies, which were based on consumption, imports of unnecessary goods, imports of agricultural produce, and so forth. This was followed by a presentation of the policy worked out under the Bazargan government (February–November 1979) by a Commission for Plan Studies led by the minister of agriculture, Dr. Izadi. It stated that "first priority is given to production to the extent that it makes our society ... independent of others" (p. 2).[2]

The more they let their economic policy become wreathed in international missionary zeal, the more vehemently Bazargan's successors in office insisted on retaining self-sufficiency as a priority. It was the first declared aim in the draft of the Islamic state's initial five-year plan, approved by the Council of Ministers on July 12, 1983. According to the plan, the "great significance" of "self-sufficiency" is the reason for conferring "on agriculture the status of axis of development policy" in the Islamic Republic.[3] When, for reasons to be discussed below, approval was not granted for this plan, parliament took the initiative. In 1985 it obliged the government to work out a bill within three months to ensure autarky, in accordance with which the government was to instigate a program helping "essential agricultural produce" to reach "the level of self-sufficiency." Essential agricultural produce was understood to mean wheat, rice, fodder, sugar, cotton, vegetable oils, and animal and vegetable products rich in proteins.[4] Although this draft landed in the wastepaper basket despite the three-month deadline, self-sufficiency remains the prime objective of agricultural policy.

4.2 Achieving Independence from Imperialism

Above all, self-sufficiency is considered the means of achieving independence from the "tyrannical rulers of the world," but it is scarcely regarded as a separate development objective. During the twelfth session of the assembly that elaborated the constitution of the republic, the cleric Ali Tehrani even declared that self-sufficiency should be understood to mean independence.[5] In the same session, Bani Sadr, the former president, endorsed this point of view, saying: "Autarky is the translation of independence." Even in the aforementioned draft plan by Dr. Izadi, where the politicization of the economy was given as one of the main causes of the shah's legacy of mismanagement, the argument for autarky was based on the requirements of the anti-imperialist struggle. Cereals, in particular corn, were designated as "the political and economic basis of dependency on imperialism." It was stated that with the increase in production the country was "to create a supply for the battle for independence" (Izadi plan, p. 4).

The more imperialism was seen as the main cause for the existing *malheurs* and the more forcibly the new state's position as forerunner of the worldwide anti-imperialist struggle was emphasized, the more self-sufficiency was touted as the objective of agricultural policy. Here, too, Bazargan's successors differ from him. This reasoning was specifically mentioned in all the documents of the time in which self-sufficiency was proclaimed as the aim of agricultural policy. For example, in his speech to introduce the bill for the first development plan to parliament on August 16, 1983, Prime Minister Musawi said: "As achieving economic independence is the objective of the Islamic Republic of Iran, priority will be given—within the scope of the forward-looking policy which aspires to alter the structure of production in the country—to such efforts as are aimed at increasing agricultural production so as to attain self-sufficiency in agricultural produce."[6]

The same idea is to be found in the draft plan, where the attempt is made to define self-sufficiency and/or independence. They are only attained

(1) when essential mass consumer goods and other strategically important goods are produced in the country.
(2) when semifinished products that are needed for the factories to work at full capacity are mainly produced in the country.
(3) when the capital goods, skills, and technologies necessary for the development of the economy are available in the country.
(4) when foreign trade is not merely exporting national resources and importing manufactured goods.

"In other words," the draft plan continued, "economic independence is only attained if the economy of the country does not collapse but can continue to function even if the importation of goods is interrupted" (DP, p. 1/5). Achieving independence was the main reason for passing the law "requiring the government to work out a bill to attain self-sufficiency." This goal was distinctly emphasized during the debate on the law's first and second reading in parliament.[7]

Other statements in this connection are too numerous to be quoted here. As just one example, I cite a declaration made by Khomeini toward the end of 1984. He said: "We can only become independent if we are economically self-sufficient. Self-sufficiency and economic independence are only achieved if we increase our agricultural production."[8]

Self-sufficiency was to assist not only in attaining independence but also in exporting the revolution. For Ayatollah Montazeri it was the prerequisite for achieving this aim,[9] and according to the former president, Khamene'i, it would make exporting the revolution easier and ensure that the Islamic model for development was received positively in other countries.[10]

The purpose of increasing production was not only to guarantee autarky and thus independence but also to export agricultural produce. A statement by Ayatollah Khomeini on February 6, 1982, typifies such wishes: "May Allah grant that we can achieve self-sufficiency and beyond that also export agricultural produce. May God grant that we shall in future have a blossoming agriculture which is in a position to bring our industry forward."[11] But even the declared aim of exporting seemed to be considered a means of helping to achieve independence. Agricultural exports were to help end the one-sided dependence on the oil "monoculture." The draft of the first development plan stated: "[R]edressing the country's dependency on oil exports is one of the most important aspects when considering the export of products from industry, agriculture and traditional crafts.... The Islamic Republic is not willing to allow this dependency on oil exports to continue" (DP, p. 1/16). However, the plan admitted that replacing oil with agricultural produce could not be accomplished to any great extent and that achieving self-sufficiency would be the priority for the first ten years.

4.3 The Prospects for Self-sufficiency

There are contradictory declarations on the extent and the time period involved in formulating self-sufficiency as the aim of agricultural policy. The minister of agriculture in the Bazargan government, Dr. Izadi, said, "God willing, we shall perhaps achieve self-sufficiency in wheat this year."[12] Apart from his unfounded optimism, the tendency was in line with a report presented September 17–22, 1979, by the Organization of Planning and Budget at a seminar called "Examining the Economic Problems of Iran." The meeting was intended to work out economic solutions, and there was talk of "relative self-sufficiency," which could only be achieved in the long term.[13] Six years later, a member of the central committee in the Ministry of Jahad-e Sazandegi (Holy War for Construction) repeated the two-year deadline but was a little more generous, emphasizing that in 1987 self-sufficiency would be achieved "at least in the essential products such as wheat and barley."[14] The minister himself extended the deadline again ten months later, saying, "The gateways to self-sufficiency and independence opened for us today. The hope that we shall achieve self-sufficiency once and for all will gladden our hearts in the future too.... In respect of the most important agricultural products ... we shall have attained self-sufficiency in wheat, barley and maize once and for all by 1991."[15] The minister of agriculture, Dr. Zali, mentioned the same time frame two months later but thought that self-sufficiency could only be achieved in wheat by then.[16] The development plan, due to start in 1983, also envisaged self-sufficiency by the beginning of the 1990s, more precisely at the end of the second five-year plan—i.e., by the end of 1372 (March 20, 1993).[17] But self-sufficiency should be reached by the end of the first five-year plan in some products, with a wheat surplus of 428,000t and surpluses in legumes, potatoes, onions, vegetables, and melons.[18]

These deadlines were not met. The first five-year plan wasn't sanctioned into law until the beginning of 1990. It aims for self-sufficiency in wheat by the end of the first phase (March 1994) and in other products five years later.[19]

The functionaries of the Islamic state would not discuss self-sufficiency if they were not convinced that it could be achieved, but this conviction was partly based on an optimistic assessment of land and water capacities and partly on wishful thinking. The overview of agriculture in the first development plan[20] contained an example of the former. It calculated that there were 53m hectares of good and medium land for agriculture and that only 68.5bn cubic meters of water were being used for agricultural and other purposes out of 365bn cubic meters of precipitation, 95bn cubic meters of groundwater, and 84bn cubic meters of subterranean water sources. These figures suggested that irrigation could be increased and intensified to cultivate the ample area available (DPA, p. 25f). Minister of Agriculture Zali gave similar details in a letter to Khomeini, describing agriculture as "the axis of economic development in the Islamic Republic of Iran." The minister estimated that between 105bn and 130bn cubic meters of groundwater and surface water could be used annually for irrigation, whereas at present only 51bn cubic meters were being used, and unproductively at that.[21]

The regime's belief in the possibility of extensive self-sufficiency remained unbroken throughout the postrevolutionary era despite some unfortunate truths. Population growth was higher than expected and the necessary funds were either not available at all or only in amounts far too small to achieve the goal. By now, most experts either denied the possibility of self-sufficiency altogether or seriously doubted that the targets for quantities and deadlines could be met.[22] The Organization of Planning and Budget estimated that at best 6.5m hectares could be irrigated using present water resources but that at least 8m hectares would have to be irrigated by 2002 in order to achieve the level of self-sufficiency required to provide enough protein and 2,700 calories a day for the increased population. This prognosis dates from September 1979 and is based on a 3.1 percent population growth rate.[23] An analysis by Farhad Maher for the Center for Rural and Agricultural Research also questioned the population-growth and water-use data on which the first development plan was based and concluded that self-sufficiency, even in its most limited form, could not be achieved in the given period.[24] The view expressed by a farmer in a letter to Ayatollah Beheshti is also of interest. He thought farmers ought to concentrate on cultivating those crops that grow well in Iran and can be exported. He continued, "What is there against planting pistachio trees in favorable areas, selling the pistachios to the USA and Japan for $800 a ton, and buying corn for $129 a ton for it?"[25] For whatever reason, the politicians nevertheless clung to their ideal. President Khamene'i still hoped at the end of 1987 that the country might one day be able to feed double its then population of 52m,[26] while Ayatollah Montazeri thought that, despite negative estimates (which he said were influenced by the imperialists), Iran's agriculture would be able to supply 200m people.[27]

Some politicians and functionaries made self-sufficiency dependent on fulfillment of several preconditions. For example, one member of parliament said that "self-sufficiency cannot be achieved if the income gap between town and country is not closed";[28] another that it could not be attained until cultivation of individual crops was concentrated in the most suitable areas.[29] Ayatollah Montazeri stated that "we need accurate statistics if we want to be self-sufficient,"[30] and many people shared the prime minister's view that achieving self-sufficiency depended on solving the question of ownership of the land.[31] The minister of agriculture often complained about the lack of funds needed for an increase in production, giving it as the reason for the failure to achieve self-sufficiency.[32]

This failure to invest the funds needed, implement the necessary measures, and achieve self-sufficiency gave the Musawi government's opponents in the ruling clique the opportunity to attack it. Having, in his own words, counted the reasons for the failure of seven years of agricultural policy on his fingers, a member of parliament by the name of Yusefpur lamented that "at this rate of development, achieving self-sufficiency is nothing more than a mirage."[33] The chairman of the parliamentary agriculture committee, Dr. Angaji, expressed similar views: "Unfortunately, self-sufficiency never left the frame of a catch-phrase after the revolution." Instead, "we have daily been witnesses to how the substance of our agriculture has collapsed due to bad policies."[34] The limited space available here does not allow me to quote all the frequent assessments made in the same vein.

As self-sufficiency is considered by all those in power an almost holy aim, it has been used to legitimize all sorts of projects that did not have very much to do with it—e.g., to justify a policy of restricting land ownership—and nearly all the relevant bills have stated that, because it is impossible to realize self-sufficiency without land reform, large estates must be limited on the basis of the principle of necessity contained in the sharia.[35] There also has been no lack of attempts to legitimize opposition to a policy directed against private property by invoking the need for self-sufficiency. For example, the bill on the Limits and Type of Productive Activity in the Private Sector stressed the need to encourage the private sector, as it would not otherwise be in a position to guarantee productive self-sufficiency.[36]

Notes

1. See K. McLachlan 1986 and 1989.
2. Hereinafter IP.
3. See 1983 development plan (hereinafter DP), first section, pp. 1/5 and 2/2. In his speech on submitting the plan to parliament, the prime minister stated that "achieving self-sufficiency in food is among the most important aims of the country's agrarian development" (PP, August 16, 1983, p. 23). The agrarian produce needed for industry was included in the plan somewhat later in his speech.
4. PP, April 15, 1986, p. 21; December 12 and 15, 1985.
5. Majles-e Shoura-ye Eslami 1985, vol. 1, p. 298f.
6. PP, August 16, 1983, p. 21.
7. PP, December 12 and 15, 1985, April 15, 1986.
8. Speech by the prime minister in *Kayhan*, November 28, 1984.
9. *Kayhan*, June 20, 1986, and June 20, 1987.
10. *Kayhan*, December 13, 1986, and *Keshawarz* 65 (1984).
11. *Keshawarz-e Emruz*, February 6, 1982.
12. *Ibid.*, November 13, 1979.
13. This report was mimeographed under the same title. Cf. Chapter 1 and the section on water resources.
14. *Barzegar*, September 15, 1985.
15. *Resalat*, June 14, 1986.
16. *Ibid.*, July 30, 1987.
17. DP, pp. 3, 26, and 41.
18. *Ibid.*, p. 55.
19. *Resalat*, February 19, 1990.
20. The DPA contains an overview of agricultural policy, followed by numerous volumes dealing with specific areas of agriculture and the appropriate measures proposed.
21. See p. 6. It was mimeographed by the Ministry of Agriculture (no date, but probably in the first months of 1984).
22. See McLachlan 1986 and 1989.
23. See p. 2 of the "irrigation" section in the report submitted to the seminar in September the same year (mentioned above). The 1365 (1986/7) census gives annual population growth as 3.7 percent, but the true rate is uncertain, official figures varying from 3.2 percent to 3.9 percent.
24. 1983, pp. 1, 5, and 10ff.
25. *Keshwarz-e Emruz*, November 29, 1979.
26. *Kayhan*, December 10, 1987.
27. *Ibid.*, December 22, 1987.
28. PP, November 15, 1985, p. 22.
29. PP January 7, 1986.
30. *Kayhan*, October 9, 1986.
31. *Ibid.*, November 28, 1984.
32. *Ibid.*, June 20, 1986; *Barzegar*, December 15, 1984.
33. PP, March 6, 1985, p. 18.
34. *Ibid.*, August 8, 1985, p. 18f.
35. Cf. A. Schirazi 1988, pp. 83, 146, 154, and 236. See also Chapter 9.4 on the principle of necessity.
36. *Ibid.*, p. 291.

5
The Position of Agriculture in Economic and Social Policy

5.1 Agriculture as the Axis of Economic Policy

As shown in Part 1, agriculture became a less important part of the shah's economic policy after the beginning of the fourth five-year plan in 1968/9. This fact was subject to even louder criticism after the revolution than before it. The shah and his development plan were accused of pursuing an illusion of industrialization, which not only failed to create industries in the country but also destroyed its agriculture. The regime had done so despite there having been good reason to believe that Iran neither could nor should become an industrial nation.[1] "The unequal competition which this regime staged between agriculture and the unproductive construction sector in particular could have had no other result than the destruction of the bases of rural life and agrarian production."[2]

According to Dr. Zali, minister of agriculture until September 13, 1988, the shah's neglect of agriculture was noticeable in several respects. Agriculture's share of GDP dropped, pricing policies favored the towns, the gap between town and country widened, and intersectoral exchange always came at the expense of agriculture.[3] These and similar arguments were made in the foreword to the draft of the 1983 development plan. Several tables showed how agriculture's share of the national economy had fallen between 1959 and 1979, how less and less had been allocated to the agricultural sector, and how its contribution to the national product had dropped in both absolute and relative terms (DPA, pp. 18ff).

Even this limited criticism makes it clear that, after the revolution, the new powers-that-be intended to reverse this relationship. Izadi, the minister of agriculture under the Bazargan government, was in favor of giving the agrarian sector preference; others merely wanted to put it on an equal footing with industry. In his book *Nejat* (Deliverance), published in 1983, the minister listed a number of points intended to back up his support of agriculture: the vastness of the country, the abundant resources of water, the

300 days of sun a year, a population with a liking for agriculture, the independence that could be achieved through self-sufficiency, the high quality of Iran's agricultural produce, environmental protection through agriculture, and various factors against preferences for industry. For these reasons, he said, "agriculture should be granted priority over industry."[4]

However, the priority the new rulers wanted to give agriculture was not primarily based on the considerations listed above but rather on their love of independence. Even the quote by Dr. Izadi above makes it clear that this legitimation is of particular importance.[5] The link was made even clearer in the 1983 development plan: "By reason of its strategic significance for the achievement of economic independence, agriculture is to be considered as the main axis of development in the first development plan of the Islamic Republic of Iran."[6] A parliamentarian said, "So that we do not have to lean on others for food, we must award agriculture the role of an axis in development."[7]

Later, another reason was added for the priority of agriculture—namely, that it was less dependent on foreign currency than other sectors and could develop relatively independently into a source of foreign exchange earnings through exports. These considerations, in part well-founded and in part based on wishful thinking, were accompanied by the idea that promoting agriculture would curb the rise in unemployment.[8]

The pivotal position accorded to agriculture in the 1983 development plan was the culmination of a series of tributes paid to it during the preliminary stages of preparing the plan. For Khomeini, agriculture was just as important in Islam as religious services.[9] Dr. Zali, the minister of agriculture, quotes him as having "thrice" said: "Agriculture must be at the head of things—industry must serve agriculture."[10] According to the speaker, Rafsanjani, devotion to rural life was the "soul of the Islamic revolution"[11] and in his view "the path to the economic development of the country" could only lead through villages.[12] Finally, the former minister of agriculture, Mohammad Salamati, thanked God for the decision to make agriculture the axis of development.[13]

Contrary opinions about the significance of agriculture were also expressed but seldom published. The Organization of Planning and Budget's September 1979 report (see Chapter 4.3) came out clearly against prioritizing agriculture, saying that self-sufficiency was impossible and that over the long term the country would be dependent on exporting industrial goods in order to be able to import food. Industrialization ought to be accelerated for this reason, said the report, and because "a productive and stable agriculture cannot exist without an effective industry." The reduction in oil revenues meant that a balance-of-payments equilibrium could not be guaranteed by agricultural development, because of its limitations, so industrialization was imperative while the country still lacked oil-export income.[14] An article in *Kayhan* five years later summarized the arguments of those opposed to making agriculture the axis of development as follows: Choosing it as the axis of development in the 1983 development plan had been a reaction to the neglect of this sector under the shah. The strategy lacked any theoretical foundation and displayed ignorance about the limits of agricultural development. Accelerated and independent development in agriculture, they said, presupposes both the existence of an industrial infrastructure and also the provision of advanced technology. Further, self-sufficiency in agricultural produce alone does not guarantee independence—the technological dependence of the underdeveloped countries must be eliminated at the same time. "In view of this fact," the article resolved, "agriculture should only be allocated the place due to it within the framework of a strategy to develop industry, namely heavy industry."[15]

Other authors noted that agriculture's backwardness undermined its central role in development plans. For instance, M. Nuri, a member of the Association of Iranian Economists, raised the point (see *Barzegar,* July 20, 1984), as did those experts who before the revolution had given priority to the industrialization of the country.[16] Still, those opposed to emphasizing agriculture were a small minority, the most prominent among them being the minister of heavy industry, Behzad Nabawi. Their weak position was the reason the draft of the 1983 development plan guaranteed agriculture a pivotal position for the first ten years. It provided for agriculture, which before the revolution had growth rates of 1 to 3 percent, to increase production by about 7 percent annually by 1993 (some 2.2 percent above the average for the economy as a whole). Its contribution to GDP, which had dropped to 8.5 percent by 1977, was to rise to 20.9 percent by 1987 and to 19 percent by 1993.[17] The actual development was quite different, as will be shown.

5.2 Agriculture Yields Priority to the War

The actual degree of priority agriculture enjoyed in practice over other sectors of the economy will be discussed below. What is certain, however, is that, as of September 1980, the war with Iraq succeeded in diverting all attention and investments away not only from agriculture but from the economy as a whole.

With the glorification and mystification of the war, agriculture soon lost the priority it enjoyed in official parlance. By the time the draft of the 1983 development plan, which had allocated priority to agriculture, was approved by the Council of Ministers, it already read: "The government will ensure that the priority of the war is not subject to any restriction until final victory."[18] Formally according first priority to the war, as was already the case in practice, left agriculture only with second priority at best. This demotion was officially decreed and made public a number of times. For example, in July 1986 the minister of agriculture stated: "The economic council has decided that agriculture takes second priority to the war."[19] This assurance was repeated almost one and a half years later by President Khamene'i[20] and was repeated on every appropriate occasion thereafter.

The war had soon eclipsed agriculture in importance to such an extent that the war had to be enlisted to remind people of the importance of agriculture. The minister of agriculture thought it necessary to emphasize its "equality" with the war, commenting, "We cannot fight if we do not farm,"[21] and saying on another occasion, "Just as the war is the number one problem, we must emphasize the importance of the production of food. Just as the possession of reinforcements is vital to the warriors, our people must produce enough food if it does not want to become dependent and through its dependence does not want to give a weapon into the hands of the enemy, a weapon which he could use against us."[22] In this vein agriculture was not infrequently called a "defensive front,"[23] and the villages with the most war "martyrs" were honored as being exemplary.[24] Organizations engaged in rural construction and the promotion of agriculture were remodeled for the war effort, the best example being Jahad-e Sazandegi, which will be examined in Chapter 7.

In conjunction with the general reduction in funds caused by the drop in oil revenues, war expenditures quickly led to a situation in which very few resources at all were available for other purposes. The lion's share of them had to be earmarked for the "satisfaction of general needs," mainly food imports, which consumed part of the government's foreign exchange earnings. As a result, not much remained for investments in development. As shown in Chapter 3, the tendency to reduce the funds allocated for development in recent budget proposals is very clear.

Agriculture has not even received the proportion of the massively reduced investments that would have been required to confirm its priority. Since 1980/1 it has ranked only fifth or sixth, in terms of allocations, behind transport, oil, industry, energy, and water. It had been in third place the previous year when its share of the total investments for development amounted to 16 percent. In 1985/6 it amounted to 10.6 percent and a year later to 12.3 percent of the total.[25]

5.3 The Postwar Development

The ending of the war with Iraq in August 1988 caused the bulk of the population, including many experts, to hope that the country's entire resources would be devoted to reconstruction, thus giving agriculture the "first priority" it deserved. "Now It's Agriculture's Turn" (the title of the lead story in the July 30, 1988, edition of the journal *Barzegar*) was characteristic of this expectation, voicing the hope that it would now be possible to provide agricultural development with adequate funds and restore it to its pivotal position in development policy.

This hope was at first confirmed by those in charge. President Khamene'i stated on October 8, 1988 that agriculture must take precedence, and he gave an assurance that Imam Khomeini was of the same opinion.[26] Some weeks previously, Prime Minister Musawi had announced that agriculture was at the top of the agenda in the reconstruction plan.[27] The minister of jahad-e sazandegi thought it ought to stay at the top for the first and second five-year plans because the independence of the country depended on it.[28]

However, the actual priorities in development policy were very different despite these assurances, as the cessation of hostilities did not mean that the defense budget could be cut significantly. The way the war had ended, the continuation of the enemy's hostile attitude, and the need to rearm for the contingency of a renewed outbreak of fighting all obliged the government to spend a considerable proportion of its revenues on maintaining the state of alert at the front. As a consequence, there was no increase in investment expenditure in the 1368 (1989/90) budget proposals over the year before.

Moreover, the government had to devote time and money to eliminating the war damage. The measures taken were in fact directed to this end, which is why there was talk of implementing a *re*construction rather than a construction plan. Agriculture did not top the list of priorities in this plan, approved by parliament and the Council of Guardians on February 1, 1990, which caused the ex–minister of agriculture, Dr. Zali (voted out of office on September 13, 1988), to complain that the government was still continuing to deny it the necessary support.[29] Salamati, another former minister of agriculture, stated that the plan accorded it a sort of second priority rather than a "pivotal position" and added that not even this priority was guaranteed when funds were allocated.[30]

5.4 Criticism of the Neglect of Agriculture

Those favoring top priority for agriculture often criticized the fact that it had been supplanted but, indicatively, went to pains to avoid mentioning the war as one of the causes. Instead, they often linked the neglect with a lack of will on the part of the minister, the incompetence of the ministries, or—though less frequently—with unacknowledged interference in agricultural questions by the state. One member of parliament said: "By reason of the direction taken by the Ministry of Planning and Budget, agriculture is not only not the pivotal position in the country but we would be happy if it could take the tenth or fifth position."[31]

Such accusations were primarily leveled against the minister of agriculture, but he rejected any blame and joined the ranks of the critics, knowing full well that it would only have been possible to guarantee the pivotal position of agriculture if "the entire machinery of state had been geared to this aim"—which had by no means been the case.[32] Toward the end of 1984 he complained, "All funds were put at the disposal of the war. If the supply of bread or water poses problems in Tehran, all powers are given to solve them; if the problem of the Mobarake steel works requires a solution, all funds are made available for this purpose." Agriculture was the only exception.[33] A year later, he asked parliament how it was possible to speak of the priority of agriculture when it was not even possible to obtain the plastic material needed to pack rice and dates.[34] He expressed himself in a similar vein in October 1987: "[H]ow can we maintain that agriculture is the axis of economic development if our farmers have to complain about the lack of fertilizers, pesticides, and spare parts?"[35] His endorsements of the criticisms did not exonerate him from the blame his opponents were trying to pin on him in order to have somebody to carry the can. On September 13, 1988, after nearly five years in office, the minister was given a vote of no confidence by parliament.

Notes

1. According to Dr. Izadi, minister of agriculture in the Bazargan government, in *Keshawarz-e Emruz*, October 21, 1979. He expressed the same view in his book, *Nejat*, 1983, pp. 618ff and 635ff.
2. IP, p. 2; RS, p. 4, agriculture section.
3. See p. 4 of his letter to Khomeini, op. cit.
4. *Ibid.*, pp. 629 and 636ff.
5. He considers independence the most important of all the reasons he gives; cf. Izadi, *Nejat*, p. 630.
6. DP, pp. 3/2 and 1/11; DPA, p. 2f.
7. PP, August 16, 1983, p. 14.
8. Dorri Najafabadi, spokesman of the parliamentary committee for planning and budget (PP, March 7, 1987, p. 23) and Kabiri, spokesman of the agricultural committee (PP, March 15, 1987, p. 37).
9. *Payam-e Enqelab*, May 25, 1983, p. 6.
10. *Barzegar*, July 31, 1982.
11. *Jomhuri-ye Eslami*, March 2, 1983.
12. *Ibid.*, July 9, 1983.
13. The Council of Ministers decided it in connection with the draft of the first five-year plan of 1983, but the plan itself was rejected by parliament. Interview in specialist journal *Zeytun*, November 25, 1982.
14. Sections: water resources, p. 3f, and industry, p. 4. *Kayhan*, October 24, 1985.
15. *Kayhan*, October 24, 1985.
16. Sazman-e Barname, "Fourth Construction Plan of the Country," pp. 31f and 38; cf. Izadi, *Nejat*, p. 624f.
17. DP, p. 2/15f.

18. *Jomhuri-ye Eslami*, July 12, 1983.
19. *Resalat*, July 30, 1986.
20. *Kayhan*, December 24, 1987.
21. *Ibid.*, June 17, 1986. He also stated in parliament: "We must understand agriculture as if it were a matter of war." PP, November 15, 1985.
22. *Kayhan*, December 1, 1988.
23. *Resalat*, October 8, 1986.
24. *Ibid.*, September 30, 1987.
25. Markaz-e Amar-e Iran 1984, p. 692, and 1988, p. 440; B. Farnush 1984, p. 51, and 1988, p. 103; and H. Refahiyat 1986, p. 56, and 1987, p. 95.
26. *Resalat*, October 8, 1988.
27. *Kayhan*, September 3, 1988. At the same time the minister of agriculture was insisting that "agriculture must form the axis of development." *Barzegar*, September 10, 1988.
28. *Resalat*, January 31, 1989.
29. Zali's open letter to parliament in *Barzegar*, October 22, 1988. The draft had only had its first reading at the time, but even at the second reading agriculture was not given top priority.
30. *Kayhan*, November 26, 1989.
31. PP, June 6, 1985, p. 19; and December 12, 1985, p. 31.
32. p. 11 of letter to Khomeini.
33. *Barzegar*, December 15, 1984.
34. PP, January 14, 1986, p. 22.
35. PP, October 21, 1987, p. 30.

6
Planning Agriculture

6.1 The Need for Planning

The previous chapter's discussion about the position of agriculture makes it clear that the Islamist rulers are convinced that development policy has to be planned. Agriculture ought to have been assigned a pivotal position in any development plan. Article 44 of the constitution of the Islamic Republic emphasizes the need for a planned development policy, stating that "the economic order of the Islamic Republic of Iran is based on the state, cooperative and private sectors as well on orderly and correct planning."

The Islamist rulers' conviction that planning is needed has never been explained in terms of economic theory or relevant discussions among experts. It is highly probable that they are convinced of the need for planning because Iran's economy has been planned, to a greater or lesser degree, since 1947. For years there has been an Organization of Planning and Budget (OPB), and it was kept on after the revolution.[1] It seemed self-evident, within this tradition, that the organization should draft a new development plan soon after the revolution, especially as the old one had expired in 1977.

The positive reception accorded this approach by the Islamists in power was further supported by a simplistic, even naive logic that rendered superfluous any reference to the relevant theoretical discussions. For example, an Imam leading the Friday prayers said, "A people without a plan is like a ship heading for port without a compass."[2] Khomeini's recommendation of December 9, 1982, was similar: "It is impossible to administer a country without a plan. So we need a plan."[3] In the preamble to the draft of the ill-fated 1983 five-year plan, planning was equated with the obligatory religious services that society is duty-bound to hold. The minister of planning and budget put it more succinctly: "Without working out an overall plan, it is impossible to establish a logical and coordinated connection between the individual areas [of a society]." In this connection, he suggested that an overall plan be drafted for a twenty-year period.[4]

Another argument for planning was that it would be impossible to implement a distinctly Islamic form of development without a plan. After having given details about some of the reasons planning was needed, the prime minister, Musawi, addressed this point during the presentation of the first Islamic development plan to parliament:

> Another reason for requiring socioeconomic planning in the newly founded Islamic Republic lies in the assurance which must be given to the world's dispossessed that the Islamic Republic of Iran—because it is based on religion and because it was able to hold its own politically and militarily—is also economically in a position to determine the direction it will take. This enables it to make—at [the] international level—its convincing, dynamic and precisely elaborated plans available to the dispossessed as a signpost and to encourage them—with unbroken will—to continue the struggle for liberation from the dependence vis-à-vis Western and Eastern imperialism.[5]

Without a plan, the speech continued, it would be impossible to establish the Islamic economic order provided for in Article 44 of the constitution. The spokesman of the Parliamentary Planning Commission expressed this last idea in more general terms two years later, saying that "the movement in the direction of the Islamic order desired will certainly encounter great difficulties if it is not planned."[6]

Many other high-ranking functionaries in the Islamic Republic have put forward similar arguments throughout the postrevolutionary years. However, the ruling Islamists may have been practically unanimous in their public conviction of the need for planning, but some of them reputedly voiced doubts, based on Islam, about any sort of planning. Musawi alluded to such objections in his speech before parliament, saying, inter alia: "There was a dangerous school of thought which was of the opinion that no planned and organized measures to safeguard the common good are possible or useful before the resurrection of the hidden twelfth Imam." He added that the dissenters would stop at nothing to negate planning: They were circulating letters, spreading rumors, and denouncing planning as a U.S. foible.[7]

Indeed, the process of getting an actual plan approved and implemented proved more difficult than anybody would have imagined. Efforts to draft a plan began within months of the shah's overthrow, but not until 1983, four years later, was one ready to be submitted to parliament. That plan was never approved, nor was a more limited plan, submitted in 1987, designed to achieve agricultural self-sufficiency. It was not until 1990 that the Islamic Republic finally put into effect its first five-year development plan.

6.2 Working Out the 1983 Development Plan

The first steps toward working out a development plan were taken by the Bazargan government. In September 1979, the Organization for Planning and Budget held a seminar to discuss a new "comprehensive development plan" and presented a report that dealt with many relevant questions. The report began with a foreword that not only criticized planning under the shah but also briefly outlined the fundamentals of a new development plan. (These fundamentals will be dealt with in detail shortly.) Its criticism of planning under the shah was that it was based on revenues from oil exports and thus exploited national resources with the aim of distributing the revenue among capitalists at home and abroad (p. 2). The report went on to say that the shah's planning was governed not by considerations of development policy but by the requirements of politics (p. 5). The result was an economic order whose characteristics the report summarized as follows:

1. The discrepancy between the country's financial and nonfinancial resources had increased, resulting in inflation.
2. A considerable proportion of the financial resources had been wasted by inflation.
3. The government had proved incapable of counteracting these developments.
4. The bureaucracy was overblown, and an ever-increasing proportion of the state budget had to be spent on personnel.
5. The banking system served a small group of capitalists who were dependent on foreign interests; the report termed this group the "politico-financial oligarchy."
6. The planners had been incapable of creating a harmonious and effective relationship between the individual sectors of the economy and the individual regions of the country.
7. Investment in agriculture was not encouraged, so agriculture was unable to keep pace with developments in other sectors of the economy, leading to an ever-growing need to import agricultural produce.
8. The gap between the towns and the country was widening, with severe consequences for the towns.

This criticism of development policy and planning under the shah formed the basis for the concepts underpinning the report's new development plan. It stated, among other things, that development ought to be pursued simultaneously at the economic, social, and cultural levels, as its main aim was to satisfy the basic needs of the poor classes in the population (p. 2f). The report also suggested working out a plan that in addition to proposing short-term solutions to pressing problems, should contain longer-term solutions to structural problems. Some of the short-term measures envisaged were establishing the state's responsibilities and the private sector's limits in the economic field; overcoming the legal, politicoeconomic, and administrative uncertainties the revolution had caused in connection with construction projects started by the shah; reducing current expenditure in the state budget; and avoiding the bureaucratization of the credit system arising from the nationalization of the banks (pp. 12–14).

The long-term measures were intended to relieve the crisis in the economy by means of structural changes aimed at reducing dependence, diversifying production, and ensuring relative self-sufficiency. To this end, it was thought necessary to precisely define areas of dependence and diversify the development of the economy, at first using technologies suitable for alleviating unemployment. Dependence on oil was to be reduced in such a way that satisfying the basic needs of the poor was still possible. Investments were to be restructured to create the conditions enabling domestic production to satisfy a large part of the country's consumer demand. The tax system was to be reformed so as to reduce dependence on oil and ensure social justice, with higher incomes being heavily taxed and the taxes strictly collected (pp. 15–20).

A detailed critical analysis of the situation in the individual sectors of the economy followed, linked to proposed solutions for the problems identified. This section addressed agriculture, rural construction, water management, industry, energy, traffic, communications, housing, urban construction, education, medical care, and hygiene.

In its economic and sociopolitical orientation, the 1979 report, which experts from the Organization of Planning and Budget had drafted with only scant regard for the Islamic revolution, took the same general line as the Bazargan government had. It recognized the difficulties involved in development planning in the Islamic Republic, summarizing the most salient points as follows:

1. The country's economic order had still not been determined, nor had the government's attitude on property and the limits of the private sector.
2. The number and diversity of centers of power had weakened the government and increased insecurity.
3. Production and investment were sluggish.
4. In view of the enormous tasks confronting the state in this phase of the revolution, the executive organs were slow to take action.
5. Some sociopolitical problems, such as the relationship between employers and employees, were having a negative effect on the economic stability of the country.

6. The failure to fully utilize capacity in the production and service sectors was making investment even more difficult.
7. Wage rises and import restrictions were increasing the danger caused by rising inflation (p. 11).[8]

This first try at working out a development plan was unsuccessful. The failure was caused by, in addition to the factors listed in the report, the struggle for political power that had flared up between the various Islamist groups, hindering or preventing decisions on development policy. It was only in the second half of 1981, after Bani Sadr had been deposed and the suppression of the People's Mujahidin had eliminated the last Islamist opponents of the ulamas' monopoly of power, that it was possible to begin development planning again. Work started immediately, initially under the government of Hojjat ol-Eslam Bahonar (August 5–30, 1981), and continued under the government of Ayatollah Mahdavi Kani (September 2–October 19, 1981). In order to emphasize the urgency of the task, the year 1361 (1982/3) was declared "Planning Year." Throughout the country, 5,000 people organized in 96 planning panels and 500 expert committees were employed in working out the plan.[9]

Work on the plan produced initial results in the spring of 1982 in the form of a draft. Although not quite complete, the draft was nonetheless approved by both the Economic Council and the Council of Ministers and subsequently published as "Major Trends in the Economic, Social and Cultural Development of the Islamic Republic of Iran and the Principal Quantitative Targets for 1361–1381 (1982/3–2002/3)." The planners had been set a huge task. In an interview with the daily *Kayhan* on July 10, 1982, the former director of the planning organization, M. T. Banki, indicated that "the final aim of Islamic society" had been taken into consideration in the draft—i.e., "perfecting humankind to the point of liberating it from all non-Gods and impelling it towards Allah." The economic, political, and cultural development envisaged in the draft served "to remove those obstacles preventing humankind and Islamic society meeting with God."

Work on the first development plan finally concluded in 1983 with the complete draft of the "First Economic, Social and Cultural Development Plan of the Islamic Republic of Iran 1362–1366" (DP), which was approved by the Council of Ministers on July 12, 1983. The prime minister sought approval for it during a speech in parliament on August 16, 1983. The plan ran to 4,500 pages in 36 volumes. The mere completion of such a mammoth task filled the leaders of the Islamic Republic with hope. The work was widely praised. Speaker Rafsanjani declared that "the government's drafting of the plan in conditions of war and economic blockade represents one of the wonders of the world."[10] Prime Minister Musawi called it proof of the workability of the Islamic development model and a signpost for the independence movement of the dispossessed of the world.[11] In a postscript to the first volume of the plan, it is characterized as serving God with the aim of founding a community of worshippers which, for the first time in the fourteen centuries of the history of Islam, would succeed in properly Islamizing itself (p. j.).

Before moving on to the substance of the first development plan in detail, we should first look at the efforts made to create a special program related to agriculture in the period prior to July 12, 1983, both parallel to and within the framework of drafting the plan.

6.3 Planning Agricultural Policy

Drafting a master development plan is traditionally a matter for the planning organization. But after the revolution, a variety of groups and individuals became very politically active, especially during the liberal phase, publishing a number of rudimentary programs intended to reform or revolutionize agriculture, industry, and other aspects of society. They contained some strange assertions, which betrayed them as political propaganda or the result of personal naiveté. For instance, in a televised debate with Bani Sadr (who later became president), the spokesman of a Trotskyite group declared that he would solve the problems in agriculture within three days if he were given the necessary powers.[12]

At the state level, various agencies (including the Ministry of Agriculture and Rural Construction and the newly founded Jahad-e Sazandegi organization) were also trying their hand at drafting a development program for agriculture. Dr. Izadi, the minister of agriculture in the Bazargan government, was responsible for one of the first documents on the matter as early as May 1979 (see Chapter 4). This summarized program of twenty-four pages produced by the Special Group for Planning Studies[13] began with a criticism of agricultural policy under the shah and found fault with, among other things, Iran's dependence on agricultural imports, agriculture's loss of status, and the rural exodus. It also considered the Ministry of Agriculture to be confronted with two basic tasks: first, to "eliminate the large-scale destruction in the productive sector" and "remedy the deplorable state of affairs in the rural areas"; and second, "to take measures to redress this situation." These measures were crystalized in twelve points dealing with almost all aspects of agricultural policy. These points will be dealt with later in greater detail.

It is noteworthy that the authors of this program made no great effort to cast it in an Islamic frame of reference.[14] It clearly bore the stamp of the Barzagan government's liberal economic and political policies, only displaying an interest in land reform to the extent that it related to the reclamation of uncultivated land and wasteland. It aimed to reduce government intervention in agriculture to providing assistance and services, envisaged private investment in agriculture, and placed considerable emphasis on a combination of traditional and modern procedures to reform the organization of production.

Dr. Izadi and his closest colleagues further expounded their policy in interviews and at seminars.[15] In a letter to the Revolutionary Council, Dr. Izadi made it clear that he wanted to base his policy on the principle of profitability, intending to combat the accumulation of wealth through measures that could be based on the Islamic poor tax (zakat)—to which end he even submitted draft legislation (Proposed Legislation on the Establishment of Rural People's Banks) to the Revolutionary Council. The bill mandated that interest-free credits and loans be made available to needy peasants from the funds collected from these religious taxes.[16] Measures to implement this program are to be found in numerous laws enacted by the Revolutionary Council before the fall of the Bazargan government in November 1979. These will be examined in detail in later chapters on individual agricultural measures.

The era of moderate, liberal economic policy ended with the fall of the Bazargan government. The populist course of its successors is clear in their agrarian program, which is primarily concerned with land reform. The radical restrictions on private land ownership sought by those in charge at the Ministry of Agriculture, above all Reza Esfahani, met with stiff opposition and created a political atmosphere that pushed the formulation of a program for the rest of agriculture into the background. This program, which was only made known in September 1980, contained fourteen points. The one dealing with land reform ranked first, underlining the most significant difference between it and Izadi's program. Another important difference was the incorporation of a measure already instigated under the shah—i.e., the regionalization of specific crops. The program was too brief for further differences to be seen.[17] Such differences became clearer when the new minister of agriculture, M. Salamati (who took office in September 1980), explained the program in detail. Interviewed by the journal *Barzegar* on November 1, 1980, he declared that under his leadership ideology would take precedence over technical expertise. Asked whether he was ready to make use of the experience of the farmers to implement his program, he (though not an expert himself) answered that he would "put greater store on ideological soundness than on experience and expertise." He went on to express his intention of calling the peasants' attention to forgoing profitable crops in the interests of the revolution and planting ones considered "essential"—meaning wheat. Another difference, which became clear in the course of the land reform legislation, was in the priority given to the government-controlled establishment of a new form of producer cooperative known as mosha'; in Dr. Izadi's program private initiative was to have determined the type of operation.[18]

Salamati's fourteen-point program constituted the first formal guide to agricultural policy under his leadership. Somewhat later, five points were added, mainly the result of the subdivision of some of the points in the first program. The establishment of mosha's was specifically mentioned. It is interesting to note that the supplement mentioned the need to coordinate agricultural policy measures, a reference to the problems resulting from the split in agriculture at the administrative level created by the establishment of Jahad-e Sazandegi organization.[19] In addition to working on the short and the long versions of the program, the Ministry of Agriculture was, under Salamati, also busy formulating his contribution to the first development plan.[20]

6.4 The 1983 Development Plan

6.4.1 Basic Data

The first development plan, which was to be "neither Western nor Eastern" but "Islamic" as well as "thoroughly cultural and spiritual," was submitted to parliament on August 16, 1983. It consisted of a broad agenda to develop certain specified areas of social life over a period of twenty years and a somewhat more concrete strategy for the five years immediately after 1983. Its aim was not only to define the activities of the state in these areas and for this period but also to include private sector investment in the plan, thus ensuring the participation of the people in its implementation.

The plan began with criticism of the economic developments in the three decades before the revolution, decrying the same deplorable state of affairs and the same misdirection criticized in the seminar report of September 1979. There followed a list of aims for the future: improving and promoting education and culture, achieving economic independence, ensuring social security, increasing food production and housing, and combatting unemployment, among others. Particular attention was given to safeguarding the interests of the dispossessed (pp. 1/5ff).

The plan outlined the policy for implementing the objectives as follows:

1. Encourage investment and counteract consumerism
2. Make agriculture the axis of development
3. Increase research
4. Create more part-time jobs for peasants and nomads with the aim of improving their income
5. Link economic sectors
6. Develop engineering and the production of intermediate goods
7. Change the economic structure of the towns

8. Prevent overspill in the cities
9. Ensure utilization of existing production capacity
10. Improve utilization and maintenance of machinery and equipment
11. Increase exports from industry, crafts, and agriculture
12. Step up planning
13. Protect the environment (pp. 1/11ff)

This qualitative list of aims and the description of the corresponding political measures were followed by details of quantitative equivalents. From 1982/3 to 2002/3, GDP (at factor cost) was to increase from 9,348bn to 39,825bn rials (at base-year prices) at annual averages of 4.8 percent, 9 percent, 8.7 percent, and 7.5 percent, respectively, in the four five-year periods. The growth rate for agriculture was to be 7 percent in the first ten years, 5 percent in the third five-year period, and 3.1 percent in the fourth, equal to an increase from 1,768bn to 5,170bn rials at base-year prices (p. 2/15). Agriculture's share of GDP was to increase from 18.9 percent in the base year to a peak at 20.9 percent and then drop back to 13 percent by the year 2003. Industry's share was to grow continuously from 16 percent to 45.2 percent over the same period. The service and oil sectors were to decrease continuously, from 47 percent to 36.7 percent and 18.1 percent to 5.1 percent, respectively (p. 2/16). Clearly, investment in general and particularly in the individual sectors had to keep pace (p. 2/17). State revenues were to increase by a minimum of 5.5 percent and a maximum of 7.6 percent annually at constant prices. Oil was to become less important as a source of state revenue, with zero growth in the third five-year period and negative growth in the fourth. There were three scenarios for state revenues from oil. The most pessimistic assumed that the price of oil would stay at $29 a barrel for twenty years from 1982; the second was based on an annual price rise of 5 percent, to approximately $73 a barrel in 2002; and the third envisaged oil costing only $66 a barrel by then (p. 2/3). The state's budget deficits were to disappear by 1992/3 (p. 2/27). The development plan assumed an average population growth rate of 3.1 percent (p. 2/1).

The third part of the draft plan in the first, generally worded volume dealt with the projected development of the economy over the first five years. Although it attempted to be very realistic, the planners were wide of the mark even for this short period, as I shall show when presenting my criticism of the plan.

Irrespective of this aspect, it is interesting to discover how "the Islamic society" would have looked if, in the first phase of development, the Islamic Republic had succeeded in achieving its targets. The main features of the rosy picture the plan painted are as follows:

It will be an independent society which can itself satisfy its basic needs with respect to agricultural and industrial goods as well as in the field of defense. . . . It will be a society whose members tread the path of God in full awareness. . . . In this society there will no longer be poverty and unemployment and its members will do productive and useful work. . . . In this society each family will have adequate housing in which the basic pillars of the family are strengthened and Islamic upbringing is enforced. . . . It will be a society in which the foundations are laid for the further development and continued growth of the Islamic community by raising aware, thinking people and by the establishment of infrastructural institutions and basic industries. (p. 1/10)

This picture was to have become reality in five years—i.e., by 1988.

6.4.2 The Development Plan for Agriculture

The draft of the master plan devoted a volume of 365 pages to agriculture in the first phase, entitled "Five-year Plan for Development of Agriculture." This summary was mimeographed by the Coordinating Committee for Sectoral-Regional Planning at the Ministry of Agriculture in December 1982. It began with a lengthy quotation by Khomeini testifying to the need for planning and recommending that it should be supervised by the clergy to ensure that, "heaven forbid, nothing be decided contrary to Islam." If that were to happen, the plan would be rejected by parliament and/or the Council of Guardians. The Islamic character of the plan was reiterated in the foreword, written by Salamati, the minister of agriculture. He spoke of a planning movement, inspired by Islamic values, that would continue the Islamic revolution. Indeed, its success would bring about the "defeat of imperialism on all fronts"; in addition, because the plan aimed to "achieve self-sufficiency as soon as possible," it would "deal a powerful blow, in the mouth, to all those who think that we cannot provide for ourselves."

The introduction and foreword were followed by a criticism of the shah's agricultural policy (pp. 1ff) that broadly corresponded to the criticism expressed in the seminar report of September 1979 mentioned above. The draft then analyzed the state of affairs in detail and the capacities available for development. This analysis was quite positive about natural capacities (p. 26). On the other hand, the description of the current state of affairs, which formed the point of departure for the first phase of the development plan, was intended to highlight the difficulty of the task undertaken by the officials at the Ministry of Agriculture. Although it did so, the planners' evaluation of the results of the agricultural policy in the first years after the revolution was so negative that they considered it advisable to blur the line between the pre- and postrevolutionary eras. "The current state of affairs" thus meant the state of affairs prior to 1982, not prior to 1979.

The next section was devoted to determining the "objectives of agricultural policy." When specifying the aims, a distinction was made between the general qualitative aims for the coming decade, the general qualitative aims for the first five-year plan, and the quantitative aims, which could be valid either for the first five-year plan or for the coming decade.

The quantitative targets will be detailed and compared with the actual results in the analysis of specific areas of agricultural policy in the Islamic Republic of Iran in subsequent chapters. The draft outlined the qualitative aims projected for a period of ten years as follows:

1. Self-sufficiency is to be achieved by means of the production of essential agricultural produce that is used for food and as raw material for industry . . . with the aim of liberating the country from dependence and ensuring sovereignty.

2. Production is to be increased to such an extent that agricultural produce can be exported. Some of the foreign currency required for the economic development of the country is to be obtained in this way, thus making unnecessary any support for agriculture that is financed by oil.

3. Farmers' incomes and standards of living are to be raised so as to bridge the gap between town and country as well as between the agricultural sector and the other sectors of the economy. The pace of the rural exodus is to be reduced to a reasonable level by creating opportunities to absorb manpower into agriculture.

The twenty-two measures to achieve these aims were listed in this part of the plan and touched on more or less the same issues as Dr. Izadi's twelve-point program and Salamati's fourteen- and nineteen-point ones.

The third section of this part of the plan contained detailed particulars of the individual steps to be taken in the first five years for all branches of agriculture, along with precise details of the results expected and the investments planned (pp. 85–121). As in the two previous sections, the exposés contained a series of tables that included the relevant target figures (pp. 122–212).

In the fourth section, the necessary conclusions were drawn from the statement that agriculture ought to occupy a pivotal position in planning development, inasmuch as the demands that the development of agriculture makes on the other sectors of the economy were listed. The Ministry of Water and Energy was to ensure that agriculture received the projected quantities of water and electricity; industry was to deliver suitable machines, equipment, fertilizers, and pesticides; factories were to undertake the processing and packing of agricultural produce; universities and other educational or research establishments were to provide experts and technology; and the legislative organs were required to pass the necessary laws as soon as possible. The tables provided indicated the quantities in question (pp. 293ff).

The "Rules of Procedure and the Systems of Implementation in the Agricultural Sector" were determined in the last section of the agricultural part of the plan. This section contained ideas for "the establishment of an organizational system" to be "set up as soon as possible on the basis of the objectives and political measures determined"—failing which it would prove impossible to implement the plan. It is significant that a plan was made whose implementation was to be accomplished by an administrative system not yet in place—a problem still confronting the Islamic state when it passed the 1990 plan, as will be shown.

Some of the guiding principles that were envisaged as becoming effective in connection with the administrative and procedural reforms read as follows: decentralization of the administration; orientation of politics toward the needs of the producers, whose trust was to be gained and whose readiness to cooperate was to be enlisted; minimization of production costs; education of the rural population, for which the cooperation of the ulama was to be ensured; coordination of the work of the various state organizations; cooperation of the Islamic Village Councils to mobilize the rural population; trust that the population would carry out the work; motivation of graduates in agricultural disciplines and encouragement of expatriate experts to return; where necessary, collaboration with foreign experts; and shortening of the chain of command.

6.5 Criticism of the Development Plan

From the very beginning, the first development plan and the part of it dealing with agriculture encountered massive criticism even among the staff of the OPB and the Ministry of Agriculture. One example is Farhad Maher's 1983 document, which was mimeographed as "Criticism of the Quantitative Targets for Agriculture in the Period 1983/4–1992/3" by the Center for Rural and Agricultural Research. The criticism expressed in this eighteen-page document covered five points:

1. The targets were unrealistic. For example, achieving self-sufficiency in the allotted period was impossible because of the high growth rate of the population and other uncontrollable conditions (p. 5). The data on which the targets were based could only be termed illusionary, as for example the projected increase in the area under irrigation (p. 10). The plan suffered from the fact that the conditions confronting the government did not permit the aims to be achieved (p. 1).

2. The objectives were contradictory. Mechanizing agriculture was incompatible with stemming the rural exodus (p. 5). Rehabilitating over-

grazed pastures ran counter to the aim of basing the organization of animal husbandry on the traditional methods, which had caused the overgrazing that was being complained about (p. 13). The establishment of the mosha' cooperatives could not be enforced by the state without running counter to the aim of reducing state intervention in agriculture (p. 9).

3. Some of the measures that should have been implemented in the period prior to the plan were still waiting to be put into effect. For example, the establishment of the Centers for Rural, Agricultural and Nomadic Services had not made progress as expected because of a lack of qualified personnel (p. 15).

4. The plan did not deal with "one of the most important points in agriculture"—i.e., land reform.

5. The plans for individual agricultural branches such as forests and pastures were exactly the same as the ones that had been gathering dust in the administration for some considerable time; they dated from before the revolution (p. 17).

A more detailed critique, whose authors wished to remain anonymous, originated in the Organization of Planning and Budget. The manuscript, probably written in 1983, contained some seventy pages of detailed arguments about the master development plan.[21] Its main criticism was reserved for the impossibility of planning for a society that lacked the prerequisites for planned development. "The disunity and disintegration" of the society in the postrevolutionary era, the lack of an unequivocally political decision-making machine, and the serious shortcomings in the economy (the lack of physical and financial resources or, equally, the decline in the number of experts) made it seem absurd even to attempt any planning (p. 1/7). There was also the grave circumstance that the postrevolutionary regime had still not clarified the status of private property and of the private sector in the Islamic Republic (p. 1/7), causing the confusion apparent in the draft plan (pp. 58–71). This confusion kept the plan from delineating the boundary between the state and private sectors with reasonable clarity—even the nationalized banks and industrial enterprises had been classified in the "nonstate" sector (p. 61). For all that, the plan assumed that a considerable number of its projects would be carried out by the private sector, which was scarcely to be expected in the circumstances.

Even in setting targets, the plan clearly was based on wishful thinking (pp. 10 and 37) inasmuch as it ignored or underestimated a number of negative tendencies and conditions. For example, it ignored the war and its consequences, as well as the priority the Islamic Republic's leaders had given it in their political deliberations (p. 13). The plan was full of contradictions: Although it assigned the function of axis in the master plan to agriculture, for instance, many other politicoeconomic strategies were also designated as basic, including establishing and developing industry and expanding housing construction and mining (pp. 12ff); it wished to curb government expenditure and at the same time aimed to improve the training system and social welfare (p. 18); it assumed an increase in government tax revenues and a curb on private consumption and on the private sector in general (p. 18); and it aimed to export agricultural produce while declaring as its primary objective increasing the production of the supposedly "strategic" products to the level of self-sufficiency (p. 26). This list of the contradictions could have been continued—suffice to say that the authors create the impression that the plan is fatally flawed. They also take the planners to task for having ignored the actual development of the economy in the postrevolutionary era (pp. 35ff and 57ff). The planners' ignorance of established facts included, according to the authors, choosing as the base year for their estimates 1361 (1982/3), a year for which they had also made an estimate. If they had opted for the previous year they would have had no choice but to lower their sights (pp. 20, 23, and 32).

6.6 The Development Plan in Parliament

Similar negative reactions were expressed, and to an extent published,[22] by experts both before and after the plan was debated in parliament. There it was subjected to its harshest criticism, partly thanks to the impression the experts had created by rejecting it. The plan was submitted to a special parliamentary commission for consideration in the fall of 1983. After thirty-five sittings, the commission decided to reject the plan because it (1) was based on subjective data; (2) had no clear aims; and (3) did not specify the level of state investment required for it to be implemented.[23]

As a consequence, the plan was not even deliberated on the floor of the house. This rejection occurred during the parliament's first legislative period, which lasted until June 1984. However, the Musawi government did not give up and urged parliament to reconsider the plan. The appropriate special commission subsequently worked on the plan for another thirty-five sittings. The modified version was debated on the floor of the house in January 1986 and approved at first reading—but the plan parliament approved was very different from the government's draft. The differences can be summarized as follows.

First, the approved draft contained no (or very little) quantitative data on the proposed aims and performance. It contented itself with presenting long-term qualitative aims and strategies for the general development of the country. The spokesman for the commission thought the objectives that had been decided on would suffice for a period of between fifty and seventy-five years—i.e., for a corresponding number of five-year plans—thus determining the manner of establishing the ideal society in advance.[24]

The approved version did include detailed data on the development aims and strategies envisaged in the first five-year plan. But these aims, too, were only stated in qualitative form. According to the commission spokesman, they were based on the constitution of the Islamic Republic, on Islamic principles, on the guidance of both the Imam and the "venerable jurist" (meaning Ayatollah Montazeri), and on the holy aims of the Islamic revolution, so that they "did not tend toward the East or the West."[25] The new draft called for the government to take appropriate measures to prepare for implementation of a quantitatively determinable plan in later periods (appropriate measures being legislative reforms, etc.). In addition, it was to determine the actual potential for development, in particular in agriculture; curb inflation; step up investment in infrastructure; repair the war damage; reach a decision with respect to appropriate technologies; close the gaps in its statistics; decide on a foreign trade policy; estimate oil revenue; and determine the boundaries between the state, private, and cooperative sectors.[26] The commission's plan stipulated that all 850 national and 1,800 provincial projects begun under the shah but not yet completed were to be finished before any new projects were started.[27] The plan did not contain any quantitative data because, according to the spokesman for the commission, there were, among other things, "drastic differences of opinion" between the commission and the government on the issue. It was hoped that an agreement could be reached before the plan's second reading in parliament.[28]

According to the minister for planning and budget, however, the principal difference between the two draft plans lay in the development strategy for the country as conceived by the government on the one hand and the parliamentary commission on the other. "The government was concerned to achieve the greatest possible growth on the basis of oil revenue, to rapidly expand the country's infrastructural and productive potential . . . and to considerably expand the social services. It assumed that it was in a position to rapidly solve the structural, administrative and institutional problems at the economic and social levels and to collect considerable revenues." The commission, however, thought it would "be impossible to achieve the ideal society overnight" and that the country should concentrate on completing unfinished projects, organize investments more productively, and refrain from promising to satisfy basic needs. It was more important "to elaborate the criteria and guidelines on which the satisfaction of basic needs should be based." Whereas growth and needs determined the direction of the plan for the government, the commission was guided by capacities. There could be no talk of "self-help"[29] for agriculture or of the primacy of this sector until the key points of agricultural development had been determined on the basis of specific conditions in the individual regions and until it could be guaranteed that the implementation of new cultivation patterns would be based not on coercion but on measures to motivate the peasants.[30]

Compared to the government's plan, the commission's appeared much more realistic. However, this realism disappeared when the problematic circumstances facing the government and the administration—the bodies responsible for implementing the plan—were factored in. Seen in this light, the commission's plan also had to be considered unrealistic, at best a plan of programmatic, doctrinaire importance. This accusation was in fact made in parliament and was one of the main reasons a large minority of members spoke out against the commission's plan. One of them stated that the plan offered nothing more than a series of generalities and watchwords.[31] With its very general language, it was a poor copy of the constitution[32] and merely represented an attempt to produce a literary text.[33] One parliamentarian concluded his criticism of the plan by noting that it spoke of virtuousness, bravery, justice, and self-sacrifice and wondering whether it was merely "storing snow" instead of dealing with wheat production.[34]

Despite this massive criticism, the commission's plan was approved at first reading. However, the plan's opponents proved to be more realistic. Having passed at first reading, the plan, in due form, was referred for further deliberation back to the commission, where it disappeared forever. It never returned for a second reading. For a long time it was said that the government and the commission were in the process of jointly rewording it. Later, there was some talk of other development plans, which will be dealt with below.[35]

6.7 The New Economic Policy

The work of preparing a development plan, as has been shown, was taking place in very unfavorable circumstances, with the war and the fluctuations in the government's financial position making planning extremely difficult. For a long time, though, these factors and the limitations they inevitably imposed on targets were not taken into consideration in planning or even acknowledged officially because of ideology, power politics, and lack of experience. The government continued to insist on targets that could not be achieved under these unfavorable conditions, if at all. It was mid-1986 before the Islamists finally proclaimed a "New Economic Policy" that took account of these negative factors, in particular the war. Now a war economy was officially proclaimed, which was to be taken in hand in order to ensure victory in spite of the "world powers." The reduction in oil revenues was put down to a plot hatched by the "powers that dominate the world" to force Iran to discontinue its war policy.[36] Despite this conspiracy, the war was to be given first priority in the New Economic Policy; everything else must be subservient. The prime minister declared, "The first aim that we have set ourselves within the framework of the New Economic Policy is to satisfy all the needs originating with the war. Proclaiming this as our aim means that, to the best of our ability, we shall make sure that nothing—neither the allocation of foreign currency earnings and national resources nor measures concerning industry, technology and other areas—prevents us from putting all of our facilities in the service of the war."[37] According to this plan, the funds required by all the other areas of the economy were to be provided only if (1) the expenditure seemed indispensable for the war; (2) and if, after deducting the foreign currency required for the war and for procurement of the most urgent consumer goods, funds remained (which could then be spent to import raw materials, intermediate goods, etc.); (3) and if these areas were themselves earning foreign currency and were not dependent on foreign currency.[38]

The practical consequences of the new policy were in fact evident long before it was officially announced. As shown in Chapter 3.3, the estimates of war-related expenditures were raised vis-à-vis all other budgetary items. Industrial production, which according to the new plan was to have been switched to the production of war material, dropped off considerably; for many factories, the new policy meant either abandoning or at least extensively reducing output.[39] The plan intended to counteract additional unemployment by exporting redundant labor, particularly experts.[40] In conjunction with the extractive sector, agriculture was now—in addition to becoming self-sufficient, which task still had high priority—to bring in foreign currency. To this end, exports of agricultural produce were to be stepped up. At the same time, there were more and more complaints about the lack of artificial fertilizers and the other inputs needed for agricultural production. It was no longer possible to import these materials in the same quantities as before because of the preferential allocation of foreign currency for the war.[41]

Even the provision of basic foods could not be guaranteed at the time, and the occasional shortages that cropped up were the subject of rumors that even the dailies published.[42] In his report on the state of the economy and the New Economic Policy, the prime minister was obliged to emphasize that the supply of bread to the population was assured.[43] In view of this situation, the government had no alternative but to proclaim the "satisfaction of basic needs" as priority Number 3 in the New Economic Policy. At the same time, it tried to turn necessity into virtue by declaring that the people must change their patterns of consumption: They were to economize on the use of imported goods, and "artificially induced consumer habits" were to be abandoned. This modification of consumer habits was given fifth priority in the New Economic Policy, and a Panel for the Reform of Consumer Patterns was set up for the purpose.

Another consequence of the New Economic Policy was to be seen in the attitude of the Musawi government, which on the whole had an etatist orientation toward the private sector. Concentrating state expenditure on the war made it necessary to adopt a more moderate tone toward the private sector, which was now being called on to offset reduced state investments.

The private sector now came to be thought of as "the people," whose participation was being recommended as the best means of ensuring the full utilization of production capacities, increasing investments, and stepping up production. This change in the government's attitude toward the private sector, dictated by necessity as it was, was seen as a good sign by the advocates of private enterprise. The newspaper *Resalat* made no secret of its joy on the "death of etatism which the reduction in oil revenue has finally brought about."[44]

This war economy determined (if it is even possible to speak of orderly politics in the Islamic Republic) the behavior of the government until it accepted UN Resolution 598 in August 1988. The concentration of the government's energies reached such an intensity that the prime minister could only describe it with the words: "We were absorbed in the war."[45] Nevertheless, the Islamic regime was unable to mobilize enough funds and strength to bring the war to a successful conclusion. Khomeini was soon forced, as he himself said, to drink the goblet of poison represented by the acceptance of the armistice. Although the reasons for this about-face were to remain an official secret, it is obvious that the main one was the exhaustion of the country's resources, both human and material. Those in positions of responsibility in the regime occasionally concede as much in terse statements.[46] Their reluctant acceptance of the armistice, linked as it was to a clear defeat, and the concomitant ending of the war show that the New Economic Policy—whose main aim was to win the war—was an unmitigated failure.

6.8 State Budget Planning

Despite this conclusion, some officials in the Islamic regime continued to maintain that they had the economy under complete control. Prime Minister Musawi often said that his government had worked out a particular development strategy for every conceivable level of state revenue from oil—even the lowest level—and that development policy in the Islamic Republic thus could always be conducted according to plan.[47] This statement did not go unchallenged, however, as a great many contrary opinions were expressed, both in the newspapers and in parliament.[48]

The failures in development planning became so apparent that some policymakers took the view that it might be better to dispense with long-term planning for a while. Planned state budgets, which would only be valid for one year, were considered as an alternative. This question was probably discussed for the first time by the Special Parliamentary Commission for Planning in connection with the debates on state budgets for 1986/7. It was proposed that the still incomplete construction projects left over from the prerevolutionary era should be classified according to the time needed for completion so that the government could include them in the yearly budgets and gradually finish them.[49]

Accordingly, the 1986/7 budget proposals envisaged completing 280 projects by the end of the year, for which 86 percent of the total state investment in development was earmarked. However, by the end of the year the government was shown to be incapable of planning its work, even for such a short period: Half of the projects remained incomplete.[50] The 1988/9 state budget directly acknowledged this incompetence: Note 22 in the corresponding law obliged the Ministry of Planning and Budget to provide funds for the projects that "ought to have been, but were not, completed by the end of last year."[51] Each year, construction projects scheduled for completion in the state budget have suffered a similar fate. It did become clear during parliamentary debate that there has always been an almost unbelievable discrepancy between the projected funds and those actually allocated. The following table makes the point evident.

Table 6.1 Projected and Actual Funding to Complete Projects (in billions of rials)

Year	Projected	Actual
1982/3	200	14
1983/4	150	22
1984/5	20	12
1985/6	40	15
1986/7	80	20

Sources: Morteza Alwiri, Parliamentary Secretary of State, Ministry of Planning and Budget (PP, March 1, 1987, p. 23); Speaker of the Parliamentary Commission for Planning and Budget (PP, February 23, 1987, p. 19); Alwiri (PP, February 23, 1986, p. 19); PP, February 23, 1986, pp. 18ff.

The discrepancy between the proposed and actual amounts occurs not only in individual budget items earmarked for the completion of smaller projects but also—or, to be more accurate, logically enough—in the estimates for larger sums. Some examples of these discrepancies were mentioned in Chapter 3 in connection with the fluctuations in oil revenues; further examples could be given for any particular year. Because it would not otherwise have been able to pay its employees' salaries or make other urgent payments, the government presented a supplementary budget to parliament toward the end of each year. When, as happened on January 18,

1989, a "weeping" member of parliament took the minister of planning and budget to task for this bad habit and asked where the government was leading the country, the latter answered: "We knew from the outset that we would fall short of the projected revenue."[52] He thus put the blame for this misfeasance on parliament, which every year places additional items of revenue on the government's budget estimates. But parliament would not put up with being censured like that. Opening the debate on the 1986/7 budget proposals, the spokesman of the appropriate parliamentary commission, Dorri Najafabadi, declared that the commission had made the preparation of realistic budgetary estimates its number one priority.[53] That same year, however, the discrepancy amounted to 50 percent of the state budget.

The idea of presenting a budget "according to plan" finally lost its appeal and persuasive force. It had become increasingly clear that the budget could not replace a development plan[54] and that it was impossible to prepare "planned" budgets as long as there was no development plan.[55] These contradictions finally assumed such drastic proportions that, contrary to established custom, the government decided not to make a statement on the figures for the current fiscal year when presenting its budget estimates for the coming year. According to *Enqelab-e Eslami,* the 1987/8 budget was only approved by the Council of Guardians under pressure from Khomeini. The government reputedly proposed to pass the budget by state decree (hokm-e hokumati) so as to avoid being embarrassed in parliament (February 13, 1988, p. 6). Although this decree was not made, the parliamentary debates on the budget estimates were remarkably short. The government also attempted to keep its estimates for a supplementary budget in 1987/8 secret, but leaks and parliamentary obstacles finally led to an abandonment of this approach.[56]

The failure of attempts to prepare a development plan have been unable to shake the faith in the necessity of such an undertaking. Responsible officials in the Islamic regime remain convinced of the validity of the assumption, which they have now raised to an ideological maxim, that no progress is possible without a plan. As late as March 1988, the minister of planning emphasized that "the use of a master plan must be the agenda of the holy system in the Islamic Republic" and voiced the hope that "the atmospheric problems in planning" (such as, in his opinion, "the uncertainty about the principal objectives of our development"—that in the tenth year after the revolution!—and the "uncertainty about how comprehensive the plan should be and the uncertainty of calculations due to the war") would soon be resolved.[57]

6.9 The Self-sufficiency Plan

Toward the end of 1985, the standstill in the work of completing the development plan gave the Parliamentary Commission for Agriculture the opportunity to prod the government into addressing another issue: how the country could achieve self-sufficiency in the so-called strategic agricultural products. The corresponding legislative proposal had its first reading on December 12 and 15, 1985. In essence, it read: "The government is obliged in three months at the latest to submit to the Islamic parliament a legislative proposal which contains a plan for increasing the production of essential agricultural produce (wheat, barley, rice, fodder, sugar beet, products rich in proteins, milk products, and oil-rich plants) to the level of self-sufficiency. Plans for the individual products are to be worked out separately. The increase in production is to be achieved by raising the yield per hectare and by expanding the area under cultivation."[58] The usual reasons were given by the commission spokesman for this legislative initiative, not least the belief that it was impossible to achieve the "holy aims" without a plan. All the previous failures were due to the lack of a plan—hence the need for the government to present the desired plan within three months.[59]

During the debate in parliament on this initiative, it also became clear that its supporters were primarily interested in setting a time limit for achieving self-sufficiency so that attaining this aim could not be postponed time and again. During the debate, the minister of agriculture stated how much of each product would have to be produced by 1992 in order to achieve self-sufficiency by then. But he was aware of the obstacles. First, he believed that an agricultural plan could not succeed if it was not an integral part of a master development plan, which would have to be realistically adapted to circumstances. Second, it would have to be determined how to grow more potatoes if, for example, it is more profitable for the peasants to work in town selling potatoes than to grow them in the village; if the minister is not given the necessary funds to provide the peasants in time with the foil for packing their produce; if the peasants have to worry about not being able to sell their cotton or rice; and so forth.[60] Despite such remarks, the minister promised to comply with the legislative initiative. One member of parliament stated: "Our brothers from the Ministry of Agriculture have said that they already have a plan for self-sufficiency and that they would present it to parliament as soon as they have cognizance of the law—i.e., in one or two months."[61] The minister himself assured parliament that as soon as the proposed initiative had been given approval at the first reading, he had instructed several groups of experts to prepare the plan so that it could be presented after the final enactment of the law, "God willing."[62]

The initiative encountered little resistance in parliament. Only one lobbyist (for the Ministry of Jahade-e Sazandegi) considered it necessary to point out that achieving the aims set by the legislative initiative would exceed the capabilities of the Ministry of Agriculture and that it would be better to leave agriculture in peace than to constantly burden it with such decisions.[63] Be that as it may, the initiative was approved by parliament on

April 15, 1986. But despite the three-month time limit, the plan was only completed in May 1987. It was submitted to the Council of Ministers on June 21, 1987, as it needed their approval before being put to parliament.[64] The Council kept it waiting for approval until it was no longer relevant, having been made redundant by the new draft of the first comprehensive development plan (1989/90–1993/4).

The self-sufficiency plan (SP), presented in twenty-three big volumes and officially titled the "Plan to Increase the Production of Agricultural Produce 1987/8–1996/7" (also known as the "Obligation Plan" because of the government's obligation to prepare it), was similar in structure and content to the agricultural part of the 1983 development plan discussed in Chapter 6.4.2. The most conspicuous difference between the two is that commencement of the newer plan is scheduled for the year in which the implementation of the 1983 plan was to have been completed. As the older plan was unable to be implemented, the self-sufficiency plan logically had as its point of departure data that differ considerably from those designated as targets for the first five-year period in the 1983 development plan. According to the self-sufficiency plan, the same—or similar—targets were only to be achieved many years later. The following examples make this deferment of targets obvious.

Table 6.2 Deadlines for Implementation, DPA and SP

Product	Year	Yield per Hectare (in tons)		Total Area (thousands of hectares)		Output (millions of tons)	
		DPA	SP	DPA	SP	DPA	SP
corn	1987/8	2.4	1.9	2,395	2,200	5.7	4.2
	1993/4	NA	2.4	NA	NA	NA	5.7
	1996/7	NA	NA	NA	2,500	NA	NA
rice	1987/8	4.3	3.0	520	481	2.2	1.4
	1996/7	NA	4.1	NA	525	NA	2.2
sugar	1987/8	28.1	28.0	225	171	6.3	4.8
beets	1992/3	NA	NA	NA	NA	NA	6.3
	1996/7	NA	NA	NA	233	NA	NA

Sources: 1983 development plan, 1987 self-sufficiency plan.
Note: NA = not applicable

Comparable figures can be observed for the quantities of other products specified in the two plans: In almost every case, the same or similar targets were used, and the deadline set in the development plan was simply deferred. However, things were different regarding the details of the funds to carry out the plans: The SP allocated much higher amounts than the DPA did. Whereas state investments came to 36bn rials in the DPA, 54bn rials were considered necessary for the first five years of the SP. The sum earmarked for 1987/8 in the SP was 7.4bn rials higher than in the DPA. Although the SP seemed to be the more realistic of the two when it came to setting deadlines for attaining the targets, it was the more illusory when it came to giving figures for the funds to be invested. This fiscal wishful thinking becomes even clearer when one compares the figures in the SP with the actual investments and results, as will be done below.

There were further significant differences between the two plans. Whereas the DPA was drafted at a time when belief in the absolute priority of agriculture was still being proudly proclaimed, the SP's authors could not ignore the fact that the pivotal position of agriculture had existed in word only (p. 5, foreword).[65] However, even for them, assigning high priority to agriculture constituted the main precondition for achieving self-sufficiency. The foreword to the first volume of the draft the SP stated: "The principles of the revolution, their deepening and widening, and lastly the exporting of the heavenly Islamic regulations by means of the Islamic revolution in Iran require us to raise agriculture to the axis of any economic and social development strategy" (p. 9). Both plans prefaced the presentation of their aims with an analysis of prevailing circumstances. The assessment was extremely negative in each case: Both the shah's agricultural policy and (although not explicitly) the postrevolutionary situation in agriculture drew unfavorable reviews. The SP was also critical of the competing agency, the Ministry of Jahad-e Sazandegi. Alluding to the activities of this ministry, it asked what sense there could be in improving village roads if they only helped to depopulate the villages (pp. 21ff).

Significantly, in determining agricultural policy, the SP emphasized that the state should not intervene in production (p. 141) but ought to encourage private investment; that experts should be consulted about the completion of projects; and that the trust of the population should be gained (p. 142). It attached rather more importance to decentralizing the agricultural organizations while consolidating control of the regional organizations (p. 143). It was banking on regional implementation of the scheme to determine production patterns and hoped to give a lot of assistance to producers. These provisions either were not contained in the DPA at all or were not as unequivocally stated as in the SP.

The SP also contained separate reports on two large-scale projects for water and land utilization linked to the formation of the so-called agricultural poles (qotb ha-ye keshawarzi). They were not included in the DPA.

The comparative terseness of the references to Islam in the SP were significant, too. This brevity was due, perhaps, to the SP's having been mostly drafted by experts and officials with executive functions so that—as is emphasized at one point—it would be realistic and feasible (p. 9). Finally, it must be pointed out that the draft of the SP was much bulkier than the agricultural part of the DP, consisting not of twelve but of twenty-three volumes.

Additional differences between the two plans will become obvious when I present and analyze individual agricultural policy measures and plans in the following chapters. However, a few other special features of the SP ought to be mentioned here. Although it sets a limit of ten years for achieving its aims, not all of the products mentioned in the original 1985 legislative initiative will have reached the level of self-sufficiency by then. For instance, domestically grown oil-rich plants will only be able to satisfy 40 percent of the demand by 1996/7. Self-sufficiency can nevertheless be expected for some of the products even before the limit expires. Such was already the case for potatoes in the base year (1987/8). Other products, such as legumes, rice, and corn, are to reach self-sufficiency by 1991, 1992, and 1995, respectively. In addition to the products mentioned in the legislative initiative, the SP includes legumes, wood, and potatoes.

According to the SP, production has to rise by 6 to 7 percent a year to meet the targets (p. 121f), assuming a population growth rate of 3.2 percent. However, according to the results of the 1986 census, Iran's population is growing by approximately 3.9 percent.[66] The plan makes attaining self-sufficiency dependent on a number of other conditions, including actual preference for agriculture in the allocation of state investments (p. 5) and actual implementation of the "infrastructure" measures deemed necessary in the development plan as revised by the special parliamentary commission. Among these measures are

1. establishing the legal and administrative limits for private property;
2. ensuring law and order on the basis of Islamic principles and the constitution;
3. setting up a suitable system to provide the statistical data required;
4. working out a pattern of consumption for the population;
5. deciding on suitable types of business and development patterns;
6. assessing the capacity for employment in agriculture;
7. determining a suitable organizational structure for the SP; and
8. creating a suitable basis for effective and comprehensive participation by the population.

The SP also assumes that the attempt to increase production will fail without appropriate, simultaneous measures in the areas of land use, research, training, services, mechanization, availability of inputs, insurance for agricultural produce, and relevant financing, which is why the corresponding programs are included in the plan (pp. 139ff and 208ff).

The SP stipulates the appointment of separate panels that are to work within the framework determined for each product. Seen in this light, the SP represents the totality of all the various projects for the individual products (p. 89). The overall plan was budgeted for total investments of 9,543.3bn rials over ten years, of which 5,763.4bn rials are to be provided by the private sector and the banks. The state's share thus amounts to 3,779.9bn rials (p. 12f).

The self-sufficiency plan has been condemned to oblivion since being submitted to the Council of Ministers, despite the fact that the Ministry of Agriculture is quite convinced of its uniqueness (p. 19f). There have been occasional indications of its fate. It was reported on October 2, 1987, for example, that the Council of Ministers was just in the process of approving the figures. On January 7, 1988, the dailies reported that the Council of Ministers had considered the agricultural situation and the SP in the presence of President Khamene'i on the fifth and sixth of that month (*Kayhan*). In his new year address, the minister of agriculture reported that the plan had been supplemented by additional projects in the year just ended and that, during the above meeting, an interministerial commission had been charged with scrutinizing the plan. He voiced the hope that "God willing, with the final approval of the plan by the Council of Ministers, the way has now been cleared for the employment of the population in agriculture."[67]

But statements by others make it clear that God is not at all well disposed toward the plan. One member of parliament, for example, reported that in the opinion of the minister of planning and budget, the SP was not feasible. The same member claimed that the prime minister himself, in a letter to the Ministry of Agriculture, had written that a plan should be drafted that could be implemented on earth rather than up in the clouds. The minister of planning and budget confirmed the details given by this parliamentarian by stating during the same session that the investments earmarked for the SP were 5.7 times greater than the state's total investments since the revolution.[68] However, this plan is no less realistic than the 1983 plan, about which the same minister spoke in such glowing terms. Thus, we may safely assume that the struggles between the various factions in the Council of Ministers must have played a more decisive role in creating the fatal delay for approval of the SP than any pertinent assessment of the matter.[69]

6.10 Planning in the Postwar Era

One of the main factors on which the leaders of the Islamic Republic had blamed the development policy fiasco ceased to exist at the end of the war. As soon as UN Resolution 598 was officially accepted, they began to take every opportunity to express their satisfaction that development would now be able to enjoy top priority. Speaker Rafsanjani voiced his hope that "all the funds that were being spent on the war could now be devoted to reconstruction."[70] A few months later, he declared the second postrevolutionary decade the "decade of construction," in which "achieving independence and uprooting dependence" would become reality.[71]

In the opinion of the rulers, construction and reconstruction could not be effected without a plan, so talk of the need to continue planning was widespread. The spokesman for the relevant parliamentary commission stated that without a plan, "leading the country was like [taking] a step in the dark."[72] The chairman of the same committee argued that a plan was needed because of the "responsibility which we have assumed as a development model for the rest of the world."[73]

The first steps toward a resumption of planning were not long in coming. After intensive work, the new plan was finally submitted to parliament for its first reading on October 11 and 16, 1988, and was approved by a large majority. But this proposal was merely the first part of a draft that still had to be worked out in detail. Broadly speaking, it contained the same "qualitative" statements as the DPA. The targets and guidelines for comprehensive development were determined with a view to "instructing and transcending the people on the basis of the exalted and universal Islamic values so that the conditions for their material and immaterial development on the path to God can be ensured without prejudice to their nobility and enlightenment."[74] The detailed plan was to be ready and voted on by March 21, 1989, i.e., the beginning of the Iranian year 1368. In view of the fact that this was the date set for implementation of the plan, the Parliamentary Planning Commission's spokesman had to promise to comply.[75] He was, however, unable to keep his promise. The same forces that had previously prevented clear decisions or their implementation remained in effect and delayed the drafting of a detailed plan. Ideological differences, a doctrinaire approach to the task, personal and factional power struggles, and the continued war mania ensured that even if decisions were made they could not be carried out.

The arguments about the plan merely continued after the war and concentrated mainly on the question of how large a contribution other countries and/or foreign capital ought to make toward the Islamic Republic's development policy. The debate stemmed from the widespread belief that it would be impossible to implement a plan that would show results quickly with only domestic resources. A number of leaders, including Rafsanjani, favored bringing in foreign capital or arranging loans on the international money market. Many of them correspondingly attached great importance to normalizing relations between the Islamic Republic and the West in particular. However, the exponents of a more extreme policy declared that the country should attach greater importance to independence than to "prosperity and consumption." "For independence, one would have to put up with inflation and [economic] pressure [for the short term]," declared Prime

Minister Musawi.[76] To prevent this normalization with the West, the radicals took any and every opportunity to bang the anti-imperialist drum as loudly as possible. The anniversaries of the taking of hostages from the U.S. embassy and of the publication of Salman Rushdie's book *Satanic Verses* were, among others, well suited to this purpose.

Another point of disagreement, as before, was the question of the role the private sector should play in the implementation of the expected plan. The advocates of further concessions to the private sector attempted to encourage it by opening up some additional activities to it, such as foreign trade and the stock exchange (for participation in future investment). Their opponents argued that profiteering should no longer be tolerated and wanted parliament to pass laws increasing the controls on private wholesale and retail trade.[77] *Kayhan* in particular led a campaign against the investment companies, which had supposedly made inadmissibly large profits out of the Islamic form of contract known as mozarebe.[78]

Delays also occurred over the question of whether, in view of the extensive damage caused by the war, planning should be devoted mainly to reconstruction of the devastated areas or whether these areas should be dealt with in the framework of a more comprehensive construction plan. Though the circles close to the prime minister were in favor of the latter solution, Khomeini issued a decree at the beginning of September 1988 to set up a special panel just for planning reconstruction. This panel, which was parallel to the authorities employed in preparing the development plan, comprised the heads of the executive branch, the judiciary, and the legislature. Subordinated to them was a series of "advisory commissions" that did the actual work, which was coordinated by two clerics.[79] The establishment of this new panel must primarily be interpreted as the result of the crippling factional struggles, and it only created even more confusion in the attempts to work out a new draft plan. The panel's decisions were ignored by the executive whenever possible. As a result, complaints began to appear in the papers shortly after the panel announced its first decisions benefiting the private sector, such as easing import restrictions on certain goods.[80] This overlap in planning continued for a few months, until in May 1989 the decision was made to coordinate reconstruction and construction planning and entrust both to one body.[81]

The war mania, which continued unabated even after the end of the war, made a change of attitude toward one better suited to development and development planning more difficult. Defeat had not led to a reshuffling in the highest offices of the ruined country, and the leaders of the republic were fully occupied with justifying their handling of the war to themselves and the nation. In their eyes, maintaining the war mood must have seemed a good way of accomplishing this end. It also provided an excuse for devoting a large share of the state budget to strengthening the military might of the Islamic state, whose leaders continued to believe in the idea of exporting the revolution. This idea was also not very conducive to construction.

Khomeini's death on June 4, 1989, and the revision of the constitution, concluded on August 6, 1989, together with the reshuffling at the top of the Islamic state following these events, permitted a shift in favor of those circles better disposed toward the private sector. Khamene'i succeeded Khomeini as leader of the regime. Rafsanjani formed a cabinet whose members' attitudes were by and large close to his own. The shakeout in the administration further strengthened the position of this camp.

This new situation allowed work on the draft plan to continue with less friction,[82] and soon the number of progress reports began to increase. The Council of Ministers began the work of checking the plan, which was completed on August 31, 1989, and approved it on October 9, 1989. The parliamentary debate on the relevant legislation began on December 10, 1989, and it was finally passed on January 31, 1990. Eleven years after the establishment of the Islamic Republic, the almost equally long struggle to draft a development plan and have it adopted as law was brought to a close. This victory did not, however, mean that it could be successfully implemented. Strong skepticism was registered from all sides, both before and after parliament enacted the plan. Two points were doubted most: first, the revenue the planners had earmarked for financing the plan, including around $27bn that was to be procured abroad and revenues in excess of $85bn the government hoped would flow into its coffers from oil exports;[83] second, the ability of the Islamic Republic's administration to act according to plan.[84] This second point was brought up by none other than Rafsanjani himself when he stated that the country's administrative system would have to be reformed if it was to be expected to implement the five-year plan.[85] The problem remains that an administration that is so in need of reform must implement a development plan whose high-flying aims would be beyond the capabilities of even a reformed administration. Nor should the still powerful opposition of the etatists and populists among the leaders of the Islamic Republic be overlooked: Even if they have lost some of their influence since Khomeini's death, they are still more than strong enough to put almost insurmountable obstacles in the path of a plan based on funding by foreign "Satans." To this must be added the fact that, even under the leadership of Rafsanjani and Khamene'i, the Islamic Republic cannot succeed in gaining the participation of the indispensable elements in the population—intellectuals, experts, merchants, workers, and so forth—as long as the regime clings to its exclusivity and monopoly of power and is unable to reach a consensus with the rest of society.

Of course, the new plan also contains calculations for future developments in agriculture. Quantitatively determined progress is to be made in all fields. Artificially irrigated arable land, for example, is to be expanded from 6.3m to 6.5m hectares, wheat production is to be raised by 9.5 percent annually, and rice production is to increase from 1.7m tons in 1988/9 to 2m tons in 1993/4. Funding for the whole project in the agricultural sector amounts to $10bn for the necessary imports and domestic expenditure of 800m rials. An overall annual growth rate of 6 percent in production is expected, of which 3 percent is compensation for the population growth.[86] Agriculture loses its oft-promised "pivotal position" in the new plan and is accorded a level of priority shared by education, oil, defense, and a number of other branches. This decision was a disappointment to people who had expected that after the war agriculture would finally get the attention they had wanted it to receive for so long.[87] This disappointment led to some harsh criticism, which was probably also voiced in the cabinet. In the opinion of the editor-in-chief of the journal *Jahad,* which is published by the Ministry of Jahad-e Sazandegi, agriculture's lack of primacy is the "main problem of the current plan." He compared the plan with the fifth five-year plan of the shah's reign and stated that in allocating state funds for investment, the shah's policy attached more importance to agriculture.[88]

Notes

1. After the revolution it was transformed into a ministry but regained its former status under Rafsanjani.
2. *Kayhan,* December 29, 1982.
3. DPA, vol. 1, foreword.
4. *Kayhan,* December 29, 1982.
5. PP, August 16, 1983, p. 19.
6. *Ibid.,* January 2, 1986.
7. Some of the functionaries and experts I interviewed confirmed these details. Their opponents were of the opinion that the Quran and Khomeini's law books were adequate for conducting an Islamically oriented development policy and that Islam was not dependent on planning.
8. The draft of a more programmatic plan worked out by planning experts for the Office for Revolutionary Projects was put to the Bazargan cabinet in August 1979. Discussion in S. Behdad 1989, pp. 115ff.
9. DPA, pp. j and b; interview with the chairman of the Organization of Planning and Budget, *Kayhan,* August 10, 1982.
10. *Kayhan,* August 17, 1983.
11. PP, August 17, 1983, p. 18f.
12. *Kayhan,* June 3, 1980.
13. Dr. Izadi and Hushang Keshawarz kindly placed this document at my disposal.
14. The authors, who were not obvious Islamists, were in the main experts previously employed by the Ministry of Agriculture or the University of Tehran who had been brought together for the purpose by Dr. Izadi. Dr. Izadi himself has Islamist tendencies but was at the time a member of the secularist National Front. The author was able to obtain more detailed information on the body in interviews with two of its members, Hossein Malek and Hushang Keshawarz.
15. See, for example, the report on a seminar held by the Ministry of Agriculture in Tehran in October 1979 to discuss agrarian problems and work out

proposals for overcoming them in *Keshawarz-e Emruz*, October 21, 1979; also Dr. Izadi's letter to the Revolutionary Council, December 28, 1979, and interview with him, October 13, 1979.

16. *Keshawarz-e Emruz*, October 21, 1979. Izadi deals with the same subject in his book, pp. 467ff and 733ff.

17. For details, see *Barzegar*, September 6, 1980.

18. Interview with Salamati in *Masa'el-e Keshawarzi* 2 (Spring 1982), p. 18.

19. For details, see *Barzegar*, August 12, 1981.

20. *Kayhan*, April 8, 1982; also Zali's letter to Khomeini, p. 15.

21. One of the authors of this manuscript, whose name and position are known to me, indirectly provided me with an unbound copy without a title.

22. Inter alia: N. Sedaqat 1987; Sabet Qadam 1987; Mohtasham Sarmadi 1984.

23. According to the spokesman of the commission, M. Mahluji, in PP, January 2, 1986, p. 21.

24. PP, January 2 and 7, 1986, pp. 20 and 24.

25. *Ibid.*, January 2, 1986, p. 20.

26. *Ibid.*, January 7, 1986, p. 22.

27. *Ibid.*, January 2, 1986, pp. 24ff.

28. *Ibid.*

29. According to the government plan, self-help (khod etteka'i) is one rung below self-sufficiency (khod kafa'i) and is to achieved for agriculture at the end of the first five-year plan, creating a basis for realizing self-sufficiency in the second phase.

30. PP, January 7, 1986, p. 21f.

31. *Ibid.*, January 2, 1986, p. 22.

32. *Ibid.*, p. 30.

33. *Ibid.*, p. 23.

34. *Ibid.*, p. 25.

35. The main reason given by the functionaries and experts I interviewed for the plan's failure to get parliamentary approval was that it did not take the country's real possibilities into account and was based on ideals. One interviewee thought it failed because of the maliciousness of some members of parliament, but another put it down to ignorance of the significance of the planning. Two of them pointed out that some parliamentarians thought the plan had been drafted by members of the Communist Tudeh Party and was leftist, so they had rejected it. Three of them put the neglect of the plan down to the incompatibility of the positions and the inability to reach a consensus.

36. According to Prime Minister Musawi (*Kayhan*, June 25, 1986), and Minister of Planning and Budget Zanjani when explaining the "New Economic Policy" (*Kayhan*, June 17, 1986).

37. *Kayhan*, June 25, 1986.

38. PP, March 7 and 8, 1987, pp. 18 and 22.

39. According to a report by the Ministry of Heavy Industry, the production index of all the state industrial enterprises it managed dropped to 74 points, equivalent to reductions in production of 26 percent, 34 percent, and 37 percent for 1983/4, 1984/5, and 1985/6, respectively.

40. According to Zanjani, minister of planning and budget, *Kayhan*, June 17, 1986.

41. See, for example, *Resalat*, September 7 and December 11, 1987; and *Kayhan*, January 1 and 10, 1988.

42. For example, *Resalat*, October 21, 1986.

43. *Kayhan*, June 25, 1986.

44. *Resalat*, June 14, 1986.
45. One member of parliament later objected: "We have still not been absorbed in the war." Another member demanded that the government be more absorbed in the war, *Resalat*, July 2, 1988.
46. Khamene'i in *Resalat*, December 7, 1988.
47. *Kayhan*, June 25, 1986; *Resalat*, June 13, 1967.
48. *Kayhan*, September 7, 11, 21, and 22, October 9, and December 1, 1987.
49. PP, February 17, 1986, p. 22; March 3, 1986, pp. 22ff; and March 7, 1987, p. 22.
50. PP, March 7, 1987, p. 22.
51. PP, March 9, 1988, p. 33.
52. PP, January 18, 1989, p. 25f.
53. PP, February 17, 1986, p. 18.
54. Minister of planning and budget in *Resalat*, March 10, 1988.
55. View expressed by a member of parliament, PP, March 7, 1987.
56. If the bill had been debated in closed session it would have needed a two-thirds majority for approval, which the government did not think it could get.
57. *Resalat*, March 8, 1988.
58. PP, December 12, 1985, p. 30; and April 15, 1986, p. 27. Oil-rich plants were only included as essential products at the second reading.
59. PP, April 15, 1986, p. 27.
60. PP, December 15, 1985, pp. 20ff.
61. PP, December 12, 1985, p. 34.
62. PP, April 15, 1986, p. 28.
63. PP, December 12, 1985, p. 31.
64. *Resalat*, June 22, 1986.
65. Quotations here regarding the SP are taken from the first volume. It is a summary of the other twenty-two volumes but adequate for our purposes.
66. This growth rate cannot be considered accurate, as discussed above. Figures from the Central Statistical Office vary between 3.2 percent and 3.9 percent, the latter probably including the Afghan, Kurdish, and Iraqi refugees.
67. *Resalat*, March 26, 1988.
68. PP, July 6, 1988, pp. 26 and 36. Investment must thus have totalled 1,000bn rials.
69. Of the fifteen functionaries and experts asked about the reason for the rejection of this plan, six did not reply; others put it down to the plan being "naive," "senseless," or "unrealistic;" did not think that enough funds were available to implement it; or thought that it was based on inadequate studies and lacked coordination with other sectors of the economy.
70. *Kayhan*, September 17, 1988.
71. *Ettela'at*, January 4, 1989.
72. *Resalat*, October 12, 1988.
73. *Resalat*, January 3, 1989.
74. See the text of this draft in *Resalat*, October 12, 1988.
75. *Kayhan*, October 24, 1988.
76. *Kayhan*, March 4, 1989.
77. Parliament approved an urgent initiative to combat hoarding and profiteering on November 12, 1989. On December 4, 1989, it decided to seize the fortunes of profiteers pursuant to Article 49 of the constitution, which deals with illegally acquired fortunes. Two days later, it reopened the debate on the long-forgotten, disputed initiative on the cooperative system in the Islamic Republic, which was intended to compete with the private sector. See the relevant newspapers and parliamentary protocols.

78. This campaign began at the end of October 1991 and lasted for several months.
79. *Kayhan,* September 4, 18, and 21, 1988.
80. *Resalat,* September 19, October 26 and 27, and November 1, 1988.
81. Rafsanjani announced this decision on May 15, 1989.
82. The chairman of the reinstated Organization (ex-Ministry) of Planning and Budget stated on September 3, 1989 that the multiplicity of decisionmaking centers and the disagreements within the cabinet that had been responsible for the lack of success in planning had been removed. See *Kayhan,* September 3, 1989.
83. The minister of oil's hopes have meanwhile risen, and he has announced that oil exports are expected to earn $1,000bn in the five years of the plan. See *Kayhan,* February 4, 1990.
84. *Kayhan,* August 10, December 5 and 9, 1989.
85. *Kayhan,* February 7, 1990.
86. Minister of Agriculture Kalantari in *Ettela'at,* September 4, 1989. See the draft of "The Five-Year Plan of the Islamic Republic of Iran 1989/90–1993/4," part 1, p. 13, plus statements by the chairman of the planning organization on the new plan's agricultural program in *Resalat,* August 20, 1989. For the text of the plan, see CL 1368 (1989/90).
87. Because of its significance, this was the first point in the resolution by the National Congress to Investigate the Problems of Agricultural Development held in Tehran at the end of February and beginning of March 1989 and attended by all the ministers for economic resources. See *Resalat,* March 2, 1989.
88. *Jahad* 123 (November/December 1989), p. 2f. Former minister of agriculture Salamati, who can be counted among the etatists in the Islamic Republic, made the same comparison in *Kayhan,* December 5, 1989.

7
Reforming Agricultural Administration

7.1 General Characteristics of Administrative Reform

With respect to administrative reform, the Islamic Republic has made more progress in agriculture than in other economic and social areas. But at the same time, the most conspicuous contradictions to disrupt the administration exist in agriculture. The reform shares several characteristics with the efforts at administrative reform in other areas.

To begin with, it is not an organic part of a general administrative reform policy. Essentially, administrative reform of agriculture was drawn up and implemented piecemeal, which is one of the reasons for many of its contradictions. Some of these stem from the fact that the other areas of the administration have not been reformed. Although those in positions of responsibility in the regime think general reform is necessary, they have not even been able to present a concept to date. The constitution of the Islamic Republic provides for "the establishment of a proper administrative order" (Article 3, Clause 10); however, an initiative passed by parliament on February 7, 1982, that obliged the government to work out a suitable proposal "for thoroughly restructuring the existing administrative order in accordance with the holy aims of the revolution" and submit it to parliament within six months has not yet been complied with.[1]

Second, the reforms most ardently pursued concern the appointment to leading government posts of supporters of the system of rule by the jurists, irrespective of their qualifications. The decrees issued and laws passed from the first year after the revolution provide the necessary authorization,[2] and so a major step has been taken toward the "Islamization" of the state administration. The penetration of the administration by "Islamic Societies" (anjoman-e eslami) is a further decisive step in this direction. The main task of these societies is to ensure that Islamic tenets are observed at work and to report deviations to the authorities.[3]

What this means in practice is clear from a speech Prime Minister

Musawi gave at a seminar held by the Islamic Societies at the beginning of June 1983. Musawi commended the societies for dealing the "gang of deviationists" a decisive blow.[4] The new appointments on a massive scale and the penetration of the state organizations and ministries by the Islamic Societies presented an opportunity to oust not only opponents of the regime but also dissenters within the ranks of the ruling Islamists. This purge explains the frequent complaints in parliament and in the press about the dismissal of supporters of Hezbollah, as all of the groups among the ruling Islamists occasionally call themselves.[5]

Establishing so-called Revolutionary Institutions (Nahadha-ye Enqelab) is a third characteristic of administrative reform in the Islamic Republic. There are sixteen or more of these institutions, depending on how they are defined, and they often cause a duplication of responsibility in the administration of the areas concerned. Here the negative consequences are best illustrated by the example of the dualistic administration in agriculture, which was brought about by the establishment of Jahad-e Sazandegi parallel to the Ministry of Agriculture.

The failure of administrative reform is best characterized by the representatives of the regime themselves. In his speech to parliament on June 28, 1988, Prime Minister Musawi called the bureaucracy "unrestrained" and declared that it has "decisively reduced the country's executive power." He went on to say that "the clients of the state authorities are usually named as the principal victims of its red tape although the executive agencies themselves are the worst victims of the administrative chaos."[6]

7.2 Reform at the Ministry of Agriculture

7.2.1 The Centers for Agricultural, Rural and Nomadic Services

Setting up the Centers for Agricultural, Rural and Nomadic Services (Service Centers for short) was by far the most important reform at the Ministry of Agriculture and Rural Construction taken over from the shah's regime. The measure was primarily a response to the main criticisms of the ministry in the prerevolutionary era: that it was located in the capital and the other towns and that it served the large-scale commercial enterprises rather than the peasants. The magnificent glass skyscraper in which the ministry resided at one of the finest addresses in the capital was regarded as a symbol of its alienation from its real tasks.

This criticism continued after the revolution[7] but now was made openly. Detractors issued demands to decentralize the ministry, to send its staff out into the villages, to stop it from interfering in matters relating to peasant holdings, to put it at the service of the peasants, and to greatly improve its services to the rural and nomadic economies. Setting up the Service Centers was intended to meet these demands.

The idea of the Service Centers dated from before the revolution. A mixed commission had already worked out a plan for the economic development of Khorasan province in 1972 on behalf of the Organization of Planning and Budget that included details for setting up centers to provide various services for the peasants and their farms. This project—whose similarity to comparable projects in India is unmistakable—formed the basis in 1977 for a program, commissioned by the same organization, that was to be realized experimentally at eleven locations. Similar attempts were in the pipeline at the Ministry of Agriculture, culminating in 1978 in a project to set up Centers for Agricultural Services, which were very similar to the project taken in hand shortly after the revolution. The centers envisaged in this project were intended to replace the Farm Corporations, which had been liquidated even before the revolution.[8]

The postrevolutionary plan to set up the Service Centers had already received a lot of attention in the draft on agricultural policy that was prepared in May 1979 at the Ministry of Agriculture under Dr. Izadi. This draft promised that the ministry would relocate in the district villages (dehestan) in order to get closer to the land (p. 3). Centers for Agricultural, Rural and Nomadic Services were to be established and would concentrate on "meeting the basic needs and demands of the rural population," avoiding all bureaucratic and technological confusion. The centers were to distinguish themselves as the "driving force of the harmoniously organic development in the rural areas" (p. 9). The intention was not to arbitrarily choose the district villages where the centers were to be located but rather to select villages that had already developed into centers for the surrounding region.

Each center was to be organized around a panel that included representatives from the District Village Council. The District Village Council, comprising representatives from the Village Councils, was to inform its Service Center about local needs, set priorities, and determine the resources available from the villagers themselves. Through the presence of its members on the Service Center panel, the District Village Council was to ensure that "funds are discussed and plans drafted and carried out on the basis of the stated needs" (p. 11f). This arrangement was designed to get the rural populations to participate in making the decisions affecting their lives and work. The Ministry of Agriculture declared its policy to be "based on the principle of noninterference. . . . This is the reason the District Village Councils have been given the main power" (p. 12).

The center in each district village was to provide services in the fields of culture, production, construction, and social security. Teachers, counselors, and social workers trained to perform these tasks were to be stationed in the villages. The teachers were to conduct reading and writing programs, raise the cultural level in the villages, and give the villagers an Islamic character. Their task was also "to remind the rural population of its forgotten knowledge, to emphasize its inherent importance and to

Figure 7.1 Dr. Izadi's Plan for Administrative Reform in the Ministry of Agriculture

Level	Administrative Unit	Representative Oversight Body
National	Ministry of Agriculture	Supreme Council for Agriculture
Provincial	Administrative Unit on Provincial Level	Provincial Council
County Town	Centers for Agriculture and Rural Improvement	County Town Council
District Village	Centers for Agricultural, Rural and Nomadic Services (Service centers)	District Village Council
Village		Village Council

reactivate it. The centers are to make use of all the village's buried skills and abilities. The teacher loses his conventional and formal role here and is transformed into a factor inducing mutual understanding and instruction among the inhabitants that ensures movement in the direction of creation" (p. 13).

According to the plan, the counselors for agriculture and construction were to rely not just on their own knowledge but also on the peasants' experience. "They [are to] attempt to create an optimal mix of old and new technologies based on indigenous know-how and regional possibilities and to apply it with the help of the rural population." The social worker's duties included promoting hygiene and environmentally sound practices. Further, it was envisaged that in the long term the villagers would become independent of the need for government to provide these services and would integrate the relevant functions into their economic and social life (p. 13).

According to the plan, the centers at the district village level were to be subordinated to Centers for Agriculture and Rural Improvement in the county towns and were to consist on the one hand of groups of resident experts and on the other of groups of itinerant experts who could be sent to the district villages to provide particular services as required. Agricultural Councils were to assist the centers in the county towns "to ensure the coordination and supervision of the relevant projects." At the county town level, plans were to be worked out and measures taken with due regard for the general objectives of agricultural policy and for the needs the centers in the district villages had established (p. 14).

The Agricultural Organizations and Agricultural Councils were to be at the next highest—i.e., provincial—level but were not to have any executive functions. They were to be centers for "considering, planning, checking and determining aims at the regional level and allocating funds to implement them." The Agricultural Councils at this level were also to coordinate and supervise the relevant projects (p. 15).

Finally, there was to be the central machinery of the Ministry of Agriculture at the national level. Its tasks were to be planning, coordination, procurement and allocation of funds, supervision, research, collating statistics, and so forth. Restricting headquarters to these tasks meant that many of the ministry's branch offices, whose tasks had resulted in interference in production and rural life, were now to be less intrusive. An Agricultural Council with planning, supervisory, and decisionmaking functions was to assist the ministry (pp. 16ff).

Additional information about the Service Centers and the ongoing plans for administrative reform can be gleaned from interviews with Dr. Izadi. On October 22, 1979, he expressed the hope that a total of 1,573 centers could be set up if sufficient funds were available (*Kayhan*). Nine days previously, he had spoken of the centers replacing the "Extension Corps," which had been set up under the shah. Comments in the specialist journal *Keshawarz-e Emruz* based on an interview with Dr. Izadi indicated that he wanted to divide the whole country into ten agricultural regions, which were to be subordinated to the same number of Agricultural Organizations at the provincial level, each headed by a deputy minister with the authority to make decisions. The deputy minister was to have as many deputies as the minister in Tehran, and they would be responsible for different tasks. The idea of subdividing the country was based on considerations of the regional differences, which required separate management in the respective provinces (October 12 and 20, 1979). "In this way, the administrative centralization in agriculture disappears. All affairs at the regional level are handled by the officials responsible for agriculture on the basis of cooperation with the Agricultural Councils and the Service Centers."[9]

The project for the centers was not dropped after the fall of the Bazargan government. It was kept on in the programs and plans announced by Izadi's successors—e.g., in Minister Salamati's fourteen- and nineteen-point programs,[10] in the agricultural section of the 1983 development plan (pp. 49f, 291ff, 364), and in the self-sufficiency plan (p. 16). In 1987 Minister of Agriculture Zali announced that even such greats as Ayatollah Beheshti, Hojjat ol-Eslam Rafsanjani, and former president Reja'i supported the project.[11]

The project became law when the Revolutionary Council approved the Proposal for the Establishment of Centers for Agricultural, Rural and Nomadic Services on June 4, 1980. The centers, as outlined in this decree, largely corresponded to the concepts in the Izadi plan, but their tasks were specified in greater detail. They included all the services the government could provide for expanding agriculture and improving the rural areas. The rural population's actual needs as determined by the appropriate councils were to be decisive, as in Dr. Izadi's plan. The district villages in which centers were to be set up would be selected "with regard to natural, geographical, traditional and ethnic conditions and on the basis of local custom" (Article 1, note 1). In the performance of their duties, the centers were to form independent administrative units, with the number and composition of the staff to be decided on a case-by-case basis (Article 1, note 2). In view of the wide range of services to be provided by the centers, the various ministries concerned were obliged to "plan and implement their projects, in as far as they relate to the rural population in areas where centers have been set up, with [the centers'] assistance" (Article 1, note 4). "The Ministry of Agriculture and Rural Construction" was obliged to "undertake its own reorganization in conformity with this decree."[12]

Broadly speaking, the administrative regulations, which consisted of eighty-eight articles and notes, reflected the lines laid down in Izadi's plan, except for the principle of nonintervention by the state, which was not mentioned because of the populist-etatist orientation of the post-Bazargan governments. The administrative regulations pertaining to this decree were approved thirteen months later by the Council of Ministers. (The reasons for the delay are dealt with later.)

Almost half the administrative regulations were devoted to listing the tasks the centers were to perform either by themselves or in cooperation with the local Islamic Village Councils. Article 10 summarized these tasks as follows: the provision of general, technical, and infrastructural services, plus services related to the credit system; training; research; welfare; marketing; counseling; planning; assisting with setting up Islamic Service Councils; investigating local land ownership; encouraging the peasants to form production collectives and to set up small industrial enterprises; and so on. Article 13 stated that "the centers at the District Village level represent a nucleus for planning, implementing, research, training and counseling which . . . drafts the necessary plans on the basis of the needs determined by the Islamic Service Councils and of their order of priority and submits them as proposals to the head office in the County Town."

Taking account of the needs submitted to it, the county town was to adopt the appropriate measures to fulfill the plan if the district village centers could not. The resident and itinerant groups of experts mentioned above were to be available to it. The centers in the county towns were to gradually replace the equivalent organizations of the Ministry of Agriculture and the Revolutionary Institutions at the same level (Article 49). They were also to have planning functions, although these were based on proposals received from the district village centers and councils and the county town councils submitting their proposals to the provincial centers (Article 63). In other words, planning was to go from bottom to top until it finally reached the ministry. There it would be made consistent with the government's overall agricultural policy and the country's human, financial, and physical capacities and take the road back down (Article 64).

Each center working at the district village level was to have at least three staff members possessing the expertise necessary at this level. There was to be a minimum of approximately nineteen staff at the county town level, although this number could vary according to local conditions and needs. The centers in the county towns were to be set up even if there were not enough qualified staff (Articles 68–74).

The administrative regulations dealt at length with the Village Councils (Articles 51–61). The lowest level at which councils were to be set up was the village or a nomadic unit, with the district village center playing an active part in establishing them. There was to be parity representation for all ranks in the village. The District Village Council was to comprise those in positions of responsibility in the district village center, including one member of the staff and seven representatives from the plenary meeting of the District Village Council, which in turn comprised one representative from each Village Council. The Village Council was intended to be the link between the rural population and the Service Center in the district village and to help it carry out its tasks. It also was to perform certain public functions, such as arbitrating disagreements.

The District Village Council was to play an oversight role. According to Article 57, it was "the official agency at this level for planning activities related to production, services and welfare." Article 56 stated that these councils were merely "advisory and technical" agencies in matters provided for in the relevant laws and administrative regulations. According to Article 67, the Service Center in the district village was to carry out the plans approved by the District Village Council. All the center's financial operations had to be submitted in advance to the District Village Council for authorization (Article 83). Other than these points, the functions and tasks of the District Village Council were identical to those of the Village Council; they were simply implemented on a wider scale. Both these types of councils were to play an active part in establishing and reforming property and usufructuary rights for water and land in their catchment areas.

The administrative regulations mentioned both a County Town Council and a Provincial Council (Articles 58f), making it unclear how things were to be regulated at these levels. The last few articles were devoted to resolving a conflict that was partly responsible for the tardiness in setting up the centers—namely, the question of whether they were to come under the Ministry of Agriculture, as initially planned, or under the Jahad-e Sazandegi organization, which had begun to set up similar units with the same tasks in rural areas. The disruptive effects of this massive duplication of effort still await a solution, which the regulations cannot provide. They state on the one hand that the centers come under the Ministry of

Agriculture (Articles 84ff) but on the other declare that "Jahad-e Sazandegi is to supervise and coordinate the entire project. The Ministry of Agriculture has been given the option of relinquishing such tasks to Jahad-e Sazandegi. In this case, the latter is responsible for implementing the project. The budget and all the funds provided for implementing the project then devolve upon it" (Article 87).[13]

Despite the fact that the new regime adopted this prerevolutionary project very early on and despite its central importance for reforming the state's agricultural and rural organizations, it remains far from complete. As noted above, Dr. Izadi promised to establish 1,573 centers. According to the 1983 development plan they were to be set up by the beginning of 1367 (March 20, 1988) in 1,703 district villages and 190 county towns. Implementation was to have proceeded so rapidly that only eighteen would remain to be set up in the final year of the plan.[14] Reports in the newspapers and official communiqués indicate that the work is actually moving ahead much more slowly.

On October 13, 1979, Dr. Izadi stated that the investigations required to establish the district village centers had been completed and that a commission had been dispatched to the appropriate regions to set them up (*Keshawarz-e Emruz*). However, by autumn 1980 only seventy-three centers were in operation.[15] Even at the time, the specialist journal *Barzegar* commented that the peasants had "still not had anything" from the centers (August 22, 1981). A year later Minister Salamati told parliament that there were already 350 centers in existence.[16] However, in a letter to Khomeini, his successor, Dr. Zali, complained that "with the stagnation of his ministry's organizational reforms," the setting up of Service Centers had fallen into a state of disarray (p. 11). He wrote this after having reported that steps would be taken to set up 538 centers by the beginning of 1983 (p. 11). According to another statement by Zali, there were 683 centers in district villages and 116 in county towns by August 1985;[17] two years later he said there were 677 centers in district villages and 118 in county towns.[18] For an idea of the readiness with which such contradictory figures were tolerated, consider that the draft of the self-sufficiency plan completed that year (1987/8) claimed that 730 district village centers had already been set up.[19]

But even this last figure was some 58 percent below the target for 1987/8 contained in the 1983 development plan. Ex-minister Salamati put this neglect down to the fact that "the positive and useful experience of setting up the centers had already lost the support of the government by 1983," even though "the centers have succeeded in establishing a creative, close and effective link with the rural population, a fact which has made an important contribution to mutual understanding with the rural population, to their earnest cooperation, in particular in matters of infrastructural services . . . and has strengthened emotional and human ties between them."

He added that "the centers are a revolutionary system with great effectiveness in the service of the people" and are "based on the general policy in the Islamic Republic."[20]

However, experts evaluate work of the centers somewhat differently. Mrs. Sabet Qadam, an expert with the Organization of Planning and Budget and one of the signatories to the administrative regulations pertaining to the law establishing the Service Centers, presented the results of her study in February 1983. Her criticism of the work accomplished begins with the statement that "none of the Centers set up so far . . . conforms to what was envisaged in the original plan" (p. 12). The first difference was that the responsible agencies had begun to establish the centers where the "Farm Corporations, which were considered as the archetype of the failed projects to solve the organization of enterprises in agriculture, had been wound up." This placement, she argued, was intended to ensure the survival of an imported organization model that had been unable to hold its own despite twelve years' experience and considerable state subsidies.[21] The Ministry of Agriculture, she claimed, was secretly trying "to present this model as the best type of enterprise in Iran." Nor did the staff at the ministry want to give up the privileges they derived from the FCs (pp. 15 and 30).

Sabet Qadam then went into the details of her general criticism, establishing in several instances that funds had either not been spent at all or had not been spent in accordance with regulations (pp. 16ff). Many of the measures taken had nothing to do with the real needs of the peasants (p. 19), and no poll of the rural population had been conducted concerning these measures (pp. 20, 28, and 31). The Village Councils, which could have helped the staffs at the Service Centers collect information about their areas of work, had not been set up (p. 28). The requirements of the staff had been decisive in selecting the villages in which to locate the centers, and their houses had been built near the towns instead of among the rural population, as stipulated (pp. 20f and 26). Clinics, workshops, and so on had been built, but no experts were hired to work in them (pp. 22f and 27). Center employees distinguished themselves by lack of responsibility and initiative and got the better positions through connections (p. 25). Contrary to the spirit of the project and against regulations, they clung to the idea that the government—the Service Centers, in this case—had to decide everything (p. 19). Thus, continuing the practice of the Farm Corporations, they interfered in peasant affairs (p. 28). Not appreciating the traditional skills and know-how or customs and values of the rural population, the staff had even interfered without cause in those areas where the peasants had all along performed certain tasks themselves (p. 30). There had been no attempt "to make use of the rural population's active, all-around participation in determining the problems, in planning, in taking decisions, in implementing, supervising and making use of the technical and economic opportunities" (p. 31). No Service Centers had been set up in nomadic regions. There was also strong competition with Jahad-e Sazandegi. "The Ministry of Agriculture is attempting to occupy all the district villages in the country at short notice in order to prevent any progress in Jahad's work; this is happening although in practice there is not the slightest similarity between the centers formed in this way and those envisaged." And a group of staff members at the ministry had monopolized the implementation of the project, which explains why other officials were resisting measures to implement it even though they were of the opinion that setting up the centers was "the only way to the agricultural, rural and nomadic development of the country" (p. 32).

In his 1986 book, *The Sociology of Development and Underdevelopment of Rural Regions of Iran,* rural sociologist M. Azkia gave a different appraisal of the lessons learned from the Service Centers. His assessment was based on studies of the established centers conducted by the University of Tehran and the Ministry of Agriculture before the end of 1983. The author himself took part in these studies.

Some of Sabet Qadam's appraisals can also be found in Azkia's comparatively balanced evaluation, although he expressed them in a more differentiated and qualified way. In a few instances he came to positive conclusions, which were also qualified. He made a positive assessment of the Service Centers with respect to the provision of funds and the implementation of measures for the "expansion of the area in agricultural use, for transforming areas irrigated naturally into artificially irrigated land and for raising the per-hectare yield in several areas." But he added that such successes were not far-reaching (pp. 320ff). He, too, stated that regional specifics were overlooked when siting the centers (p. 300) and that the population was not consulted, resulting, among other things, in services being unevenly distributed (p. 301). In some places the center consisted only of a sign, which had been waiting for the necessary personnel and equipment for four years (p. 304). Where they actually existed, the centers were mostly staffed by poorly qualified experts who were unaware of the program's aims. Most of the staffers were strangers to the area and did not live in the local village but in the towns. In one case, the staff only worked from 8 a.m. to noon because of poor communications (p. 303). In most cases, their training had nothing to do with their work; either training courses were ignored or, even worse, the staff did not know about them. The few experts available were unevenly distributed and missing where they were needed most. Staff were badly paid, and poor amenities were causing more and more of them to give up the job (pp. 303ff).

Azkia also reported on the competition between the various state organizations offering the rural population the same services in the same place at the same time. "In most of the areas investigated, it was possible to ascertain an overlapping of work between the centers on the one hand and the Ministry of Agriculture's local organizations on the other." This overlap was due to the fact that, contrary to regulations, government officials in the local organizations were refusing to dissolve them and integrate them into the centers (p. 302).

Regarding the relationship between the Service Centers and the Village Councils and rural population, Azkia came to the following conclusion: "The staff at the Centers usually have no concrete knowledge of the villages in their area" (pp. 305 and 316). "The scanty knowledge of the Centers' aims and tasks on the part of the members of the Village Councils is primarily the result of a lack of constant contact between them and of the council members" (p. 310). On this basis, it was impossible for the rural population and its councils to participate in decisionmaking. Apparently contradicting himself, Azkia nonetheless spoke of such participation in several centers. Where the rural population was informed, there was a growing readiness to grasp the opportunities. In this respect, however, "the state organizations and institutions in rural areas have taken no positive steps" (p. 316). Azkia seemed to have observed widespread participation by the rural population in implementing projects decided on by the Service Centers. The Village Councils and the rural population were not satisfied with the centers' work, complaining about the uneven distribution of fertilizers, tools, and other supplies and about the influence of the well-off villagers on the centers (p. 319f). These influential individuals normally received preferential treatment, but it was only to be expected that "in a society in which there is a great discrepancy between the social classes," the well-off would reap the benefit of the centers' work (p. 319).

Azkia also reported how the competition between the centers and Jahad's local organizations disrupted the relations between them as well as with the District Village Councils and the Village Councils. As the Village Councils were usually influenced by Jahad, the Service Centers went to great lengths to make sure that the District Village Councils were composed of representatives not from the Village Councils but from among the residents of the district village. Thus, functional contacts between these bodies did not materialize (pp. 311 and 316).

Though Azkia and Sabet Qadam's appraisals were based on studies conducted before the end of 1983, there is no reason to believe that things have changed much since then. The former minister of agriculture, Salamati, was quoted above as telling parliament in March 1987 that the centers only lost government support after 1983. Most of the centers that have been set up to date were already in existence by then—477 according to Azkia (p. 297).

Another study of the Service Centers, completed in March 1983, referred to a case in which nine former Farm Corporations on the Moghan Plain in northwestern Iran were replaced by three centers. This field study was commissioned by the Ministry of Agriculture's Institute for Agricultural and Rural Research and undertaken by M. Rawanbaksh. It came to the same conclusions as above, i.e., the centers did not meet the region's requirements; in the centers, those in positions of responsibility did not understand the aims or tasks of the project; they had no statistics on the villages they were supposed to serve; they were not properly trained; there was a lack of funds, machines, equipment, and tools; transferring staff to the villages was a problem; the centers had been completely unable to gain the rural population's confidence; some of the staff used the same bureaucratic methods as the previous regime; there was absolutely no cooperation between the various local state organizations; and the unresolved question of land ownership was causing problems (pp. 18ff).

In 1987 many people used the lack of progress on this project as an argument for abolishing the Ministry of Agriculture. But before moving on to that, I wish to report the opinions expressed by the experts and functionaries in the Islamic Republic during interviews conducted at the beginning of 1990 on the state of the Service Centers. Three out of nineteen interviewees were unable to answer the question as to what extent setting up the centers had led the Ministry of Agriculture's administrative machinery to move into the villages. One functionary maintained that this move had been 70 percent achieved. Nine others asserted that any changes were minimal. Three thought that they could determine a partial relocation (60 percent at most) at the province-county town-district village levels but not at the capital-district village level. One expert pointed out that implementation of the project was at a standstill because of rivalry with Jahad. Another admitted that the shift could not be quantified but deemed the progress achieved "not bad."

7.2.2 Other Reform Measures

A series of other administrative reforms was tackled within the Ministry of Agriculture, but they are much less significant than the setting up of the Service Centers. Accordingly, I will address here only the measure that is of significance for the functioning of the ministry and the conducting of any sort of agricultural policy. Other reforms and changes will be taken up in the next section during the discussion of individual measures relevant to agricultural policy.

Radical purges of officials, particularly those in leading positions, not loyal to the ruling Islamists were conducted at the Ministry of Agriculture, as in all other government agencies. It is difficult to be precise about the extent, though the figure given for the number of Hezbollahi at the ministry—intended to ward off criticism that there were too few—permits some assumptions about the extent of new appointments. Some 20,000 supporters of the Party of God were reported to have joined the ministry after the revolution.[22] For comparison: 54,000 people worked for it and its affiliated organizations in 1983.[23] In 1987 Dr. Zali announced that 1,500 Hezbollahi engineers were working at his ministry, adding that it had taken on more of them than had any other ministry or nonrevolutionary institution.[24]

The purges resulted in a considerable loss of trained, qualified staff. Complaints in parliament and elsewhere indicated that this loss was not advantageous for the functioning of the ministry.[25] There were also experts who left voluntarily because of the Islamization or the bad pay. According to Zali, salaries at the Ministry of Agriculture were lower than at any other ministry,[26] which explained why most graduates in agricultural disciplines looked for work elsewhere.[27] These factors resulted in a constantly widening gap between the number of experts required by the ministry and the number actually employed there. In 1983 Zali stated: "We have 3,200 experts at present, although we need 15,000 to 20,000 to implement the five-year plan. This fact belies the axial position of agriculture."[28] It should be borne in mind that even if the targets in the five-year plan were to be achieved, Iran would still only have one expert for every 81ha—Hungary, by comparison, had one for every 4ha[29]—and this huge shortage of experts would continue for years. The draft of the self-sufficiency plan came to the same conclusion in May 1987 (p. 119). In February 1990, the minister of agriculture reiterated that "one of the biggest problems hampering our planning is the lack of capable experts."[30]

Thus, based on the available sources and interviews with experts, the impact of the administrative reforms at the Ministry of Agriculture has been meager indeed. Nobody has described the sorry state of affairs that existed at the ministry ten years after the revolution better than the new minister of agriculture, Dr. Kalantari:

> Unfortunately, from the point of view of the people who have made sacrifices for the revolution, we have in the past been unable to create a successful administrative order. I have often warned the heads of department [at the ministry] to desist from obstructing the work and from handing round the working people.[31]

> The administration of agriculture is at present in the poorest of states in respect of the provision of services for farmers and stock-breeders and stewardship of the natural resources.[32]

> Unfortunately, the administrative system in agriculture has been transformed into an office for procuring material in which the question of expanding production represents an unknown link in the chain.[33]

7.3 Genesis and Development of Jahad-e Sazandegi

7.3.1 Jahad as a Revolutionary Organization

If the Service Centers represented a moderate reorganization of the existing administration, a move supported by the reformers among the ruling Islamists, then setting up the Jahad-e Sazandegi organization was a revolutionary act. It aimed to establish an administrative system based on the mobilization of the masses; refused to be fettered by bureaucracy; was to be run democratically; raised the participation of the population to a principle; and intended to put an end to all sorts of privations in the countryside. In the language of the revolutionaries, these were the reasons Jahad was needed. The obstacles encountered in setting up such a Revolutionary Institution will be shown below, as well as how, despite its considerable achievements, the agency created additional problems for the reorganization of the state agricultural administration. The achievements will be dealt with later when I present specific agricultural measures.

The decision to establish Jahad was made in the first few months after the revolution "in the framework of the informal talks" held every Friday by the Council of Ministers. On May 8, 1979, the proposal was submitted to the Conference of Provincial Governors, which approved it. The government informed Khomeini of the decision a few days later and requested that he call on the population to cooperate in implementing it. He complied on June 17, calling on "all the classes of the people to take part in this movement, to unite in order to begin this holy struggle for construction." He also appealed to the government and the clerics to help, emphasizing that according to the sharia such cooperation was more meritorious than the pilgrimage to Mecca and Medina. He also warned of the need to ensure that the opponents of the revolution—i.e., the left—did not use the opportunity to go out into the countryside and conduct anti-Islamic propaganda.[34]

Immediately after his appeal, offices were set up to organize the expected storm and register "all the brothers and sisters, all the specialists, engineers, students and experts in the disciplines of agriculture, irrigation technology and vetinary medicine" who wanted to volunteer. The announcement was published in the newspapers on July 2, 1979. The response was positive; volunteers signed up everywhere. Even the government did its bit to expedite the "holy struggle for construction." Funds were made available, offices were organized, and so on.[35] The organization's charter was published in the gazette of the Islamic Republic on October 24, 1979.[36]

According to this charter, Jahad was called into existence with the aim of mobilizing the existing "potential and resources of the people and the state to cooperate in effectively and rapidly elaborating and implementing the construction projects and in reviving society in all its material and spiritual dimensions while taking into consideration and emphasizing the needs of the villages and the remote regions of the country" (Article 1). Jahad's organizational structure was to comprise a head office in Tehran as well as provincial and county town offices. Each office was to be composed of a steering council, an executive committee, and operational units and groups of experts (Article 5) responsible for doing cultural, hygienic, therapeutic, economic, technical, or construction work (Article 18). Various bodies at a higher level were to deal with managerial, planning, and supervisory tasks. Although Jahad specifically emphasized that it would organize its work according to the real needs of the villages and regions (Articles 1 and 3), the projects would be decided not at the village level but at the top (Articles 3.11–19), the lower levels only being permitted to suggest projects. Great store was nonetheless placed on the organization's working "with simple instructions for action that are immediately effective, decentral and far removed from obstructive guidelines and regulations" (Article 2). "Elaborating and approving the necessary projects" was to be realized independently and in smooth cooperation with state authorities and private organizations, but using its own funds and on its own responsibility (Article 3). Additional funds were to be made available by the government or procured by "voluntary donations from the population" (Article 4). Jahad's tasks would be directed toward the realization of Islamic values and serve the purpose of creating "a Godly unity" in Iran (Preamble), to include not just material but also "spiritual aspects of development" (Article 1.3). Therefore, Jahad considered it particularly important that its staff comprise individuals who had no doubts about the legitimacy of the Islamic revolution (Article 2). This ideological purity was to be ensured by the Imam's representatives, who, as "trusted locals," had a seat in all the organization's agencies and had the privilege of deciding who could become a member of the local bodies (Articles 8ff and 18).

At this point, unlike later, Jahad was defined by its charter as an organization concentrating mainly on rural improvement work. Other tasks, such as providing cultural services or creating jobs in rural crafts, were to be performed on the side. Jahad was represented at the village level by its executive organs. Substructures similar to those in the Service Centers were not provided for in the charter at this stage. Jahad was an interministerial organization, presided over at the decisionmaking level by representatives from the ministries concerned, including the Ministry of Agriculture (Articles 6 and 8f).

7.3.2 Jahad's Hypertrophic Development

The transfer of political power to the populist-extremist forces of Islamism after Bazargan's resignation also led to a change of direction in Jahad's development. The obstacles to developing its purview were gradually removed, and, as a Revolutionary Institution, it was encouraged to incorporate areas previously within the jurisdiction of the Ministry of Agriculture and other ministries. Responsibility for the construction of village schools, along with the appropriate funds, was removed from the Ministry of Education and Training and assigned to Jahad. The same thing happened to the Ministry of Transport with respect to building country roads. The procurement, production, and distribution of tractors and pesticides was soon transferred in the same way. Similar decisions were made about seed corn, negotiating loans, and various other issues.[37]

The high point in assigning new tasks to Jahad came in the second draft of its charter, which was debated by parliament from November 22 to 29, 1982, in an effort to sanction in law Jahad's penetration of various ministries' purviews. The first article authorized Jahad to cooperate in expanding agriculture and animal husbandry, doing rural improvement work, spreading Islamic culture, and "creating the conditions for the development of the rural population's sublime human personalities by involving them in village activities and supervisory work."[38] These tasks were detailed in other articles of the charter. Articles 2 and 3 called for Jahad's "participation in the implementation of state 'extension' policy and the provision of agriculturally necessary services (setting up base and field workshops, distribution of inputs and fodder, training peasants and nomads)."[39] Article 9 determined that all the Ministry of Agriculture's tasks relating to rural construction were to be transferred to Jahad, and Article 5 did the same for the drainage of underground canals. Jahad was to cooperate in implementing irrigation projects and participate in planning work to ensure the water required for agriculture in the villages and nomadic areas. Article 6 empowered Jahad to issue vouchers to the peasants entitling them to loans for agricultural purposes or authorizing them to participate in relevant planning.[40]

The arguments put forward by the strong parliamentary lobby for approving this charter are of interest. One member of parliament pointed to Jahad's character as a Revolutionary Institution that was ideologically sound, unlike the other (state) authorities. It acknowledged the principle of welayat-e faqih and was thus fit to mobilize the power of the people for construction.[41] As an organization based on Islamic principles, it could not only tackle additional tasks but was also to serve as a model for reorganizing the entire state administration and be provided with the necessary authority to do so.[42] Culturally its work was of great importance: bringing the message of Islam to the villages and disarming the counterrevolution in the rural areas. It ought therefore to be entrusted with cultural tasks.[43]

It should not be forgotten that in many places clerics were in charge of Jahad, making the mullahs' propaganda work easier in the countryside. The mere fact that it had already set up 14,000 Islamic Village Councils and 10,000 Quran schools and had distributed 7,000 volumes of Islamic texts demonstrated the importance of its cultural work.[44] It ought to be borne in mind that the mere existence of a ministry was not enough to accomplish the enormous tasks facing agriculture, the less so as agriculture, being the axis of development, demanded more zeal. Clearly, the Ministry of Agriculture had not succeeded in introducing the necessary administrative reforms.[45] Consideration should also be given to the fact that Jahad was already at work in all the areas provided for in the proposed legislation for the charter.[46]

Jahad's parliamentary lobby was supported by similar arguments in the newspapers, but in parliament the members who sympathized with its rampant growth encountered very strong opposition. The main argument against Jahad was that its expansion was resulting in authority being exceeded everywhere, which made success more difficult and responsibility unclear.[47] In particular the clerics in parliament denied Jahad's right to interfere in their affairs—i.e., propagating Islam in the rural areas. One cleric explained that it was necessary to "draw on experts in Islamic matters" to carry out such tasks; in order to teach Islam, it was necessary to have subjected oneself to the rigors of a religious academy and to have acquired a precise knowledge of the religion.[48]

As the opponents of expansion had a majority, they were able to defeat the offending articles or water them down to such an extent that they only provided for Jahad's "cooperation" in the areas concerned. Apparently not having foreseen this development, Jahad's lobby protested loudly and managed to have the bill referred back to committee.[49] Nine months later, the Jahad lobby made a second attempt to push the new charter through parliament. So as to avoid the expected resistance, they declared that the revised charter precluded any overlapping with other authorities but did provide for Jahad being transformed into a ministry. The reason they gave for this provision was that the Council of Guardians was against Jahad's acting like a government agency but having a shouralike structure[50] as well as its not being responsible to parliament. If it were organized like a ministry it would be accountable to parliament.[51]

Despite strong opposition, the new charter received parliamentary approval at its first reading on August 4, 1983. However, at the second reading, from November 16 to 30, 1983, some deletions and amendments were made in an attempt to limit Jahad's authority and prevent it from encroaching upon other ministries. An effort was made to keep Jahad's tasks within the bounds of rural construction. The same arguments for and against were raised at the second reading as at the first one. The only tasks that had nothing to do with rural construction but were still assigned to Jahad without provoking a single dissenting voice were its war services. Because of their significance, these will be dealt with separately.

Despite the various deletions, the charter approved at the second reading still gave legal sanction to Jahad's actual concentration of powers. Its responsibility for production, or for "arranging conditions leading to an increase in production," was confirmed in more or less vague wording (Article 2), and Jahad was thus able to encroach upon areas previously reserved, at least formally, for the Ministry of Agriculture. Its activities in spheres for which other ministries had previously been responsible were also confirmed, including establishing rural industries, carrying out irrigation projects, running reading and writing programs, collating statistics, and fulfilling military tasks (Article 5). Responsibility for rural construction was transferred from the Ministry of Agriculture to Jahad (Article 4). As a sop to the opponents of Jahad's expansionism, a proviso was made that the organization was only to offer its cooperation or to become active if requested to do so by the other ministries (Article 5). Appropriate regulations, which were to be drafted within six months, were to ensure careful delimitation and coordination in joint operations (Article 6). So that Jahad would not fall prey to bureaucracy, it was given leave—in spite of its expansion and transformation into a ministry—to lay down its own unbureaucratic regulations, independent of those in force for other ministries, in financial, personnel, and administrative matters. Corresponding proposals were to be drafted within three months of the minister for jahad being appointed (Article 9).[52]

Jahad's expansion, however, did not end with the passage of its charter and its transformation into a ministry. It subsequently succeeded in taking over other areas, as graphically illustrated by the regulations approved by the Council of Ministers on September 30, 1984. Like Article 6, these regulations were intended to define and coordinate Jahad's and the Ministry of Agriculture's respective purviews. However, the sole purpose of the coordination defined in these regulations was to transfer additional tasks from the ministry to Jahad, including land reclamation, some of the work on irrigation projects, the reclamation and preservation of pastures in nomadic areas, and a number of other tasks—animal husbandry, beekeeping, poultry breeding, traditional fishing in southern waters, and growing wheat or animal fodder on naturally irrigated land.[53]

Further steps incorporating additional tasks into Jahad's purview followed the delimitation regulations. On October 9, 1987, the Council of Ministers decided to transfer the entire fishing industry to Jahad.[54] Some one and a half months later, Zangane, the minister for jahad, stated that his organization was intending to found a university offering courses in all the disciplines relating to rural industry, agriculture, natural resources, combat engineering, and war management.[55] On June 1, 1988, the papers reported that Jahad's first naval students had graduated and were now ready to obey Imam Khomeini's orders anywhere in international waters or in the Persian Gulf. Note 24 in the state's budget estimates for 1367 (1988/9) was a discretionary clause permitting the implementation of all national and international construction projects to be transferred to Jahad.[56] There were also reports that Jahad had undertaken to produce all the agricultural appliances suitable for mass production.[57] On its tenth anniversary, Jahad launched its first landing craft.[58] Similar reports are legion.

As in many other cases of administrative reform in the Islamic Republic of Iran, Jahad's expansion resulted in multiple organizations having the same or similar tasks. As the secretary of state at the prime minister's office declared, this duplication had gone farthest in agriculture, where two rival ministries were locked in combat on the backs of the rural population.[59] The conflict was most apparent where Jahad had started to set up organizations called jahad-e dehestan (District Village Jahad) that were similar to the Ministry of Agriculture's Service Centers. According to the minister for jahad, Zangane, there were 800 to 900 of them,[60] most located in the same district villages as the Service Centers and needlessly competing with them.

This untenable state of affairs led the leadership of the Islamic Republic to conclude that the two ministries ought to be merged. Because of the majority view in the Council of Ministers, this merger, in effect—and in view of previous revolutionary practice—had to mean abolishing the Ministry of Agriculture and incorporating its functions and affiliated organizations into Jahad.

The idea of a merger had been under consideration at the ministerial level long before the Council of Ministers reached its decision and submitted the proposal to parliament. Three years previously, Dr. Zali had predicted that if Jahad's expansion continued, a proposal would be made to merge the two ministries.[61] According to Prime Minister Musawi, the idea had been in the air since the start of the revolution,[62] and talks had been held about it since the end of 1364 (March 20, 1986) among the Ministry of Planning and Budget, the prime minister's office, and the authority responsible for administration and personnel matters.[63] The Council of Ministers reached a decision on March 1, 1987, and the proposal was debated in parliament on July 6 and 7, 1987, where it was rejected at the first reading.

There were plausible arguments for the decision by the Council of Ministers to favor merging the two ministries: avoiding the personnel and financial burdens of duplicating staff; debureaucratizing services provided by the state; coordinating same; and avoiding parallel purviews, which blurred the responsibilities of the individual ministries and rendered supervision impossible. All these problems hampered planning and gave the peasants and nomads new grounds for dissatisfaction.[64] But the Council of Ministers actually based its position on arguments that were not convincing, at least not for its opponents. The prime minister saw the decision as being based on the fact that Jahad was a Revolutionary Institution that had adopted the "values of the revolution" and was thus very close to the rural population.[65] The minister for jahad confirmed this argument by stating that a mere 10 percent of the Ministry of Agriculture's staff were in close contact with the rural population—i.e., working in Service Centers.[66] Two officials from the ministry under attack affirmed his view in a newspaper article in which they put their ministry's bureaucracy down for imitating Western forms of organization—a fate that might befall Jahad if it were transformed into a ministry.[67] One member of parliament expressed the view that all the ministries ought to be reorganized along the lines of Jahad. Another one declared that Jahad was more successful than the Ministry of Agriculture and that it was intolerable for Jahad to be given dangerous tasks such as the conduct of the war, even though other people, including those in charge of the Ministry of Agriculture, benefited.[68] The Ministry of Agriculture's failures were yet another argument made in favor of Jahad and were illustrated with statistics comparing the per-hectare yield in Iran with that of other countries: Iran came off badly even in comparison with Ethiopia and Afghanistan. Even the "centers the said ministry is so proud of are unable to submit a record of services that is in a reasonable relationship to the means which have been placed at their disposal."[69]

The opponents of a merger (at least, of a merger to the benefit of Jahad) gave several seemingly credible reasons for their position. The problems that had surfaced at the Ministry of Agriculture, such as excessive bureaucracy, they said, were symptomatic of a malaise affecting the entire apparatus of state, including Jahad, and so could not be solved by a mere merger. The government had no real program for organizing the merger; thought was to be given to the regulations only after the merger was agreed upon. It was impossible to reform the administration in the agricultural sector without a decision on agricultural policy and how to plan it being made first.[70] The former minister, Salamati, declared that merging the Ministry of Agriculture with Jahad would be detrimental to the latter's work, overburdening its organizational structure and distracting it from its revolutionary tasks.[71] It ought also to be remembered that neither Jahad nor its top officials had the necessary know-how to take over the Ministry of Agriculture, which had 5,000 experts; Jahad had at most 500 of dubious standard.[72]

Most of the opponents of a merger attested to Jahad's good work and were merely resisting its expansion, but some were very critical of the organization. One member of parliament pointed out that Jahad had dismissed a great many specialists or given them menial tasks simply because they were not members of the Party of God, replacing them with unqualified people. Many of the achievements Jahad was proud of were useless— for example, building roads for uninhabited villages. One member of parliament voiced his fear that the merger could give Jahad too much power, especially in rural areas, which it might abuse to influence the elections.[73]

The opponents of the merger put forward their own proposals for solving the Ministry of Agriculture's problems. According to former minister Salamati, Jahad's methods could be introduced at the ministry. It was also advisable to relieve it of many of its subordinate organizations, such as the "Meat Marketing Organization," which only distracted it from its real tasks.[74]

The pros and cons of a merger split the ruling Islamists into two main camps,[75] but not along the usual line—i.e., populist etatists versus lobbyists for the private sector. Although those in favor of a merger had a majority in the government, they did not in parliament, where only "a small number" of the 200 members present approved it. Anticipating this result, the minister of jahad said that even if the proposal were to be rejected the merger would be complete in two years.[76] Since then, many attempts have been made to implement a de facto merger by transferring more and more tasks to Jahad—some of the transfers listed above were made after the merger was rejected. For a while, there was even talk of the government putting the rejected proposal to parliament again.

The discussion about a merger was taken up again after the war. Prime Minister Musawi demanded a merger in a speech to the National Congress to Investigate Problems of Agricultural Development,[77] but no practical steps followed. The new minister of agriculture, Dr. Kalantari, speaking on March 8, 1989, raised the possibility of completing a merger in the first half of 1368 (i.e., by September 22, 1989). The summarized quotations of his statements suggest that he felt a merger would be to the advantage of his ministry.[78] About seven months later, a parliamentary initiative proposed conjuring up a "Ministry of Jahad for Agriculture" from a merger of the two ministries.[79] A few weeks later, there were reports that a proposal would soon to be presented in parliament with the aim of defining the purviews of three ministries. Jahad was to be made responsible for the organizations dealing with forests, pastures, fishing, land and water use, rural improvement, and rural industry; the Ministry of Agriculture was to be left in charge of farming and animal husbandry; and the Ministry of Water and Energy was to look after electricity supplies and construction of large dams.[80] Parliament took the seemingly final decision in the matter on September 2, 1990, by approving draft legislation submitted by the Council of Ministers, according to which the Ministry of Agriculture was to retain the administration of matters pertaining to farming as well as local land and water use. Jahad was responsible for all natural resources (forests, fishery, pastures, supraregional water utilization) as well as animal husbandry, rural construction, rural crafts, and so on (see the dailies). The fact that Jahad's lobbyists made a fresh attempt in parliament in January 1991 to expand its jurisdiction at the expense of the Ministry of Agriculture makes it clear that this division of duties was not the last word on the subject.[81]

7.3.3 The Bureaucratization of a Revolutionary Institution

Many critics see in Jahad's expansion and its transformation into a "super ministry," which seems like the "establishment of a new state," the danger of it losing its original revolutionary character and becoming bureaucratic. This transition could happen if it were no longer to function as a Revolutionary Institution but rather as a ministry, forcing it to abandon its shoura-based way of working. Jahad's successes have been put down to its not having been "a ministry with the corresponding spirit, red tape and disruptive guidelines."[82] Bureaucratization was a great danger, declared a member of parliament, regretting even in 1985 that Jahad and "many other revolutionary, holy institutions . . . are gradually being exposed to immobility in the bureaucratic channels of rigidity."[83] When the discussion about the proposal for a merger between the Ministry of Agriculture and Jahad began, many people were convinced that the bureaucratization of Jahad was already a fact; the organization originally associated with the hope of transforming all state organizations into unbureaucratic structures, it seemed, had itself succumbed to bureaucracy.[84]

Jahad's lobbyists put down its transformation into a ministry to pressure from the Council of Guardians, as noted above. This view was used to repudiate the opposition's arguments. Jahad's transformation was the logical consequence of its own expansion, and many of its leaders saw great benefits in it, benefits they did not want to give up. One member of its central staff contended that Jahad "establishes the necessary contact with the country's administrative order . . . and is present in the decisionmaking centers."[85] In an attempt to achieve this aim in full, a proposal was submitted to parliament on December 11, 1986, providing for the minister of jahad to attend many of the supreme councils of state just as the other ministers do.[86]

Jahad's lobbyists and leaders also saw the danger of bureaucratization. To counter it, they had themselves granted the right, in the charter approved in December 1983, to draft their own guidelines and regulations independently of the other ministries in financial, personnel, and other administrative and organizational matters. This freedom was not only intended to protect Jahad from bureaucratic peril but also to serve as a model for how the other ministries could be transformed in an equally revolutionary manner.[87]

These 1983 regulations and guidelines were supposed to have been drafted very quickly—i.e., within three months. However, it actually took one year in the ministry itself, eight months in the Council of Ministers, and fourteen months in parliament to complete them. The corresponding legislative proposal was passed by parliament at its first reading on November 25 and 27, 1987, and at its second reading on January 8, 1988, and was finally approved on April 12, 1988, after having been amended to meet the demands made by the Council of Guardians.

Appreciating the significance of the delays, contemplating the regulations and guidelines that were finally approved, and following the relevant debates in parliament, it is impossible not to conclude that these reforms have failed to achieve their objectives. As it is impossible to analyze this text of ninety-seven articles and as many notes here, a few examples will have to suffice.

The main difference between the Ministry of Jahad and the other ministries is that it is organized on the basis of a shouralike order. The 1979 charter provided for Jahad to be constituted down to the county town level in councils (shoura) having the authority to make decisions and manage their own affairs. However, the regulations, as finally approved, severely restricted this shoura system. The proposal by the Parliamentary Commission for the Institutions of the Revolution, which was prepared on the basis of the draft proposed by the Council of Ministers and submitted to parliament, provided for a Central Committee "to perform the tasks of the ministry in due form, to ensure the coordination considered necessary in matters affecting Jahad and to guarantee uniformity [of procedures]" (Article 2). The committee was to consist of reliable individuals proposed by a Panel of Responsibles, itself composed of members of the Provincial Councils plus those in positions of responsibility in Jahad's central organizations and affiliated branches (Article 2, Notes 1 and 2). The spokesman for the commission termed this arrangement "a novelty" in the Islamic Republic "devised by the upright children of the revolution and diligent members of Jahad"; in the future it could become a model for the reform of the entire machinery of state.[88] The advantage of this system, according to the minister of jahad, was that it guaranteed participation by those members of the staff "who want to apply themselves wholeheartedly to their work and from whom it would not be good to demand obedience."[89] One member of parliament emphasized that because Jahad is a revolutionary organization, it ought to be organized on a shoura basis.[90]

Many members of parliament spoke out against this arrangement during the debate on the new regulations and guidelines, quoting the constitution of the Islamic Republic, which stipulates that the minister, not a committee, should be answerable to parliament for the ministry.[91] The response to this objection made it clear that even the supporters of the shoura order did not seriously want to defend it. They tried to calm their opponents with the assurance that the committee envisaged had no powers of decision; these were exclusively a matter for the minister, whom the committee was to assist in a purely advisory capacity. "We don't want to bring in a system of soviets," said one member of parliament.[92] The proposal was amended accordingly and passed. The Central Committee stayed, its members picked by the minister from among the "responsible and competent members of Jahad"—i.e., no longer on the advice of the panel mentioned above but after consultation with those in positions of responsibility in its provincial offices (Article 2). It was stipulated that the minister would be answerable to parliament (Article 3) and that the Central Committee's decisions would only be valid if approved by the minister (Article 4).

Another regulation intended to guarantee Jahad's revolutionary character concerned the intention expressed in the proposal to exempt the organization's financial matters from the laws applying to public accounts. The relevant articles (13–15) were rejected by parliament in late December 1986.[93] The third regulation intended to preserve Jahad's unbureaucratic character was the commercialization of its services in rural and nomadic areas (Article 7), an attempt to simplify financial transactions by circumventing bureaucratic regulations. That other ministries had already commercialized their services by setting up companies—for example, the postal service and the railways—was glossed over, because the main reason was always to free the state from the costs, not to free the services from bureaucracy. This motivation is clear if it is remembered that such companies have a monopoly but remain state-owned enterprises. The opponents of this arrangement point to the negative experience with the state-owned and nationalized commercial companies after the revolution. One member of parliament said, "Such companies, because they need fear no competition, form monopolies; they increase prices" and added, "please don't turn Jahad, this holy organization, into a commercial company . . . don't turn Jahad into a contract company."[94]

Those in charge of Jahad argued that special rules to counter bureaucracy could only work if administered by members of the Party of God and wanted such a requirement enshrined in the proposal. Thus, it was announced with pleasure that, according to the new rules, a representative of the Imam would have a seat and a vote on the Central Committee and be vested with a number of specific powers (Article 2). Another of the special rules dealt with Jahad's flexibility, which enabled it to respond to the requirements of the war. According to the spokesman of the relevant parliamentary commission, Jahad was to be enabled to offer the armed forces powerful support and to operate at the front by concentrating its strength at the provincial and county town levels. The minister of Jahad added, "We must organize our forces so that we are in a position to send some of our people to the front; our work must not come to a standstill because of this measure."[95] Article 11 made this operational readiness binding on Jahad.

No special rule was discernible for debureaucratizing Jahad with respect to its personnel structure. The legislative proposal put the "salaries and allowances of the dear Jahadis" on a par with those of the other ministries. Staff working in hardship zones were to receive a special allowance (Article 60). Bonuses were stipulated for staff who distinguished themselves by good work (Articles 61f), with up to one month's holiday guaranteed each year (Article 66). Jahad was not permitted its own medical insurance scheme. It was pointed out that other officials were also insured with the state-owned insurance company and that it was impossible to grant Jahad this particular privilege.[96] So Jahad was put on a par with the other ministries in this respect, too. Only the faintest of traces of a Revolutionary Institution could still be made out.

7.3.4 Jahad's War Services

All the Islamic Republic's leading personalities have repeatedly praised Jahad's great achievements. According to Prime Minister Musawi, it plays an "enormous part" in cultivating the revolutionary culture in the country's rural areas.[97] The late Ayatollah Beheshti called the Jahadis the "ambassadors of the Islamic Revolution."[98] Jahad embodied "the miracle and the value of the revolution" for Rafsanjani;[99] to Khomeini, the holy fight as fought by Jahad was the best of all holy fights, and he often praised it for its great zealousness in the war against Iraq.[100] In December 1988 he wrote this message to a Jahad seminar. "The uninterrupted efforts of the Jahadis ... for our holy defense are among those things which cannot be put into words." Even the opponents of Jahad's encroachment upon other ministries were full of praise and admiration for it during the parliamentary debates on the bills dealing with it and its charters.

It owed this praise and the great support its expansion enjoyed primarily to the part it played in the war against Iraq. This role is generally described as "engineering in war," by which Jahad meant building roads, bridges, canals, and lines of defense; repairing equipment and weapons; and supplying the front with electricity, water, and everything else. Jahad was entrusted with these tasks mainly because of the experience it had gained in construction work in rural areas and because it had machines and equipment that could be used in the war.[101] But its services far exceeded these tasks and included mobilizing and dispatching so-called volunteers to the front; producing equipment for the war; collecting money, clothes, and food; providing medical facilities; and producing and distributing Qurans and propaganda material for the war, as well as building mosques and houses of mourning. It also handled field security at the front. In 1986 it prepared to assume an active role in the fighting by forming its own combat units.[102] The extent of the services rendered by Jahad was considerable—by June 1982 they included the following:

> building 2,543 kilometers (km) of roads, 318 bridges, 63 runways, 170km of canals, 11 field hospitals, 7 field mosques, 535 field baths, [and] several thousand bunkers; laying 1,529km of water mains, 61,800km of cables; providing 66,000 drivers, mechanics and experts; donating 1,662,489,299 rials; producing 3,743 tanker lorries; distributing and installing 148 generators; repairing and maintaining 63,445 light and heavy machines and vehicles and 217 deep wells; maintaining 9,500 light and heavy items of war equipment; supplying water in 266 cases; collecting and supplying 30,844 tons of food and 1,894,472 blankets or items of clothing; dispatching several hundred groups of doctors; [and] distributing several hundred thousand Qurans, prayer books and newspapers.[103]

This service was maintained and even increased after 1982. By September 1985 Jahad was reported to have donated 50bn rials and dispatched 150,000 "specialists" to the front,[104] including at least 2,800 "martyrs" who had lost their lives for Jahad.[105] A member of Jahad's central staff announced in mid-1986 that if necessary the agency could provide combat engineers for 100 divisions; at present it was doing so for thirty of them.[106] Five days later, eighty batallions of its combat engineers were reportedly ready to be dispatched to the front.[107] A report dated June 3, 1988, stated that Jahad had set up fourteen garrisons in various provinces for the purpose of training the necessary combat engineers.[108]

Jahad's war services have been repeatedly acknowledged. The head of war propaganda said: "Organizing the conduct of the war would be impossible without Jahad."[109] General S'adi, the army commander, thought Jahad "played an essential part for the front."[110] A member of parliament stated: "We would not have been able to achieve success on many fronts, perhaps on all fronts, if it had not been for Jahad's effective and drastic actions."[111]

Jahad's war operations naturally reduced its opportunities to be effective in rural improvement and other constructive activities. This reversal of effort reached a point where it could be said that Jahad's forces made the greatest impact "where they were employed to support our fighters against the aggression of the war forced upon us."[112] In November 1984, the minister of jahad stated that the war was claiming "a huge proportion" of its funds and added the agency was "not in a position to accomplish all the improvement work in question with such reduced means."[113] Three years later, when it was officially announced that all the country's resources were to be allocated to the war, Jahad declared itself willing to act upon the appropriate instructions. When the total mobilization failed to achieve the desired victory and Khomeini had to announce his readiness to drain the "poisoned chalice" and swallow a truce to end the war, Jahad took none of the blame. Its official "front hymn writer" attributed this (in his opinion) unwelcome turn of events to the fact that the other ministries, organizations, and institutions had not followed Jahad's example and placed all their might at the disposal of the war effort. In the same passage he spoke of a symbolic Jahadi "who leaves his poor village to go to the front, thus giving up the struggle against poverty for the fight against unbelief"; the peasants wait for him to come back from the war "so that he can take up the struggle against poverty again, but after some time they catch sight of his corpse so they forget their poverty and go to the front themselves."[114]

These words exactly describe the psychic change imposed on the Jahadis by their active service and by the organization's new functions in the war. Following this reorientation and after the war had ingloriously ended, the same front hymn writer plaintively and woefully expressed his war nostalgia in the monthly *Jahad*. The following excerpt from the poem depicts the extreme intensity with which Jahad was engrossed in the war:

> I'm talking to you, you to whom the lovers give their trust,
> You who trumpets out the hardships of the barefooted,
> You who have become the toy of the worldly politicians.
> You are the place where the lovers of the martyr's death meet. . . .

> You are witness to the fight against unbelief,
> To the fight which makes the lovers of freedom come to power,
> Who now rest in the marriage bed of the holy war and martyrdom,
> You whose music was the song of the angels,
> And your shouts the trumpets of the fire which came forth from unbelief.
> It's you I'm talking to,
> You must wake up,
> This is no time to sleep,
> Silence is not worthy of the revolution...

In another poem in the same edition, the war is praised in the following words:

> Here beauty has its home at the front,
> Overflowing with buds of volunteers, flowers of Jahadis
> and fragrance of martyrs' death.
> Ugliness has with all its despotic force opened the front to it, ...
> Here the martyr's death is the buttress of beauty ... with
> what strange appearance,
> Beauty in barricades of love,
> Marching through the fronts in the south and east and west, emerging.
> Here life becomes beautiful only through passing away....
> Here death becomes beautiful as a game,
> Here the war loses, despite its unpleasantnesses, its
> bitterness through beauty,
> Which belongs to the movement of fighters for Islam,
> It is sweet, till the duty which is God's mission, is fulfilled,
> Standing on the barricades tastes like honey,
> As long as the movement is led by those commanded to rule.[115]

7.4 Other State Organizations Administering Agriculture

The Ministry of Jahad-e Sazandegi was not the only state organization duplicating the Ministry of Agriculture's administration. There was also overlap with those organizations that came into being outside the traditional machinery of government after the revolution, such as the Foundation for the Dispossessed (bonyad-e mostaz'afan), the Sevener Commissions (hey'atha-ye haft nafareh), and the Imam's Relief Committee (komite-ye emdad-e emam). Others, such as the Martyrs' Foundation (bonyad-e shahid), were also active in agriculture and rural improvement. These organizations will be sketched below, but only in connection with the questions that are of concern here.

7.4.1 Sevener Commissions

The Sevener Commissions came into being in connection with land reform, which they were charged with carrying out. The relevant legislative proposal, drafted by the Bazargan government and passed by the Revolutionary Council, provided for a network of three-man commissions to be subordinate to the Ministry of Agriculture and entrusted with carrying out land reform.[116] But carrying out land reform was politically and socially too important for the powerful men and institutions in the Islamic Republic not to want to intervene. This meddling gave the commissions the chance to become more independent of the ministry, as their composition after the first bill—passed after the fall of the Bazargan government—makes clear. They were composed of the following representatives: two from the Ministry of Agriculture; one from the Ministry of the Interior or the provincial administration; one from Jahad-e Sazandegi; one from the Ministry of Justice; and one from the Village Council concerned.[117]

Because of the increased importance of the clerics in the state apparatus, the representative from the Ministry of Justice was replaced in later proposals by one from the "religious judge and ruler," and it was emphasized that the representative from the Village Council had to be confirmed by him.[118]

The Sevener Commissions formed at the local level came under a central office in Tehran composed of one representative from the "religious judge and ruler," two plenipotentiaries from the Ministry of Agriculture, and one representative from each of the ministries mentioned above. From the very beginning, the ruler's representative was Hojjat ol-Eslam Fazel Harandi, of whom a great deal will be heard in the next chapter.

The Sevener Commissions' tasks were laid down as follows: (1) solving the controversial questions arising over land reform (in matters pertaining to the ruler's powers, only his representative was authorized to make a decision—as land reform dealt with the existing ownership of land, which is supposedly a matter of direct concern to the sharia, the powers of the representative of the ruler overshadowed those of all the other members of the commission); (2) overseeing transfer of estates; and (3) determining the suitability of individuals for credit and agricultural assistance during land reform.

As the estates that were to be taken away from their previous owners and transferred to the peasants had not been surveyed for this purpose by the land registry, a great deal of surveying devolved on the Sevener Commissions. In addition, there were tasks connected with arranging loans for peasants, supplying them with farming equipment and means of transportation, and related functions. It would have been impossible for the landless peasants who were being given wasteland to reclaim or cultivate it without this assistance. Taking on such services led to overlap with all the other organizations that provided the same services, particularly Jahad and the Ministry of Agriculture.[119] The peasants were not allowed to decide for themselves which form of management the transferred estates should have;

the relevant legislative proposals stipulated that these enterprises were to be organized "in the form of partnerships, cooperatives and enterprises with undivided property." A number of other conditions restricted the peasants' rights to the land they had been assigned. The Sevener Commissions were entrusted with ensuring that the restrictions were enforced and also with establishing the enterprises with undivided property, called mosha'. This last task alone took them into areas otherwise under the Ministries of Agriculture and Jahad.

Other Sevener Commission activity that collided with that of other state organizations and Revolutionary Institutions included setting up Islamic Village Councils,[120] ensuring that opposition groups could not gain a foothold in rural areas,[121] and instructing the rural population in the principles of Islam by giving lectures, distributing posters and banners, and so forth (an encroachment on Jahad's tasks).[122] The commissions were at the center of the controversy surrounding land reform, the number one topic in the agricultural policy of the Islamic Republic until October 1986. They took sides on the issue, the majority of their members initially being for radical reforms and attempting to enlarge their scope of action in the hope of achieving their aims. In 1982 some commissioners suggested that their system be transformed into a Ministry of Land Reform, explaining that they would be unable to coordinate their work if it got caught up between various ministries.[123]

7.4.2 Imam Khomeini's Relief Committee

Planning for this committee was reputedly in hand even before the revolution,[124] but it was only founded—as a Revolutionary Institution—on Khomeini's orders on March 5, 1979, three weeks after he came to power. Its task was to provide the poor, the dispossessed, and others in need with various forms of assistance. Like other Revolutionary Institutions, it was soon being funded by the treasury, which earmarked the items in the budget, and it, too, succeeded in extending the scope of its activities over time. A report issued on the committee's tenth anniversary stated that it was active in nineteen different fields. By 1987/8 it had 1,100 branches throughout the country, providing assistance that year to 1.5m people living in the towns and in 53,000 villages. It reported supporting 529,162 peasants at the end of 1366 (March 20, 1988) and providing over 114bn rials' worth of assistance in cash and kind to some 452,950 peasants over the age of sixty. The work was done by 4,000 salaried and 8,000 volunteer staff.[125]

The committee was also economically active, owning a number of manufacturing plants (including in the agricultural sector) that were placed at its disposal by the Foundation of the Dispossessed, the fund set up with the fortunes confiscated from members of the shah's regime. Its activities in agriculture and rural improvement included granting loans for rural crafts, animal husbandry, and farming; it also engaged in farming itself. At the beginning of 1989, it was said that the committee wanted to reclaim 480,000ha of land in the provinces of Sistan and Baluchistan.[126] The committee operates under the Imam's direct influence, as its name makes clear, and serves—as do many other Revolutionary Institutions and similar semi-state organizations that came into being after the revolution—to aggrandize the person controlling it.

7.4.3 Foundation of the Dispossessed

This foundation (bonyad) was established as an institution of the revolution on March 5, 1979, on the basis of a decree by Khomeini. Its assets consisted of the fortunes confiscated from members of the shah's regime immediately after the takeover of power. In 1986 these assets comprised 140 industrial plants, 230 commercial enterprises, 12 big stock and poultry farms, 270 orchards, 90 cinemas, thousands of hectares of land, a number of houses, art collections, jewels, and so on. The foundation employed 150,000 manual and clerical staff.[127] Its activities in the agricultural sector are varied and include the production and sale of agricultural produce as well as the sale of farming implements, machinery, and other inputs. It conducts an independent agricultural policy within its own sphere of influence, planning and implementing its own projects. At the beginning of 1989, it was renamed the Foundation for Disabled War Veterans and then shortly afterwards the Foundation for the Dispossessed and Disabled War Veterans.[128]

7.4.4 Martyrs' Foundation

A decree by Khomeini set this foundation up on March 12, 1980, at the beginning of the second year after the revolution; it, too, is a Revolutionary Institution. Its task is to provide various services to the dependents of the men who fell during the revolution and the war, or who are missing in action or were taken prisoner of war. The aim is to bind these dependents to the Islamic regime and make them its loyal supporters. In addition to the funds it is allocated each year in the national budget, the foundation finances itself through its own economic activities. In 1984 it owned 141 enterprises in industry, agriculture, construction, and commerce,[129] including 17 large companies engaged in stock breeding and farming as well as 140 orchards and estates.[130] In 1986/7 its profits from the sale of agricultural produce came to 9bn rials.[131] This foundation obtained its initial assets from the riches confiscated from members of the shah's regime.

Notes

1. PP, March 6 and 9, 1982, and April 7, 1983.
2. The Revolutionary Council issued the first decree to this end on August 28, 1979. See CL 1979/80, p. 131.
3. See the relevant regulations in CL 1984/5, pp. 245ff, which are based on the Law on the Activity of Parties, Political Leagues and Associations, the Islamic Societies and Associations of the Religious Minorities, approved on August 28, 1981. See CL 1981/2, pp. 92ff.
4. *Jomhuri-ye Eslami*, June 11, 1983.
5. Such statements are too numerous to be dealt with exhaustively here. Some examples: *Kayhan*, November 5, 1983, April 11, 1984, July 21, 1985, and July 8, 1986.
6. *Kayhan-e Hawa'i*, July 6, 1988.
7. See DP, p. 3; Zali's letter to Khomeini, p. 11; Dr. Izadi's speech on the subject in *Ettela'at*, October 24, 1979, and *Keshawarz-e Emruz*, October 31, 1979; and interview with Salamati in *Barzegar*, November 1, 1980.
8. See M. Azkia 1986, p. 278f, on the history of the idea.
9. *Kayhan*, October 24, 1979.
10. See *Barzegar*, September 5, 1980, and August 22, 1981.
11. *Resalat*, June 30, 1987.
12. CL 1980/1, pp. 135ff. See the translation of this law in Schirazi 1988, pp. 240ff.
13. These regulations are not contained in the appropriate year's CL. My source is Sabet Qadam 1983, pp. 57ff, which includes them as an appendix.
14. DPA, p. 50.
15. *Ettela'at*, November 10, 1980.
16. PP, November 25, 1982, p. 16.
17. *Kayhan*, August 22, 1985.
18. Zali in PP, July 6, 1987, p. 31.
19. p. 16. In all, 742 centers had been established at the district village and 142 at the county town level by March 20, 1991, according to Rasulof in *Resalat*, April 24, 1991.
20. *Kayhan*, March 31, 1987.
21. See Chapter 10.4.2 on these companies.
22. PP, July 5, 1987, p. 29.
23. See interview with Dr. Zali in *Barzegar*, February 26, 1983.
24. PP, July 6, 1987, p. 31.
25. Mo'ezi MP complained about experts with twenty years of experience being sent to the provinces and recruiting people who had completed their degrees two years previously to replace them in PP, July 5, 1987, p. 30.
26. *Barzegar*, February 26, 1983.
27. Zali's letter to Khomeini (1984), p. 19.
28. *Barzegar*, February 27, 1983; DPA, pp. 298 and 315.
29. Zali's letter to Khomeini, p. 20f.
30. *Resalat*, February 21, 1990.
31. *Kayhan*, February 2, 1989.
32. *Resalat*, March 9, 1989.
33. *Resalat*, June 1, 1989.
34. This depiction of Jahad's genesis comes from Bazargan and his party, Nehzat-e Azadi (Freedom Movement). In answer to those who considered him and

his government liberal, he went to pains to emphasize that the establishment of such Revolutionary Institutions as Jahad was the result of an initiative by his government and that its revolutionary character was thus beyond question. See Bazargan's letter to Ayatollah Gilani of May 29, 1982, in Nehzat-e Azadi, *Shesh Name-ye Sargoshade* (Six Open Letters), (Tehran, 1983), pp. 11ff.

35. See Schirazi 1988 for information on this and the relevant legislative measures.
36. *Ibid.*, pp. 98ff.
37. On this reorganization, see *Barzegar*, October 4 and November 8, 1980, August 22, 1981, and January 2 and July 31, 1982.
38. PP, November 22, 1982, p. 22.
39. PP, November 25, 1982, p. 15.
40. *Ibid.*, pp. 21, 24, and 26.
41. PP, November 22, 1982, p. 25.
42. PP, November 23, 1982, p. 16f.
43. *Ibid.*, p. 19f.
44. *Ibid.*
45. PP, November 23, 1982, p. 23; and November 25, 1982, p. 15f.
46. PP, November 23, 1982, p. 24.
47. PP, November 23, 1982, p. 22f; and November 25, 1982, pp. 15f, 18f, and 24ff.
48. PP, November 23, 1982, p. 18.
49. PP, November 25, 1982, pp. 15ff.
50. Here shoura (council) is any body whose members not only participate in deliberations but also have the right to vote. This development contradicts the traditional Islamic understanding of shoura, where decisions are made by the head of the body after consultation with the other members. See Chapter 9.
51. PP, August 4, 1983, p. 2.
52. Complete text of charter in CL 1983/4, pp. 433ff.
53. CL 1984/5, pp. 251ff.
54. *Barzegar*, October 3, 1987.
55. *Resalat*, November 18, 1987.
56. PP, March 7, 1987, p. 34.
57. *Kayhan*, February 13, 1989.
58. *Kayhan*, June 18, 1988.
59. *Kayhan*, March 5, 1987.
60. *Kayhan*, March 5, 1987.
61. PP, July 7, 1987.
62. *Kayhan*, March 8, 1987.
63. Zangene in *Kayhan*, March 5, 1987.
64. PP, March 5, 1987; *Kayhan*, March 11 and 12, 1987.
65. *Kayhan*, March 8, 1987.
66. *Ibid.*, March 5, 1987.
67. *Kayhan*, June 24, 1987.
68. PP, March 5, 1987, p. 31; and March 6, 1987, pp. 27 and 34.
69. PP, March 5, 1987, p. 33; and March 6, 1987, p. 14.
70. PP, March 5 and 6, 1987, pp. 25, 28f, and 34; and March 6, 1987, p. 25. See also Nehzat-e Azadi's 1987 brochure on the subject.
71. *Kayhan*, March 1, 1987.
72. PP, March 5, 1987, p. 32.
73. PP, March 5, 1987, pp. 30ff; and March 6, 1987, p. 31.
74. *Kayhan*, March 31, 1987; see also PP, March 5, 1987, p. 35.

75. *Kayhan,* April 8, 1987, makes out two pro and three contra groups.
76. PP, March 6, 1987, pp. 34 and 36.
77. *Resalat,* February 26, 1989.
78. *Resalat,* March 9, 1989.
79. *Kayhan,* September 25, 1989.
80. *Ettela'at,* January 28, 1990.
81. *Resalat,* January 7, 1991.
82. PP, August 4, 1983, p. 22f; Nehzat-e Azadi 1987a, pp. 8ff.
83. *Kayhan,* July 16, 1985.
84. Nehzat-e Azadi 1987a, p. 8f.
85. *Kayhan,* June 13, 1984.
86. CL 1986/7, pp. 507ff.
87. According to the minister of jahad in parliament. See PP, August 4, 1983, p. 22f; and November 28, 1983, p. 24f.
88. PP, November 25, 1986, p. 28.
89. PP, November 27, 1986, p. 26.
90. PP, December 17, 1986, p. 29.
91. PP, November 26, 1986, pp. 29ff; and December 17, 1986, p. 29.
92. PP, November 26, 1986, p. 29f; November 28, 1986, p. 25; December 17, 1986, p. 30; December 20, 1986, pp. 23 and 25f.
93. PP, December 29, 1986, pp. 23ff.
94. PP, November 25, 1986, p. 31.
95. PP, November 25, 1986, p. 28f; and November 27, 1986, pp. 28ff.
96. PP, January 5, 1987, pp. 23ff.
97. *Kayhan,* September 14, 1983.
98. *Jomhuri-ye Eslami,* June 13, 1983.
99. *Kayhan,* June 16, 1983.
100. *Ibid.,* and *Kayhan,* December 5, 1982.
101. On this and Jahad's tasks in the war, see the interview with "brother engineer J'afari," head of Jahad's central staff for support and engineering in war in *Jahad* 120 (September 1989), pp. 30ff.
102. *Kayhan,* June 7, 1986.
103. *Kayhan,* September 29, 1982.
104. *Barzegar,* September 14, 1985.
105. The new minister of jahad, Foruzesh, announced the figure in *Kayhan,* February 12, 1989. It is doubtful whether it is correct.
106. *Resalat,* June 17, 1986.
107. *Resalat,* June 22, 1986.
108. *Resalat,* June 18, 1988.
109. *Kayhan,* July 2, 1988.
110. *Kayhan,* July 4, 1986.
111. PP, August 4, 1983.
112. *Kayhan,* June 13, 1984.
113. *Kayhan,* September 19, 1984.
114. *Jahad* 112 (November 1988).
115. *Jahad* 110 (July 1988), pp. 36ff.
116. CL 1979/80, pp. 188ff; Schirazi 1988, p. 89.
117. CL 1979/80, pp. 546ff; Schirazi 1988, p. 147.
118. CL 1980/1, p. 13f; Schirazi 1988, p. 169.
119. See Azkia 1986, p. 302.
120. They reportedly set up 15,318 Village Councils by September 1981; see *Kayhan,* September 7, 1981.

121. *Kayhan*, February 10, 1981.
122. Azkia 1986, p. 265.
123. See the interview with Salamati in *Barzegar*, June 10, 1982.
124. According to the committee's administrator (*Resalat*, May 18, 1987).
125. *Resalat*, June 9 and August 31, 1988, and March 4 and 5, 1989.
126. *Resalat*, March 2 and 5, 1989.
127. *Karname-ye Jomhuri-ye Eslami* 1984/5, p. 517f; *Kayhan*, March 5, 1986.
128. *Kayhan*, January 7, 1989.
129. *Karname-ye Jomhuri-ye Eslami* 1984/5, p. 517f.
130. *Barzegar*, November 16, 1985.
131. *Kayhan*, March 11 and 12, 1989.

8
The Reform of Land Tenure

Land reform retained its central importance in the Islamic Republic's agricultural, social, and economic policies until 1986, when the issue was almost settled. It was a tense period. On the social level, the battle was between peasants and private landowners. In the economic sphere, the debate revolved around how best to utilize land and maximize agricultural output. And in the religious realm, various factions of Islamists fought to bring land reform into line with their particular interpretation of Islamic law. The interplay of these various forces caused the reform to change directions numerous times and often thwarted final resolution of the issue.

8.1 The Spontaneous Action Phase

The structure of land ownership in the period immediately before the revolution caused deep dissatisfaction among peasants with little or no land. In many areas, they expressed their desire to reform property rights by occupying large estates, and some medium ones, and driving off the owners and/or their stewards during the collapse of state authority just prior to the revolution. Some national forests and pastures were occupied, too. The peasants' actions were widespread, with heavy activity in the northeast regions of the country and in the western provinces inhabited by Kurds. Similar actions were reported from the Central province as well as from the provinces of Kerman, Fars, Lurestan, Khuzestan, Yazd, Gilan, Isfahan, and Hamedan.[1] A study of the peasant movement in this phase established 285 cases in which land was occupied, ranging from peaceful mass actions (84 percent) to violent mass confrontations (16 percent). These actions involved peasants with anywhere from no land to 30ha, which resulted in differing demands being made. Whereas the poor peasants were fighting for the redistribution of land (19.9 percent), the others were demanding more water, machines, and implements for their farms or better hygienic facilities, electricity, schools, and so on for their villages.

These actions were widely supported and violent in those places where the shah's land reform policy had led to severe disadvantages for the peasants. In the Gorgan and Gonbad regions, for example, members of the shah's regime had taken illegal possession of peasant and state lands to plant large orchards,[2] working them with resettled Zabolis from southeast Iran. These plantations often caused great poverty or even unemployment among the local Turkmenic peasants, and even those who still owned their land were in constant dread of further usurpations and competition.

With the overthrow of the shah's regime, which was accompanied by the flight of many of the owners of large estates, Turkmenic peasants with little or no land grasped the opportunity to take possession of the land they wanted. This seizure happened on a large scale. The peasants formed councils to defend and jointly administer the land they were on. A central council, known as the Turkmenic People's Cultural Staff, soon came into being to deal with matters of concern to all the councils.

The leadership of the peasant movement in Gorgan and Gonbad was soon taken over by local left-wing intellectuals, who in turn were influenced by the supraregional communist organizations. Setting up the central council, extending its purview beyond agriculture, and introducing collective forms of landholding all testify to this influence. The peasant movement in this region was also affected by the ethnic conflicts, on the one hand between the local Turkmen and the Zaboli migrants from the provinces of Sistan and Baluchistan, on the other between the Turkmen and the central administration, which was run by other ethnic groups. The peasant movement in this area had thus acquired a significance far exceeding the issue of land—it had established a local ethnic power base whose existence, let alone expansion, the government was not prepared to tolerate.

The spontaneous peasant movements in the provinces inhabited by Kurds soon became part of the wider political movement. The overriding concern of the ethnic Kurdish parties, such as the Democratic Party of Kurdistan and the Revolutionary Organization of Workers in Iranian Kurdistan (KUMELE), and the nonethnic political organizations active in this area was to achieve autonomy for the Kurdish people. This aim reduced the peasants' specific demands to a secondary role.

At this stage, the efforts of the former owners of large estates were directed at regaining the privileges they had acquired as a result of the shah's land reform. They invoked Islam, which in their opinion guaranteed the sanctity of property rights, to justify the various forms of action they took. Peasants were either driven from their land and settlements or forced to pay arrears for the years after the land reform. In some places, the former owners placed themselves at the head of the local revolutionary movement and set up their own revolutionary committees, forming armed gangs or making use of local armed groups to enforce their demands against the peasants. Such actions were reported mainly from the Kurdish and Turkmenic regions but also from such provinces as Kerman, East Azerbaijan, and Fars.[3]

The peasants' actions were in many cases either supported by the radical Islamist groups and the newly formed Revolutionary Institutions or exploited by them for their own ends. Members of Jahad-e Sazandegi and the Revolutionary Guards were reported to have taken over some land and given it to the peasants.[4] The total area of the land which changed hands in this phase is estimated at between 800,000 and 1m hectares.[5]

8.2 Land Reform Under the Bazargan Government

From the very start, land reform under the Bazargan government was influenced by the conditions created by the actions of the peasants. The new rulers had to react to the repossessions and squats as well as to the demands for recourse by the previous owners. This reaction had to include some sort of answer to the political demands of the groups that had succeeded in bringing the peasant movement under their control *and* had to fit in with the new rulers' concepts about agrarian, social, and economic policy. Each of the factions among the Islamists who had come to power in the revolution had a different solution to the problem. The final decision would depend upon which faction was able to gain the upper hand.

Infiltrating the peasant movement, splitting it from its leftist leadership, and pacifying it was undertaken largely by extremist circles among the clerics with the assistance of the Revolutionary Guards, the Revolutionary Committees, and the other newly founded Revolutionary Institutions. The system of councils in the Turkmenic region was bloodily crushed and brought under control by February 1980. The Kurdish autonomy movement suffered a similar fate later, although this clash involved a much greater effort and higher losses. It became increasingly clear that the ruling Islamist currents were not even prepared to tolerate legal opposition, to say nothing of a non-Islamist movement demanding regional autonomy and so questioning the Islamists' monopoly of power. In order to suppress both the autonomy movement and independent peasant actions, Islamist extremists made use, where necessary, of local landlords, either turning a blind eye to the weapons they and their gangs of thugs already had or even helping to arm them.[6]

Under Bazargan, the extremist Islamists were much too concerned with suppressing the non-Islamist, leftist, and autonomist opposition to put their own concepts for land reform to the government or the Revolutionary Council. They were occasionally involved at the local level in supporting squats. Reports of their protests against the Bazargan government's attitude toward the existing structure of land ownership became more common toward the end of this phase.[7] The Revolutionary Council approved all the bills concerning the question of land ownership submitted to it at the time, although the majority of its members would later approve radical proposals on this question.[8]

The land reform envisaged by the Bazargan government, specifically by Izadi, was detailed in the Legislative Proposal on the Method of Transferring and Reclaiming Estates in the Islamic Republic of Iran,[9] approved by the Revolutionary Council on September 17, 1979. The decree's preamble stated that it was based on "the principles of the holy Islamic law, which state that the riches of nature belong to God the Almighty and that mere mortals are only entitled to use them if they perform useful work to satisfy human needs and communal self-sufficiency." Based on these principles, Article 2 of the decree stipulated that the rights of private individuals concerning cultivated estates (arazi-ye dayer) remained valid and must be respected "irrespective of whether they were acquired by reclamation, conclusion of a contract, purchase, conveyance from other individuals, transfer of state domains or private property or in consequence of the land reform." Contrary to this stipulation, which was aimed at maintaining the status quo, Note 2 to the same article empowered the government "with the permission of the ruler [hakem-e shar'] and by issuing decrees to take measures at any time to limit the amount of agricultural land a single person may possess and to determine its maximum size." So as to avoid any misunderstandings about the term "useful work" in the preamble, Article 3 emphasized that the rights to cultivated land did not necessarily have to be acquired by personal work but could equally be based on cultivation "with the help of machines, hired laborers or farmhands" or be acquired as a result of sharecropping contracts (mozare'e) and the like.

As the aim of the Bazargan government's policy was to ensure that existing agricultural land was cultivated, only its restrictions on property rights for *un*cultivated land were fairly radical. According to Article 4, "Land which is usually cultivated falls within the category of uncultivated land (arazi-ye bayer)" and would be treated as such "if it is left uncultivated for three years in succession without good reason." The owner was given five years to begin cultivating it again, after which it fell to the state for assignment to peasants in accordance with the appropriate regulations (Article 8).

This proposal made various categories of state land, other than confiscated estates, available for assignment to peasants or others (Article 7). Privately owned wasteland (arazi-ye mawat) had to be cultivated within two years; otherwise it fell to the state, which released it for assignment (Article 8.9). The land was leased at first, and the leaseholder was obliged to carry out certain projects on the plot. Ownership was only transferred if the projects were completed within the prescribed period (Articles 13–15). The rental or purchase price was paid to the state (Article 14).

The September 1979 decree outlined above corresponded to the ideas of the Bazargan government, in particular to those of the minister of agriculture, on private property, on how to achieve social justice in rural areas, and on land reform. Dr. Izadi, the minister of agriculture, was firmly convinced that the rights of legally acquired property must be inviolable, and he resisted any measures to question this maxim. He considered land reform under the shah to have been one of the reasons for the ruin of agriculture in Iran[10] and thought that honoring private property was the only way to rehabilitate it.[11] He was also of the opinion that distributing cultivated land would only lead to encroachments on individual liberty and cripple personal initiative and creativity. It was absurd, he thought, to limit private property simply to take the wind out of the left's sails; this would be like committing suicide to avoid being murdered. Moreover, there were no feudal lords in Iran, despite all the talk to the contrary. Izadi was just as adamant about refusing to acknowledge other motives for restricting private property rights,[12] which is why he resisted efforts to have a clause included in the proposal affirming such restrictions. He reacted hesitantly to pressure from the Revolutionary Council, postponing decisions as far as possible and preferring to leave them to the government that was to be formed after the opening of parliament. In an interview with the author, he stated: "I didn't want hasty decisions to be made," adding: "I didn't think restrictions [on private land ownership] would come into effect in the end because I'm convinced that Islam doesn't limit private property, unless it's illegal. . . . the limits on private property are only qualitative in nature." He went on to say that distributing cultivated land would not solve the problem of rural poverty or landlessness because there was simply not enough of it. Even if it were possible to solve the problem by redistributing land now, what could be done in the future when Iran's population would be 100 million? "For my part," he said, "I don't consider that everyone ought to own land." Anyway, the problems of landlessness and rural poverty could be better solved by reclaiming the wasteland: "We should encourage the landless to reclaim the uncultivated land, make the necessary capital and knowhow available to them and awaken a love of agriculture in them by assuring their futures."[13]

According to Dr. Izadi, Islam had better ways of ensuring justice and the livelihoods of peasants, such as the zakat (poor tax). Taking up this idea, he submitted a proposal to the Revolutionary Council to set up "Bayt ol-Mal" funds in the villages to make interest-free loans and grants available to needy villagers. The money was to be provided from a fund financed jointly by the villagers' own religious taxes and government aid.[14]

The Revolutionary Council issued a series of decrees dealing with the question of land ownership that were broadly compatible with the Bazargan government's attitude toward private property. A commission was set up on the basis of a legislative proposal passed in April 1979 and amended four months later to "negotiate and settle amicably" the disputes caused by land squats and other infringements of existing property rights.[15] According to a proposal of the Ministry of Agriculture approved in September 1979 by the Revolutionary Council, "all estates, including installations and crops, in the area irrigated by the Dez Dam are to be transferred to the Ministry of Agriculture and Rural Construction." (The reference was to estates that had been forcibly taken away from the peasants under the shah and leased long-term to Agribusinesses. The proposal annulled these leases.) Pursuant to new guidelines, the estates in question and their installations were to be assigned "on lease to Iranian citizens (individuals and corporate bodies) as plots suitable for cultivation," with preference given to those individuals "whose property or usufructuary rights to the soil of this region have been transferred to institutions of the state, or to such persons as were employed in agriculture in the region."[16]

In September 1979 the Revolutionary Council also approved a bill aimed at settling property disputes on the Gorgan Plain and in Gonbad by arbitration "in as far [as] they relate to estates appropriated by the stooges of the previous regime or by other individuals or corporate bodies, which were appropriated and taken possession of by premeditated illegal methods or by transfer to the administration of the former crown lands," irrespective of whether the appropriation had been carried out by the present occupant or a previous one who had then transferred his "rights" by sale or other lawful acts to the present occupant. In each individual case the arbitration commission was to determine the rightful owner on the basis of the proof presented. As the state claimed to be the rightful owner in many cases, property transferred to the state in this way was to be assigned to the peasants and farmers in accordance with the appropriate special directives.[17]

The Bazargan government used this proposal to try to settle legally the disputes in the Turkmenic regions of Gorgan and Gonbad mentioned in Chapter 8.1. It was one of a number of measures aimed at confiscating the property of those who had been close to the shah and/or his regime. Khomeini had already issued a more generally worded decree in this matter on March 5, 1979: "The Islamic Revolutionary Council is hereby ordered to confiscate on behalf of the needy, the workers and poor officials all the chattels and estates of the Pahlavi dynasty and its branches, stooges and members which were embezzled from the national domain of the Muslims during the reign of this unlawful dynasty."[18] A large part of the fortunes "taken back" were allocated to the Foundation for the Dispossessed, including 100,000ha of land that was gradually made available for assignment to peasants.[19]

The Bazargan government's position on land reform was revealed by the fact that it established Agricultural Councils that were to be composed of "farmers, stock-breeders and the owners of such enterprises and which are to advise the government on agricultural matters."[20] As the landowners' lobby, the councils for a time played an important part in the discussion about land reform. The left-wing groups saw them as proof of the Bazargan government's counterrevolutionary attitude.[21]

This description about the Bazargan government's approach to land reform is confirmed by the fact that the topic is not mentioned in their documents on general agricultural policy. The report to the September 1979 planning seminar speaks of the necessity for complete stability in matters of land ownership as the precondition for stimulating agricultural activity (p. 5), and the Izadi plan drafted in April/May 1979 does not deal with the problem. When listing the agricultural problems at the start of the revolution, Izadi merely criticized the shah's land reform program without putting forward any concepts for a better one.[22]

8.3 The Disputes About Radical Land Reform

The fall of the Bazargan government on November 7, 1979, ushered in a third phase in the reform of property rights. Populist Islamists took over the leadership of the state and adopted a course midway between the liberal/conservative and left-wing currents.

The assumption of power by the populist Islamists was preceded by massive pressure on the Bazargan government. Various public conflicts were staged by peasants seeking an extensive redistribution of land and, so they said, the removal of the feudal lords. The actions continued throughout the radical phase (November 7, 1979–October 12, 1980) and were accompanied by a number of pronouncements about a radical reform. A day after the fall of the Bazargan government, the same Revolutionary Council that had approved the legislative proposal of September 1979 declared that it would introduce "effective measures to resolve the land question for the peasants and to fight feudalism."[23] In some places, particularly the Turkmenic regions of Gorgan and Gonbad, the proclamation of a radical reform was accompanied by some practical steps.[24] In other places, Jahad-e Sazandegi, the Revolutionary Guards, and the Revolutionary Committees encouraged the peasants to take possession of the estates of the "feudal lords" and cultivate them themselves.[25] Some revolutionary courts made their contribution to the expropriation of land acquired "illegally" by "feudal lords."[26] Protests by peasants and students completed the picture.[27]

The struggle in the administration for a radical reform was led by Reza Esfahani, the secretary of state at the Ministry of Agriculture responsible for land reform. He announced the implementation of "a fundamental land reform" in which the land was to belong to those who tilled it.[28] In a number of interviews he informed the public about the details of his plan,[29] which had already been submitted to the Revolutionary Council by about the end of 1979[30] and was approved by it on February 27, 1980.

According to the plan, all uncultivated land in private hands was to be transferred to the state immediately; it was considered uncultivated if it had not been worked for three successive years without reasonable cause. Large cultivated estates were subject to different regulations, depending on whether the owners worked in agriculture. Those who did were to be left a plot of land equivalent to the "customary local smallholdings"; those who did not were to be given the choice between taking another plot of land somewhere else or accepting as payment the prevailing rental (ojrat olmesl), provided they had no debts. A plot of cultivated land was defined as large if it was three times as big as "local custom" ('orf-e mahal) considered necessary to support a farmer and his family. Cultivated land could be confiscated entirely if justified by the "interests of society," and the government could assign the owners uncultivated land suitable for reclamation "if this is in harmony with the public good." However, cultivable state lands and confiscated estates were to be preferentially assigned to peasants. Other than in exceptional circumstances, these assigned estates were to be operated as companies, cooperatives, or collectives with joint land rights (mosha'). Title was only to be transferred if certain conditions were met: The land should not lie fallow, the choice of crop must meet the needs of society, the peasants were to observe both the boundaries of the leased land and the layout of the fields and were not to acquire land other than that assigned to them as a result of the proposed legislation. The proposal also set up the Sevener Commissions, whose main task was to handle the assignment procedures.[31]

Esfahani's proposal encountered massive resistance from those who opposed any reform aiming to restrict existing "legitimate" land rights. This opposition is probably why the proposal was not made public despite having been approved. Khomeini's reaction was to have a panel of three jurists examine whether the proposal accorded with Islamic law.[32] He chose Ayatollahs Beheshti, Montazeri, and Meshgini, who were among the leaders of the regime. They submitted a slightly modified proposal to the Revolutionary Council, which was approved on March 2, 1980.[33] The modifications concerned the definition of uncultivated land: It now had to lie fallow five years instead of three to qualify. The owners of such land could keep that part of it on which they had made installations required for the land itself. The installations had to be sold to the state if they were used for agricultural purposes. Owners of cultivated estates retained an area equivalent to three times the local custom.[34]

Neither the three ayatollahs' approval of Esfahani's proposal nor its watering down appeased its opponents. Further modifications became necessary. Within less than one and a half months, the same Revolutionary Council approved two other bills, whose main difference was that they dropped the demands in the February 27, 1980, bill by degrees. It attempted to save as much of the earlier bill as possible by appealing to arguments in Islamic law.

Finally, a bill was approved on April 15, 1980, that provided for the owner of cultivated land to retain a plot equivalent to twice the customary size even if he was not a farmer. The remainder was assigned to local landless peasants who "cannot acquire title to land by any other means" (Article 4). The same applied to the owners of uncultivated land provided they began to cultivate their fields; otherwise it came under state control for allocation (Article 2). Land used for animal husbandry was an exception—it could be retained by its owners (Article 4).[35]

But even these concessions were not enough to silence the proposal's opponents—they simply showed the tremendous pressure being exerted on Khomeini and the Revolutionary Council. The resistance took many forms: discussion in the press with the proponents of a radical reform; masses of protest telegrams, letters, and resolutions to Khomeini, the Revolutionary Council, or Ayatollah Montazeri;[36] and a number of demonstrations, sometimes violent (several members of the Sevener Commissions were killed). Large and medium landowners were the mainstays of the resistance. They organized themselves into Agricultural Councils, which had been reinstated by the Bazargan government.[37] They got effective support from the conservative clerics, among them such grand ayatollahs as Golpaygani, Qomi, and Rohani, who in their fatwas and other pronouncements declared restrictions on legitimate land ownership to be illegal and even communist.[38] The opponents of the land reform even succeeded in obtaining a fatwa from Khomeini; though worded in general terms, it strengthened their position. Because of the grand ayatollahs' negative attitude, in many cases no clerics offered their services to the Sevener Commissions, declining to legitimize the commissions' decisions concerning matters of Islamic law.[39]

The resistance of the reform's opponents was finally successful and in October 1980 Khomeini ordered that implementation of the law with respect to cultivated land be discontinued. The order was released to the press in a communiqué by Ayatollah Rabbani Shirazi, a member of the Council of Guardians and himself an opponent of the reform.[40] He explained that the measure, which was initially considered temporary, was aimed at reducing tension in the agricultural sector but added that the war and counterrevolutionary activities in the country were other reasons. He also mentioned the decrease in production and was confirmed in this by Ayatollah Meshgini.[41] Ayatollahs Jennati and Hojjat ol-Eslam Rafsanjani put the suspension down to improper implementation of the legislation,[42] an allusion to excesses supposedly committed by overzealous members of the Sevener Commissions. Ayatollah Beheshti even went so far as to say that Khomeini had not approved of some details of the legislation from the start.[43] Such declarations served to play down the real reason for Khomeini's decision, although it is obvious that the reasons given were not unimportant. A report in *Barzegar* claimed that shortly before Khomeini issued his order, Ayatollahs Montazeri and Meshgini had advised him to continue implementing the reform (November 8, 1980). Hojjat ol-Eslam Fazel Harandi was the most skillful in covering up the real reason—he stated that the partial suspension of implementation was based on the same tenets of Islamic law that had led to its being approved in the first place.[44]

The advocates of radical reform had taken the opportunity, prior to the October 1980 order, to implement the controversial legislation as far as possible. The regulations relating to the April 1980 bill were drafted with unusual speed (by May 21, 1980) and approved by the Revolutionary Council.[45] Within weeks some thirty-five Sevener Commissions had already been set up and had begun preparing to assign land to the peasants. By the time Khomeini ordered the reform suspended, they had succeeded in assigning 150,000ha of wasteland and 35,000ha of cultivated, uncultivated, and confiscated land to the peasants.[46] They undertook the supervision of over 800,000ha of land squatted by peasants, although the relevant legal ruling only came into effect in October 1986, and they managed to create the conditions for later allocations in 20,112 villages and to set up 18,556 Village Councils, with whose help they hoped to be able to press ahead with distributing plots.[47] The commissions also established about 4,300 mosha' enterprises, which were to be the actual recipients of the land.[48]

The Sevener Commissions were occasionally overzealous and exceeded their purview, which gave the opponents of the reform grounds for complaint. They reportedly started work by allocating cultivated land,[49] even though the law only provided for recourse to such measures if there was insufficient uncultivated land or if the wasteland was unsuitable for allocation. When offsetting the owners' religious debts against the price of the land taken from them, they set the debts so high that the former owners were left empty-handed.[50] In addition, they were said to have arbitrarily determined the size of plot needed to support a farmer and his family.[51]

A series of legislative proposals dealing more or less directly with the question of land ownership were approved in this phase by the Revolutionary Council and parliament. The measures included annulling ownership of wasteland within Tehran city limits;[52] solving the problems caused by winding up the Farm Corporations (see Chapter 10); reorganizing the enterprises slated to be put under state administration;[53] and a series of decisions benefiting the peasants who had been affected by the shah's land reform.[54] Some regulations were put into operation to subdue the unrest in rural areas, to prevent trespassing, and to punish offenders.[55] A decree designated such offenses counterrevolutionary and put punishment in the hands of the revolutionary courts.[56] It also provided for nonlocals who committed crimes in groups of two or more—i.e., were actively propagating their own ideas of reform—to be punished.[57]

The punishment of nonlocal leftist propagandists—a permanent feature of the ruling Islamists' policies—throws some light on one of the motives for the populist Islamists' radical approach. Dr. Izadi's explanation for that approach (in his letter to the Revolutionary Council, noted above) was later confirmed by the radicals themselves in a Survey of Feudalism and the Efforts of the Sevener Commissions (subtitled "Political and Economic Results of the Sevener Commissions' Activities"). There, suppressing the influence that "American stooges"—i.e., the non-Soviet left—had attempted to gain was given pride of place. Not only did the populist Islamists force the left out of the rural areas, they also gained support for their apparently radical policies from some leftist groups.[58]

Ousting the left from the rural areas, and thus from politics in general, was not, of course, the only reason the Islamists supported a radical land reform. The populists were convinced (contrary to Dr. Izadi, his staff, many experts, and the landowners) that putting Iran on its own feet agriculturally depended on implementing land reform as they envisaged it. This argument seemed all the more convincing as production was actually falling, although this decline must be put down to the squats, postrevolutionary social and political unrest, the lack of legal regulations for land ownership, and other peripheral factors. It would be possible to quote any number of declarations made between the revolution and October 1980 in which members of the extreme wing of the ruling Islamists linked land reform with self-sufficiency. Statements to the contrary from this camp only came later, e.g., when Hojjat ol-Eslam Kho'iniha denied any such link in April 1986.[59]

It can be assumed that many radical Islamists' support for land redistribution benefiting peasants with little or no land was based on their concept of justice. Some were aware that land redistribution could not solve the problems of landlessness and rural poverty, including Minister of Agriculture Salamati (although he was nevertheless an ardent supporter of it).[60] These problems could not even be solved by a much more radical limit on land ownership, say of 10ha per inhabitant. According to calculations by M. R. Hosseini Kazeruni (1982, p. 18), setting the upper limit at 50ha, which would be more realistic, would leave 2,136,450ha to be divided among 1.7m needy peasants. The average-sized plot would thus be well below the minimum needed to support a farmer. According to calculations by A. Ashraf (1982, p. 44f), if the minimum set is based on the April 1980 law, only 1m hectares would be available for redistribution. But the proposals backed by the radicals nevertheless stipulated that every needy peasant was to be given a plot of the "customary size" so as to ensure his and his family's livelihood. This feat could only be achieved by releasing the wasteland. It will be shown below that this undertaking also encountered great difficulties.

8.4 The Struggle over Land Reform in Parliament

The fourth phase of the struggle for Islamic land reform lasted until January 18, 1983, when the Council of Guardians rejected a bill that parliament had already passed. This phase was conducted mainly in Islamic parliament, which first met on May 27, 1980.

The dispute kept resurfacing and was argued on religious and socioeconomic grounds both in the committees and on the floor of the house. The external pressure for a more extensive reform came mainly from the Sevener Commissions, which received broad support in the now state-controlled press.[61] Its opponents were increasingly organized in the Agricultural Councils, from where they tried—with the vigorous support of conservative clerics—to influence legislative procedures. They all felt vindicated by Khomeini's October 1980 order.[62] The war that had broken out between Iran and Iraq contributed to a lessening of the violent conflicts over land reform, as did the leadership's readiness to suppress such acts and not to provoke them itself. After October 1980, the Sevener Commissions were only allowed to allocate state-owned wasteland or confiscated estates that had previously been given to the Foundation of the Dispossessed. Hence, even less land was available for redistribution, certainly not enough to satisfy the peasants' need for cultivable land, which the local commissions had been able to assess. In particular, those peasants who had occupied land in the spontaneous action phase pressed for the legalization of their squats. The need to solve the problems caused by these squats became the driving force behind the untiring efforts for land reform; and that need was reinforced by the fact that the government was in the process of drafting its first development plan, for which a solution to the property question was considered a necessary prerequisite.[63]

An attempt was made in parliament and the agricultural committee to find a compromise between the various drafts of the reform. In autumn 1981 the government presented a draft that only differed slightly from the April 15, 1980, legislative proposal.[64] At almost the same time, the committee received a legislative initiative from sixteen conservative-legalist members of parliament in which restrictions on the private ownership of land could only apply to property acquired illegally within the meaning of Article 49 of the constitution (i.e., through usury, fraud, theft, etc.) or with funds that should have been used to pay religious taxes.[65] Their draft provided for the state to administer uncultivated land if it was shown that the owner(s) had not made use of the property rights.[66] The draft envisaged the government helping peasants with little or no land by allocating them state wastelands, pastures, and legally confiscated land.[67] Twenty-five other members of parliament submitted a different proposal to the committee (I have been unable to obtain a copy of it to date).[68]

The compromise worked out by the agricultural committee on the basis of these drafts was presented to parliament and passed at its first reading on March 2, 1982,[69] but it failed to satisfy either the opponents or the proponents of radical reform. Discussions continued both in and out of parliament without effecting any significant modifications. The draft presented for second reading contained watered-down regulations (by comparison to the proposal of April 15, 1980), which were defused even further in the debate in parliament.

As in the proposal of April 15, 1980, state and abandoned wasteland as well as confiscated and nationalized estates represented the bulk of the land available for redistribution (Article 4). Owners of uncultivated land were given one year to begin cultivating a plot equivalent to "three times the customary size"—failing which, this plot would also be made available to the state for allocation to peasants. They were to get a fair price for it, to be paid out after deduction of "lawful debts" (Article 5). The period of grace could be extended if reasonable cause was shown for noncompliance (Article 5, Note 2). Parliament added a further note obliging the government to provide such landowners with financial and technical aid to cultivate their land (Note 3).

As in the April 1980 bill, the owners of cultivated land were allowed to keep a plot of land two or three times the customary size, depending on whether they worked in agriculture or not. However, the definition of "agricultural activity" was widened to include "direct and effective management," and it was emphasized during the debate that the owner could assign the task to someone else. An owner who did not work in agriculture was permitted to retain a plot twice the customary size if he had no other source of income (Article 6), but this provision was later deleted. The owners were to receive a fair price for their land after deduction of debts (Article 6).

The notes to Article 6 toned the reform down even more. Note 4 read: "Owners whose total agricultural estates amount to less than four times the customary size do not come within the scope of this law" if they work in agriculture either directly or as direct and effective managers. This clause was deleted during the debate, as was a note providing for the estates of private foundations to be reallocated. Market gardens, nurseries, and fully mechanized enterprises continued to be exempt. The clause limiting the exemption for market gardens and nurseries to those planted before the approval of the April 1980 proposal was deleted, as was a clause exempting fully mechanized enterprises and agribusinesses if dividing them up was contrary to "the interests of society." Should the owners and peasants agree on a sharecropping or lease contract, the cultivated estates were exempt from reallocation (Note 1). Each partner in a company was to receive the minimum, provided that none of them was liable to maintain the others (Note 6). Article 10, Note 2 weakened the reform still further by stating that the owners' descendants should be given preference during reallocation if they met the relevant criteria (i.e., neediness, etc.).

The proposal said land reform was needed because it could contribute to making Iran self-sufficient, wiping out poverty, and curbing the rural exodus (Article 2). These same reasons were put forward during the debate, when it was also claimed that the bill aimed to distribute property equitably and make the peasants landowners in order to escape the pressure from the squatters. It was also necessary to free the land from the grip of "traitors" and "opponents of the revolution," as well as from those who had acquired it illegally.[70] The advocates of this line were thus against any exemptions and any other restrictions on distributing land, as envisaged by the parliamentary committee's proposal. They prevailed with respect to Article 15, which made it possible to challenge the legality of any claim in court.[71] This provision did not make much sense because the proposal presumed, as the committee spokesman emphasized, that all landed property with which it was concerned had been acquired legally and that illegally acquired land ought to be regulated under another law.[72]

The reform's opponents countered that land distribution, "as is well known," lowers the hectare yield, reduces total production, and thus is detrimental to the aim of self-sufficiency.[73] Neither would it in any way prevent the rural exodus, as the peasants were leaving their villages not because of land scarcity but because of the lack of social amenities and other welfare benefits. For this reason, preference should be given to reclaiming wasteland, not to distributing cultivated estates. To achieve self-sufficiency, it would be more sensible to make state wastelands available to those with capital so that they could reclaim it.[74]

During the debate, the reform's opponents exploited the Sevener Commissions' excesses in reallocating land, insisting that the proposal should forbid such acts. This argument led a clause to be added to Article 10 emphasizing that both cultivated and uncultivated land was only to be reallocated if there was no state wasteland available in the locality. Offending Sevener Commissions were to be prosecuted.

The reform's opponents demonstrated an almost allergic reaction to any form of state intervention in agricultural affairs. This attitude became very clear during the debate on Article 11, which sought to impose a series of conditions on peasants who were assigned land: They were not allowed to decide which crops to plant—these had to meet the "requirements of society"; the reallocated land was not to be transferred, sold, or used for purposes other than agriculture; cultivation must correspond to local custom; as in the April 15, 1980, bill, land was to be allocated to collectives rather than to individual peasants (Note 1); personal facilities were not to be erected on this land (Note 4); and the heirs of a person who had been allocated land were only entitled to it if they cultivated it or would agree to cultivate it, failing which it would be allocated to someone else (Note 5). The reform's opponents were up in arms against this clause, and they succeeded in deleting Notes 1, 4, and 5.[75] The reform's advocates tried to counter them with the argument that Islamic justice could not be guaranteed without these conditions;[76] they were intended, so the opponents of the reform claimed, to create in the Islamic Republic conditions comparable to those in a Soviet *kolkhoz* or *solkhoz*.[77]

Both sides tried to consolidate their positions during the debate in parliament and the accompanying discussions in the press with arguments from Islamic law (these will be dealt with in Chapter 9). It was mainly these arguments that the Council of Guardians cited when, on January 18, 1983, it announced its rejection of the bill on the grounds that it contravened both the sharia and the constitution of the Islamic Republic.[78] This decision put land reform back by years.

8.5 Reducing Land Reform to the Unavoidable

The fifth phase of the land reform quest, lasting to October 1986, was characterized by many government functionaries as a period in which the legal vacuum concerning landed property prevented any measures for improving agriculture or curbing the rural exodus.[79] Although there was a legal vacuum in other sociopolitical areas as well, it is significant that whenever the subject was raised, agriculture was always the example cited. For all that, there was no legislative movement on the issue in the two years after the rejection of the proposal in January 1983. Everything seems to indicate that the Islamic Republic's legislators were deadlocked and would have preferred to overcome it behind closed doors. Their endeavors surfaced as polemical attacks on each other in public.

The Council of Guardians was the target of the criticism by the reform's advocates in this phase. Speaker Rafsanjani led the most violent attack, accusing it of having exceeded its authority.[80] Even if this particular accusation does not seem justified, the Council of Guardians had shown itself to be a power that, from the position of the dominant Islamic legal tradition, was thwarting many of parliament's decisions, not only on property ownership but also on all the other vital questions of social and economic policy. It was thus blocking policies agreeable to the government or the majority in parliament. But at the same time it was, as an institution, too firmly anchored in the concept of welayat-e faqih (governorship by jurists) not to be shielded at the highest level from growing criticism. Khomeini was obliged to come to its defense several times. On January 24, 1983, he told the members of parliament that their decisions must be worded so that the Council of Guardians need not reject them.[81] A year later he warned the

Council's opponents that insulting and weakening the Council was endangering the country and Islam.[82] He did, however, consider it necessary to urge the Council of Guardians in the interests of Islam not to lose sight of the possibility of permitting urgent reforms on the basis of the so-called secondary decrees (ahkam-e sanawiye).[83] He was referring to the Muslims' right, laid down in the Quran, to ignore the precepts known as the primary decrees (ahakm-e awwaliye) in emergency situations. It is possible for the Imam to issue secondary decrees within the realm of constitutional law according to the requirements of Islamic rule.

The focus of debate about land reform shifted from parliament to the press. The dailies, which were largely controlled by advocates of reform, reported the course of events with a clear bias, mirroring both the pressure being exerted by leading functionaries of the Islamic state to speed up a decision in the matter and the numerous complaints about the lack of appropriate measures and its devastating effect on agricultural production. The press constituted a forum to put forward the social, economic, and Islamic legal arguments for land reform—opponents of reform went largely unheard.[84] The debate about the permissibility of making the principle of necessity the basis for land reform, which was already very heated in the third phase, continued unabated.

The Sevener Commissions continued to try to exert pressure on the opponents of reform with all the means at their disposal. They threatened to refuse to accept responsibility for about 800,000 ha of squatted land they were charged with supervising, while the transfer of peasant squatting into property was the cause of continual disagreement.[85] Such a refusal would have given rise to the danger of serious unrest among the peasants, and the commissions finally rescinded their threat on the urging of the reform's proponents.[86] The commissions published details of their work more than once, reporting on July 14, 1984, transfers as follows:

Table 8.1 Land Transfers by Sevener Commissions, to July 14, 1984 (in hectares)

Cultivated land	154,224
Uncultivated land	6,236
Confiscated land	28,470
Wasteland	381,845
Land for nonagricultural purposes	120,922
Total	691,697

Source: Sevener Commissions.

The area of land squatted is reported as 791,922ha.[87] Comparison with the figures they published in February 1981 makes the extent of the progress in transferring cultivated land clear, although it is unclear whether the progress was the result of having transferred confiscated, squatted, or state estates or whether it was the result of ignoring Khomeini's October 1980 order.

It began to look like a compromise had finally been reached in the spring of 1985. Parliament sat on May 14–15 and June 2, 1985, to debate a proposal that had reputedly been worked out through the mediation of Ayatollah Yazdi after discussions with Ayatollah Montazeri in a special parliamentary commission whose meetings were also attended by members of the Council of Guardians. It was also said that this proposal was essentially the legislative proposal of December 1982 with revision in "all" the points objected to by the Council of Guardians.[88]

The proposal contained no restrictions on landed property with respect to uncultivated land provided that within one year it was cultivated by the owner himself or by a tenant or sharecropper. Failing this, it would be sold at a "fair price" by a commission specially set up for the purpose, the proceeds going to the owner. The requirement to till the land was all-important here; property rights were not called into question (Article 5).

Article 6 regulated the property rights for land occupied before March 20, 1980 (March 20, 1985, in Kurdistan). If the squatters were local peasants with little or no land and no other means of ensuring their livelihood, property rights were transferred to them, and the owner was paid a "fair price" after deduction of his legal and religious debts. If the squatters did not meet these conditions, the land was returned to the owner, who was then dealt with in accordance with Article 5. If it was shown that the owner himself worked in agriculture and had no other means of ensuring his livelihood, then his land would be returned to him in full or in part.

Those squatted estates administered by the Revolutionary Institutions[89] were to be dealt with as follows. If the title to the property was in dispute, the owners had to ensure that a court of competent jurisdiction validated the legitimacy of their claim. If, however, the title was not in dispute, the land was handed over to the owners if they were in the country, and a decision about cultivation was taken in accordance with Article 5. Article 5 also applied to those owners who were abroad but whose claim to the property was undisputed, provided their land had not already been reallocated. Disputed title deeds were to remain under the administration of the Revolutionary Institutions until the courts decided about them.

Unoccupied cultivated land remained unaffected by this compromise proposal (Article 7). According to the Council of Guardians' reasoning, as long as wasteland and state and confiscated land had not been reallocated, it was impossible to ascertain whether the transfer of cultivated and uncultivated land was so necessary that the sanctity of property would have to be violated. Parliament had to bow to this argument.

These and a few less significant amendments to the December 1982 bill rejected by the Council of Guardians were approved by parliament, Articles 5 and 6 by a two-thirds majority, which meant, pursuant to a decree issued by Khomeini on August 6, 1984, that they could no longer be rejected by the Council of Guardians. According to this decree, any resolution that invoked the principle of necessity and was passed by parliament with a two-thirds majority no longer required the approval of the Council of Guardians. But even this watered-down proposal failed to become law because the Council of Guardians defeated it, pointing out eight discrepancies between it and the sharia in its June 2, 1985, notification of rejection. But the decisive reason for its rejection was a procedural point: The proposal ought not to have been dealt with as an amended version of the December 1982 bill but as a new legislative initiative, which had to run the full gamut of parliamentary procedures and so could only be passed at its second reading.[90]

The matter nevertheless remains puzzling, because at the start of the debate on the proposal the spokesman of the parliamentary committee had reported that the Council of Guardians had agreed to it. The public was not informed of the rejection. It can be inferred from various indicators that battle was joined behind the scenes to satisfy the Council of Guardians. The spokesmen for the opposing sides tried to blame either parliament or the Council of Guardians for the delay. Speaker Rafsanjani urged the Council of Guardians not to put off amending the rejected bill;[91] a member of parliament said the Council had already handed its proposals to parliament and that they had disappeared under a pile of papers there, along with other important bills.[92] Both bodies were requested to bring about a decision as quickly as possible. Khomeini was increasingly petitioned to take on the task himself, one parliamentarian stating that it was necessary to turn to him in view of the disunity prevailing among the Islamic jurists over such vital questions.[93] A letter with the same demand was written to Khomeini during a seminar held by the Ministry of the Interior,[94] the representatives of the "exemplary Islamic Village Councils" expressing similar views at a rally in Tehran two months later.[95] But the public was left in the dark about his response, if any, to these undoubtedly not quite spontaneous calls.

The impossibility of pushing through a comprehensive land reform and the fact that the fate of the squatted land could no longer be left in the balance finally forced the leaders of the Islamic state to agree to legitimize the squats. In view of the fact that most of this land had been in the squatters' hands since 1979 and that handing it back to the original owners might cause unrest, a proposal was submitted to parliament providing for the transfer of "all cultivated and uncultivated land which in whatsoever form came into the possession of persons other than the owner after the victory of the Islamic revolution but prior to March, 20, 1985, in Kurdistan or March 20, 1980, in the other parts of the country." The transfer was to be completed if the squatters were local peasants with little or no land and having no other visible means of support and if they paid the owner a fair price for the land given to them, with payment to be made in installments. The owner received this fair price after deduction of legal and religious debts.

The bill was passed by a two-thirds majority on October 30, 1986, but only after having been watered down even further. Note 2 of the proposed legislation, which was submitted as a single article, excluded land belonging to owners who had concluded sharecropping or lease contracts with squatters or had reached another form of agreement that did not contravene the sharia. Note 5 provided for rightful owners with no other source of income to recover a plot three times the customary size. The squatter who had to give back land was to receive, if possible, another plot appropriate to his needs (Note 6).

The bill was based on the principle of necessity and thus was only valid for three years, meaning that the transfer of the squatted land had to be completed within this period.[96] The reason for the rejection of the May 1985 bill was made public for the first time during the debate on this proposal. The Council of Guardians' proposed solution to the problem also became known—i.e., the October 1986 bill dealing only with squatted land.[97]

Detailed reasons for transferring the squatted estates were given during the debate on this bill and the May 1985 bill. The reasons were mainly of a political nature but were backed up by Islamic law; basically, they argued that returning this land to its owners would cause a disruption of the political order and place the regime in an awkward and distressing position.[98] Such a decision would permit the counterrevolution in Kurdistan to claim that the Islamic Republic was on the side of the feudal lords. The transfer of the squatted land was therefore unavoidable if the counterrevolutionary arguments were to be defused.[99] It was also important not to offend the numerous peasants involved in the war against Iraq and on whom the continuation of the war was so dependent: They might turn their backs on the front. The Imam, the president, the speaker, and the prime minister had for the past seven or eight years promised 120,000 peasants that the squatted land would be transferred to them. What would happen if the peasants were suddenly to be given "a pill of despair" instead of "this painful pill of promises"; what would be the consequences for the war?[100] In order to emphasize the urgency and indispensability of transferring the squatted land, a member of parliament listed how many times this promise had been referred to between March 1980 and September 1986: by Khomeini, 7; Montazeri, 6; prime ministers, 35; ministers of agriculture, 65; members of parliament, 335; and others in positions of responsibility in the Islamic Republic, 45.[101]

Reducing land reform to transferring only the squatted land caused a great deal of resentment among those favoring more comprehensive, radical steps. One member of parliament expressed his feelings in the following words: "In this country peasants and farmers deprived of their rights find no succor; here feudal lords are defended, with a loud voice they are spoken up for."[102]

The conflicts about the redistribution of land were not entirely on the verbal level. There were mass actions and occasional press reports of violence between owners and peasants,[103] though many fewer than in the past. *Kayhan* reported a peasant demonstration on December 18, 1985, and the Mazanderaner peasants' demonstration on January 9, 1986. On November 8, 1985, Hojjat ol-Eslam Kho'iniha, in his capacity as attorney general, ordered the sequestration of 8,000ha of land on the Caspian Sea that under the shah, it was alleged, had been unlawfully transferred to members of the regime.[104] The same month, at the urging of the peasants, a judge in the province of Kerman overturned a previous ruling in which 7,000 lease contracts relating to land owned by private foundations had been declared void.[105] Reports of sequestrations and confiscations were much less common than ones about returning such estates, with or without legal effect. There were thirty-nine such reports in *Kayhan* alone from 1363 to 1365 March 21, 1984–March 20, 1987), being particularly frequent in 1364 (1985/6). Acts of sequestration and confiscation were also more common that year, and the reports about them were often accompanied by complaints about the return of the "feudal lords," decisions made by courts in their favor, and the maltreatment of peasants.[106]

8.6 The Transfer of Squatted Land Since November 1986

The area of land squatted is usually given as 700,000 to 800,000ha[107] dotted throughout fourteen provinces. Topping the list are Gorgan and Mazanderan (130,000ha), followed by Kurdistan (120,000), Hamedan (85,000), Fars and Bushehr (82,000), and Zanjan (82,000). Last on the list is Hormozgan (3,000).[108] The land originally belonged to 5,600 owners, not all of whose estates could be termed large; they included farmers with 2–10ha whose land was obviously quite arbitrarily occupied.[109] Of the owners, 78 percent live in towns, 8.8 percent live in the country, 1.8 percent commute to and fro, 8 percent are expatriates, and it is unknown where the remaining 5 percent live.[110] The number of squatters is given as 120,000,[111] although the chairman of the Central Office for the Transfer of Land cited 90,000.[112] This discrepancy is probably due to peasants who returned land they had squatted. It is assumed that 125,000ha still have to be handed back.[113] In 1985 about 40,000ha were in the hands of Revolutionary Institutions.

Most of the squats occurred, as mentioned above, in the first few months after February 1979, but the law covers those that took place before March 20, 1985, in Kurdistan or March 20, 1980, in the rest of the country. The later date for Kurdistan is due to the fact that government troops only gradually succeeded in bringing the areas controlled by KUMELE and the Democratic Party of Kurdistan under their control after 1982. A parliamentary report in May 1985 stated that "even today a (small) part of Kurdistan is under the heel of the enemies of the people."[114] In many places, these "enemies of the people" had given land to the peasants, and the central government could scarcely permit the land to be taken away from the peasants again.[115] The situation was much the same in the Turkmenic areas of Gorgan and Gonbad or even Khuzestan. A state that considered itself to be revolutionary or the state of the dispossessed could scarcely reverse the occupations initiated on behalf of the downtrodden.[116]

The administration of these estates presented the government with great difficulties. On the one hand, the owners were trying to get their land back with the help of the courts, in particular after 1982/3;[117] on the other, the peasants were exerting pressure on the government to counter these attempts. The protracted battles to determine their legal status often prevented these parcels from being cultivated. The government found a way out of the dilemma in a decision by the Supreme Council of Justice in 1980 that allowed the peasants to till the land without permitting them to call it their own. Khomeini supposedly confirmed this decision in writing, extending it each year.[118] This ruling is why the official term for the squatted land is "estates of temporary cultivation."

The October 1986 law provided the clarity required in this respect, and the Sevener Commissions had a free hand to begin the definitive transfer of land that had previously been made available to the peasants on a temporary basis. First the obligatory administrative regulations were drafted, receiving the approval of the Council of Ministers on February 18, 1987.[119] They contained a number of regulations that supplemented the law. Nurseries with a certain number of commercial or fruit trees were to be excluded from the transfers—i.e., returned to their owners (Article 1). The peasants had to pay a fair price for the land they had received and for the water they had used in twelve annual installments (Article 7) and also had to pay for the plant, tools, and machines they had used since squatting (Article 8, Note 1). The fair price was to be based on the market value (including state tariffs) on the date of transfer and take into account details supplied by local experts on soil quality, but it was not to include appreciation due to improvement work undertaken by the squatters (Article 8, Note 4). Article 9 mandated that only the owner's legal debts were to be deducted from the sale price. Transfer was to be formalized by a conditional contract of sale, which meant the government imposed certain conditions on the peasant, such as not using the land for nonagricultural purposes or parceling it up. Failure to comply with these conditions rendered the contract void. Cultivation had to comply with the cultivation plans and technical guidelines of the Ministry of Agriculture (Article 10). Article 13 obliged the Revolutionary Institutions to transfer the estates they held to the Sevener Commissions within two months for reallocation to peasants, primarily those forced to return their land pursuant to Article 5 of the law (Article 14). Article 23 stipulated that the transfers of cultivated and uncultivated land effected prior to Khomeini's October 1980 decree remained valid. Estates donated to foundations by their owners prior to being squatted were not covered by the October 1986 law (Article 24). Approval of the regulations was followed by a series of other measures to prepare the actual transfers, due to begin on December 27, 1986, or a few months later.[120]

In practice the transfer work encountered a series of obstacles, which the central and local leaders of the Sevener Commissions complained about in a number of interviews and lectures. These obstacles ranged from a lack of staff to inadequate funds to successfully cultivate the land, but the main problem was the reluctance of the ministries and other agencies to cooperate. The Ministry of Justice and the courts in particular were accused not only of making the transfer work more difficult by delaying registration procedures but also of returning to their owners, by court order, the estates earmarked for transfer. To all appearances, a decision by the attorney general on May 27, 1987, forbidding the courts to hand down similar judgments (*Resalat*) was ignored, because even after this date such cases occurred.[121] Some courts even revoked transfers effected by the Sevener Commissions.[122] This attitude on the part of the Ministry of Justice and the courts provoked Hojjat ol-Eslam Afzali (representative of the Imam to the commissions in the Gorgan, Gonbad, and Sari areas) to call the ministry a "stagnating factor in the order of the Islamic Republic," an organization that had shown itself unable to become "the bearer of Khomeini's fundamental concept." One of the Sevener Commissions' leaders pointed out the reason for the judiciary's behavior: "Some of the judges are themselves landowners and that is the reason this ministry is causing difficulties even about the transfer of wasteland."[123]

Another reason given for the delays was that because all members of the Sevener Commissions had a vote, decisions could only be made after lengthy consultations. This might sound somewhat strange, but it is in fact directly linked to the legalist Islamists' understanding of the way decisions ought to be made—i.e., by individuals, not councils (shoura). This attitude became very clear during the discussion about revising the constitution of the Islamic Republic in 1989, causing the passages covering decisionmaking based on shouras to be altered accordingly (see Chapter 11).[124]

The delays confirmed what had been assumed from the start—namely, that three years (which represents the time limit on the principle of necessity and thus applied for this law) would not suffice. The Council to Determine the Interests of the (State) Order, or Determination Council, had been set up in the meantime and was authorized to enact legislation over the heads of both parliament and the Council of Guardians. It solved the problem by extending the period by two years, until the end of September 1988.[125]

The Determination Council solved another problem that had arisen in connection with the transfers by approving, on March 21, 1989, the following additional comments to the October 1986 law: "In the event that a plot of land which was occupied jointly by several persons and is being tilled jointly by them is to be divided, it is to be divided into equal lots, if no other relevant, specific criterion applies" (Note 10). "The price of the squatted land is determined on the basis of the market value at the time of implementation of the law" (Note 11). "So that large areas [in excess of 100ha] . . . are not parceled [as a result of the transfer], the occupiers are obliged, although retaining their property rights, to cultivate their land cooperatively, i.e., as a mosha'" (Note 12). Note 13 dealt with extending the period, as mentioned above. The rider included two additions to the administrative regulations aimed at preventing the registration bottlenecks that were blocking the transfers.[126]

The insistence on cooperative forms of management for the land was the most conspicuous of the changes made. The obligation to form such cooperatives contained in the December 1982 bill had been declared contrary to the sharia, but the Sevener Commissions nevertheless continued working on setting up the mosha' cooperatives (see Chapter 10.3.2). The legalization of these measures was thus retroactive, even if it only applied to mosha's set up on large squatted estates.

The effects of the obstacles to the commissions' work become very clear when one looks at the results of the transfer work to date: Preparations for transfer had only progressed to the point of issuing final title deeds for 270,000ha by the eleventh anniversary of the revolution in February 1990.[127] Things apparently speeded up that year: It was reported that deeds for 450,000ha had been drawn up and handed over by December 1990. According to Harandi, another 400,000ha were to be allocated by the end of 1370 (March 20, 1992).[128]

Legalizing the squats in the October 1986 law reduced the land reform originally sought by the radical Islamists to a rump legitimized only by the fact that rejecting it would have endangered the Islamic state order. Prime Minister Musawi was nevertheless unable to resist the temptation to call it a "revolutionary law which will play a large part in solving the land question. . . . It will destroy the feudal order throughout the country at a blow and pave the way for growth, grandeur, and freedom to replace the landlords' oppression."[129]

8.7 Other Decisions and Additions to Land Reform

The October 1986 law closed the chapter on land reform in the Islamic Republic, the minister of agriculture announcing somewhat later that "from now on no more difficulties of any sort will arise for land ownership." He was all the more emphatic so as to assure landowners that they could now "invest in their own land" without fear.[130] In addition, various authoritative sources proclaimed the government's readiness to make land available to investors for setting up agricultural enterprises. The influential Hojjat ol-Eslam Harandi instructed the Sevener Commissions to make available to people who declared that they were ready to invest in agriculture as much (waste) land as they could cultivate. He specifically mentioned the fact that Ayatollah Montazeri had agreed to this procedure and pointed out at the same time that the concept of "local customary size"—long the criterion for setting the permissible size of plots—had been dropped.[131]

The decision to transfer land to investors had originally been made under the Bazargan government: The first land reform bill (September 1979) provided for transfer to applicants who were prepared to invest in agriculture (Article 10), and the appropriate steps actually were taken at the time. A specific limit for the size of such transfers was not stipulated then, but the administrative regulations—only approved by the Revolutionary Council after Bazargan's fall—established different limits, ranging from 10 to 150ha for various regions of the country.[132]

The legislative proposals approved after Bazargan's fall also provided for transferring land to such applicants, but the amount was determined by the "local customary size." This limit was first exceeded in the regulations appending the April 15, 1980, bill: Article 31 stipulated that "for the purpose of providing assistance to establish and expand installations for animal husbandry, poultry and fish breeding, and the associated enterprises, the Ministry of Agriculture and Rural Construction is entitled to screen the projects of resident individuals and corporate entities and, if approved, to ensure the transfer on lease of estates from nationalized or other state estates suitable for the project approved."

Initially, however, no practical measures were taken to implement this regulation. The political atmosphere was so charged with radical slogans and actions that no investor would have dared put his money into any such undertakings. There was renewed movement only when the October 1986 law put an end to the controversies about land reform. Large advertisements calling for private investment appeared in the newspapers in November[133] and gave details of projects already planned (including estimates of costs and profits) and up for transfer, offering a range of additional inducements.[134] The head of the responsible section at the Ministry of Agriculture, Rasulof, told the journal *Barzegar* on December 13, 1986, that 1m hectares of land were to be checked for investment by the private sector within six months and 600,000ha made available for transfer to applicants. Suitable applicants would be graduates in agricultural disciplines, experts, and investors who were ready to work more with their own funds and less with state aid. He added that the policy was intended to ensure self-sufficiency and independence, cope with population growth, and curb the rural exodus; therefore, it was absolutely essential to mobilize the people and involve them in agricultural projects.

To implement this policy, Investment and People's Participation Centers were to be set up in various provinces. They were to plan projects in conjunction with the Ministry of Agriculture's provincial offices and the Service Centers and make sure that private investors were ready to implement them, prizes being offered to people who worked out suitable projects.[135] There were even reports in September 1988 that the Bank for Agriculture was ready to invest in such projects together with private investors who could not raise enough capital, then pull out as soon as the private partners were ready to buy out the bank's share.[136]

State and nationalized estates were supposed to be made available for such projects on a lease basis pursuant to Article 31 in the regulations noted above. But in order to increase private investors' interest, the government stated that it was prepared to sell these estates, and the necessary legislation was approved at its first reading on July 3, 1989.[137]

Further steps to encourage private investors were taken after October 1986. The government stated its willingness to sign contracts with individuals who had arbitrarily taken possession of estates of natural resources if such action was in the interests of the Islamic Republic.[138] In December 1988, *Barzegar* quoted Rasulof as stating that the restrictions on the buying and selling of land for which the occupier only had usufructuary rights would soon be lifted so as to "attract investment in the direction of agriculture."[139] Such decisions were accompanied by calls from high places for the private sector to acknowledge the government's good intentions and profitably invest its idle capital in agriculture. Kalantari, the new minister of agriculture, in a statement made not long after he took office on September 20, 1988, promised that protecting private investments was a firm part of his policy and that landed property would in future no longer be touched.[140]

But all the promises, assurances, and encouragements were far from enough to create the political climate needed to get the capital circulating in commerce to be invested in production. Radical tones could still be heard from the cabinet, where the majority of ministers were known etatists and extremists bent on cultivating this image. The Investment and People's Participation Centers were failures, as the people refused to give their participation. On July 1, 1989, Rasulof stated that "we are unable to register movement concerning the participation."[141]

The October 1986 law ignored the problem of uncultivated lands, as the Council of Guardians' rejection of the May 1985 bill had resulted in decisions about their ownership being deferred. But no policy, however conservative, could do without regulations for reclaiming it. The Determination Council fell back on the May regulations and on August 16, 1988, issued a decree placing uncultivated land under state administration if the owners did not exercise their rights. If within a year—which period could be extended by a further year—they ensured that their land was cultivated, they would be allowed to keep it with no conditions attached; otherwise the Sevener Commissions were entitled to sell the land for a fair price on their behalf and give them the proceeds after deducting legal and religious debts. If action were instituted in respect of title, a court competent to deal with questions pertaining to Article 49 of the constitution would decide the case in question.[142] Issuing this decree was the Determination Council's final act (so far) with respect to land reform, despite the many promises that it would progressively solve problems in proposed legislation relating to controversial social and economic policies.[143] On October 1, 1988, Hojjat ol-Eslam Harandi explained that the Council had already made all the decisions demanded of it by the Sevener Commissions.[144]

The following review of the estates transferred by the Sevener Commissions by the end of 1990 shows the results of more than a decade of battle over the land reform.

Table 8.2 Land Transfers by Sevener Commissions to December 1990 (in hectares)

National and state wasteland	600,000
Squatted land	450,000

Source: Central Office for Transferring the Estates, in *Resalat,* December 8, 1990.[145]

Some 220,000 peasant families had come into possession of a plot of land by December 1990 and were reportedly united in 10,309 mosha' cooperatives. Adding all the cultivated and uncultivated land already transferred and still to be transferred on the basis of the October 1986 law gives a total of 850,000ha that have changed or will change owners to the benefit of peasants with little or no land. This total is 40 percent of the 2,136,450ha[146] they would have received if land reform had applied to the estates of all enterprises with more than 50ha (excluding large state and cooperative enterprises), which would have been more in line with what the radical

Islamists wanted. To a certain extent, their ideas did not prevail because of the Islamic legal arguments their opponents used. These arguments are dealt with in more detail in Chapter 9.

Notes

1. Such actions were reported by the leftist press in particular. See, for example, consecutive editions of *Kar, Ayandegan,* and *Etehad-e Chap,* as well as A. Amini 1986, pp. 186f and 215; and Gil Azar 1980.

2. Hozhabr Yazdani alone owned 30,000ha in this region, and the shah's family owned 10,000ha. *Ibid.,* p. 183.

3. Such reports reappeared, especially in the left-wing press (see, for example, *Etehad-e Chap,* June 6 and 23, 1979, July 21, 1979, April 12, 1980), but were also frequent in the nationalized newspapers (see, for example, *Ettela'at,* July 12, 1979, October 8, 1979; *Kayhan,* March 4, 1979, and April 7, 1979; and PP, March 2, 1982, p. 25. Further reports: Amini 1986, 182ff; Bafekr 1982, pp. 52ff.

4. Spokesman of the parliamentary committee on agriculture in PP, May 16, 1985, p. 26f; and October 21, 1986, p. 24f. Gil Azar (p. 77) says 69 percent of the peasants' actions were led by religious and nonreligious political organizations and that only 19 percent were spontaneous.

5. Peasants took possession of some 800,000ha, which were later called "estates of temporary cultivation." Another 100,000ha were estates that had previously been confiscated or sequestered by the state.

6. See Amini 1986, p. 185f; *Etehad-e Chap,* July 7, 1979.

7. See, for example, the report of the criticism of Izadi by the Islamic Student Societies calling on him to expropriate the feudal lords and resolve the land question in *Kayhan,* October 26, 1979, and the critical report on October 17, 1979, by *Jomhuri-ye Eslami* on the seminar "Problems of Agricultural Development" held by the Ministry of Agriculture in October 1979, at which calls were made for radical restrictions on landed property in *Keshawarz-e Emruz,* October 21 and November 16, 1979.

8. On the constitution of the Revolutionary Council at this time, see Bazargan 1983, p. 25f.

9. The decrees issued by the Revolutionary Committee were known as "legislative proposals" because they had not been approved by a legislative body. It was intended that they be examined by a constitutional legislature to be convened later and, if approved, passed into law. These decrees are sometimes referred to as "bills" in this work, although this term is normally reserved for draft laws presented to parliament by the government.

10. See his letter to the Revolutionary Council in *Keshawarz-e Emruz,* January 25, 1980.

11. *Keshawarz-e Emruz,* October 27, 1979.

12. See his letter to the Revolutionary Council in *Keshawarz-e Emruz,* January 25, 1980.

13. In *ibid.,* and in an interview with the author, Izadi said that Khomeini supported him in his attitude to the property question and that he had often spoken with him about the September 1979 bill and obtained his approval for it. "Khomeini was against the restriction of property and against its division." *Keshawarz-e Emruz,* October 6, 1979.

14. See the text of this proposal in *Keshawarz-e Emruz,* October 20, 1979; an

interview with Izadi in the October 6, 1979 edition; and the October 27, 1979 edition.

15. CL 1979, pp. 4f and 83ff; Schirazi 1988, pp. 45f and 69ff.

16. CL 1979, pp. 162ff; Schirazi 1988, pp. 73ff.

17. CL 1979, pp. 164ff; Schirazi 1988, pp. 77ff. On the measures taken by the government with respect to these estates before approval of this bill, see the statements by Secretary of State Pur Tabataba'i in *Ettela'at*, September 19, 1979.

18. *Kayhan*, March 1, 1979.

19. The Sevener Commissions transferred 43,007ha of these estates to peasants by September 1988. See *Resalat*, February 13, 1989. According to an announcement (which was only published at the end of November 1991), the foundation was holding a total of some 2m hectares in 1,200 villages that had belonged to the royal family. They were now to be transferred to peasants within ten years. See *Resalat*, December 1, 1991.

20. The corresponding bill was approved on April 14, 1979. See CL 1979, p. 1, and administrative regulations pp. 3ff; Schirazi 1988, pp. 44 and 58ff.

21. See, for example, K. Ma'sumi 1980, pp. 68ff; *Keshawarz-e Emruz*, October 21, 1979, contains a different opinion. In an interview with the author, Izadi rejected the accusation that the Agricultural Councils were to represent the interests of the owners of large estates. Every farmer was entitled to become a member of the Councils. The Councils were set up with the aim of leaving agriculture to the farmers, preventing government interference in their affairs "so that it was possible to create security for the maintenance of the peoples' economic independence and thus for their political freedoms." See the position of the Councils in the overall plan as envisaged by Izadi in Chapter 7.2.

22. *Keshawarz-e Emruz*, October 21, 1979.

23. Announcement by the Revolutionary Council on November 8, 1979, in *Kayhan* of the same date.

24. See *Keshawarz-e Emruz*, December 9 and 30, 1979; *Kayhan*, November 20 and December 4, 1979.

25. As in Khuzestan by the Revolutionary Guards. See *Keshawarz-e Emruz*, December 23, 1979; *Kayhan*, November 17, 1979.

26. *Kayhan*, January 25, 1980.

27. On December 26, 1979, *Kayhan* reported a demonstration by 10,000 people against the "feudal lords." According to *Ettela'at* of February 22, 1980, peasants occupied the courthouse in the town of Shiraz to underline their demands. *Keshawarz-e Emruz* of December 23, 1979, and January 21, 1980, reported the "murderous anarchy" that broke out after the first speech by the secretary of state at the Ministry of Agriculture responsible for land reform, Reza Esfahani. Many farmers from around Tehran took part in a demonstration on December 30, 1979, in his favor, according to *Kayhan*. Similar actions followed in 1980.

28. *Ettela'at*, December 8, 1979.

29. *Ibid.* and *Kayhan*, January 1, 1980.

30. *Keshawarz-e Emruz*, January 6, 1980.

31. See the text of the bill in CL 1979, pp. 546ff; and Schirazi 1988, pp. 134ff.

32. This information comes from Ayatollah Beheshti. See *Ettela'at*, June 13, 1981.

33. Ayatollah Beheshti told *Ettela'at*, (March 27, 1980) that with due consideration of the opinion of the jurists, Esfahani's bill was approved "with some amendments."

34. CL 1979, pp. 585ff; Schirazi 1988, pp. 153ff. In the discussion on the land reform, "local custom" came to mean land equivalent to the customary local size. The assumption was that a plot of land of this size was sufficient to ensure the livelihood of a peasant and his family.

35. CL 1980, pp. 13ff; Schirazi 1988, pp. 167ff.
36. *Barzegar* printed most of them—see, for example, the September 13, 1980 edition.
37. *Ibid.*, September 20, 1980. *Kayhan* (January 10, 1981) reported the opponents' actions. See also Ashraf 1982, pp. 34ff; Pur Karim 1981, pp. 23ff; and *Keshawarz-e Emruz*, December 29, 1979.
38. See *Ettela'at*, March 12 and April 22, 1980, on the declarations by Ayatollahs Qomi and Rohani, respectively. The weekly *Mojahed* printed a copy of Golpaygani's fatwa on the subject in its October 27, 1983 edition.
39. See the interview with Ayatollah Rabbani in *Barzegar*, December 13, 1980, which states inter alia that in Esfahan three clerics had quit the Sevener Commissions following Grand Ayatollah Golpaygani's fatwa rejecting the reform. Hojjat ol-Eslam Harandi reported similar occurrences in the province of Fars in *Ettela'at*, February 16, 1981.
40. *Ettela'at*, October 23, 1980.
41. *Ibid.*, and *Barzegar*, December 13, 1980.
42. *Kayhan*, July 22, 1981; *Ettela'at*, June 2, 1983.
43. *Barzegar*, November 29, 1980.
44. *Ettela'at*, February 16, 1981.
45. CL 1980, pp. 59ff; Schirazi 1988, pp. 180ff.
46. Ashraf 1982, p. 33. Figures vary considerably, as usual. *Ettela'at*, September 7, 1981, reported that over 61,000ha of cultivated land had been transferred before the order. *Kayhan*, July 22, 1981, quoted the representative of the ruler in the province of Kermanshah as stating that the Sevener Commissions had transferred 80,000ha of cultivated land temporarily or permanently by November 12, 1980.
47. *Kayhan*, February 10, 1981.
48. Bafekr 1982, p. 65.
49. According to Ayatollah Rabbani Shirazi in *Barzegar*, December 13, 1980.
50. See *Barzegar*, June 11, 1980, on complaints by owners.
51. Telegram from landowners in Kermanshah to Montazeri in *Barzegar*, September 13, 1980.
52. CL 1980, p. 26f; Schirazi 1988, p. 172.
53. CL 1980, pp. 138f and 250; Schirazi 1988, p. 213.
54. CL 1979/80, pp. 297, 450f, and 626ff; 1980/81, p. 282f; and Schirazi 1988, pp. 120, 137, 163, and 210f.
55. CL 1979/80, pp. 283f and 291; 1980/81, p. 282f. See also Schirazi 1988, pp. 115, 118, and 174.
56. CL 1979/80, p. 291; Schirazi 1988, p. 118.
57. CL 1979/80, p. 284; Schirazi 1988, p. 115.
58. The periodical *Masa'el-e Keshawarzi*, which published the Tudeh Party's views on agriculture, was the best example of this in the two years it appeared.
59. *Kayhan*, April 19 and 20, 1986.
60. See his statements in PP, December 2, 1982, p. 21; and December 8, 1982, p. 19.
61. Time and again it printed interviews with the heads of the Sevener Commissions and other advocates of the reform, plus its own reports and analyses against the "feudal lords." See, for example, *Kayhan*, February 3, 4, and 10, 1981; *Ettela'at*, June 9, 1981.
62. A head of the Sevener Commissions made this assertion; see *Ettela'at*, February 9, 1981.
63. The government's attempt to get a bill defining the limits of the private sector through parliament came in this phase but failed because of the resistance of

its opponents both in and out of parliament. See PP, January 15–November 24, 1985, and Schirazi 1988, pp. 274ff.

64. See the text of the draft in Schirazi 1981, pp. 222ff.

65. See the text of this initiative in *Barzegar,* November 8, 1981, and Schirazi 1988, pp. 227ff.

66. This refers to the rule of avoidance ('eraz) in Islamic law, which is subject to differing interpretations. The subject is dealt with in Chapters 9.5 and 2.3.1.

67. In his criticism of the draft, Hojjat ol-Eslam Harandi pointed out that "1) we do not have enough wasteland available that can be transferred; 2) we need the pastures for cattle breeding; and 3) determining the illegality of landed property is an extremely difficult task." *Barzegar,* November 21, 1981.

68. See PP, March 2, 1982, p. 21, for a reference by the spokesman of the Parliamentary Commission on Agriculture to the existence of such a draft.

69. See *Barzegar,* March 6, 1982, for the text of the draft.

70. PP, December 8, 1982, p. 24; December 13, 1982, p. 16.

71. PP, December 26, 1982, pp. 17ff.

72. At the time the commission's spokesman was Hojjat ol-Eslam Harandi, who also represented the Imam in the Central Staff of the Commissions for Transferring the Estates. PP, March 2, 1982, pp. 21 and 25.

73. PP, November 30, 1982, p. 16; December 8, 1982, p. 16.

74. PP, March 2, 1982, p. 27; November 29, 1982, p. 21. Minister of Agriculture Salamati countered this argument by pointing out that the reclamation of wasteland was not so easy in view of the lack of water. See PP, November 29, 1982, p. 22; and November 30, 1982, pp. 17ff.

75. PP, December 19, 1982, pp. 20ff; December 20, 1982, pp. 17ff; and December 21, 1982, pp. 15ff.

76. PP, December 9, 1982, p. 24f.

77. PP, December 21, 1982, p. 17. See Schirazi 1988, pp. 234ff, for the text of the bill.

78. *Jomhuri-ye Eslami,* January 18, 1983; Schirazi 1988, p. 247f; S. J. Madani 1987, vol. 4, p. 274f.

79. According to Ayatollah Musawi Ardebili, for example, in *Kayhan,* October 16, 1984.

80. PP, August 14, 1984, p. 19f.

81. *Jomhuri-ye Eslami,* January 24, 1983.

82. *Kayhan,* May 16, 1984.

83. *Kayhan,* September 3, 1984.

84. For examples of press activity in this connection, see *Kayhan,* January 24 and 29, June 15, November 8, and December 1, 1984; *Ettela'at,* May 3, 1983, January 16 and October 20, 1985, January 7 and 25, and February 24, 1986.

85. *Kayhan,* August 6, 1984.

86. *Kayhan,* October 21, 1984.

87. Setad-e Markazi-ye Hey'at ha-ye Haft Nafare 1984, p. 7.

88. PP, May 14, 1985, pp. 28ff; May 15, 1985, pp. 22ff.

89. Reputedly amounted to about 40,000ha at the time. PP, May 16, 1985, p. 30.

90. Madani 1987, vol. 4, p. 285f; and Chapter 9.4.

91. *Kayhan,* July 29, 1986.

92. *Resalat,* May 28, 1986.

93. *Kayhan,* March 17, 1986.

94. *Kayhan,* April 24, 1986.

95. *Kayhan,* June 22, 1986.

Reform of Land Tenure 199

96. See the text of the bill in CL 1986/7, p. 364f; and PP, October 21, 23, 28, and 30, 1986.
97. PP, October 23, 1986, pp. 25 and 28.
98. PP, May 16, 1985, p. 27.
99. PP, May 19, 1985, pp. 21ff; October 21, 1986, p. 29f.
100. *Ibid.*
101. PP, October 21, 1986, p. 26.
102. PP, May 16, 1985, p. 26.
103. *Kayhan*, October 9 and December 31, 1985, and January 12, 1986.
104. *Kayhan,* November 9, 1985.
105. *Kayhan,* November 2, 1985.
106. See, for example, *Kayhan,* January 14 and 20, February 18, March 3, 12, and 18, 1986.
107. Harandi once quoted 1m hectares (*Kayhan,* May 11, 1989). The spokesman of the Parliamentary Commission on Agriculture quoted 750,000ha (PP, March 9, 1987, p. 19). The experts I asked put the inconsistencies down to such factors as a lack of coordination between the various "reporting" agencies and the fact that their figures were based on inaccurate and incorrect estimates.
108. *Resalat,* July 21, 1987.
109. PP, May 16, 1985, p. 30; October 28, 1986, p. 20.
110. PP, October 23, 1986, p. 28.
111. PP, May 16, 1985, p. 30.
112. *Resalat,* November 24, 1986.
113. According to the spokesman of the parliamentary commission (PP, March 9, 1987, p. 19). *Resalat,* June 15, 1985, spoke of one-fifth of the squatted estates being given back.
114. PP, May 19, 1985, pp. 21ff.
115. *Ibid.*
116. See the statements by Hojjat ol-Eslam Musawi Tabrizi on this subject in PP, October 28, 1986, p. 20.
117. According to Hojjat ol-Eslam Harandi, the courts in Mashhad, Fars, Saweh, and Kurdistan had attempted to return the squatted estates to their owners and had had a large number of peasants flogged or put in jail. See PP, October 23, 1986, p. 24.
118. *Ibid.*
119. See CL 1987/8, pp. 619ff.
120. *Resalat,* November 24, 1986. One of the responsible officials thought the transfers had actually commenced at the beginning of 1366 (March 21, 1987), *Kayhan,* November 14, 1987.
121. The head of the Sevener Commissions complained about it at a seminar held from October 1 to 3, 1988. See also *Resalat* of the same dates.
122. *Ettela'at,* May 20, 1989.
123. *Resalat,* October 16, 1988.
124. Experts and functionaries I asked quoted similar reasons for the slow work by the Sevener Commissions: "Negative attitude of some of the factions in power," "deficiencies in the legislation," "lack of preparation," "uncertainty in matters of private landed property," "influence of landowners in the administration," and "political opportunism." One interviewee even thought that the Sevener Commissions were already doing their transfer work too fast.
125. *Resalat,* October 1, 1988.
126. *Ettela'at,* June 21, 1989.
127. A total of 550,000ha had been checked and recognized as estates falling under the law. *Resalat,* February 6, 1990.

128. *Resalat,* December 8, 1990.
129. *Kayhan,* March 12, 1987.
130. *Resalat,* July 12, 1988.
131. *Kayhan,* February 3, 1988. In Harandi's case this was a change of mind that could be traced back to the debates on the December 1982 bill and that made out of a proponent of more radical land reform a man who was now satisfied with the reduction of the original project. In a mid-April 1990 interview carried on radio, TV, and other media, he stated that the government had abandoned the transfer of smaller areas and intended to transfer larger areas to those interested in investing in agriculture, adding that the existing laws would be modified accordingly, alluding to the April 1980 bill. See *Barzegar,* April 21, 1990.
132. CL 1979/80, p. 61; Schirazi 1988, pp. 124ff.
133. See, for example, *Resalat,* November 19, 1986.
134. See, for example, *Barzegar,* October 26, 1987.
135. *Barzegar,* December 12 and 26, 1987.
136. *Barzegar,* October 8, 1988.
137. *Resalat,* July 4, 1989.
138. The minister of agriculture made the corresponding decision in October 1988 (*Barzegar,* October 8, 1988).
139. *Barzegar,* December 12, 1987.
140. *Kayhan,* October 19, 1988.
141. *Resalat* of the same date.
142. *Barzegar,* October 6, 1988.
143. At the time President Khamene'i had promised that the Council would break the legislative deadlock, See *Resalat,* June 2, 1988.
144. *Kayhan* of the same date.
145. A representative of the Sevener Commissions said (July 19, 1992) that out of 850,000ha squatted land, 670,000ha were transferred to peasants. The remaining 180,000ha were given back to their owners (*Salam*). The daily *Salam* reported on April 20, 1992, that 610,000ha wasteland had beeb transferred to 102,361 peasant families.
146. Calculation taken from Hoseini Kazeruni 1981, p. 18.

9

The Debate About Land Reform in Islamic Law

The land reform issue made for a lively debate among theorists of Islamic law and doctrine. Whereas their arguments had mainly been formulated in categorial and formal conceptual terms before the revolution, they subsequently took on more concrete forms and were applied to problems that needed to be solved immediately.

The Islamization of politics forced everyone who was interested in changing or maintaining existing property rights to try to portray his position as the only Islamic one. Even some experts with Leninist or liberal opinions used this language.[1]

The divergence of Islamicized positions was evident in almost all questions relating to land reform. (The only exception was the estates of the religious foundations, on which there was a conspicuous harmony, at least among the ruling Islamists.) These differences will be examined below with respect to four issues: confiscation and sequestration of estates; determination of the illegality of existing land ownership; applicability of the principles of necessity or state interest to legitimize land reform; and the disposition of wasteland. These controversial questions actually require more detailed treatment than it is possible to give them here and should be the subject of a separate study.

9.1 Confiscation and Sequestration of Estates

The main confiscations of land and other assets took place in the first few months after the revolution but were void of any basis in law at the time. As a result, before the Law on Administering Article 49 of the Constitution of the Islamic Republic came into force on August 8, 1984, any religious judge, whether or not in a revolutionary court, could deliver a verdict on this point according to his own interpretation of the sharia. Such decisions, however, were often influenced more by the revolutionary mood than

Islamic law. Later statements by Ayatollahs Meshgini and Beheshti to the effect that these verdicts had been reached on the basis of Article 49 of the constitution[2] cannot disguise the arbitrariness of such judges as Hojjat ol-Eslam Khalkhali. Indeed, some of the decisions reached in these circumstances were later declared null and void. Arbitrary confiscations had reached such proportions in 1979 that Khomeini was obliged to "issue an order to all those in positions of responsibility, committees, courts and Revolutionary Guards to prevent these illegal acts with all their strength and purposefulness." He continued, "This is an Islamic country and the principles of Islamic law must be respected here."[3] One conservative member of parliament later demanded that the estates seized in this manner be returned to their owners.[4] Several years later, Ayatollah Ardebili, chairman of the Supreme Council of Justice, put these "misjudgments" down to the speed with which they had been given in the year after the the revolution.[5] The chairman of the Revolutionary Tribunal, Ayatollah Gilani, quoted protests from the grand ayatollahs about such decisions,[6] and Ayatollah Sadduqi, the attorney general, described how in one case it had been decided to seize the assets of 209 people, in another case of 39 people, at one stroke. He voiced his doubts about the legality of these assets to Khomeini, who replied that in that case they must be given back, adding: "Should they demand of us that we blindly approve such decisions with disregard for the principles of the sharia and for the provisions of Islamic law, we should not lend ourselves to it, even in a hundred years; even if they put us in front of machine-guns, we should not lend ourselves to it. . . . We carried out the revolution in order to install Islam, not communism."[7]

Various statements on the question of confiscations reveal some of the criteria that may have formed the basis for some of these judgments or were later used to justify them. They include misappropriation of wasteland, usury, failure to pay the Islamic taxes, and collaboration with an illegitimate regime, according to Ayatollah Beheshti.[8] The former religious judge Hojjat ol-Eslam Musawi Tabrizi gave the "crime" of the landowners concerned as the reason without specifying what crime, although he did refute the assertion that such decisions were based on Article 49 of the constitution.[9] Zawarre'i, an ex–state prosecutor at the Revolutionary Tribunal, cited "plundering state assets."[10] The "crimes" laid at the door of the "Jewish capitalist" Elqanian to justify his execution and confiscate his assets were: "Friendship with the enemies of God and enmity with God's friends." He was allegedly an "enemy of God," a "messenger of the opponents of Islam," and was supposed to have brought "ruin on earth" by "destroying economic resources," "obstructing the development of Islamic and human values," and committing a number of purely political crimes.[11] Landowners were frequently accused of being the "originator of ruin on earth" (mofsed-e fi al-arz) or of "illegal seizure of property belonging to others or the state." Khomeini's March 5, 1979, decree (see Chapter 8.2) provided further details of the relevant criteria, such as embezzlement of state assets, to justify confiscating the fortune thereby accrued. In the same decree, the assets concerned were termed "booty" (qana'em, plural of qanimat), which in Islamic law means it was captured in war against the enemies of Islam, and one-fifth was to be conferred on the Imam.[12]

Some of the estates that, together with other assets, were placed at the disposal of the Revolutionary Institutions could not be confiscated without further ado—they belonged to individuals who had left the country during or after the revolution and whose ties to the shah's regime were too minimal (or nonexistent) to warrant deeming their property illegal. The real problem with such sequestered assets was that the ruling Islamists found it difficult to decide whether they should remain confiscated or be given back to their owners. A first attempt to regulate it was made when the Property of Refugees, Disposition of Assets Bill was debated and passed at its first reading on October 4–5, 1982, and at its second reading on January 10–11, 1983. The proposed legislation, drafted as one clause, stipulated that all individuals residing abroad must apply in person to the Supreme Court of Inquiry of the Revolution within two months so that a verdict might be reached about their sequestered assets, failing which the Attorney General of the Revolution was entitled to sell or lease the movable and immovable property of such refugees. After deducting the expenses incurred by the state in looking after these assets, the proceeds were to be deposited with the treasury for safekeeping. Should the courts decide that the ownership of these assets was lawful, the property or the proceeds from selling it would be returned to the owner. The reason given for this bill was the need "to protect the public interest and to prevent the squandering of assets or their unlawful removal from the country."

The spokesmen for the Parliamentary Justice Commission and the Ministry of Justice emphasized more than once during the debate that, first, the bill was based on the premise that the ownership of the assets concerned was lawful and, second, its only purpose was to end the uncertain legal status of these assets because looking after them was causing the state considerable expense.[13] An assurance was also given that the final decision about the legal standing of these assets would be made by the courts, which would institute appropriate proceedings upon application in person by the owner to the Supreme Court of Inquiry of the Revolution.

But the bill's proponents expected more from it, hoping that it would establish once and for all that the refugees were part of the counterrevolution and thus leave the way clear to confiscate their assets. For them, the mere fact of having fled the country was sufficient proof of the counterrevolutionary attitude of those concerned. There was also an accusation that these people were conspiring against the revolution from outside the country and were financing actions against the regime with income from their assets in the country. The parliamentary state secretary from the Ministry of Justice described the Iranians who had fled the country in these words: "The refugees consist of a gang of counterrevolutionaries who support the Pahlavi regime, who took part in slaughtering the people and in plundering its wealth and today are active[ly] working abroad against the Islamic Republic. A second group consists of counterrevolutionaries who belong to the circle of God's mortal enemies. A third group includes the debauched, lascivious gluttons for whom the ethical code of the Islamic Republic represents an obstacle to pursuing their dissolute delectations."[14]

The bill's opponents protested that even an individual's participation in a counterrevolution did not prove the illegality of his assets; even if the person concerned had been sentenced to death on this account, it was still possible for the property to have been acquired lawfully.[15] In Islam, even an apostate's property is not seized but given to his heirs.[16] Moreover, they argued, none of the refugees would dare return to Iran just to sort out their assets; the sharia did not require a personal appearance in court; and the sharia had enough regulations to confiscate the assets if they had been acquired illegally. If they proved to have been acquired legally, it would be better not to touch the assets at all.[17]

The debate on this bill did not last long. It was passed and four days later submitted to the Council of Guardians, which decided unanimously on January 20, 1983, that it contravened the "principles of the sharia." The reason given was: "Fleeing the country and residing abroad do not, according to the sharia, satisfy the regulations mentioned in the bill." Further, the bill contradicted Article 20 of the constitution, which reads: "Each member of the nation, whether woman or man, is protected by the law and enjoys the full political, economic, social, and cultural rights of humans with due regard for Islamic principles."[18] So the bill failed. No attempt was made to amend it, and uncertainty about the sequestered assets and estates remained.

A second attempt at a legal solution to the problem was made with the May 1985 bill on the transfer of estates. This failed, too, because of resistance from the Council of Guardians. The courts have since returned to their previous practice—namely, deciding how to deal with the sequestered assets on a case-by-case basis. This approach has led to sequestrations being both upheld and lifted. The frequent complaints about such sequestered assets being returned to their owners indicate that such outcomes are not uncommon. The parliamentarian Khalkhali, speaking during a debate on April 30, 1989, about the need for a purge in the Ministry of Justice, stated: "Judges and magistrates who were earlier in the forefront of the counterrevolution now have a beard and wear an overcoat, become revolutionaries and decide in most cases, God knows it, in favor of the landowners and of the wealthy. I have heard they want to give industrial enterprises, gardens and estates back to these people" (Parliamentary Protocols, p. 19). Contrary decisions are, however, no less common.

The Supreme Council of Justice made a far-reaching decision about the sequestered assets at the end of June 1988 to the detriment of the owners. The decision was probably intended to relieve the treasury, which was being crushed by the burden of the war costs. The Council decided to make the sequestered assets available for this purpose and simplify confiscation.[19] The newspapers have since occasionally reported such verdicts, but they are uncommon. The "interests of the state order," which has been an established part of the repertoire of constitutional justifications used by the ruling jurists since early 1988, is the only tenet in Islamic law that might support such decisions (see Chapter 9.5).

9.2 The Legality or Illegality of Landed Property

The proponents of radical restrictions on landed property used a contention widely accepted among Islamists—namely that property is reserved for God—to qualify the individual's rights to the same or reduce them to mere usufruct. According to this interpretation, God transfers his right to all mankind, to the community, the Muslims' state, or to the individuals chosen by Him to rule over others. As the last in this chain of God's stewards, the individual has little control over the soil. His status is determined by his superiors, leaving him only usufructuary rights, if any.[20] Even work does not establish property rights, merely usufructuary ones—which do, however, give him preferential claim to cultivating a plot of land.[21]

The advocates of private land ownership also accepted that property rights are reserved for God.[22] They sometimes considered the power of the Imam, as God's representative on earth, to be so absolute that they were prepared—despite their vehement advocacy of the right to private property—to accept restrictions on it if such restrictions should be ordered by the Imam or legitimized by the Islamic system of government.[23] It was, however, mainly the advocates of radical land reform who cited the exclusivity of God's property rights to support their own arguments.

Restricting man's right to usufruct did not necessarily preclude a quantitative limitation such as customary size, which is why the limit had to be constantly emphasized. This point was equally true of property rights, if they are acknowledged as permissible. When restricting usufructuary and property rights, the difference lay between quantitative and qualitative limitations. All Islamists considered the latter to be permissible; Islam has restricted property rights qualitatively by banning so-called illegal deals (makaseb-e moharrame) and permitting any assets accruing from them, even indirectly (i.e., with money made from illegal deals), to be confiscated. Confiscation was often advocated or tolerated for landed property whose acquisition was made possible by the owner's failure to pay the taxes laid down in the sharia. This is the reason much of the proposed legislation discussed above provided for the owner to be paid the price for reallocated land after deduction of his religious taxes. There were disagreements about the extent to which this criterion should be applied. The reform's opponents argued that arbitrary determination of the debt was often used to circumvent the owner's rights; those in favor of the reform said the owners never paid their religious taxes anyway and that the amount due was so large that it justified confiscating the property without more ado.[24] Khomeini was often quoted in this connection—he considered it improbable that "such people have ever paid their religious taxes"[25] and was reported to have calculated in a fatwa that if the tithe was not paid, then the debt accrued in geometric progression and that it was thus lawful to confiscate all the assets of such people.[26]

Those who also advocated quantitative limitations on land ownership under Islam put forward various arguments, "ensuring justice" being one often heard. According to Ayatollah Meshgini, "justice in distributing the land among the people is the most important form of justice."[27] Ayatollah Musawi Ardebili based his support for quantitative limitations on a hadith, quoted by Khomeini, that "poor people share in the riches of the wealthy."[28] Sheikh Ali Tehrani thought that in Islam everyone has the right to property according to his needs, although he understood "rights" to mean usufructuary rights. According to Hojjat ol-Eslam Morteza Razawi, an extreme left-winger among the radical Islamists, "not much land remains for private property or usufructuary rights anyway if one bears in mind that Islam counts 90 percent of the surface of the earth as communal and/or state property [enfal]. Individuals only had the possibility of competing with one another [for the acquisition of a share] in respect of the remaining 10 percent."[29] Reza Esfahani stated, "The limits which the manifesto [of the Communist Party] has envisaged for private property are childish when compared with the limits and conditions set by Islam."[30] Together with Meshgini, Montazeri, and Razawi, many other Islamists saw a basis for the quantitative limitation of private landed property in the Islamic rules below:

1. The zarar (refrainment from damage) rule, which bans any act inflicting damage on other people. As the large-scale private ownership of land presupposes the exploitation of other people, it must be limited, according to this rule.
2. The 'otla (closure) rule, which prohibits leaving land uncultivated, the owner losing all his rights to the property if he does so.
3. The kanz (hoarding of wealth) rule, which forbids one person to concentrate wealth in his hands or a few to monopolize it.[31] The rules of necessity and ruling are often mentioned in this connection and will be dealt with later in this chapter.

The demand to restrict private ownership of land was put much more strongly when it was based on the argument that personal work is the only source of wealth or property in Islam. This argument was based on a verse from the Quran—"And that man is allotted nothing other than that for which he strives [during life on earth]" (53/40)—which was interpreted to mean that a person only owns what he has acquired by personal work.[32] Anything else was considered the product of exploitation, which Islam condemns.[33] Rafsanjani was quoted as saying, "Land ownership which is based on exploitation contradicts Islam."[34] A more credible advocate of this point of view was the oft-quoted Reza Esfahani, who acknowledged as owners only those people whose property has been "acquired by the sweat of their brow." (It should not be forgotten that, according to him, land ownership is merely a preferential claim to till the soil.)[35] In 1979 the Revolutionary Guards in the province of Khuzestan encouraged the peasants to occupy the land on the grounds that "only those people are the owners who personally work on the land."[36] A participant at the October 1979 seminar mentioned in Chapter 4 demanded that "the soil must be transferred to those who cry to Heaven from the pain suffered working in the fields if one touches their wounded heels, and not to the farmers on whose ties and curls the dust of the earth has never settled."[37]

Another saying the advocates of land reform liked to quote was "al zar' li il-zare'" (land to the tillers), which was ascribed to the Prophet, although its authenticity was disputed. The first radical land reform bill's stipulation that the owner would be left a plot of land only if he did agricultural work stemmed from the view that work is the only lawful basis for owning land. But as shown above, the definition of agricultural work was widened by the legislators to include management.

Another argument in Islamic law cited to negate private landed property rights was applied to estates claimed to be in areas once conquered by the Islamic army. Because they belonged to the category of land that the Muslims took by force (maftuh al-'anwa land), they were the property of the community of Muslims and in accordance with the sharia must be placed under the authority of the Imam.[38] Other large estates appropriated by their owners were in the enfal category—i.e., land that according to the sharia belonged to the Imam or the state. There was also waqf land, which the owners of large estates had unlawfully taken possession of and which must be given back. According to Hojjat ol-Eslam Khalkhali, such great jurists as Sheikh Tusi, Ebn al-Edris, and Mohaqqeq Helli established the boundaries of the land conquered by force: from Musel in the North to Turkhan of Abadan in the South and from Qadesiye in the West to Nahawand in the East, including the lands on the shores of the Caspian Sea, the Persian Gulf, and the Gulf of Oman. Foundation land was scattered throughout the country—for example, in the provinces of Gilan and

Mazanderan. He concluded that these estates would have to be rededicated to their original purposes in religious law.[39]

Some considered the existing pattern of land ownership to be the result of illegal transfers or appropriations in recent decades or the last century. Individuals could be named whose ownership of land was traced back to the conversion of state lands, state gifts, or the forcible usurpation of land that belonged to other people.[40] When it was argued that because the state had given these estates to the people concerned for cultivation, the transfers were thus in accordance with the sharia, the reformers countered that the Ghajaren dynasty could not be termed an Islamic state and that only an Islamic state was entitled to transfer land for the purposes mentioned.[41]

The reform's opponents presented their own arguments, also based on Islamic law, to counter this attempt at justifying such limitations on land ownership. According to Hojjat ol-Eslam Miyanji, all the Islamic rules on property condone private property in principle—even the ones that call on Muslims to pay taxes, to refrain from unlawful business deals, and to desist from illegally usurping the property of others confirm in essence the right to private property. Islam merely affirms man's propensity for private property, "for Islam is the religion of the natural predispositions."[42]

Even many of those championing land reform, such as Ayatollah Beheshti and Hojjat ol-Eslam Harandi, did not dispute that Islam condones private property. They emphasized that the March 2, 1980, bill they codrafted acknowledged the "principle of property."[43] It would be impermissible to restrict the right to private property, which is based on the principles of Islam, other than by the limitations on legitimacy or by reasonable state intervention as defined by Islam itself. Ayatollah Yazdi stated that one of the reasons he had rejected the December 1982 bill was that work was the only criterion it acknowledged as a foundation for property. However, he argued, "we in Islam have many legitimate business activities—such as leasing, sharecropping, insurance, and commission dealing—in which profits can be made in a legitimate manner by concluding appropriate contracts. Here the capital, to use these gentlemen's words, appears as concentrated work and yields added value. In the cases sanctioned by the sharia, the profit realized in so doing is legitimate."[44]

The illegitimacy of a proposed reform is often so clear to its opponents that they consider it enough to simply point out this fact. During the debate on Article 6 of the May 1985 bill, Hojjat ol-Eslam Fahim said that approving such stipulations was the same as capitulating to theft and usurpation.[45] Hojjat ol-Eslam Wa'ezi, complaining about the illegality of the December 1982 bill, added, "Yesterday we still avoided the [usurpation] of even one hair of a camel; today we swallow the camel together with its load."[46] He went on to say that, whereas the aim of such measures was to shake the principle of property, what was really necessary was to guarantee property's safety.[47]

The proponents of the reform were not infrequently considered Communists; even Khomeini made similar allusions when he denounced the illegality of some confiscations. The cleric Allah Bedashti claimed that to say "the soil belongs to whoever tills it . . . can only confirm communist but not Islamic thinking."[48] Ayatollah Rabbani Shirazi put the Revolutionary Institutions' excesses against existing landed property down to the supporters of non-Islamic schools of thought who were attempting to cause mischief in the name of Islam.[49] The reform's proponents fought such accusations by claiming that the Islam their opponents are so concerned about is U.S.-influenced and that the true Islam aims to put the bloodthirsty landowners on trial.[50]

The opposition to the so-called Instances of Emulation (marja'-e taqlid)—i.e., the grand ayatollahs—carried considerable weight in Islamic law, equaling that of the sharia for many believers. It has already been shown that pressure from this quarter was partly to blame for suspension of the April 1980 bill with respect to cultivated estates, as Grand Ayatollahs Golpaygani, Mar'ashi, and Rohani had openly expressed their disapproval.[51] Rohani, explaining this view, noted that in Islam there could not be a reform that wanted to make the rich poor instead of the poor rich and stated that according to the constitution of the Islamic Republic it was the ulama—not Reza Esfahani or Bani Sadr[52]—who decided what was or was not Islamic. Mar'ashi observed that there were no limits on lawful property in Islam.[53] Golpaygani asserted the April 1980 land reform bill's incompatibility with the sharia in a telegram expressing his wish that "God may guide those people [onto the right path] who in the name of Islam are hacking out the roots of Islam and disseminating communist ideology in Iran."[54] Grand Ayatollah Khomeini, whose October 1980 decree halted the transfer of cultivated estates, should also be mentioned in this connection. Reja'i, president at the time and one of those in favor of the reform, commented, "We have to submit to this decision. The Imam decides about the Islamic principles. We must emulate him."[55]

The grand ayatollahs did not sanction the way supporters of the reform interpreted certain rules in Islamic law, such as the zarar rule mentioned above. Ayatollah Meshgini reported that the grand ayatollahs were of a different opinion on the matter. "They say: Owner is owner. The soil belongs to him; it is his property, immaterial of the ensuing consequences. Hence property may not be limited."[56]

There was also controversy about the interpretation of the yad rule[57] regulating current control over a thing. For the reform's detractors, this rule was proof enough of the legality of existing ownership, whose nullity can only be declared by a court on the basis of proof provided by the plaintiff.

The reformers emphatically rejected this interpretation. Hojjat ol-Eslam Razawi even said: "Those who defend the landowners with the aid of yad are worse than Saddam Hussein."[58]

Another very controversial question concerned the proper degree of state intervention in matters of private law. Whereas the proponents of the radical reform bills wanted to make transfers of land dependent on various conditions concerning its cultivation, its opponents emphatically objected, citing the fact that Islam says little about public law—i.e., that state intervention in such questions should be kept to a minimum.[59] The latter view was supported by the Council of Guardians, which rejected the December 1982 bill because it "contradicts Article 44 of the constitution, as in the last resort it makes agriculture a matter of state. It contradicts Article 2, Sentence J of the constitution because it gives the Ministry of Agriculture control over the farmers."[60]

The reform's advocates, in general etatists, campaigned against this point of view with economic arguments and Islamic morality, maintaining that without the state it was impossible to practice Islamic justice (qest).[61] However, they pushed through the terms they wanted with the help of the doctrine by which Islamic law permits conditions to be included in agreements made "by mutual consent."[62] Any condition the contracting parties agree to include in a contract recognized in Islamic law (shart-e zemn-e 'aqd) is in accordance with the sharia. This was the basis on which the government succeeded in imposing its conditions on the peasants when reallocating land to them.

9.3 Recourse to Article 49 of the Constitution

The dispute about the legality of land reform led radicals to abandon relatively quickly the general negation of landed property or large estates. Restrictions were based on the principles of necessity and rule (see Chapters 9.4 and 9.5). Article 49 of the constitution—or, more accurately, the law to implement it—was to decide the fate of illegally acquired land. Article 49 obliged the government "to return to its rightful owner or, if he is unknown, transfer to the state" any assets acquired illegally from him—i.e., assets "acquired through usury, misappropriation, bribery, fraud, theft, gambling, abuse of the foundations or state contracts and transactions, sale of wasteland and natural resources, running [of] an immoral establishment, and other acts forbidden by the religion."

Hojjat ol-Eslam Harandi commented on this way of handling the land question in May 1981 at the first reading of the December 1982 initiative, saying:

> The legislative initiative [being debated] is based on the legality of property, on the fact that all property is lawful. . . . On this basis, we recognize

ownership of cultivated and uncultivated land. We place great store on the right to property because the principle of property belongs to the inalienable foundation of Islam. Whoever has the wrong idea about property in Islam . . . makes his Islam suspect. . . . We trust that everywhere where there are signs of property . . . this property is legitimate unless we can prove under Article 49 of the constitution that this person's property is unlawful.[63]

The references to Article 49 date to before March 1981. We have seen how the confiscations made immediately after the revolution were justified with its help, some after the event. The administrative regulations of the April 15, 1980, bill were also based on Article 49. These provided for special procedures to check the land usurped and squatted by peasants and authorized the Sevener Commissions to determine the illegality of land tenure.[64] The initiative by sixteen members of parliament discussed in Chapter 8.4 was largely based on the understanding that only estates acquired illegally within the meaning of Article 49 would be affected by the reform.

The hopes of eliminating injustice placed in Article 49 were varied, as were the assessments of its suitability for the purpose. Those who signed the initiative wanted to minimize reform, whereas the advocates of an extensive reform hoped to be able to achieve great success using this article. On the one hand, Khalkhali, a member of parliament, said that Article 49 would make it possible to confiscate all the land that, going back to the first Islamic conquests, he called common or state land.[65] On the other hand, the Council of Guardians would have preferred to return the squatted estates to their former owners if their title proved to be lawful under Article 49.[66]

These diametrically opposed hopes and expectations were the cause of at least some of the difficulties associated with implementing the article. Other snags were caused by the fact that establishing whether the existing property titles were illegal was in most cases quite a problem. Ayatollah Meshgini pointed out that it was impossible to demand that ownership of a plot of land once conquered by the first Muslims (so becoming public property) be annulled after so many centuries.[67]

The difficulties in implementing Article 49 began in the preparatory stage. Only on August 11, 1981—i.e., after two and a half years of sequestrations and confiscations—did the legislature require the government to fulfill this constitutional obligation.[68] Although the government was only given four months to comply, the bill had to wait three years for final approval in August 1984.[69] The Law on the Method of Implementing Article 49 of the Constitution of the Islamic Republic assumed the legality of all existing "assets of individuals and corporate bodies, unless the contrary be proved" (Article 2). Evidence was to be heard in special revolutionary courts after the public prosecutor initiated proceedings or a plaintiff gave notice of appeal to the court (Articles 3 and 5). All ministries and other state agencies were obliged, within one year, to begin investigations into the crimes of their executive staff and business associates relating to government contracts, to compile the appropriate reports, and to notify the proper authorities (Articles 4 and 5). The public prosecutor was obliged to prosecute any individual who might have acquired his fortune by illegal acts and deals under the old regime. The law divided the government officials and businessmen concerned into thirteen categories ranging from members of the security and intelligence services organization under the shah (SAVAK) to the owners of cinemas and film studios (Article 5). Illegally acquired assets were to be returned to their rightful owners (individuals or the state) or, in the event that the owners were unknown, placed at the disposal of the "bearer of authority." If the illegal portion of an otherwise lawful fortune could not be determined, the decision was to be made on the basis of a settlement. If the rightful owner of this portion of the title was unknown, the bearer of authority was to receive one-fifth of the assets (Article 8). The other articles mainly dealt with cases in which illegal assets may have been transferred to third parties. Article 13 threatened plaintiffs with punishment if they gave notice of appeal out of maliciousness.[70]

During the debate it was emphasized that the law had been worded after consultations with the ulama, was firmly based on the sharia, and served not only to dispossess unlawful owners but also to preserve justice, counter the accusations made by the left against the Islamic Republic, punish wrongdoers and absolve them from their sins, and create an atmosphere of confidence for the assets to which it did not apply.[71] Various objections were raised that the law would be of no practical value; that most of those with illegal assets had already transferred them abroad and fled the country; that the cost of prosecuting them bore no relation to the probable outcome; that the number of actions would probably exceed the capacity of the courts to deal with them; and that the courts that had been designated were not qualified to render judgments in financial affairs as, according to the sharia, only a mojtahed was competent to do so.[72] There are even today not enough mojtahedin who could be taken on as judges in the courts of the Islamic Republic, and so the posts are filled with clerics of lower rank, which contravenes Islamic principles.[73]

More important for the question of land reform was the fact that the law made almost no mention of landed property: Article 1 only defined "derelict land" and "natural resources" and stipulated that the nonexercise of property rights on derelict land must be proved in court. Apart from this, there was no mention of landed property, never mind the illegality of same or of appropriate regulations. Some parliamentarians protested this omission, one remarking that parliament had been referred to the Law on the

Method of Implementing Article 49 time and again during the debates on the bills related to the land reform, always with the promise to put an end to illegal landed property; now the time had come for appropriate clarification. The answer was always the same: The law was worded broadly enough to include illegal landed property. One parliamentarian said that the matter was dynamite and required specific mention of landed property, but a motion proposing a rider to this end was defeated via a strange result to the vote.[74]

The law on the implementation of Article 49 was put into practice no less sluggishly than it had been drafted and approved. A year after it was approved, the time limit the law had set for conducting investigations at state agencies had to be extended. On August 8, 1985, the minister of justice stated in parliament that the responsible officials had no idea of the wrongdoings they were supposed to be investigating. "They do not know how public funds are squandered, how bribery is carried out; in short, they are unfamiliar with such abuses, which is why they first have to become acquainted with them before they can uncover such deeds" (Parliamentary Protocols, p. 21). The extension was granted, but there was still no consistent attempt to implement the law. In the last few months of 1985, Hojjat ol-Eslam Kho'iniha, the attorney general, started a campaign to do so, but the results were meager—very little action but lots of propaganda, with those in charge occasionally telling the press about the successes already achieved. On December 21, 1986, Hojjat ol-Eslam Ramezani, administrator at the Supreme Court of Inquiry, stated that 4,000 people to whom Article 49 applied had already completed the appropriate questionnaires.[75] On November 23, 1987, a few parliamentarians complained that the Supreme Council of Justice had still not submitted its report on the implementation of Article 49, one of them saying: "I fear this session of parliament will come to an end and we shall still not have heard of a case which deals with the implementation of Article 49" (Parliamentary Protocols, p. 20). Implementation was temporarily speeded up in connection with the government's efforts to put the war-weary treasury back on its feet, but they failed to score any appreciable success.

By and large, the implementation of Article 49 did not result in any significant progress for land reform. Individual reports of any measures taken have already been discussed in previous chapters.

9.4 Emergencies to Justify the Forbidden

The more the advocates of land reform felt themselves pressed to acknowledge existing land ownership as lawful and the more they perceived it as inevitable that they would have to approach their objectives from this premise, the more urgent became their need for other grounds in Islamic law on which to justify their venture. The principle of necessity was an obvious choice.

This rule, which was formulated late in Islamic law in the words "necessity justifies the forbidden,"[76] is derived from a number of verses in the Quran that permit the faithful to circumvent previously issued edicts, or primary edicts. Following the list of things the faithful are forbidden to eat in 2/173 and 6/145 comes the passage: "But if someone finds himself in a predicament without . . . coveting [something forbidden] he is not to blame" if he eats the forbidden meat. This emergency provision, or secondary edict, was raised to a principle in the post-Prophet era and used to justify any and every act that was doubtful or illegal within the meaning of the primary edicts. It was not infrequent for such justification to continue for so long that the original ban was forgotten. The increasing frequency and duration of such acts through the centuries and the endorsement or at least tolerance of them by religious authorities indicates the preference for resorting to the principle of necessity.

Nevertheless, primary edicts are only permitted to be suspended temporarily—i.e., for the duration of the emergency—as stipulated in the clause "the extent of the necessities must be taken into account."[77] The primary edict concerned retains its validity "for all Muslims in all places at all times."[78] In addition, the principle of necessity can only permit banned acts if they are not coveted but are committed with reluctance, as the Quran makes clear.

Appeals to the principle of necessity to justify land reform were expressed in almost all the legislative proposals submitted to and approved by the Revolutionary Council and parliament after the fall of the Bazargan government. But the longer the struggle about its permissibility continued, the more limited became the types of estates it was to apply to. In the bill of March 19, 1980, both cultivated and uncultivated estates were, "if necessary," to be placed under state control "on the orders of the ruler" and "with consideration for the requirements of rule" and afterward transferred to needy peasants. The Sevener Commissions charged with implementing the bill were to bear in mind that decisions based on this principle had to be reasonable and that they were not to take land away from anyone if there was no need locally. They were only to requisition cultivated and uncultivated land if the transfer of state land, confiscated estates, and wasteland was insufficient to meet the need.[79]

In the April 1980 bill, necessity was only explicitly mentioned in connection with cultivated estates, but its scope became more comprehensive in the December 1982 initiative, which gave the necessity for land reform as the reason for approving the bill in its entirety. In consideration of the ephemeral character of the emergency situation, the bill was made valid for five years (Article 2), and the order in which the estates were to be transferred was arranged with due regard for necessity (Article 10). Deviations from these enactments were to be punished (Article 10, Note 3).

But the Council of Guardians' rejection of the proposal was also legitimized by the principle of necessity—specifically, with reference to mistakes by parliament in applying it. To wit:

1. It was not necessary to invoke the principle of necessity to transfer wasteland and state or confiscated estates, as they could be transferred on the basis of Islam's primary edicts.
2. It was only possible to establish the necessity for transferring cultivated and uncultivated estates once other types of land had been transferred and it had become clear that they were insufficient to obviate the emergency.
3. The system of the Islamic Republic could not be organized on secondary edicts, temporary regulations, and the clauses of Imam Khomeini's decree of October 11, 1987.[80]

The Council of Guardians' disapproval minimized subsequent use of the principle, and general invocation, as in Article 2 of the December 1982 initiative, was dropped in the May 1985 bill, which only asserted the need for cultivating the uncultivated estates. This provision resulted at worst in the land being sold and the owner being given the proceeds. As the principle of necessity needs a time limit, the May 1985 law was only valid for ten years: Cultivated estates could only be transferred of necessity if they had been squatted by peasants and recovering them would cause the disruption of the Islamic system.[81] The October 1986 law only invoked the principle of necessity to legitimize the transfer of squatted estates, using the same argument. Application of the principle was retrospectively encouraged on August 16, 1988, when the Determination Council voted in favor of transferring uncultivated land as provided for in the May 1985 bill.

The emergency cited to justify restricting private land ownership was variously described in the relevant bills. The simplest forms of justification were the requirements of rule and the need to resolve the land question.[82] The "needs of society," the "self-sufficiency of the country," and "protecting the livelihoods of the peasants" created the March 19, 1980, bill's emergency. The December 1982 legislative initiative contained further emergencies: the need for achieving "economic independence for the country," "preventing the rural exodus," "eliminating poverty," and meeting all the aims and programmatic concepts in Articles 3, 43, and 44 of the constitution. The May 1985 bill spoke of the need to cultivate uncultivated land. Here and in the October 1986 law, the emergency given was the danger to Islamic rule that would result from recovering squatted land from the peasants. The need to have arguments to defuse the counterrevolution, to preserve the peasants' readiness to serve at the front, to observe the Islamic precept of justice, and so on were further factors intended to underpin the permissibility and indispensability of land reform under Islamic law.

Both radicals and conservatives raised objections to invoking the principle of necessity. The former objected that it would only be legitimate to apply secondary legal regulations derived from the principle to questions of property rights acquired lawfully in accordance with the sharia.[83] But as not all rights were so acquired, it would be much better to legitimize land reform with the help of the primary edicts. Hojjat ol-Eslam Mahallati stated: "The government is seeking refuge in the secondary edicts because it is incapable of implementing the primary edicts" and added that it would not do that "we ignore all the primary edicts and turn to the secondary edicts." He then asked whether people thought "the primary edicts [would] not suffice for running society."[84]

Ayatollah Emami Kashani, spokesman for the Council of Guardians, also thought the primary edicts would be better suited to resolving the question. However, the Council differed with Mahallati over which primary edicts were appropriate for restricting or protecting existing property rights. Kashani quoted Ayatollah Montazeri: "It would be an insult to Islamic law and God's rules if we wanted to have everything portrayed as an emergency. Although the secondary edicts are also God's word, the primary edicts form the basis."[85]

One of the conservatives' criticisms of the principle of necessity was that it merely restricted land ownership, whereas what was really needed was to ensure that the uncultivated land was cultivated. Therefore, it was most sensible to leave the owners their land and simply encourage them to make sure that it was cultivated. This argument was later adopted by such moderate supporters of land reform as Hojjat ol-Eslam Harandi,[86] and, as we have seen, it was successful to the extent that the May 1985 bill dealt with uncultivated estates accordingly.

The ephemeral character of the principle was another weak point. Emami Kashani stated: "What is decided on the basis of secondary edicts may not take the shape of a law with no time limit on its validity."[87] For this reason, implementation of the laws concerned was limited to five or ten years. However, the antinomy remained that these laws did not merely provide for land ownership to be suspended for a temporary period but annulled it for an unlimited period. Thus, the time limit did not apply to the substance of the decision, only to the period of its implementation. The owner of squatted land lost his property rights forever upon implementation of the law.

Another point of contention was the question of how well the government had established that an emergency existed. It was repeatedly accused of not having substantiated its claims with details of the distribution, types, and quality of land in different parts of the country.[88] The Council of Guardians insisted that, to be on the safe side, decisions about the transfer of both cultivated and uncultivated estates were only to be made if it could be shown that additional transfers were still required once other land had been transferred.

The relationship between primary and secondary edicts was also in dispute. Hojjat ol-Eslam Musawi Tabrizi took the line that the primary edict "man is the master of his property" becomes invalid in an emergency; thus, in this case no primary edict has been repealed if land is expropriated. Ayatollah Yazdi countered this assertion by speaking of his regret that a "very esteemed scholar from the religious academy [at Qom] . . . is so pointedly questioning property before such a holy assembly [i.e., parliament]."[89]

The question of which authority was entitled to establish that an emergency existed figured large in deciding when to invoke the principle. It was clear to supporters of the jurists' rule that the bearer of authority, Khomeini in this case, had this right; in fact, they said, all the fuss about land reform would not have been necessary, in a formal sense, if he himself had made a decision about this question in the interest of the system of rule he had established. He was constantly bombarded with petitions to do so, but he consistently refused to make any direct use of the powers vested in him to solve the problem, delegating them instead to others. Initially, Ayatollahs Montazeri, Beheshti, and Meshgini were chosen to decide about the legality of the proposals passed by the Revolutionary Council.[90] In October 1981, Khomeini delegated the decision about whether or not there was an emergency to parliament, saying in a letter: "Parliament is entitled to pass and implement any measure effecting the maintenance of the system of the Islamic Republic whose omission leads to decay and gives cause for distress, if the majority in parliament determines [the existence of such a] case and if it is clear that the decision is temporarily valid and is automatically annulled when its cause disappears."[91]

Parliament originally attempted to push through the initiative of December 1982 with the help of this authority and tried to legitimize it by establishing the existence of the emergencies noted above. But by rejecting the initiative, the Council of Guardians made it clear that the power Khomeini had granted was not a carte blanche to make decisions it considered to be contrary to the sharia. One Council member, Ayatollah Jennati, later explained the rejection by saying that a narrow majority in parliament is not entitled to establish that there is an emergency, especially when at least some of the legislators do not possess the appropriate expertise in Islamic law.[92]

This opinion resulted in the powers being revised. Khomeini met the Council's demands to the extent that he made parliament's right to establish the existence of emergencies dependent on a two-thirds majority in each individual case. If a bill was passed with this majority, it no longer needed the approval of the Council.[93] Those parts of the May 1985 bill that dealt with establishing the existence of an emergency were in fact passed by a two-thirds majority, but the Council nevertheless rejected them. Its explanation showed that it knew enough wrinkles in Islamic law to defeat even a bill passed by this majority. The bill assumed the existence of an emergency, but in Article 11, Note 3 it forbade under penalty the transfer of cultivated and uncultivated estates if other land was available for transfer. If other land *might* be available for transfer, then the need for a law to transfer *private* land could not have been established. "The establishment of a current emergency here exceeds the limits of the Khomeini decree," the Council concluded, denying that "the laws which the Council of Guardians has ascertained as being in contradiction to the sharia can be approved and legitimized by invocation of the principle of necessity even when the lack of such necessity has been admitted in the very same law. It surely cannot have been the Imam's intention . . . to let initiatives and bills be passed that are returned to parliament by the Council of Guardians because of their illegality under the sharia." Further, the expropriation and sale of uncultivated estates could not be justified on the basis of an "emergency" need for cultivation, as such reasoning clearly contradicted the rule stipulating that "necessities must be taken into account according to their scope." The Council ascertained further contradictions between the sharia and the bill and rejected the latter in its entirety.[94] Commenting on the rejection, Council spokesman Emami Kashani noted that although Khomeini's decree meant that parliament could arrive at a decision by a two-thirds majority, it nonetheless remained the task of the Council of Guardians to discover whether there was something fishy about the assertion of necessity.[95]

However one is inclined to interpret the Council's arguments, it is evident that it had enough strength to argue about Khomeini's decrees. By relying on this strength, the Council did in fact succeed in minimizing the principle of necessity's usefulness in implementing land reform and passing legislation in general. This principle was intended to protect the Islamic state from dangerous disturbances, not to allow the state's leaders and the legislature to conveniently carry out reforms.

9.5 State Interests to Justify the Forbidden

The Council of Guardians was successful not only in blocking the land reform legislation and watering down decisions by parliament but also in stalling all other matters of social, political, and/or economic relevance in the legislation of the Islamic Republic. It only approved thirty-three out of sixty-four "essential" bills passed by parliament in its first period (May 28, 1980–May 27, 1984), with 25 percent of all bills foundering on its resistance. This proportion was scarcely better in the first three years of the second legislative period, when the Council refused to approve 102 out of 231 bills (44 percent) passed by parliament.[96]

To remedy the situation, Khomeini adopted a measure on January 7, 1988, that seemed very radical: He declared the state to be "the outcome of the absolute rule of the messenger of God and one of the primary rulings of Islam." The decisions made by the state were thus above all the "derived rulings of Islam," including "the duty to pray, to fast and to go on pilgrimage to Mecca. The state can unilaterally annul the contracts which it has concluded with the people on the basis of the sharia as soon as they contradict the interests of the state and of Islam. It can stop any act that runs counter to the interests of Islam, regardless of whether it is an act of worship or not" (*Kayhan*).[97]

Declaring the power of the state to be absolute and raising it to the rank of a primary ruling was intended to end the blockade of the legislature and was greeted with great enthusiasm. The day it was announced, Rafsanjani was noticeably triumphant and, with an eye to the Council of Guardians, said: "I ask the gentlemen nominated by the Imam to take the Imam's views seriously and to no longer obstruct implementation of the Imam's views with their own views and those of others," because with the Imam's decree "the way is blocked for deceptions and hypocrisy and also for obstructing the state in its acts in the name of Islam" (*Kayhan*). Ayatollah Musawi Ardebili remarked that "all problems, such as the Labor Law one ... could be solved with it" and stated that this decree and others in a similar vein issued by Khomeini in recent months "are the most important achievements of the revolution."[98] Ayatollah Montazeri recommended that the Council of Guardians "show perspicacity and take full account of the realities of the revolution and the state" and pointed out that the Council's ruling cannot be "always no and rejection."[99] Prime Minister Musawi declared that Khomeini's message "can put the government in a position to master the complications and problems in any situation with which the international community is burdened" and announced that the government would form several commissions charged with finding solutions for controversial bills with reference to Khomeini's decree.[100] The minister of the interior rejoiced that the latest fatwa by Khomeini "has led the community of Muslims out of the deadlock."[101]

Probably under pressure from the general jubilation, the Council of Guardians announced it was ready "to review the rejected bills with due regard for Khomeini's latest fatwa,"[102] mentioning the land reform bill in this context. Hojjat ol-Eslam Harandi voiced his hope that Khomeini's decree would have an effect in matters of landed property.[103]

The invocation of the "rulership decree" (hokm-e hokumati), its applicability in legislative matters, its absolute character, and its derivation from the interests of the state order went back to the time when the first radical land reform bill was drafted (February 8, 1980). Land transfers were to be carried out "with regard to social needs and the question of self-sufficiency," and confiscation of cultivated estates was permitted "if the Islamic government determines that the interests of the community require it." Later bills approved by the Revolutionary Council were similarly worded. By order of the "ruler" the March 19, 1980, bill also based transfers on the "requirements of rule," the same being true of the April 15, 1980, bill.

In order to justify this last bill, Ayatollah Beheshti said that "the interests of the Islamic community" had played a part in the voting and added that on this Islamic basis the ruling jurist is entitled to encroach upon an individual's property rights.[104] Ayatollah Meshgini voiced the same opinion in an interview with the daily *Kayhan* on February 3, 1981, and Ayatollah Montazeri said: "On the basis of the principle of rule, the Imam may, if necessary, dispose of the assets of persons for the purpose of satisfying social needs. Control by the Imam over the assets [of individuals] is the guarantee for the maintenance of the Islamic character of the economic order."[105]

The principle of necessity came to the fore in later bills and during the parliamentary debates on them, but even then some voices considered the "rulership decree," which is based on the "interests of the community" and the "requirements of rule," to be a better instrument for legitimizing land reform. "The rule of the jurist [need not be] restricted by the principle of necessity. There is no compulsion for him to make the performance or nonperformance of his rule dependent on the existence or lack of a necessity. The interests of the Islamic community are basic to the rule of the jurist. If they require it, he can even take landed property away from its lawful owner."[106]

The same rulership decrees provided the legal basis for a number of appeals to Khomeini to resolve the land reform question and other controversies between parliament and the Council of Guardians. In this context, Khomeini and some of the other leading clerics called on the Council to consider "the interests of Islam" in its decisions.

There was some dissent among the leading clerics in the Islamic Republic about invoking the rulership decrees. When explaining why the ulama did not permit expropriating the cultivated estates and transferring them to peasants, Ayatollah Meshgini gave "the problem of the rule of the jurists" as the main reason and added:

> If we say one should take away the land of a landowner who has cultivated it and in this way has become its owner and share it among other people, this has to do with the governorship of the jurists . . . which is the same as the control of the father over his underage children. . . . Islam recognizes for the ruler and for the Imam of the community such a rule. . . . We are of the opinion that the ruler possesses this authority, naturally on condition that his directives conform to the interests of society and not those of an individual. . . . One part of our bill is based on it. Now a cleric

comes and says: No, the ruler is not entitled to do this; he can accept religious taxes, if they are given to him; he can also, if necessary, climb into the pulpit and instruct the faithful in questions of religion. His rule does not exceed this limit.[107]

Objections were heard even before Khomeini announced the decree on January 7, 1988. President Khamene'i, who clearly knew of the coming decree, warned that the "rulership decrees may not contravene the Islamic ones."[108] Some weeks previously, he had urged the Council of Guardians "to remain vigilant so that no law is passed contravening the constitution,"[109] and he made similar statements about other rulership decrees issued by Khomeini prior to January 1988. He was told off by his leader for his impertinence and subsequently apologized.[110]

Despite all the hopes, Khomeini's decree was not a turning point in legislative questions. Once more, he preferred not to personally face the consequences of having made state power absolute but to delegate the matter, specifically to a new body he created for the purpose, the Determination Council (noted in Chapter 8.6). It comprised the most influential clerical functionaries of the Islamic Republic and held its first session on February 24, 1988. It has since made some decisions in connection with a series of legislative proposals, although these have not always been among the most important, most disputed questions of recent years. There are also the two decisions on the land reform noted in Chapter 8.7.

From the start there were protests, especially from parliament, about the existence and powers of the Determination Council, which caused Khomeini to restrict them toward the end of November 1988 and put legislation back in the hands of parliament and the Council of Guardians. The Determination Council continued to exist, however; it was even written into the constitution when the document was revised, which coincided with Khomeini's death in June 1989. It thus experienced a new revolution, which probably has to do with its being the place where the most influential personalities in the Islamic Republic meet. But the Determination Council is only able to solve the questions still pending to the extent that Islamic rule or the common interests of the rulers permit. On the question of landed property, there are clearly narrow limits imposed on legislation by this form of rule.

9.6 The Position of Wasteland in Islamic Law

In the complicated process of legitimizing land reform by the principle of necessity and other instruments in Islamic law, restrictions on private ownership of cultivated and uncultivated estates were minimized. All eyes therefore turned to the remaining land, which was mainly wasteland. This tendency became pronounced after Khomeini's October 1980 decree, although even prior to this date many people had considered distributing wasteland to the needy a better solution to the land question than confiscation of estates. They were now joined by many advocates of land reform who were becoming increasingly convinced that recourse to the wasteland was inevitable. There were frequent recommendations to accept such a solution as a substitute for the failed reform project, at least temporarily.[111]

But overcoming the social, economic, and Islamic obstacles to releasing wasteland for the land reform required several years of effort by the legislature. Even before the revolution, wasteland was largely state-owned, and releasing it for transfer was not without legal problems. However, it was mainly the release of private wasteland for transfer that dragged on until almost the end of 1986.

In Shi'ite law, wasteland comes under the category of enfal (public land) and is at the Imam's disposal in its "natural, never-tilled state" (mawat al bel-asl). Private individuals can stake it off and acquire a preferential claim to cultivating it (hiyaza), and by reclaiming it they can become the owner (or, according to some jurists, occupier) or monopolize the usufructuary rights to it. The two decisive questions that have become relevant in the Islamic Republic are: (1) Is the reclamation of wasteland only allowed by the individual's own work and thus basically limited to an area that can be tilled by a single person? and (2) Does the reclamation of wasteland require permission from the Imam, or can it occur spontaneously?

A third decisive question concerns wasteland formerly tilled by a private individual who now fails to cultivate it or to exercise his cultivation rights (mawat al bel-'araz), the question being whether failure to cultivate results in the loss of rights as owner or occupier. In this third case the sources distinguish several legal opinions with differing interpretations. These different readings follow from: a) the manner in which the property was acquired (e.g., reclamation, inheritance, gift, purchase, etc.); b) whether the waiver on exercising the right of cultivation has been executed or whether this is unclear; and c) whether the owner is known.

Another factor is the length of time for which cultivation or usufruct has been neglected. In the event that the owner acquired his rights by reclamation or one of the other individual methods mentioned above, one of the sources reads: "Reclamation is permissible, even if the failure to exploit the land is not yet three years old. Deferment of cultivation until the failure to cultivate is three years old is preferable. More preferable still is to forgo taking possession until the prior owner waives his rights."[112] The reason for this cautious legal tack lies in the differences apparent in the interpretations of the appropriate passages in the Quran and the Sunna by various scholars.[113]

The similarity between wasteland and uncultivated land is a further important problem in this discourse. Uncultivated land is defined as land that was once cultivated and has since been left uncultivated for a while. The question therefore arises as to where the difference lies between uncultivated land and wasteland that was formerly cultivated; the regulations that apply to the former might also apply to the latter. There are differing opinions here, too. The classical sources permit the various interests in the Islamic Republic to justify their opinions, which are divided into two broad camps: On the one hand there are those who favor nationalizing private wasteland and on the other those who oppose it. The latter wish to preserve the difference between previously reclaimed and pristine wasteland in order to prevent the tendency to treat uncultivated land as wasteland.

The debates and relevant bills reflect these different positions. As shown above, the September 1979 bill saw the distribution of wasteland as the main element in resolving the land question. It made clear distinctions between uncultivated and pristine wasteland and between private and state wasteland. Private wasteland was to be nationalized if the owner did not cultivate it within a year (Article 8). Anyone who had reclaimed public wasteland without permission before September 17, 1979, could become the owner (Article 21). The later bills, approved between February and April 1980, did not mention private wasteland but did distinguish clearly between uncultivated land and wasteland (defined as pristine)—the latter was made subject to state control, the former was earmarked for transfer. The December 1982 bill distinguished between the different types of wasteland and placed them all under government control, declaring title deeds in the name of private individuals invalid (Article 3). Anyone who had reclaimed wasteland assigned to him by the government became the owner, provided that he complied with its conditions concerning cultivation and so forth (Article 11, Note 1). It became obvious during the parliamentary debate on the bill that strict attention was being paid to avoid allowing uncultivated land to be released for transfer as wasteland, which would be contrary to the sharia.[114] In view of such warnings, the assurance was given that the distinctions were based on Imam Khomeini's book *Tahrir al-Wasila,* which takes the view that wasteland that was previously cultivated and whose owner is known must be designated uncultivated land, never wasteland.[115] The May 1985 bill contained this proviso.

The Council of Guardians was primarily concerned that distinction between the legal provisions relating to the various types of wasteland had been taken into account in these last two bills. In the dispute about the nationalization of derelict municipal land—which had also been the object of prolonged speculation—it only approved bills on condition that the distinctions were made (among other things in that the owner of a previously used plot retained part of it)[116] and rejected an administrative regulation from the Bill Annulling Ownership of Derelict Municipal Land that did not make this distinction.[117]

As long as it appeared to have grounds for hope, the government tried to link the question of the ownership of wasteland to the larger question of a general land reform law and was ambivalent about steps toward regulating them separately.[118] But it was forced to abandon this linkage as its hopes waned. The result was the Bill on the Authority for the Determination of Wasteland and Annulling the Land Registers Concerned, consisting of just one article and seven notes, which had its second reading June 10–12, 1986, and was passed by parliament.

Pursuant to this bill, ownership of nonstate wasteland outside the towns was to be declared invalid. The land concerned had to be placed under the control of the government, which was obliged "in accordance with the regulations to take measures for the use of these estates for agricultural, industrial and public purposes as well as for creating jobs, for satisfying the requirements of the state, revolutionary and municipal institutions, for housing construction and transfer." According to Note 1, responsibility for deciding whether or not a tract of land qualified as wasteland rested with the Ministry of Agriculture, which was to delegate the task to the Sevener Commissions. Note 2 permitted the government to expropriate anyone who had reclaimed wasteland notwithstanding the relevant guidelines contained in the April 15, 1980, bill, provided the commissions established that the persons concerned "do not meet the appropriate requirements."[119]

It is noteworthy that the bill itself did not distinguish between pristine and previously cultivated wasteland, leaving this judgment call to the Sevener Commissions and thus providing them with the opportunity to annul property rights to the latter at their discretion. Experience shows that such arbitrary acts can be expected of the commissions.[120] As expected, the Council of Guardians was not prepared to tolerate this solution to the problem, stating that an executive body could not be entrusted with a task in which it would appear as both plaintiff and judge when verifying its own contentions. The Council also rejected the provision stipulating that everyone must have heard by April 15, 1980 (the date this land reform bill was approved) that only those with government permission could become the owners of wasteland by reclaiming it. The Council objected that not everyone need have known of this regulation as such, it being more important to realize that according to the sharia one could acquire ownership by reclaiming wasteland. Therefore, those who had reclaimed wasteland without permission after April 15, 1980, should still become the owners, at least in those cases in which reclamation was in the interests of the country and was not outrageous. Parliament was compelled to concede both points, dropping Note 2 and amending Note 1 to the effect that in case of litigation the final decision about the legal status of the wasteland in dispute should be left to a "competent court." On the basis of this compromise, the bill finally became law on December 21, 1986.[121]

Many positions that are familiar from the classical works on the sharia were taken in more modern form during these conflicts, both in and out of parliament. But in this case, the centuries-old religious dispute, which applied to concrete economic questions, embodied a clash between differing social interests, whose influence on the legislative process was noted time and again. Hojjat ol-Eslam Kho'iniha, the attorney general, made the most explicit reference to these interests in an interview with the daily *Kayhan* on April 19, 1986, complaining that "even today the problem of the wasteland is not solved." He thought the cause was the fact that "gangs of land speculators have transformed themselves into political currents" and were influencing legislation. Six years before this interview, Ayatollah Meshgini had drawn attention to land speculators in the Islamic Republic who had become millionaires.[122] On January 23, 1984, *Kayhan* stated that they were seriously obstructing the transfer of wasteland. Realizing the influence of the speculators on the courts, some members of parliament voted against entrusting the courts to distinguish between the various types of wasteland, remarking that they had all too often rendered judgment in favor of the speculators.[123]

9.7 Revesting the Foundation Lands

The obstacles to legislating a land reform based on Islamic law have been shown. In addition to the conflicts of interest and differences among experts, there was discord among the various positions in the Shi'ite legal tradition, all of which are seen as the word of God as confirmed in the sources and thus may not be made the subject of dispute or negotiations. Another point must be made before I conclude this elucidation of land reform in the Islamic Republic: Although the lack of a unified Islamist position blocked the reform, unity alone is no guarantee of reformist policies. Consider, for example, the unanimous decision by the ruling Islamists to revoke allocations of foundation estates made to peasants by the shah's regime.

The first steps in this revocation were taken in May 1979, when the Revolutionary Council decided "to annul *ab dato* all the contracts concluded between the foundations and the leaseholders, in as far as they concern public foundations, for the purpose of preventing the forfeiture of claims ... and for the purpose of determining a fair price for the foundation land leased and occupied." In other words, after rescinding the control exercised by the leaseholders and occupiers, the foundations would reallocate the land or other asset in question to the same or other individuals on the basis of sharecropping or lease contracts at a fair rent that took account of the harvest. The Foundation Board was "to collect all the claims lodged by the foundations against the former leaseholders or occupiers, either directly or by means of the sale or transfer of the chattels belonging to them" (Article

1). The bill also decided to replace all the members of the administration of these foundations with new ones (Article 2).[124]

On April 17, 1984, parliament passed a bill on "the annulment of the documents drawn up under the dissolute Pahlavi regime on the occasion of the sale of endowed land and water," pursuant to which "all foundation property sold without basis in Islamic law or which has passed in any fashion into the possession [of others] is to be rededicated as trust property." Documents to the contrary were declared invalid (Article 1). "If the foundation property can be leased and the occupier requests a lease, a contract is to be concluded with him having due regard for the interests of the foundation and the acquired rights of the occupier" (Note 1). All the estates used agriculturally and which as a result of the land reform under the shah's regime were transferred to the beneficed peasants will be leased to the latter with regard for the interests of the foundation and the acquired rights of the peasants. "The sums paid to foundations by the government for the purchase of these estates are deemed gifts. The payments made by the occupiers are to be set off against the market price of the land at [the time of] transfer and the difference determined."[125]

During the debate on this initiative by 116 members of parliament, it was stated to apply to 200,000 units of foundation land,[126] but the spokesman of the presiding parliamentary committee gave an assurance that the draft was so worded that it could effect the return of any foundation property, even if it had been illegally seized five hundred years before the Pahlavi regime.[127] The debates at the first and second readings were extremely short, with no significant differences of opinion. Two parliamentarians moved that the clause dealing with "acquired rights" be deleted because, in their opinion, no rights could be acquired through the illegal seizure of foundation land. However, the motion was rejected. Even the Council of Guardians had no grave doubts that might have endangered speedy passage of the initiative. A note giving the Organization of Foundations permission to "look into the social, political and moral suitability of the usufructuaries of foundation property and to expropriate them upon determination of the lack of suitability" was dropped at the Council's request. The reason it gave for this request was that the organization was not authorized to interfere in matters to be determined solely by the founder or the trustee.[128]

The first of further attempts aimed at regulating the transfer of foundation land within the framework of land reform was made in the administrative regulations of the April 15, 1980, bill, which authorized the Sevener Commissions "to lease foundation estates under the supervision of the Foundation Organization and in accordance with the criteria of Islamic law" (Article 29).[129] The December 1982 initiative contained the same regulation, with the difference that they were to be "transferred in the form of sharecropping leases or in other forms." The Council of Guardians again registered its objection to anyone other than the founder or trustee being entitled to interfere in the affairs of the foundation.[130] The resulting amendments to the May 1985 bill had no effect, as it was rejected in toto.

As the advocates of land reform wanted to include as much land as possible in the transfers, they resisted the objections made by the Council and at the same time gave an assurance that the transfer of foundation land was to be in strict accordance with the sharia. However, they quoted other sources in the sharia to justify their intentions or interpreted the same sources in a manner that suited them.[131]

The Council of Ministers approved the administrative regulations to the April 1984 law on November 28, 1984, but the actual implementation encountered resistance. Rededication was less of a problem if the squatters could be considered close to the toppled regime,[132] but it was much more difficult where it concerned estates that peasants had taken possession of as a result of the shah's land reform program. In early 1985, there was some talk of the imminent implementation of the law, although the papers had already reported some activity prior to this.[133] An attempt was made to placate the peasants with promises: They had no cause for alarm, as they would not lose their land, and they only had to pay rent so that they could use the land in peace.[134] Two years prior to these promises, Khomeini's representative at the Organization of Foundations had declared the following:

> Under the previous regime the foundation estates were sold to peasants at high prices, which was not correct from the point of view of the sharia. We have decided to conclude lease contracts with the owners of these estates according to which they will pay a small sum a month as rent. They will, strictly speaking, be demoted from the position of owner to that of leaseholder, without losing the land. To date we have transferred 4,000 plots of land.[135]

The responsible agencies occasionally had to react to protests by the peasants by reversing their own revocation decisions, as for instance in the province of Kerman, where the annulment of documents from 700 plots of land was rescinded.[136] Protests were also directed against measures taken by the Holy Foundation of Imam Reza, the largest foundation in the country, which was of particular interest to the clergy and which pursued the restitution of its assets with the most determination.[137] There were even more grounds for protest when it became clear that the peasants would not only lose the freehold but also be confronted with increased demands for rent by the Organization of Foundations. A *Kayhan* report on May 4 and 5, 1986, stated that the organization had increased the rent fiftyfold and had reduced the duration of the leases from ninety-nine years to three or five. There had been similar reports prior to this one. At the end of October 1982, the peasants complained about the high rent demanded by the Holy Foundation of the Imam Reza.[138]

The clergy's propensity for recovering foundation property was occasionally unbelievable. On December 29, 1986, *Kayhan* and other papers reported the following:

> Tabris: A court has declared the foundation charter known under the title Rob'e Rashidi valid. . . . Accordingly, all the occupiers of the property concerned are to be expropriated. The foundation property will be rededicated to the purpose stipulated by the founder, i.e., establishing a scientific center.

The report added that Rashid ed-Din Fazl ol-Lah had drawn up the charter 700 years ago and that according to it property in the town of Tabris and the province of Azerbaijan, as well as in the towns of Isfahan, Shiraz, Yazd, and even Musel, belonged to the foundation. Another article on May 23, 1989, stated that the Holy Foundation of Imam Reza had claimed millions of square meters of land in northwest Tehran and that a commission responsible for the implementation of the annulment law had annulled the documents relating to the property concerned and banned transactions in respect of it until the courts reached a decision in the matter.[139] Similar reports were not infrequent.

In this atmosphere, an occasional feudal lord who had fled the country returns and, as the founder, tries to advance a claim for the return of large tracts of land to his foundation.[140] When a member of parliament complained about a similar case, observing that the individual concerned had been a member of the shah's regime, the representative of the Organization of Foundations replied that the man's membership in the former, idolatrous regime had nothing whatsoever to do with the character of his land as waqf property and that the Imam had given orders to spare foundations when seizing the estates of such people.[141]

Notes

1. The specialist periodical *Masa'el-e Keshawarzi* is the best example of the former and *Barzegan* of the latter.
2. *Kayhan*, May 29, 1980; *Ettela'at*, September 1, 1980.
3. *Kayhan*, December 12, 1979.
4. Hojjat ol-Eslam Wa'ezi in PP, November 29, 1982, p. 20; and November 30, 1982, p. 21.
5. According to him there were misjudgments in between one-tenth and three-fiftieths of verdicts on the crimes. *Ettela'at*, October 6, 1985.
6. *Kayhan*, September 29, 1979.
7. *Kayhan*, February 29, 1980.
8. *Ettela'at*, September 1, 1980.
9. PP, June 26, 1983, p. 26f.
10. *Ibid.*
11. *Kayhan*, May 9, 1979.
12. The functionaries and experts I consulted mostly thought that these confis-

cations had been carried out on the basis of the "principles of the revolution" and of the "decisions of the political leaders." Some interviewees refuted that there was any Islamic justification for them, whereas others thought they were based on the Quran, the fatwas of the ulama, the Islamic sense of justice, the Islamic penal code, and/or the fact that the fortunes had been acquired illegally.

13. PP, October 5, 1982, p. 22; January 10, 1983, p. 17.
14. PP, October 5, 1982.
15. *Ibid.*, p. 2.
16. PP, January 10, 1983, p. 24f.
17. PP, September 4, 1982, p. 31.
18. See S. J. Madani 1987, vol, 4. p. 291. The reference to Article 20 of the constitution is not clear but possibly intended to point out the equality of individuals irrespective of their place of abode.
19. *Resalat*, June 25, 1988.
20. Ayatollah Montazeri in *Jomhuri-ye Eslami*, October 21, 1979, and *Kayhan*, April 20, 1988; Ayatollah Meshgini 1980, p. 32f; Sheikh Ali Tehrani in *Jomhuri-ye Eslami*, November 20, 1979, and *Enqelab-e Eslami*, April 28, 1981; Hojjat ol-Eslam Razawi at irregular intervals in *Ettela'at* between November 2, 1985, and March 8, 1986.
21. According to R. Esfahani in *Kayhan*, October 30, 1979.
22. The September 1979 bill on the transfer of estates is based on the premise that landed property is reserved for God and that man has the right to utilize it for useful work.
23. Ayatollah Azari Qomi is the most ardent representative of this attitude. See his series of articles on the subject of "Land and Its Fixtures" in *Resalat*, December 12, 1987, etc.
24. One member of parliament asked whether in the fourteen centuries of Islamic history the landowners had ever paid their tithe and their poor tax to the grand ayatollahs and the religious academies. See PP, March 2, 1982, p. 23.
25. PP, March 2, 1982, p. 24.
26. According to a member of the Supreme Council of Justice, Ayatollah Bojnurdi, in *Jomhuri-ye Eslami*, October 8, 1985.
27. *Kayhan*, January 8, 1984.
28. *Kayhan*, November 9, 1985.
29. *Ettela'at*, November 19, 1985.
30. *Kayhan*, October 30, 1979.
31. On this subject see, inter alia, Meshgini 1980, p. 77, and in *Kayhan*, May 29, 1980; Razawi in PP, May 16, 1985, p. 22, and in *Ettela'at*, January 25, 1986; and Montazeri in *Jomhuri-ye Eslami*, October 21, 1979.
32. Dr. Izadi rejects this interpretation of the concept "strive" (sa'i) in the relevant verse and thinks that here and in other verses it means "striving [to do] good deeds and [to get] the appropriate reward, in the moral sense of the word." See Izadi 1983, pp. 443ff.
33. According to Hojjat ol-Eslam Mahlati in PP, March 2, 1983.
34. Rafsanjani does, however, admit a role for "lawful capital" in the acquisition of property, seeing in capital "crystalized work." *Ettela'at*, September 15, 1981.
35. *Kayhan*, October 30, 1979.
36. *Keshawarz-e Emruz*, December 29, 1979.
37. *Jomhuri-ye Eslami*, October 18, 1979.
38. Razawi in *Ettela'at*, December 16, 1985; Ali Tehrani in *Enqelab-e Eslami*, April 28, 1981.

230   *Islamic Development Policy*

39. PP, December 11, 1960, p. 26.
40. PP, December 11, 1960, p. 23f.
41. According to Esfahani in *Keshawarz-e Emruz,* December 8, 1979.
42. A. A. Miyanji 1984, p. 9.
43. Beheshti in *Kayhan,* October 12, 1981; Harandi in PP, March 2, 1982, p. 21.
44. PP, March 2, 1981, p. 31.
45. PP, February 26, 1964, p. 27.
46. PP, December 16, 1982, p. 17.
47. PP, March 8, 1983, p. 15; October 21, 1986, p. 29.
48. PP, December 9, 1982, p. 17.
49. *Kayhan,* December 29, 1979.
50. *Kayhan,* July 22, 1981.
51. It is likely that Grand Ayatollahs Kounsari and Khou'i held similar views, but this could not be documented.
52. *Ettela'at,* April 22, 1980.
53. *Kayhan,* July 23, 1979.
54. *Mojahed* 175, p. 19; Schirazi 1988, p. 207.
55. *Kayhan,* February 3, 1981.
56. *Kayhan,* February 3, 1980.
57. The yad rule states that control over a thing, in the sense of property, constitutes the same unless the contrary can be proved. It is roughly equivalent to the postulate in English common law that "possession is nine-tenths of the law."
58. *Ettela'at,* January 25, 1986.
59. PP, December 20, 21, and 23, 1982, pp. 16ff.
60. S. J. Madani 1987, vol. 4, p. 285f.
61. PP, December 19, 1982, p. 25.
62. PP, May 19, 1985, p. 24f.
63. PP, March 2, 1981, p. 21.
64. CL 1980/1, p. 8f; Schirazi 1988, p. 184f.
65. PP, March 2, 1981, p. 26.
66. *Resalat,* October 2, 1986.
67. *Kayhan,* May 29, 1980.
68. CL 1981/2, p. 75f; Schirazi 1988, p. 221.
69. The first reading was in June 1983 and the second on January 16, 1984. The amendments the Council of Guardians had demanded were incorporated on August 8, 1984.
70. CL 1985/6, pp. 217ff.
71. PP, March 26, 1983, pp. 21, 25, and 29; January 16, 1984, p. 19.
72. A mojtahed is a cleric who, by studying at a religious academy, has acquired the competence to make independent decisions in questions relating to the religion or Islamic law.
73. PP, June 26, 1983, p. 27; January 16, 1984, pp. 21f and 26.
74. Of 181 members of parliament present, eighty-five voted "aye," thirty-six "nay," and sixty abstained or did not vote. The vote was repeated several times, supposedly because the result was questioned each time. See PP, January 16, 1984, pp. 25f and 29; and June 26, 1983, p. 18.
75. *Resalat* of the same date.
76. J'afari Langerudi 1984, p. 775.
77. *Ibid.,* p. 776.
78. According to Ayatollah Yazdi in *Resalat,* October 2, 1986.
79. CL 1979/80, pp. 619ff; Schirazi 1988, p. 158.

80. See the complete text in S. J. Madani 1987, p. 274f; and *Jomhuri-ye Eslami*, January 19, 1983. Khomeini's decree is discussed in Chapter 8.4. The notification from the Council of Guardians cannot be understood without the help of insiders—Ayatollah Yazdi gave this help when he explained it in parliament in comprehensible terms. See PP, May 16, 1985, pp. 28ff.

81. PP, May 14, 1985, pp. 31ff; May 16, 1985, pp. 20ff; and May 19, 1985, pp. 19ff.

82. As in many relevant bills or legislative initiatives. Even the members of the Council of Guardians recognize the right of the state to make use of secondary edicts. See Ayatollah Yazdi in *Resalat*, October 4, 1986, and Emami Kashani in *Resalat*, October 2, 1986.

83. According to M. Razawi in *Ettela'at*, January 7 and 18, 1986.

84. PP, March 2, 1981, p. 29. He explained in this connection that he had heard that the government was in the process of developing programs for the next twenty years with the help of the secondary edicts.

85. *Kayhan*, June 9, 1987.

86. Emami Kashani in *Resalat*, October 2, 1986, and Harandi in PP, December 2, 1982, p. 18.

87. *Resalat*, October 2, 1986.

88. According to Ayatollah Yazdi, for example, in PP, March 2, 1982, p. 32.

89. PP, March 2, 1982, pp. 30 and 32.

90. It is significant for an understanding of Khomeini's behavior that in doing so he left room to differ from decisions made by his representatives. In respect of the April 1980 bill, it was said later that Khomeini had given it his approval in general but not in detail, according to Beheshti in *Barzegar*, November 29, 1980, and *Ettela'at*, September 14, 1981.

91. Majles-e Shoura-ye Eslami 1982, p. 66.

92. *Ettela'at*, June 2, 1984.

93. *Kayhan*, August 6, 1984.

94. S. J. Madani 1987, p. 285f.

95. *Kayhan*, June 9, 1987.

96. According to Mohsen Alef, member of the Council of Guardians, in *Resalat*, June 6, 1987.

97. A month previously Rafsanjani had declared in respect of other similar decisions made by Khomeini that there was no more need of secondary edicts, as any law could now be passed. See *Kayhan*, December 8, 1987. See also *Kayhan*, December 26, 1987.

98. *Kayhan*, January 18, 1988.

99. *Kayhan*, January 9, 1988.

100. *Kayhan*, January 10, 1988.

101. *Kayhan*, January 13, 1988.

102. *Ibid.*

103. *Resalat*, January 24, 1988.

104. *Ettela'at*, September 14, 1981.

105. *Ettela'at*, August 9, 1980.

106. PP, November 29, 1982, p. 22; November 30, 1982, p. 17.

107. *Kayhan*, February 3, 1981.

108. *Kayhan*, January 2, 1988.

109. *Resalat*, December 12, 1987.

110. *Resalat*, October 16, 1987, and January 13, 1988.

111. Ayatollah Montazeri, for one, made such a recommendation. See *Jomhuri-ye Eslami*, March 14, 1983, and April 23, 1983.

112. See Meshgini 1980, pp. 53ff.
113. The various interpretations and legal regulations are dealt with not just in the classical law books but also in all the contemporary writings, including a series of articles in the newspapers on the subject of landed property.
114. PP, November 29, 1982, p. 18.
115. According to Musawi Tabrizi in *ibid.*, p. 19; and Harandi in PP, November 30, 1982, p. 18.
116. This bill was approved on March 20, 1982. See PP, 1981/2, pp. 195ff.
117. CL 1980/1, p. 10.
118. On May 24, 1984, the government withdrew the bill it had submitted to parliament dealing with the annulment of registries for wasteland because it hoped to push its aims through better by invoking the September 1979 bill. See PP of the same date, p. 29.
119. PP, June 10, 1986, p. 28f; June 11, 1986, pp. 20ff; and June 12, 1986, pp. 19ff.
120. Ayatollah Musawi Ardebili reported such cases. See *Kayhan*, July 11, 1984.
121. The Council of Guardians returned this bill to parliament twice for amendment. The Parliamentary Protocols do not record the amendment of the note but it is in CL 1986/7. See *Resalat*, June 9, 1987, on the Council's position on this bill.
122. *Kayhan*, May 29, 1980.
123. PP, June 12, 1986, p. 20.
124. CL 1979/80, pp. 20ff; Schirazi 1988, pp. 47ff.
125. The meaning of this sentence is unclear. Compare CL 1984/5, p. 20.
126. PP, August 11, 1983, p. 22.
127. *Ibid.*
128. S. J. Madani 1987, vol. 4, p. 328f.
129. The regulation is not included in the bill itself. See *ibid.*
130. S. J. Madani 1987, vol. 4, p. 281.
131. PP, December 8, 1982, p. 14; December 12, 1982, pp. 22ff.
132. Reports to this effect occasionally appeared in the press. See, for example, *Ettela'at*, November 23, 1982, and *Kayhan*, February 6, 1983.
133. See, for example, *Kayhan*, November 24, 1984.
134. *Kayhan*, January 13, 1985.
135. *Jomhuri-ye Eslami*, February 6, 1983.
136. *Kayhan*, November 2, 1985.
137. *Kayhan*, September 2, 1986, reported that this foundation had lost 375 of its agricultural fields (mazra'e) as a consequence of land reform under the shah, but *Resalat*, October 6, 1988, stated that 798 of its farming properties had been returned in consequence of the implementation of the annulment law.
138. *Ettela'at*, October 24, 1982.
139. The report was by the chairman of the Special Civil Courts, Hojjat ol-Eslam Kermani, and concerned cultivated and inhabited property that had changed hands several times. Some of them had been sold to a housing cooperative after the revolution for millions of tomans by the Organization of Municipal Property. See *Ettela'at*, May 23, 1989.
140. PP, April 24, 1986.
141. *Resalat*, May 3, 1989.

10
Problems of Agricultural Management

10.1 Criticism of the Status Quo

In the postrevolutionary period, changes in the managerial organization of agriculture and the relationship between owners and peasants occurred. These changes could only partially be related to Islamic law,[1] as the problems concerned did not lend themselves to a dispute in this framework. Awareness of the need for organizational reform of agricultural enterprises was expressed in criticism of the existing state of affairs, accompanied by reform proposals. The more recent the criticism, the more strongly it implicitly and explicitly complained about managerial organization as either continued or introduced in the Islamic Republic.

Izadi's 1979 program began the criticism by pointing out the ineffectiveness of the modern enterprises the state had promoted with large amounts of capital and then transferred to foreign companies or "influential citizens." These and similar measures had badly and needlessly damaged the traditional agricultural organization based on the village unit and traditional production techniques (p. 2). To reverse this trend, Izadi proposed to make the village and its traditional farming methods and techniques the basis for measures to reform the organization of agriculture and integrate modern technology. The program explained: "Institutions are available to the village, as a social and productive unit, whose promotion can not only step up production but also make it possible to benefit from its cultural structure, which is based on cooperativeness." Integrating modern methods into "small, semimechanized enterprises has frequently proved to be effective. In addition, they permit care to be exercised in the use of modern equipment which cannot be produced within the country and whose import increases the external dependence of the country" (p. 3). The document followed up this criticism and its declaration of principles with a list of individual measures to reform managerial organization. This list will be dealt with below.

By and large, the draft of the 1983 development plan took the same view as the Izadi program concerning the existing state of affairs and the list of reforms.[2] The criticism of the existing state of affairs in the 1987 self-sufficiency plan described a situation that could be considered a legacy of the shah's regime, as no significant reforms were implemented in the postrevolutionary era—it spoke of the "ineffectiveness of managerial organization" encountered in 1987 (p. 99).

Minister of Agriculture Kalantari expressed himself in the same vein a year later when he spoke to the National Congress to Investigate the Problems of Agricultural Development on February 26, 1989. He said that the managerial reform measures initiated and promoted by the government in the postrevolutionary era "have failed to achieve their original aim. The needless multiplicity of types of enterprise, the confusion in the organization of productive agricultural activity, the conversion of types of enterprise immediately after their introduction, and above all the lack of information about the success or failure of [various] types of enterprise clearly indicate that no decisive resolutions have been passed concerning the managerial organization of agriculture."[3]

This criticism also implied a turning away from the glorification of the traditional types of enterprise, as took place prior to the revolution and in the document mentioned above. The turning away was done carefully, at least in public, not only because it meant a reversal of the positions previously extolled but also because there was some uncertainty about the changeover to large types of enterprises. Kalantari expressed this uncertainty clearly, saying: "Obviously, we are of the opinion that large enterprises are more useful for our country. But we do not know how big they ought to be. We satisfy ourselves with generalities. The Ministry of Agriculture wants to support the types of enterprises chosen by the peasants. We do not want to impose a managerial order on the peasants." In the same speech, he announced the government's intention to conduct trials with all types of enterprise until the end of the first five-year plan (March 1994) in order to find out which were most suitable for Iran.[4]

10.2 Rehabilitating Sharecropping

The main references to a management organization based on Islamic law are found vis-à-vis sharecropping in the relevant laws of the postrevolutionary era. It was a highly criticized characteristic of Iranian land tenure before the land reform in the 1960s[5] and as such was largely replaced in the reform. But its image has now been rehabilitated, even if in practice it has hardly gained ground.

Sharecropping was first mentioned in Article 3 of the legislative proposal on the transfer of land approved by the Revolutionary Council in September 1979, where it was considered an indirect form of participation by the landowner in the cultivation of cultivated land, giving him the opportunity of claiming that he is fulfilling his duty and responsibility to cultivate the soil. The legislative initiative approved by parliament in December 1982 enabled the owner of cultivated land to avoid expropriation by signing a sharecropping contract with the peasant if the transaction was concluded under government supervision (Article 6, Note 1). Sharecropping fulfilled the same function in the May 1985 bill, which also protected uncultivated estates from transfer if the owner leased them to sharecroppers for cultivation (Article 5). Article 12 of the same bill provided that estates that were due for transfer could also be made available to the peasants for sharecropping. Both this legislative proposal (Article 5, Note 4) and that of December 1982 (Article 6, Note 3) permitted foundations to enter into sharecropping contracts with peasants. Sharecropping was also recommended in other laws indirectly relating to agriculture, as, for instance, in the September 1983 Noninterest-bearing Bank Transactions Act that allows banks to invest in "Islamic transactions" (Article 3).[6]

Not all Islamic circles approved of the rehabilitation of sharecropping. Though not denying that this activity is enshrined in Islamic law, the cleric Ali Tehrani rejected it as unproductive and contrary to the present needs of the country, demanding that producer cooperatives be introduced instead.[7] Reza Esfahani confirmed that early Islam permitted sharecropping because in the simple social relations of the time it prevented the concentration of wealth in a few hands. But relations today are different, he said, and, as such, sharecropping must be declared impermissible.[8] Hojjat ol-Eslam Harandi also rejected it, stating that if sharecropping were actually able to solve Iran's problems it would have no problems today.[9] However, Ayatollah Beheshti specifically defended sharecropping, seeing no problem in this relationship between the landowner and the tenant as long as the share of the product demanded by the owner is not excessive and unjust.[10] These differences of opinion in the evaluation of sharecropping surfaced time and again during the parliamentary debates on the bills noted above. During the December 9, 1982, session, one member of parliament cautiously suggested renouncing sharecropping as the practice conjured up the spirit of the landlords' old exploitation. (Parliamentary Protocols, p. 23). Corresponding motions, however, were rejected by the majority of members.[11]

Because of the lack of statistics, it is impossible to determine the extent to which sharecropping has actually been revived.[12] It is known that the Holy Foundation of the Imam Reza has sharecropping contracts with peasants,[13] with 12,000ha under cultivation by sharecroppers in the northeast region of Sarakhs.[14] Nevertheless, it is safe to say that sharecropping, at least in its traditional form, will never regain the significance it once had, even if it is sanctioned by Islam, because property and labor relationships in Iranian agriculture have changed too much to leave it much scope.

As part of the Islamization of the banking system, the Bank for Agriculture has since 1984 been offering its customers several types of Islamic options that could influence the management of agricultural enterprises by providing capital. The annual reports published by the Ministry of Agriculture on Iran's agricultural situation list the following options:

1. bank purchase of agricultural machinery and equipment at the request of the farmers, who pay for it in installments (forush-e eqsati)
2. cash preemption of the peasants' products to cover their fixed expenses and the financing of certain items (salaf khari)
3. remuneration of specific tasks commissioned by the bank (ja'ale)
4. setting up partnerships on the basis of undivided property (mosharekat-e madani)
5. sharecropping (mozare'e)

In 1984, 40 percent of the loans granted by the bank were in the form of such options, with sale on installment (34.4 percent) and preemption (6.1 percent) making up the lion's share. There were no sharecropping leases (pp. 42ff). There was about the same ratio of types of loans in the two subsequent years for which there are reports.[15] As with sharecropping, all the above options were known to and practiced by Iranian agriculture even before the Islamization of the banking system.

10.3 Establishing the Cooperatives

10.3.1 Cooperatives and the Sharia

Contrary to sharecropping, whose roots in Islamic law are not questioned even by those who oppose reviving it, the cooperative system in the Islamic Republic is still a matter of controversy. Differences have surfaced during the legislative debates about the establishment of agricultural cooperatives (called mosha') and during the debates on enshrining the cooperative system in the socioeconomic order of the Islamic Republic.

Article 44 of the Islamic Republic's constitution numbers the cooperative system, along with the private and state sectors, among the pillars of the state's economic order. All the postrevolutionary agropolitical programs and draft plans have held out cooperatives as a significant step toward the optimal utilization of production factors and strengthening of the peasants' communal spirit. Many people consider cooperatives to be a value rooted deep in the Islamic social order.[16]

Cooperatives were not unknown in prerevolutionary Iran and have been legally regulated since 1925.[17] Producer cooperatives like "bone" can be traced back a very long way in the history of the country but are not mentioned in the sharia.[18] The first attempt to draft a law to implement Article 44 of the constitution was made three years after the revolution. According to a report in *Kayhan,* the Supreme Economic Council had approved the Draft Bill on the Limits and Nature of the Cooperative Sector in the Islamic Republic of Iran on April 13, 1982, but it was only submitted to parliament for its first reading on June 8, 1983. The first reading was repeated in the second session of parliament on April 13 and 16, 1985; the second reading began on February 17, 1987, and ended on May 3 the same year. It was approved by parliament, but the Council of Guardians rejected it on the grounds that it contravened the sharia and the constitution. Parliament debated the rejected initiative anew in November 1989, corrected it, and resubmitted it to the Council of Guardians, which again objected. Once more, parliament had to correct the bill in accordance with the Council's wishes. This activity all took place at the end of February 1991.[19] But the Council was still not satisfied; the press reported its opposition on March 19, 1991. After being rejected and corrected again, it was finally passed into law toward the end of September 1991.

As a member of parliament said, the initiative aimed to establish an Islamic form of cooperative system differing from everything else known by this name in the rest of the world, especially from the monstrosities set up under the shah.[20] A large minority nonetheless spoke out against a cooperative system in general and this legislative initiative in particular, claiming that it would result in restrictions on the private sector, increase state influence on the economy, open the gates to totalitarianism, and lead to structures similar to those in the Soviet Union and China.[21]

Some objections to cooperatives and to legal safeguards for them were stated in terms of the sharia. It is a fact that the sharia does not provide for cooperatives (ta'awoni) and thus makes no reference to the corresponding forms of contract. Although Islamic law contains provisions for partnerships (sherkat), it specifically precludes those based on joint productive labor (sherkat-e abdan).[22] The opponents of the initiative used this fact to question the legality of cooperatives in principle and to demand that the regulations in the draft be reworded so that they were no longer at odds with the sharia. For example, they proposed that profits be calculated and paid after deducting costs, including the members' wages.[23] This measure would transform the cooperatives into partnerships and was followed by the remark that such transformed enterprises need no longer be called ta'awoni but could reasonably be termed sherkat.[24] Others were not satisfied with this legal device, objecting that it did not transform cooperatives into partnerships; they would still not be in accordance with the sharia and would thus have to be rejected.[25]

The proponents of the initiative also had reservations based on Islamic law. Some of them thought cooperatives could be adequately covered by Islamic company law; they, too, regarded cooperatives as only a form of partnership. The legislative initiative defined cooperatives in such terms. Other advocates drew attention to the legal problems that could arise if this argument were carried to its logical conclusion,[26] among them the fact that the sharia does not provide a form for cooperative contracts in the same way that it does for all other types of contracts conforming to it.[27] One member of parliament rejected this objection with the observation that, as Imam Khomeini remarked in his book, *Bai'* (vol. 6, p. 120), neither a written nor a verbal form is necessary to conclude a contract; one could in fact be tacitly entered into (mo'atati).[28] He and other members of parliament pointed out that even the familiar forms of Islamic contract do not represent regulations created by Muhammad (ahkam-e ta'sisiye) but are forms of transaction that were in common use before his time and were merely sanctioned by him (ahkam-e emza'iye). In consequence, completely novel forms of contract could also be accorded legal status, as the great scholars had done in the case of insurance policies.[29]

10.3.2 Setting up the Mosha' Cooperatives

Against the background of the disputes relating to cooperatives described above, its proponents attempted to set up new producer cooperatives in rural areas, to reorganize the old ones, and to promote them as far as possible in connection with, among other things, Islamic land reform. They focused their attention on establishing the so-called mosha' cooperatives.[30] Setting them up proceeded apace with the transfer of estates by the Sevener Commissions. Their proponents based their support not only on the value of cooperativeness in Islam (as cited above) and in the constitution[31] but also on economic grounds, including the benefits of the large-scale use of machinery and other assistance and services that the state would provide. It was also argued that because of this assistance, the government expected to be able to more readily persuade the cooperatives to cultivate its preferred strategic products.[32] Those in favor of mosha's were without doubt influenced by the criticism voiced by some experts about the destructive effects of the shah's land reform on the traditional form of cooperative (bone). Because of the many advantages attributed to this form, those in favor of mosha's wanted to reactivate it, but in an Islamic form.[33]

The mosha's were first mentioned in the legislative proposal on the transfer of land approved on February 27, 1980, by the Revolutionary Council, which stated: "The transferred estates take on the form of partnerships, cooperatives and mosha's."[34] The legislative proposal of September 17, 1979, still stated that preference would be given to those who "come together to form work groups or labor cooperatives (bone) or who for the purpose of cooperation decide to form companies."³⁵ All the legislative proposals on land reform approved by the Revolutionary Council before April 15, 1980, made the transfer dependent on, among other things, the peasants' readiness to form mosha's. Several aspects of the April 15, 1980, bill were moderated because of pressure from opponents of this sort of commitment; thus, the bill allowed land to be transferred to individuals in exceptional circumstances.³⁶

The mosha' was described more precisely in the April 1980 bill's administrative regulations, approved by the Council of Ministers on May 21, 1980. They stipulated that a mosha' must have at least five members, at least one of whom must be familiar with farming. Each household was to receive as much land as necessary to ensure its livelihood according to local custom. The Sevener Commissions were to determine the actual size of the plots according to the criteria detailed in Article 30 of the regulations.³⁷

The specific rules for establishing such cooperatives were based on these administrative regulations. They provided that each mosha' must have at least five and at most twenty members who participate of their own free will; each member must have an equal share of the jointly held land and must himself work in his mosha'. In addition to the soil, water and machinery were deemed joint property. The annual yield was to be divided in equal proportions among the members unless they did not contribute equal amounts of work time to production. Each mosha' was headed by a director (sarmosha') and two advisors (moshawer) to deal with the outside world, but decisions were to be made jointly by all the members.³⁸

In the further course of legislative procedures relating to land reform, the regulations dealing with mosha's were rejected in December 1982, but the mosha's were approved by the Determination Council some years later, in June 1989. However, this approval only applied to the squatted estates of more than 100ha that were due for transfer, where parceling out was seen as disadvantageous. The many thousands of mosha's established in the meantime were safeguarded by the April 1980 bill. Although it was partially rescinded by Khomeini and parts of it were called into question by the course of later legislation, this bill was quoted time and again to legitimize various decisions. The votes against mosha's during the relevant debates in parliament were based both on the negative experiences seen with this type of enterprise and on the fact that the government was more or less forcing the peasants to set them up.³⁹

The number of mosha's peaked at 12,000 (with 89,000 households)⁴⁰ by the end of 1364 (1985/6), but this figure said nothing about their true nature. A less impressive picture was painted by the figures from (1) fieldwork commissioned by the Central Office for Rural and Agricultural Research at the Ministry of Agriculture; (2) reports in newspapers; (3)

statements (some in writing) by experts, responsible politicians, or functionaries largely confirming the results of the fieldwork; and (4) a brochure put out by the central office of the Sevener Commissions. The fieldwork investigated a number of typical mosha's in various provinces one to three years after they had been set up. The results can be summarized as follows:

1. In almost all mosha's, the members showed no understanding for the joint land ownership that had been forced on them and in fact preferred to parcel it out amongst themselves. Elyasian attributed this preference to the lack of a guiding authority to hold the mosha's together.[41] He also cited other reasons for the disharmony among the members and their reluctance to leave the property undivided, such as individualism, the temptations of ownership, mistrust of the other members of the mosha' engendered by unequal workloads, and the lack of a cooperative spirit.[42] There were political reasons, too. For example, in Gorgan and Gonbad, massive government intervention in the councils set up by the Turkmen immediately after the revolution turned the mosha's into unpopular government-controlled institutions that the peasants preferred to dissolve. The same was true for mosha's "whose members desire to parcel up the undivided land and become the private owners of their land."[43]

2. Almost everywhere the "temptations of individual ownership" led to the joint property (land, water) being parceled up and the jointly owned possessions (equipment, implements) being shared out. Collective ownership was spontaneously reduced to such an extent that any further reductions were either impossible or disadvantageous. Credit from the Bank for Agriculture, for instance, was only granted to mosha's; financing of wells, water pumps, and tractors was beyond the means of the individual member. Working with tractors and monitoring and maintaining the pumps also had to be jointly regulated, and in Gorgan the costs of operating a plane to combat cotton pests and of digging and maintaining canals were also joint matters.[44]

3. The disbanding of the mosha's also manifested itself in their splitting up into working parties, with a majority of the members working either by themselves or together with family. Groups two strong were the most common. In Fesa, twenty-four out of forty-one working groups had less than five members.[45] All the groups in Baft consisted of two members.[46] The mosha' survived best if it consisted of family members.[47]

4. The mosha's were mostly given wasteland, sometimes even sandy, saline, or stony soil, which needed a great deal of work and money to make it arable. Although the peasants received a plot of the "local customary size," they could not make full use of it because of the quality of the soil and the parsimony of the loans granted. One year after transfer, only 20 percent of the land in Jiroft was able to be cultivated,[48] in Baft between one-third and two-thirds.[49] The loans brokered by the Sevener

Commissions and granted by the Bank for Agriculture were often inadequate to fund land reclamation.[50] In consequence, the peasants had to turn to middlemen and preemptioners who provided them with the remaining money at excessive interest rates.[51] The loans granted by the preemptioners often amounted to many times the state loans.

5. The work of the mosha's suffered not only from a lack of loans but also from a lack of such inputs as pesticides, artificial fertilizers, seed corn, equipment, machinery, and spare parts. The peasants could not afford the prices on the free market, where all these things were available. According to a report in *Kayhan* (November 14, 1987), there were twenty-four tractors in the village of 'Ata Abad in the Gorgan region, but most were not in working order because of the lack of tires and other spare parts.

6. Despite its poor provision of the loans and other things so necessary for production, the government pressured the peasants to cultivate "strategic" crops. But these yielded much less than the summer crops, with which the mosha's could earn good profits to help meet their capital requirements. Consequently, the peasants avoided this pressure where possible, resulting in more tension between the government and the members of the mosha's.[52]

7. Members of mosha's suffered from many other problems. Where they were given wasteland, it was often not in their own village, and they had to relocate, although they lacked the money to build new houses. Their children were unable to go to the village school because of the great distances involved, and medical care was even more difficult to get than in the villages themselves.[53]

The problems mentioned caused some peasants to leave their newly acquired land, lease it out, and earn their living elsewhere. For this reason, mosha's in Garmsar (Tehran province) were dissolved.[54] The destruction to the soil in Jiroft caused each summer by sandstorms was so great that some members of the local mosha's preferred to work elsewhere as agricultural laborers rather than as landowners in their mosha's.[55] In Fesa, 45 out of 222 members left their mosha's.[56]

The extent of dissolutions can be calculated on the basis of the numbers given at various times by the heads of the central office of the Sevener Commissions. As noted, Hojjat ol-Eslam Harandi mentioned a total of 12,000 mosha's encompassing 89,000 households as of March 1986. Maleki stated that 10,000 mosha's were established from March 21, 1980, to March 20, 1987.[57] Sharif Zade counted 10,800 mosha's with 89,000 households at the end of 1367 (March 20, 1989).[58] In order to even begin to make a reasonable guess at the total number of mosha's dissolved between March 1986 and March 1989, these figures must be adjusted to include the 1,500 mosha's established in 1366 (1987/8), according to another member of the central office.[59] This piece of information also contained an expression of regret for the fact that because none of these mosha's had received the motor-driven pumps for irrigating their land, tens of thousands of hectares were having to be left uncultivated.

The data from the field research and other sources enable us to conclude that on two counts this experiment is suffering or has even failed in terms of the original concept: First, many peasants are not prepared to be forced into collectives from which they do not expect any concrete benefit; second, the government has proved incapable of providing the mosha's with adequate resources, without which they cannot function. These observations may not apply to mosha's that were set up on squatted land—i.e., good land that was already under cultivation—or mosha's that have funds of their own and can cultivate the land reasonably successfully even without adequate assistance from the Sevener Commissions. Even these mosha's are in all probability exceptions only in economic terms, not in terms of the original organizational concept of cooperatives in which production is communal.

Despite many negative experiences, those responsible for land distribution and establishing mosha's cling to the idea of a cooperative organization for peasant farming. The number of mosha's is to increase to 20,000 by the end of the first five-year plan (March 20, 1994).[60] The proposal has been made that in order to improve the provision of state assistance and services, the cooperatives should be grouped into regional associations or service communities to provide support to all their members. Another proposal is that in addition to farming, the mosha's should take up animal husbandry to provide themselves with a further source of income.[61] It can be assumed that other proposals will be made, but postrevolutionary experiences do not permit an optimistic assessment of their feasibility or success.

10.3.3 The Dissolution of the RPCs

The members of the Rural Producer Cooperatives (RPCs) set up in the prerevolutionary era reacted differently to the responsible functionaries. The latter placed great store on forming and promoting the cooperatives, whereas in many instances the former advocated dissolution. As a result, nineteen of the thirty-nine RPCs established before the revolution were taken apart immediately after it. The members of some other cooperatives decided on a quieter process of dissolution that was obviously more advantageous to them—they went over to tilling the land on an individual basis without forgoing the benefits each cooperative's central management was able to provide (equipment, machinery, spare parts, other input factors, and so on). Sociologists and experts from the Ministry of Agriculture observed how these cooperatives were being transformed into Service Centers without being renamed.[62] This process began even before the revolution in Shahmaran, where "farming is presently being conducted on a completely individual basis. In another member village, seven out of thirteen members are working individually. This tendency is gaining ground despite the cooperative's relative success by and large, despite the peasants' traditional experience with collective work and despite the fact that the work groups came about voluntarily."[63] No collective work was observed in three of five Rural Producer Cooperatives visited in Isfahan province, and the majority of members worked alone in the other two.[64]

Despite this trend, the directors at the Ministry of Agriculture continue to believe in the supposed benefits of large-scale organization, and this belief might well explain the renewed encouragement for active revival of RPCs. A seminar titled "Managerial Organization of Agriculture in Iran," held in Mashad in early February 1990 and attended by the ministry's directors, ended with a resolution that recommended, among other things, "paying attention to and creating the necessary prerequisites for the development of Rural Producer Cooperatives in the suitable regions while taking into consideration the cooperative culture, which is deeply rooted in the rural and agricultural society of Iran."[65] At the end of October 1990, the deputy director of the department responsible for RPCs and Farm Corporations (FCs) at the Ministry of Agriculture stated that the agency had set itself the aim of bringing small landowners together in RPCs and FCs. At the same time, the director for FCs reported that twenty RPCs had already been set up that year (1369, or 1990/1) and that the establishment of another twenty RPCs was being considered. He added that 1m hectares of land were to be made available to the RPCs in the course of the five-year plan.[66]

10.3.4 Newer Cooperatives

The continued belief in cooperatives and the occasional encouragement given to them by some of the Islamists in power (as reflected in administrative regulations) have facilitated the development of new forms of cooperatives, which might more properly be termed loose associations of independent production enterprises. These include the so-called Agricultural Cooperatives (sherkatha-ye ta'awoni-ye keshawarzi, or ACs), which are active in all agriculture-related branches, from beekeeping to the manufacture of agricultural equipment. Although there were forty cooperatives of this type in existence before 1979, their number increased so rapidly after the revolution that they can be considered characteristic of the Islamic Republic. A turning point in the setting up of ACs seems to have come in 1984, their number rising from 80 in that year to 500 in 1989, with some 150,000 members.[67]

Only a relatively small number of the ACs—81 out of the 404 registered at the end of 1365 (March 1987)—were engaged in agriculture and horticulture, whereas 146 were listed as engaged in poultry farming.[68] At the regional level, the ACs joined forces in associations of specific branches of agriculture in order to be able to better represent their interests vis-à-vis the state-run Central Organization of Rural Cooperatives.[69]

The ACs and their associations owe their existence and the growth in their numbers to the fact that they could easily overcome the obstacles that the government, Prime Minister Musawi's administration in particular, placed in the way of individual private enterprises in procuring inputs (especially from abroad) and marketing their produce.[70] On the other hand, it was the government's policy of encouraging cooperatives that caused the private enterprises to form ACs. Cooperatives encountered the obstacles mentioned above much less frequently than did private enterprises, and they enjoyed additional privileges such as access to loans from the Bank for Agriculture.[71] In a 1985 report on ten "exemplary ACs," the minister of agriculture urged the government to provide all possible aid and protection. One of the ten was the AC Fath ol-Mobin, with some 3,000 members. It operated plantations managed by farmers from Isfahan on leased land in Khuzestan province and paid its peasants as sharecroppers.[72] At the National Congress of Rural and Agricultural Cooperatives, which opened on October 28, 1988, in Tehran, the head of the Central Organization of Rural Cooperatives stated that forming ACs was one of the "concrete aims" of his organization.[73]

The growth of the ACs in the Islamic Republic and the fact that they were actually organized as independently operating enterprises occasionally caused government functionaries to publicly voice their doubts about the genuineness of this type of "cooperative," the more so when it became clear that in some branches of agriculture the ACs were creating cartel-like structures, with all the ensuing consequences.[74] According to one member of parliament, Bahonar, the scale of these cooperatives exceeded that of the cartels in the capitalist countries, and he complained that they enjoyed all the benefits the government had to offer but did not pay any taxes.[75] The fact that the pistachio growers' AC exported nuts for $82m in one year made its size clear.[76]

The so-called cooperating production groups (guruhha-ye hamyari-ye toulidi) are another type of cooperative the Ministry of Agriculture has been striving to establish for some time. The necessity of taking practical steps in this direction was emphasized at a seminar held toward the end of September 1984 to examine the possibilities for this sort of cooperative.[77] The first reports about them appeared in May 1986, and there were stated to be seventy-four of them at the end of October 1988. This slow progress proves that the government had not made any great effort to ensure success in this field.[78] The information available about these production groups is still too scanty to give a clear picture of their structure or earnings. They consist of just a few members at the village level and reportedly enjoy preferential treatment in the allocation of state services. The aim of these groups is to raise their members' income and thus motivate them to stay in their villages. The special point about these cooperatives is that members are supposed to help each other with their own means, which is why they are known—literally translated—as "self-help production groups."[79]

A fourth type of cooperative was called into being in the first year after the revolution to counter unemployment among school leavers and graduates. These cooperatives were to do work in agriculture, among other things, and to this end were to be given wasteland and financial assistance in the shape of easy loans. They were to be supervised by the so-called Centers for Improving Productive and Constructive Services, which the Revolutionary Council had established in December 1979, but they never became significant. By 1985 there were 4,350 of them with 7,304 members in mining, agriculture, and industry. The lack of materials, capital, and effective management was considered the reason for the failure of this experiment.[80]

In August 1989 there was talk of a type of cooperative that had been called into being sometime before and was to be "implemented in a flash"—namely, the Cooperatives of Wheat Farmers (ta'awoni-ye gandomkaran). These were to be set up throughout the country near the Service Centers with the aim of raising wheat production from 1,560 to 3,000 kg/ha on irrigated land.[81] According to a presentation at a seminar held on the subject in mid-October the same year, the target had been exceeded, with an average yield of 3,373kg/ha on almost 500,000ha. *Barzegar* devoted an entire edition to this report, which also proclaimed the setting up of seven wheat cooperatives in Isfahan province.[82] No further information is available about such actions at present.

10.3.5 Rural Cooperatives

This overview of cooperatives engaged in agriculture in the Islamic Republic cannot be concluded without a brief word about the development of the Rural Cooperatives (RCs) in the postrevolutionary era. As has been indicated, the RCs played an important part in the life of the rural population even before the revolution by providing their members with loans, buying up their produce, and supplying them with food. However, as mentioned in Chapter 1, they had numerous shortcomings that limited their activities and services.

From the very beginning, the Islamic Republic aimed to encourage the RCs, extend the scope of their activity, and, "based on the experience of the past . . . adapt them to the needs and demands of the peasants as well as their customs and traditions."[83] The need to encourage the RCs provided proponents of a cooperative system with an argument with which they could try and justify their support of laws to implement Article 44 of the constitution. The measures designed to promote the RCs in particular reached a verbal climax at a meeting of the National Congress of Rural and Agricultural Cooperatives in October 1987, when numerous highly placed speakers emphasized the tremendous importance of the cooperative system in the Islamic social and economic order.[84] They also took the opportunity to make public, among other things, details about the state of the RCs, their associations (ettehadiye), and the Central Organization of Rural Cooperatives, which at the time included 3,111 RCs and 188 ACs with a combined 16,089m rials capital. These cooperatives provided services to 55,871 villages with over 4,164,948 members. The RCs maintained 10,000 sales outlets and the same number of agencies, which supplied peasants with paraffin only.[85] The number of RCs had risen by only nine and the number of associations by one at the beginning of 1990, but they were providing their services to some 1,129 more villages.[86]

Despite the increase in the number of villages and members served by RCs, there was in many cases a reduction in the services they actually provided, in particular with respect to the vending of sugar, soap, detergents, shoes, and textiles. For example, between 1983/4 and 1988/9 deliveries of textiles dropped from 43m to 4m meters and of shoes from 955,000 to 70,000 pairs. Some RCs, however, had considerable success buying up wheat, barley, and various other products from the rural population.[87] The RCs did not make a successful transition to carrying out productive activities, with the sole exception of a few RC associations in some provinces that took up poultry breeding or cheese production in addition to their old tasks.[88]

The RCs remained under state control, so the bureaucratic ways of the Central Organization were similar to those of a state agency, leaving the members little opportunity to participate in the administration of their cooperative. However, the Central Organization had numerous complaints and at the congress mentioned above listed the following shortcomings:

1. Lack of capital for the necessary expansion of its activities
2. Lack of infrastructure, such as warehouses and cold stores
3. Late delivery of inputs by agencies
4. Lack of funds for training programs
5. Scarcity of consumer goods required by peasant households
6. Failure to provide the products to reward the planting of wheat
7. Treatment of the RCs as profit-making organizations by state agencies
8. Delays in providing funds to grant loans needed by peasants[89]

10.4 The Problem of Large Holdings

The various economic interests and expert considerations involved have resulted in differences of opinion in the Islamic Republic about large holdings left over from the prerevolutionary era and those yet to be established, as well as about the size of holdings in general. These issues have still not been resolved years after the revolution. On the one hand, there is a tendency to break large estates down into smaller producer collectives or do away with them altogether; on the other, there are efforts to maintain them. Opinions also differ about whether they ought to be nationalized or whether the state should merely be entrusted with managing them; there is also debate about whether they should be retained by their owners or returned to them (if sequestered, confiscated, or squatted). Moreover, there are attempts to promote the establishment of new nonpeasant enterprises, both medium-sized ones and ones of unspecified size.

10.4.1 Modification by Squatting and Confiscation

Some of the large holdings were liquidated simply as a result of being squatted by peasants. The state attempted to prevent them from being split up by setting up mosha's, but, as noted above, these collectives have been spontaneously whittled down.

Some of the former large enterprises are under the control of the Foundation of the Dispossessed, the Martyrs' Foundation, the Imam's Committee, other Revolutionary Institutions, or the Ministry of Agriculture. Political forces, including the foundations, and the policy of the Islamic Republic toward the private sector will, in the final analysis, determine their fate, but the last word has not yet been spoken in this matter: The balance of power between the proponents and opponents of the private sector is still not clear. The large agricultural enterprises in the umbrella organization mentioned above have remained largely unchanged, and they continue to be run more unsuccessfully than successfully.[90]

Those enterprises with over 50ha of land that have been spared occupation, confiscation, sequestration, and other measures have in all probability been able to maintain their size and structure in the uncertain political climate concerning private property, and these might still total some 1.9m hectares of land.[91] Some of them are organized in the above-mentioned ACs and associations, and some reputedly possess thousands of hectares of land. During the parliamentary debates on land reform, they were often cited as examples of the continued existence of large estates in the Islamic Republic, with reformers even naming the names of the feudal lords, or "khans," concerned.[92]

10.4.2 Spontaneous Dissolution

As shown above, almost half the RPCs were completely dissolved at the request of the members in the first year after the revolution, and others disintegrated into smaller units, though formally still remaining RPCs. The process of dissolution was much quicker and more thorough for the widely unpopular Farm Corporations: eighty-eight out of ninety-three were liquidated under pressure from their members immediately after the revolution, some even before it. In some places, this disintegration occurred after demonstrations against them and their supporters (i.e., the state-appointed managers and the members who saw a benefit in their continued existence).[93]

From the very beginning there was a difference of opinion between the experts and the functionaries over the fate of the FCs. The experts responsible for formulating agricultural policy under the transitional Bazargan government had a poor opinion of the larger types of enterprises imposed on the peasants by the prerevolutionary government and thus did not resist the spontaneous liquidation of the FCs. However, all the experts and bureaucrats who favored collectivizing production or who for technical reasons preferred to organize it on a large scale were disposed to keep the FCs afloat. Whereas the group of experts under the minister of agriculture in the Bazargan cabinet spoke out clearly in favor of the "gradual transfer of these enterprises to entitled and competent locals" (Izadi program, p. 7), those who had come together in the journal *Masa'el-e Keshawarzi* were in favor of further collectivizing production.[94] When Dr. Izadi took over the Ministry of Agriculture, a circular dated April 3, 1979, was immediately sent to all its branches in the district towns agreeing that the fate of the FCs should be decided by the shareholders. He himself wanted them to be reorganized in such a way that all their shareholders could participate in the management of the company;[95] nonetheless, virtually all were dissolved.

Opposition to the dissolutions was expressed in a number of ways. There was massive support for the few FCs that had not been liquidated, including the allocation of funds and all sorts of concessions to the shareholders. Some of the FCs that were not liquidated nonetheless went through a process of restructuring, transforming them into a different type of enterprise. This was the case in Jiroft, for example, where small plots of land were leased to the shareholders. Small work groups jointly cultivated 6–20ha on their own account,[96] reflecting the widespread tendency on the part of the peasants to till the land alone or in small self-determined groups.

Another way in which the experts expressed their dissatisfaction with the liquidations was apparent in the attempt to rename the surviving FCs government-funded Service Centers, a move that leading officials in the FCs hoped would safeguard the officials' privileges.[97] Azkia pointed out in 1986 that many of the functionaries and experts at the Ministry of Agriculture still considered the Farm Corporation the best organizational structure for an agricultural enterprise (p. 252). They had guardedly expressed their support at a joint seminar held by the FCs, RPCs, and ABs on February 20–22, 1990. The seminar passed a resolution "to equip and promote" the existing FCs, along with the RPCs and ABs, to compare their potential and resolve the question of how best to organize agricultural enterprises. The minister of agriculture was reflecting opinion at his ministry when he said at the seminar that FCs had in many cases been successful and that it was a mistake to liquidate them: "We could solve their small problems easily."[98]

As a rule, the Service Centers took over many of the functions of the liquidated FCs, thus helping to solve the problems caused by the liquidations.[99] The main problems were the distribution of water and plant, the division of land among the shareholders, and the use of plant, machinery, and equipment. Parceling up the land caused numerous difficulties. Many of the shareholders who were not founding members were left empty-handed (55 percent in Qa'enat); local peasants with little or no land wanted to be included in the distribution of the property; and the shareholders who lived and worked in the towns also insisted on receiving a plot. Reputedly, the solutions to these problems proved so difficult to work out or were so disadvantageous that some members actually regretted having agreed to liquidate their FCs.[100]

Liquidating the FCs did not always lead to the establishment of peasant smallholdings. In some places the problems of land and water distribution plus the benefits accruing from the joint use of the plant and equipment installed by the FCs kept members together, more or less voluntarily, at a level of communality below that imposed by the FCs. For example, thirty-seven groups of between six and twenty-six members set up around their own wells in Nim Bluk-e Qa'enat after liquidation. The land was not parceled up but rather was worked communally.[101] At the time of the investigation (1983), however, the members of the groups were not completely satisfied with this arrangement. The government employees managing the FC, which now functioned as a Service Center, were involved in this solution. One of them explained: "If the center had not been set up after the liquidation of the FC, the land would certainly have lost its undivided character and have been subdivided into plots corresponding to the usufructuary right [of individual members]."[102]

In the first few years after the revolution, several attempts were made at the legislative level to solve the problems caused by the liquidation of the FCs. A legislative proposal approved by the Revolutionary Council on December 8, 1979, freed the government from its duty to set up FCs, RPCs, and so forth in "special zones of agricultural activity."[103] Another legislative proposal, approved on February 9, 1980, was intended to "solve the problems arising [from] vacating the FCs and RPCs."[104] These legislative proposals met the wishes of the members concerning the liquidation of the FCs and RPCs and held out the hope of some form of relief, such as debt relief.

Toward the end of February 1989, the minister of agriculture gave details of three new companies similar to FCs that had been set up, two in Khorasan province and one in Chahar Mahal Bakhtiyari province, "with the agreement of the peasants."[105] This step further proves that the rehabilitation of FCs has already progressed beyond the verbal level.

10.4.3 Agribusinesses

The Agribusinesses have been subjected to a variety of treatments in the Islamic Republic. A long, drawn-out to-and-fro between different points of view in respect of the state-owned ones has manifested itself in a number of ways, running the gamut from liquidation through consolidation to the establishment of new ABs.

The experts under Dr. Izadi declared early on that they were ready to transfer the state-owned ABs to "entitled and competent persons."[106] They initially upheld this point of view even after the fall of the Bazargan government. The first concrete steps taken were in connection with the Moghan Plain AB in northwestern Iran, which had been set up on large tracts of land that belonged to the nomadic Shahsawan tribe, upsetting their traditional way of life as the agricultural laborers needed were drawn from their midst. After the revolution, several reasons were put forward for liquidating the AB and transferring its estates to the by-then sedentary Shahsawan workers: It was unprofitable and located on forcibly appropriated land; it did not fit in with the people's way of life in the social milieu; the laborers were not interested in their work; and the machinery was being used inappropriately and thus uneconomically. In addition, there was the risk that the agricultural laborers would go over to the counterrevolution if the AB were not liquidated and transferred to them.[107]

In 1980, three offices within the Ministry of Agriculture (the secretariats for Productive Enterprises and Questions of Land Ownership, plus the Sevener Commissions) decided on the manner of transfer and the type of business Moghan Plain AB was to become. The first of these secretariats favored replacing the AB by a type of RPC that was to work under government supervision and direction. The other two offices showed interest in a system composed of mosha's, which would come into being at the end of a multistage process of liquidation and transfer.[108] Based on these considerations the central office of the Sevener Commissions worked out the Draft for the Transfer of the AB and the Fully Mechanized Estates in early 1981,[109] which related not only to Moghan Plain but to all state-owned ABs.

The draft aimed to find a form of organization for the ABs that "corresponds to the expectations of the Islamic Revolution" (pp. 123 and 126). It was to be founded on the "basis of Islam" and at the lowest level consist of mosha's that distributed a plot of the "customary size" to each member and were united in several RPCs. In conjunction with the Service Centers, these RPCs were to enable the mosha's to use resources that belonged to ABs due for liquidation or were made available by the government. The board of directors for the organization's central management would be responsible for the joint production program and comprise representatives from the RPCs, the Service Centers, the Foundation of the Dispossessed, and the Ministry of Water and Energy. "The aim of increasing productivity and permitting production relationships to develop on the basis of Islamic ideology" was to be "pursued by means of this order," as was "constructing a healthy society free of exploitation . . . on the way of spiritual development and the transcendence of man to the final goal, Allah" (p. 134).

It did not, however, come to that, because opposition to the plan was very strong. The two reports on such projects commissioned by the Ministry of Agriculture and compiled by M. J. Zahedi Mazanderani both took the position that the state ought to retain ownership of its ABs. As "everything today belongs to the Iranian people and the Islamic state is the trustee of the interests of the Iranian people," there was no longer any reason to question state ownership and "to take away from the Islamic state those means which are at its disposal for the purpose of the realization of Islamic aims and of the protection of the needy."[110]

This opinion prevailed, and there was little subsequent talk of transferring the state-owned ABs. The one on the Moghan Plain was maintained as a large state enterprise, where the problem of agricultural laborers could not be solved.[111] Volume 7 of the 1983 development plan detailed various measures intended to improve the work of the state-owned ABs and thus raised hopes (pp. 10 and 119), but after 1983 the only question was whether the government itself wanted to set up any additional ABs. In late 1984 and early 1985, it was said that the government did not want to invest in these companies, preferring to help the nationalized banks and the private sector set up ABs.[112] A state secretary at the Ministry of Agriculture expressed himself in a similar vein some three years later, commenting that the ABs established by the private sector did not need to be as big as the existing ones and that the industrial part of their enterprises could be set up by or with the help of other people. For financial reasons the government preferred smaller ABs.[113] On July 11, 1989, the newspapers reported that the government intended to set up seven more sugar-producing ABs in Khuzestan province with the help of foreign capital as part of the proposed five-year plan (eventually approved at the end of January 1990).[114]

Production reports for the state-owned ABs showed varying developments.[115] At the AB Haft Tappe, which produced sugar cane and refined it to sugar, a decline was observed between 1984–88 in all aspects: acreage, yield, and output of sugar cane, sugar, and by-products. The yield fell from 88.12t/ha to 68.53t/ha and output from 808,525t to 577,489t. At the AB Moghan Plain, production of some things increased (wheat, barley, maize, sugar beets) but others (fruit and cotton) declined. Similarly, at the AB Jiroft wheat output fell from 254t to 97t, while that of maize increased from 174t to 303t over the same period.[116] The AB known as Gust-e Lorestan

(Lorestan Meat) was in such dire straits by 1987 that it had to be made over to the Central Bank and refloated.[117] Other ABs are likewise under the supervision of the state banks.

The private ABs either were squatted, sequestered, or confiscated or are still in the possession of their owners. The sequestered and confiscated ones were subordinated to the Revolutionary Institutions or other state agencies.[118] The ABs owned by foreigners were the object of a great deal of attention after the revolution, in particular those set up under the shah's regime in the area irrigated by the Dez Dam. Immediately after the revolution, the government was confronted with peasants demanding the return of their stolen land, on which some of these companies had been set up. The Bazargan government was inclined to meet such demands, calling these ABs a "cancerous growth" that ought to be removed by operation.[119] Although the government did not like peasants to squat the ABs by force and often imposed punishments,[120] it was in fact preparing a legal framework for transferring these lands to the peasants, as evidenced by the "Legislative Proposal on the Appropriation and Cultivation of the Estates in the Area Irrigated by the Dez Dam and on the Annulment of the Contracts Signed with the ABs," approved by the Revolutionary Council in October 1979. Article 3 gave preference to individuals "whose property or usufructuary rights to land in this region have been transferred to state institutions."[121] As the regulations approved on January 12, 1980, made clear, this bill aimed, among other things, to recreate the region's lost village system. The estates of the ABs concerned were to be leased to peasants, initially for five years, with the land ultimately to be transferred to them if they were to cultivate it successfully, provided they organized themselves into mosha's.[122] These administrative regulations were actually implemented, though after considerable delay. Azkia reports that four of the five ABs in the area were paraceled out among the agricultural laborers and Khoshneshins (landless villagers), who are now tilling fields of between 40 and 100ha in groups of four or five.[123] It should, however, be noted that the area was badly damaged in the Iran-Iraq War.

10.5 Spontaneous Forms of Organization

The squats, the transfer of all sorts of land, and the dissolution of many large holdings in the course of the Islamic Republic's land reform further fragmented land ownership and increased the number of smallholdings.[124] By 1982/3 the agricultural census conducted by the Central Statistical Office was already showing a marked shift towards smaller holdings, as the comparison with the corresponding figures from the previous census (in 1974/5) shows:

Table 10.1 Structure of Holdings Before and After the Revolution

Size (in hectares)	1974/5				1982/3			
	Number (in thousands)	Percent	Area (in thousands of hectares)	Percent	Average Size (in hectares)	Number (in thousands)	Percent	Area (in thousands of hectares)	Percent	Average Size (in hectares)

Size (in hectares)	Number (in thousands)	Percent	Area (in thousands of hectares)	Percent	Average Size (in hectares)	Number (in thousands)	Percent	Area (in thousands of hectares)	Percent	Average Size (in hectares)
<1	734	29.6	260	1.6	0.4	863	33.5	305	2.3	0.35
1–2	322	13.0	444	2.7	1.4	406	15.3	553	4.2	1.36
2–5	542	21.8	1,733	10.6	3.2	623	23.4	1,992	15.2	3.20
5–10	428	17.3	2,953	18.0	6.9	408	15.2	2,806	21.5	6.80
10–50	428	17.3	7,501	45.7	17.5	339	12.6	5,693	43.5	14.52
50–100	16	0.7	1,073	6.5	66.0	11	0.4	718	5.5	64.73
100+	10	0.4	2,454	14.9	256.8	4	0.2	100	7.7	240.26
	2,490		16,419		6.6	2,654		12,167		4.58

Sources: Markaz-e Amar: Agricultural Censuses, 1974/5 and 1982/3.

The Kurdish provinces of Kurdistan and West Azerbaijan were not included in the 1982/3 figures, as the civil war rendered it impossible to conduct the census there. However, it may safely be assumed that the inclusion of the figures concerning these two provinces would not significantly change the following conclusions, as drawn from this table. The average area of a farm was clearly smaller in 1982/3,[125] with an increase in farms of less than 5ha and a reduction in those of larger size. The transfer of wasteland and/or squatted estates in the ensuing years can only have increased this tendency, even if the latest agricultural census (1988/9) gives the average area under cultivation as 6.02ha.[126] By comparison with 1974/5, the 1988 average has dropped, and the increase in the number of farms to 2.8m could be interpreted as an additional indication of an ongoing structural change toward smaller farms.

As has been shown, some of those in positions of responsibility within the state apparatus attempted to counter this shrinkage by setting up mosha‘s, and the results of this policy have been stated above. Independent movements initiated by peasants and/or modern farmers have been in existence since the prerevolutionary era and have resulted in the merger of peasant farms or the integration of individual peasants into larger enterprises. Azkia divides these efforts into four categories:

1. Liquidation of the peasant farm and sale of the land to well-off farmers or preemptors, in which case the peasant and his family move to town.
2. Formation of hamab (joint water-user) groups, where irrigation is conducted collectively under the leadership of an irrigation council. Individual members might consolidate their fragmented plots by exchange or sale among themselves.
3. Formation of work groups consisting of a few individuals, where cooperation continues throughout all stages of production. These came into being after the revolution in areas where the ABs were liquidated.
4. Formation of habbati groups, where the fragmented bits (habbe) of peasant land in a village are consolidated and, depending on the crop, collectively cultivated for individual stages of production (plowing, tending, or harvesting) or throughout. Well-off, dynamic farmers and a habbati council are in charge of management (1986, pp. 204ff).

These and similar types of efforts clearly show that peasants are capable of taking the initiative and entering into partnerships to deal with their needs. The effect of their helping and taking responsibility for themselves during the liquidation of the FCs, ABs, RPCs, and mosha‘s has been shown. In addition to these peasant work communities, various forms of entrepreneurial initiatives appeared both before and after the revolution, particularly among farmers in Isfahan province, Yazd, and around the city of Qom. They work on land leased from absentee landlords or from peasants who have moved to the towns. They plant summer crops using modern techniques, sometimes with financial help from preemptors, and employ seasonal workers, to whom they either pay wages or give a share of the harvest. These enterprises have different names in various parts of the country, such as moqaseme kari (partition work), tolombe kari (water pump work), and nime kari (halving work).[127]

Notes

1. Some of the functionaries interviewed consider everything the government of the Islamic Republic does to be Islamic. One said that as all parliamentary resolutions have to be approved by the Council of Guardians and the Council of Guardians does not give its approval to a law if it does not concur with Islam, all laws passed in the Islamic Republic are to be considered as Islamic.

2. DPA, pp. 10, 15f, 35, and 39.

3. *Resalat,* February 26, 1989.

4. *Resalat,* February 21, 1989. M. Mohajerani criticizes the predominant attitude of technocrats at the Ministry of Agriculture toward large types of enterprise by discerning a revival of the same positions that prevailed before the revolution. See *Resalat,* April 11 and 12, 1990.

5. This criticism of sharecropping did not come from the Islamists (see Chapters 2.3.1 and 2.3.2). Even if some of them could not condone it as practiced, they were unable to ignore the fact that it was enshrined in the sharia, so they transformed it into an ideal form that could not be realized, even after the revolution.

6. CL 1983/4, pp. 335ff.

7. *Jomhuri-ye Eslami* November 20, 1979. In his book (published in 1974), he still acknowledged sharecropping, even in the form in which seed corn is provided by the peasant and not by the owner of the land; see p. 288f.

8. *Ibid.,* November 12, 1979. See also *Keshawarz-e Emruz,* December 8, 1979, and *Ettela'at,* April 6, 1980. Before the revolution Esfahani emphasized that sharecropping as envisaged in Islamic law was vastly different from the way it was practiced in feudal societies; see Esfahani 1978, vol. 4, p. 31f.

9. *Barzegar,* November 21, 1981.

10. *Jomhuri-ye Eslami,* June 21, 1983.

11. PP, December 19, 1982, p. 22f.

12. Most of the functionaries and experts interviewed denied that sharecropping had increased, though their opinions are based only on their own experiences. One interviewee did, however, think it was widespread, and one believed there had been a 30 percent increase. A third interviewee attributed the increase in sharecropping to unemployment, and a fourth thought that landowners were unwilling to enter into such leases with peasants because they were unsure of the consequences.

13. *Resalat,* April 17, 1989.

14. *Resalat,* September 5, 1988.

15. Refahiyat 1986, p. 83; 1987, p. 90.

16. At a November 1987 seminar to justify proposed legislation to set up production cooperatives, Rafsanjani declared them to be the "manifestation of Islamic justice in the modern economic order." See *Kayhan,* November 10, 1987.

17. Sazman-e Markazi-ye Ta'won, 1971.
18. On bone, see J. Safi Nezhad 1972, and the discussion in Schirazi 1975, pp. 66ff.
19. *Resalat,* February 27, 1991.
20. PP, February 15, 1987, p. 30.
21. PP, January 10, 1984, and June 27, 1985.
22. See N. Katouzian 1984, p. 31.
23. PP, January 10, 1984, p. 23.
24. *Ibid.,* pp. 23, 28.
25. PP, June 27, 1985, p. 30.
26. PP, February 19, 1987, p. 28.
27. *Ibid.,* p. 25f.
28. *Ibid.*
29. PP, January 11, 1984, p. 30; June 27, 1985, p. 31; and February 15, 1987, p. 31.
30. Mosha' is an Arabic term for the undivided ownership of an object by several persons.
31. See the speeches given by leading politicians at the frequent seminars on the subject of a cooperative system—e.g., in *Kayhan,* August 17, 1986, and October 28, 1987.
32. PP, December 19, 1982, p. 26f; M. Azkia 1986, p. 266. According to a 1989 tract published by the central office of the Sevener Commissions, the mosha' served all the social, economic, national, and other objectives normally set for other similar enterprises (p. 23).
33. "The new house (i.e., the mosha' cooperatives) must be founded on the basis of the traditional modes of production such as bone." Setad-e Markazi-ye Hey'at ha 1989, pp. 15 and 22.
34. CL 1979/80, pp. 546ff; A. Schirazi 1988, pp. 145ff.
35. CL 1979/80, pp. 188ff; A. Schirazi 1988, pp. 83ff.
36. CL 1980/1, pp. 13ff; A. Schirazi 1988, pp. 167ff.
37. CL 1980/1, pp. 5ff; A. Schirazi 1988, pp. 180ff.
38. See M. Azkia 1986, pp. 266ff.
39. PP, December 19, 1982, pp. 24, 26, and 29.
40. According to Harandi in *Kayhan,* April 16, 1986.
41. H. Elyasian 1985, p. 526. He ignores the fact that the Sevener Commissions went to great lengths to hold the mosha's together. His opinion is probably based on the experiences with the traditional labor cooperatives in several places after the shah's land reform—they fell apart as soon as the landowner disappeared. See also M. Azkia 1986, pp. 164 and 203; and S. Amini 1985. Elyasian and others give a better explanation when they detail the social, economic, and psychic factors that determine the relationships of the peasants to each other and their work.
42. H. Bafekr 1982, p. 92; and 1984, p. 165; Fahim Kermani in PP, December 19, 1982, p. 26; Setad-e Markazi-ye Hey'atha 1989, p. 40f; and M. J. Zahedi Mazanderani 1986, p. 95.
43. H. Bafekr 1984, p. 175.
44. Bafekr 1984, p. 203f; 1982, pp. 92f and 100. Interviewed experts confirm "the practical dissolution" of the undivided ownership in mosha's. The brochure published by the central office of the Sevener Commissions in 1989 corroborates this outcome and puts it down to the "attitudes of the farmers." See pp. 29f, 36, 40f, and 45.
45. 'Alimorad 1984, p. 22.
46. A. Anoushirwani 1982, pp. 115, 118, 124, 127, 129, 131, and 137.

47. Setad-e Markazi-ye Heya'atha 1989, p. 37f.
48. Bafekr 1982, p. 86.
49. Anoushirwani 1982, p. 145.
50. The central office of the Sevener Commissions stated in 1989 that each mosha' member receives a maximum loan of 200,000 toman, which "does not suffice to solve all problems and to finance all costs, but is a good beginning" (p. 53). The members of mosha's in Baft received 36,000–54,000 toman each, See Anoushirwani 1982, pp. 115, 118, 121, 123, 126, 130, and 137.
51. The interest rate is approximately 50 percent in Jiroft. See Bafekr 1982, pp. 125ff.
52. See, for example, Bafekr 1982, pp. 132ff.
53. *Ibid.*, pp. 84ff.
54. M. Azkia 1986, p. 272.
55. Bafekr 1982, p. 85.
56. 'Alimorad 1984, p. 26.
57. *Kayhan*, July 21, 1987.
58. *Ettala'at*, August 24, 1989.
59. Rahim Zade to *Barzegar*, October 26, 1988. He could have meant the year that ended on the date of the interview. It is, however, still impossible to calculate the exact number of mosha's still in existence. Comparison of the figures would seem to indicate that the number of dissolutions is between 1,200 and 2,700. When interviewed, experts and functionaries were skeptical about the figure of 10,800 and considered it to be exaggerated. One interviewee thought there were actually about 6,500 mosha's. The interviewees also made the point that a difference must be made between the mosha's that exist on paper and those that exist in fact.
60. According to Harandi in *Ettela'at*, January 28, 1990.
61. *Barzegar*, May 7, 1988, and *Kayhan*, December 31, 1988.
62. A group of experts studied five RPCs in Isfahan province in 1984; see A. Anoushirwani 1984. Another group studied the RPCs in Shahmaran (Kerman province) in 1982; see Anoushirwani 1982. See also M. Azkia 1986 and Elyasian 1985 for observations on Isfahan province.
63. A. Anoushirwani, 1982, pp. 38ff.
64. A. Anoushirwani, 1985, p. 22.
65. *Barzegar*, March 3, 1990.
66. *Resalat*, October 31, 1990.
67. The figures on ACs are from Dr. Zali, the ex-minister of agriculture, in *Ettela'at*, July 25, 1989. There were, however, only 280 ACs in October 1988, according to the Central Organization of Rural Cooperatives in *Barzegar*, October 3, 1988. The organization's chairman counted "about 580" ACs in February 1990; see *Barzegar*, February 1, 1990.
68. *Barzegar*, October 29, 1987.
69. *Barzegar*, October 29, 1987, and February 11, 1989, carries reports on these associations; see also *Keshawarz*, February 1988.
70. *Barzegar*, February 11, 1990.
71. On September 22, 1987, one of the bank's leading officials called on the farmers and other interested parties to set up ACs, promising to provide land and credits of up to 90 percent of the required investment; see *Barzegar* of the same date.
72. *Barzegar*, October 29, 1987.
73. *Ibid.*
74. The term was used by *Resalat* in its edition of November 21, 1988.
75. PP, November 1, 1988, p. 20.

76. *Resalat*, June 22, 1988.
77. *Kayhan*, September 23, 1984.
78. *Barzegar*, October 29, 1988.
79. *Ibid.*
80. *Kayhan*, May 18, 1985.
81. According to the project's director in Azerbaijan province in *Resalat*, August 21, 1989.
82. October 13, 1990.
83. IP, p. 9; DPA, pp. 117 and 362.
84. See *Barzegar*, October 29, 1987.
85. *Ibid*. The figures given above only differ slightly from the ones in the 1367 Statistical Yearbook, pp. 381ff.
86. Figures given to *Barzegar* (February 1, 1990) by the Jabbar Khiyabani, chairman of the Central Organization of Rural Cooperatives. See also *Barzegar*, October 27, 1990.
87. Markaz-e Amar 1988 and 1989.
88. See the report on a large number of RC associations in the February 1, 1990, special edition of *Barzegar*.
89. *Barzegar*, October 3, 1988, and February 1, 1990. See also M. Azkia 1986, pp. 181ff.
90. *Barzegar* sometimes publishes large-scale promotional reports on the more successful ones. See the September 24, 1988, and February 11, 1990, editions.
91. Less the estates of the agroindustrial enterprises, the now liquidated Farm Corporations, the RPCs, and the confiscated estates.
92. One member of parliament reportedly knew of a "merchant landowner" close to the shah's court who had returned to Iran and now owned 400,000ha of land. See PP, April 9, 1989, p. 19; and October 23, 1986, pp. 23 and 27.
93. Research group 1980 in *Masa'el-e Keshawarzi* 1, pp. 46ff; also M. Azkia 1986, p. 252. The research group claims that when the small shareholders whose interests would have been better served by the continued existence of the RPCs voted for liquidation, they were influenced by the transitional government's policies.
94. See especially *Masa'el-e Keshawarzi* 3 (Summer 1981), p. 12.
95. Anoushirwani 1984, pp. 45ff.
96. M. Azkia 1986, pp. 252ff.
97. H. Sabet Qadam 1983, pp. 13ff.
98. *Barzegar*, February 3, 1990. Almost without exception, the experts and functionaries we questioned favored rehabilitating the FCs and RPCs, although some thought this should only be done in suitable parts of the country and one interviewee made his agreement conditional upon the peasants concerned.
99. M. Rawanbakhash 1983, pp. 12ff; M. Azkia 1986, p. 297; S. Sabet Qadam 1983, p. 13f; A. Anoushirwani 1984, pp. 48ff; H. Elyasian 1985, pp. 2/4ff and 3/17ff.
100. A. Anoushirwani 1984, p. 49.
101. *Ibid.*, pp. 63ff.
102. *Ibid.*, p. 57.
103. CL 1979/80, pp. 284ff; A. Schirazi 1988, p. 112.
104. CL 1979/80, pp. 477ff; A. Schirazi 1988, pp. 138ff. For more resolutions and regulations, see A. Anoushirwani 1984, appendices.
105. *Resalat*, February 26, 1989.
106. See IP, p. 7; and the report on the October 1979 seminar in Tehran, in which the subcommittee formed to discuss these and similar questions recommended transfer in *Keshawarz-e Emruz*, November 16, 1979.

107. M. J. Zahedi Mazanderani 1984, pp. 23ff.

108. *Ibid.*, pp. 26ff.

109. M. J. Zahedi Mazanderani, 1986, pp. 120ff. This is the source of the information below about this AB, unless specifically stated otherwise.

110. *Ibid.*, p. 104f.

111. This information was supplied by an interviewed expert.

112. According to the deputy minister of agriculture, Tabataba'i, in *Kayhan*, December 29, 1984, and January 1, 1985.

113. *Barzegar*, February 12, 1988.

114. Reported by Dr. Kalantari on February 20, 1990, to the seminar on large holdings mentioned above; see *Resalat*, February 21, 1990.

115. I refer to a report by the Ministry of Agriculture on "enterprises under the supervision of the Office for Production Enterprises and ABs as well as their productive activity in the years 1363–1367."

116. More information on the productive activity of these companies in *Barzegar*, February 6, 1988, February 11, and March 3, 1990. Kalantari compares the AICs to charitable organizations paying thousands without needing their work—"I told more than 14,000 laborers in Moghan: You don't need to come at all. We'll send your wages to you, plus twenty years' overtime." *Barzegar*, March 3, 1990.

117. For more information, see PP, January 20, 1988, pp. 24ff.

118. For details, see M. J. Zahedi Mazanderani 1986, pp. 49ff.

119. Pur Tabataba'i, state secretary at the Ministry of Agriculture, in *Ettela'at*, July 25, 1979.

120. See the relevant legislative proposal in CL 1979/80, pp. 4f and 83ff; and Schirazi 1988, pp. 45ff and 69ff.

121. CL 1979/80, pp. 162ff; Schirazi 1988, pp. 73ff. Several clauses were inserted on two later occasions to help clarify problems that had arisen during implementation of the legislative proposal. CL 1979/80, p. 566f; and 1980/81, p. 52f; also Schirazi 1988, pp. 150f and 174ff.

122. See the appendix in M. J. Zahedi Mazanderani 1986, pp. 115ff.

123. Azkia 1986, pp. 233ff.

124. This observation was also made by A. Malekaniyan 1986, pp. 82ff.

125. As the arable area per farm in the province of Kurdistan is larger than in other provinces, the inclusion of such figures could alter the average size for the whole country. According to the 1974/5 census, farms with less than 5ha accounted for only 28 percent of the 83,273 farms in the province but represented 66 percent in West Azerbaijan.

126. See Markaz-e Amar-e Iran: Sarshoumari-ye 'Omumi-ye Keshawarzi-ye Iran 1989, p. 1. Neither the full results of the census nor the classifications of farm sizes are available yet. The figures quoted here are based on the evaluation of a supposedly representative 2.5 percent sample of households.

127. M. Azkia 1986, pp. 209ff; A. Ashraf 1972; A. Anoushirwani 1986, p. 83; and *Kayhan*, March 25, 1985.

11

The Question of Participation

Even in postrevolutionary Iran, popular participation in the developmental process is generally acknowledged as a sine qua non for success. This acknowledgment is expressed as criticism both of the shah's development strategy and of his regime in general. Blueprints for shaping Islamic society highlight the widely differing attitudes of various Islamist currents on the question of participation.

Participation (mosharekat) is guaranteed under the constitution of the Islamic Republic, which explicitly cites "the participation of the whole people in the determination of its political, economic, social, and cultural fate" as one of the aims pursued by the state (Article 3, Point 8). The preamble to the constitution considers "the extensive and active participation of all members of society" a necessary condition for the "development of man" toward the "godly order" and for the "manifestation of the dimension of godliness in man." The avowal of the sovereignty of the people further acknowledges the principle of participation embodied in the constitution.

The importance of participation for the successful implementation of development projects is emphasized in the relevant documents. For example, Izadi's 1979 draft program for agricultural policy promised that "from the stage of passing resolutions to bringing in the harvest, planning agriculture and rural improvement will soon occur by utilizing the ideal cooperation and participation of the rural population and nomads" (p 4). The "greatest possible use of the participation of the population" in reaching individual plan targets was repeatedly emphasized in the agricultural section of the draft of the 1983 development plan[1] and in the 1987 self-sufficiency plan—which voices the criticism, inter alia, that the people did not take part in state affairs while the plan was being drafted (p. 16).

The participatory principle is expressed most clearly in the constitutional acknowledgment of the sovereignty of the people. It is also subjected to its most radical limitation there, in that the sovereignty of the people is subordinated to the rule of Islamic jurists. Accordingly, decisions made by the representatives of the people only become law if they are approved by the representatives of the Islamic jurists in the Council of Guardians. A more explicit restriction on the sovereignty of the people can be found in the theory of rule by Islamic jurists, which compares the people to underage children who have to be guided by the religious authorities.[2]

This theory in fact excludes the people from taking part in decisionmaking processes, though they may participate in implementing the decisions made at the top. Hence, the 1983 development plan only mentions the people's participation in *implementing* the plan; although it holds state intervention responsible for the failure of earlier plans and measures, the reference is to interference in the process of implementation. In addition, this interpretation of participation treats the populace as an object that must be protected from exploitation and oppression. It represents the "class" or mass of the dispossessed, whose rights must be ensured by the ruling Islamic jurists.[3] According to etatist-oriented Islamism, this protection can best be provided if state rule encompasses all aspects of social life in which the dispossessed might otherwise be exploited, and the people are properly protected economically only if state control is all-pervasive and nationalization obviates all potential spheres of exploitation. For the Islamist opponents of etatism, on the other hand, extensive state intervention in the economy in excess of control functions contradicts the principles of the sharia. They advocate entrepreneurial freedom, portraying their position as support for participation (although the conservative wing of this current pushes all the harder for restricting individual freedoms in other areas of social life, even in the private sphere).

Following Bazargan's fall, the Islamic Republic was ruled in the etatistic sense. The radicals exploited their greater weight in the government to impose a concentration of decisionmaking powers in the hands of the state, both in the economy and in other areas of society. This tendency was only restricted when other Islamists who were averse to economic etatism were able to bring their influence to bear or when the reduction in state investment opportunities made mobilizing the private sector seem essential in order to stimulate the economy. From 1986 onward, the sudden drop in state revenue made private participation in development policy seem unavoidable, and Khomeini urged the government to allow the people to become involved in trade and commerce. The government promised to obey the Imam's order, and the newspapers printed articles by influential politicians on the question of participation.[4] *Resalat* gloatingly (and prematurely) disseminated the "joyful tidings" of the "death of state rule" (doulat salari), meaning the death of state control of the economy (June 14, 1986).

But even in these circumstances, many radical Islamists in and close to the government rejected any policy that would open the gates of the economy to the private sector, insisting on a more limited interpretation of participation. During the discussion on the question of participation, the opposing sides appealed to a wide audience by accusing each other of contravening the sharia or of espousing "American Islam." Minister of Heavy Industry Behzad Nabawi characterized the Islamist opponents of etatism as people who advocate dictatorship at the political level but at the same time want a capitalistic liberalization of the economy. He himself favored a tight rein "on political freedoms, so that the Islamic order does not collapse, as well as on economic freedoms."[5]

The Bazargan government—admittedly not a solidly Islamist one—put forward a third interpretation, advocating both the political and economic participation of the people in decisionmaking processes, within certain limits.[6] Its economic liberalism was expressed, inter alia, in its concept for land reform, and the political freedoms enjoyed at the time, though limited, clearly demonstrated its political liberalism.[7] The same was true of some of the bills it presented, which (with certain reservations) were approved by the Revolutionary Council, including the Law on the Local Councils, which was to come into effect after publication in the official gazette of the Islamic Republic on July 24, 1979. This law granted the long-held wish, albeit in limited form, that local government and provincial administration should be transferred to shouras (local councils)—and it did so to a degree not seen before or since.

11.1 The Shoura System as the Mainstay of Participation

Even many Islamists viewed the setting up of the shouras as a way of enabling the people to participate in government. Article 100 of the constitution directs that "the administration of the villages, districts, towns, county towns or provinces be conducted under the supervision of an appropriate council whose members are chosen by the inhabitants of the same locality." These councils were to facilitate the "expeditious implementation of social, economic, construction, hygiene, cultural, training, and other welfare programs . . . through the cooperation of the population," who will be won over if the shouras motivate them. The spokesman of the parliamentary commission concerned stated that shouras "signify the participation of the people in the country's affairs."[8] Commenting on the first law to implement this provision of the constitution, the future president, Bani Sadr, wrote on June 21, 1979, that the Revolutionary Council had approved the law "so that the inhabitants in the various regions of the country—provinces, district towns, towns and villages—participate in their own affairs through the election of councils and become autonomous in the Islamic sense of the word." He also hoped that ensuring the participation of the people in local administration in this manner would strengthen national unity and finally defeat the dictatorial order (*Enqelab-e Eslami*). Others liked to point out that local administration on the basis of shouras would bring additional benefits: It would serve to instruct the people and educate them politically;[9] help to allow Islamic justice to be established;[10] and bear witness to the fact that the Islamic state recognizes the worth of the people.[11] The shouras were the most effective and most relevant mainstays of popular power.[12] In a decree issued shortly after the first Law on Local Councils was approved, Khomeini stated that it had been necessary to set them up because they established "the rule of the people in Iran and over its affairs."[13]

In order to legitimize the shoura system, the Islamists referred to the Quran, which recommends that the Prophet consult with the believers (3/159) and that the believers deliberate amongst themselves (42/39). The constitution of the Islamic Republic quotes such passages in Article 7. Reference was also made to the traditions of Muhammad and the Shi'ite Imams when the subject was discussed. According to Ayatollah Ardebili, Islam has respected the shoura principle for fourteen centuries.[14] Ayatollah Golzade Ghafuri took the position that Islam accords the shoura more importance than any other religion,[15] whereas Ayatollah Taleqani considered the shoura one of the most important matters in Islam.[16]

The battle for shouras as the basis of a democratic provincial and communal administration goes back to the Constitutional Revolution in Iran (1906–11). In that case, district and provincial councils were enshrined in the constitution of the monarchy (Articles 90–92). Although implementation was not accorded any great significance under the Pahlavi dynasty, the government remained committed, at least verbally, to introducing local rule, and in some towns the shah even installed town councils composed of members he had picked himself. In 1963 he had a Law on the Establishment of Village Councils passed by parliament, on which basis councils were set up in most villages with over 250 inhabitants and in many smaller ones by 1979.[17]

The February 1979 revolution initially gave free rein to the forces that favored autonomous administrations in the various parts of the country or even management of economic enterprises and government agencies by shouras. The revolution itself was partly organized on the basis of committees formed in enterprises and neighborhoods that wanted to continue working after the fall of the shah and were pressing for institutionalization. In such cases, shouras were formed under the influence of leftist and autonomist factions. The movement swept along in its stream both the town and village dwellers in Kurdistan, the Turkmenic regions, and some other areas inhabited by non-Persians. All of these groups were striving for autonomous administration in a country divided along ethnic lines. Under the influence of the movement, postrevolutionary Iran found itself in a shoura stupor.

The broad consent of the Islamists to the shoura system observed in the first few months after the revolution should primarily be seen as a reaction to this movement. Unlike liberal Islamists, who were convinced of the need for at least decentralizing the administration and so were not averse to forming local councils, the conservative supporters of ulama rule adopted the movement's demands just to take the wind out of the sails of the leftists and autonomists.[18] Their main aim was to get control of the movement and of the shouras that had already been set up, which they attempted to do by excluding non-Islamist members. At the same time, they redefined the system of councils to correspond to their Islamic concept of "shour" and their system of government. These largely successful attempts can best be followed by examining legislative attempts to regulate local administration in the country.

The first step toward implementing the relevant articles of the constitution was taken under the Bazargan government at the end of June 1979 in the shape of the Law on Local Councils, which directed that councils be formed at the village, district, town, county town, and provincial levels.[19] It was never implemented, apart from a failed attempt in some towns in October 1979.

Twenty-nine months later (November 22, 1982), parliament passed the Law on the National Organization of the Islamic Councils."[20] This law, which the Council of Guardians approved eight days after parliament passed it, provided, inter alia, for the Ministry of the Interior to draft and submit to parliament a bill for holding elections to the shouras within two months of the final approval of the law on November 30, 1982 (Article 2, Note 2). It further directed that the elections be held two months after approval of the administrative regulations to this ballot procedure bill (Article 4). However, the bill was only introduced to parliament in October 1983,[21] where both it and the law it was based on were the subject of a dispute over the local councils that lasted until spring 1986. At its first and second readings, the November 1982 law was subject to several minor amendments, but these cannot explain the long delay. The amended law and the ballot procedures were approved by the Council of Guardians on July 23, 1986,[22] and forwarded to the Ministry of the Interior nine days later for implementation.[23]

However, the law has not been implemented. Since July 1986, new dates for holding the elections have been set, mostly by the minister of the interior and his secretaries. On November 12, 1989, a date was set for spring 1990. At the same time, however, it was declared that the government had submitted proposals for amending the law to parliament,[24] which did in fact introduce some amendments in the first half of May 1990.[25] On December 19, 1990, Minister of the Interior Nuri held out the prospect of holding the elections by the end of the Islamic year (March 20, 1991) or early the year after (*Kayhan*). As of early 1993, the elections have not been held; it is said that sometime in January 1993 the Council of Ministers finished reformulation of the law of July 1986.[26]

The reasons for the government's obvious refusal to put the Law on

Local Councils into effect are to be found in the conflict between the autonomous, participatory administrations in parts of the country and the authoritarian, hierocratic state of the Islamic jurists. Differing interpretations of the relevant Islamic sources have furthered the delay.

Differences on this subject had already arisen at the Constituent Assembly of Experts. A small minority demanded a real transfer of authority leading to the autonomous administration of parts of the country by local councils elected by the people. They also sought a new administrative division of the country along ethnic lines.[27] Others did not go so far but did want the councils to be granted discretionary powers in their own affairs (not merely visitatorial rights, as envisaged by the majority)—i.e., the local executive was to *comply* with council decisions, not—as the majority put it—merely *consider* them. They also thought the local executive ought to be elected by the local councils, not nominated by central government. The Assembly of Experts rejected such notions by a huge majority, and the wording written into the constitution considerably restricted the participatory function of the shouras, even in the postrevolutionary era.[28] The representative of the provinces Sistan and Baluchistan, the cleric Moulawi, denigrated this result by comparing it to the system of shouras under the shah. Mirmord Zehi, from the same part of the country, added: "Here shoura is nothing more than decoration."[29] All the parties based their positions on Islam and the Quran.

The first law on shouras bearing Bazargan's signature (June 1979), enacted months before the constitution was adopted, granted the shouras more powers than the constitution did. The village and municipal councils elected their own mayors, and the executive organs at all levels were obliged to implement the decisions of the councils concerned. The shouras were entitled to draft and implement administrative regulations in the fields of culture, training, economy, finance, and justice within the framework of the policy determined by the central administration. They were to supervise the work of the executive. Everyone was allowed to take part in the elections, regardless of religion, race, or language. The law was adopted at a time when there was a general call for shouras, based in part on opportunism and in part on genuine democratic convictions.

Such enthusiasm for shouras had evaporated by the time the 1982 and 1986 laws were debated. The advocates of a shoura-based local administration had ceased to be a serious political force, having been completely suppressed by 1986. The memory of shouras was now an internal matter among the Islamists. The drop in support had an effect on the wording of the laws mentioned. Leaders were to be appointed by the central government except in the municipal councils, which were permitted to elect and dismiss the mayors.[30] The purposes of the councils—now known as "Islamic Councils"—were to transmit information, complaints, proposals, opinions, and reports to and from the central administration; get the rural population's cooperation for implementing projects; and fulfill supervisory functions. Decisions made by them within the authority granted them by the constitution were to be "considered" by the provincial governors. Only practicing Muslims loyal to the constitution of the Islamic Republic and "not biased toward parties, organizations, and groups that are illegal or are based on eclectic or atheistic convictions" were eligible to be elected. This provision excluded members of the overthrown regime, such as mayors and members of the former municipal councils.

The opposing positions in the discussion about the shouras slowly became clear. In 1982 Hojjat ol-Eslam Wa'ezi had interpreted the Quran passages on the subject to mean "shour"—i.e., deliberation with wise men, not an institution practicing socialist convictions.[31] Ayatollahs Yazdi and Khaz'ali later concurred, interpreting the relevant Quran verses to mean that decisions are to be made by one man who has consulted other wise men.[32] In an article in *Ettela'at* on the significance of the shoura in Islam, a scholar stated that making decisions based on the opinion of the majority renders the opinion of the majority worthless if those decisions don't comply with Islam (August 23, 1989). Hojjat ol-Eslam Razawi called the supporters of this interpretation pious Muslims who had had negative experience of the shouras.[33] The Islamic Student Association at the University of Shiraz countered that such people simply think the masses incapable of making decisions.[34] The supporters of the conservative Islamist line gradually prevailed to such an extent that the shoura-style bodies at the head of the administrative organs specified in the constitution, such as the Ministry of Justice, were replaced by one-man leadership during the 1989 revision of the constitution.

Some supporters of the councils among the legalist Islamists even found it necessary to emphasize that they did not wish to restrict the power of the ulama in any way and that they saw no contradiction between the shoura system and rule by the ulama. According to Hojjat ol-Eslam Khalkhali, one of those advocating councils, shoura only have the right to make decisions within the framework of the rules of Islam.[35] The shoura system, agreed Hojjat ol-Eslam Razawi, revolves round the axis of the Imamat: It serves it as a mediator between the Imam on the one hand and the community as the planning and executive organ on the other, but it has no legislative rights because God and the Prophet have already enacted laws.[36] According to the spokesman of the parliamentary commission concerned, the shouras should function as "the arm of the Islamic state."[37]

Only a minority of radical Islamists approved of giving councils the authority to make decisions and consider them to represent popular rule or to manifest the rule of the dispossessed.[38] Representatives of this school of thought readily blamed the lack of support for the shoura system and its incompatibility with the present form of government for the state's failure to enact the relevant law.[39] Another reason given was the aversion of the rulers to having the already heated internal conflicts worsen "because of such an unimportant question."[40] They feared that resistance by the shouras' opponents might further increase tension. Another major reason for postponing the council elections might well have been the fear that the government would be unable to control the 300,000 members of the councils to be elected. Where there are no grounds for this fear, the state pushes ahead with setting them up, even without a basis in law.

11.2 The Village Councils

Village Councils have been established at a pace completely at variance with the plodding implementation of the Law on Local Councils. There were over 25,000 of them by June 1982[41] and 35,000 by February 1986, covering some 40,000 villages.[42] In December 1987 the minister of jahad-e sazandegi announced the existence of 40,000 Village Councils, whose activities covered a total of 96 percent of the rural population.[43]

There are several reasons the Village Councils were dealt with separately and set up with such relative speed. First, the councils established prior to the revolution or later by the leftists and autonomists had to be disbanded as quickly as possible. This aim was best achieved by replacing the unwanted councils with Islamic ones or by Islamizing the existing ones and throwing out their unwanted members.[44] Second, the various state institutions and organizations involved in agricultural administration considered the Village Councils a useful instrument for implementing their own agricultural policies. This outlook resulted in a competition among the Sevener Commissions, the Ministry of Agriculture, and Jahad-e Sazandegi to set up their own Village Councils (it was won in the end by Jahad). Other reasons will be given below.

The Village Councils were part of Izadi's program to reorganize the Ministry of Agriculture by bringing the administrative apparatus closer to the people it was intended to serve. In an interview with the author, Dr. Izadi said: "By forming these councils we have set ourselves the aim of ensuring that farmers big and small decide about their own affairs themselves, because we were convinced that the state should interfere as little as possible in such matters." The Village Councils were considered a suitable instrument with which to implement the measures contained in the 1983 development plan and the 1987 self-sufficiency plan. Pursuant to the 1982 law, they had two clearly political tasks—replacing the Village Councils set up by both the shah and the opponents of rule by the ulama and helping to suppress the counterrevolution. In this connection, Article 6 of the law's administrative regulations reads: "The holy key task of the Village Councils lies in the preservation of the achievements of the Islamic revolution and in the efforts that are to be made for enforcing the line of the Imam and in the fight against all the groups that are active against Islam and the Islamic people."[45] In a speech to the president at a meeting of the Village Councils in November 1982, a representative of the councils reported on such activities, saying that they had spared no effort to uproot the counterrevolution and had also organized a lot of help for the front in the war.[46]

As the speech made clear, the war effort—including recruiting men for the front and providing all sorts of material—was one more "holy" task for the Village Councils, which is why establishing them could not be delayed. In a resolution passed at the meeting, the first point (after an affirmation of loyalty to welayat-e faqih) was that the councils considered the war their "primary concern until the infidel B'ath regime in Iraq and the other regimes in the region that are dependent on America are toppled." There followed other political tasks, such as condemning the conspiracies of the "blind-hearted hypocrites" (i.e., the People's Mujahidin).[47] In a *Kayhan* interview, the members of "exemplary" Village Councils extolled their great achievements in fighting the counterrevolution, setting up people's mobilization stations, dispatching volunteers, providing logistical support, and forming ansar units (groups to take care of war victims' dependents). One member of every council was engaged in ensuring that the needs of the front were satisfied. A total of 33,000 such war commissioners were spread throughout the country (February 8, 1989).

As political instruments and providers of material and labor for construction projects, the councils have for years come under the Ministry of Jahad-e Sazandegi, which contributed most to setting them up and knew how to use the "best arm of the government" for its own aims as well as for those of the Islamic regime. Jahad, itself an organization that shifted away from its original tasks and was placed at the service of the war, is largely responsible for inducing estrangement from its original purpose of control and representation in the Village Councils.

The little field research and the few direct studies conducted by experts and scientists confirm the observations made here about the lack of participation in the councils. Azkia investigated the relationship between the District Village Councils and the Service Centers on the one hand and the councils and the peasants on the other by examining the extent to which the latter are involved in the work of these agencies. The same question was put to members of the Village Councils to determine their participation in the Service Centers and District Village Councils above them. He used the following indicators: (1) the extent to which the peasants are informed about the work of the Service Centers and Village Councils; (2) the extent to which the peasants participate in the decisions made by these organizations; (3) the extent to which the peasants participate in implementing construction projects; and (4) the extent to which the peasants are satisfied with their participation.

Investigations were conducted in three different regions: Jiroft

(Kerman province); around Bandar Abbas at the entrance to the Persian Gulf; and Garmsar, near Tehran. Concerning the first indicator, Azkia noted that the members of the Village Councils had very little information about the work of the Service Centers with which they were supposed to cooperate through their representatives. The members of the District Village Councils were not much better informed about them (a mere 37 percent of members in Bandar Abbas were in the know) and also knew very little about the villages they supposedly represented. The major problem with respect to the second indicator was that the Village Councils in no way represent the villagers. Azkia cautiously reported some disproportionality between the social composition of the villagers and that of the Village Councils.[48] "The members do not possess adequate information about their tasks and responsibilities. In some cases they are incognizant of agriculture and have no social standing at the village level" (p. 309). The members of District Village Councils were nominated by the Service Centers,[49] and even if the former participated in the decisions of the latter it would still not mean that the peasants did so. Azkia observed that the peasants were involved in implementing the measures decided on by the government, although there were local differences. "In other words, there is a readiness to accept projects that are related to construction and infrastructure" (p. 314). The peasants' satisfaction depended on whether the councils and centers performed convincingly and whether the fruits of these labors were distributed fairly. Azkia concluded his analysis with the following words: "In respect of an aware participation based on codetermination by the population and its satisfaction above and beyond that . . . the [revolutionary] institutions and state organizations have taken no positive steps in the villages. The peasant who is a council member is one because the government wants him to be one and not because he feels the need for it" (p. 317).[50]

Although Village Councils exist in almost every village in question, their function is often affected by the delay in implementing the Law on Local Councils, which accounts for the considerable pressure exerted by its sponsors, above all the Ministry of Jahad-e Sazandegi, for immediate action. The pressure initially took the form of frequent public meetings, verbal statements, and campaigns in the media.[51] Problems can be observed most clearly when the Village Councils want to uphold their interests vis-à-vis third parties: They are unable to claim that they are organizations sanctioned by law in conflicts where a landowner appeals to the courts or in disputes involving the gendarmerie.[52] According to reports in *Kayhan*, the courts deny them any support in combatting the khans, sheiks, and feudal lords and litter the path of the councils with obstacles—for instance, by not allowing them to arbitrate in local disputes.[53] This situation and the delay in sanctioning the councils in law have caused their members to feel hopeless, to lose credibility among the peasants, and thus to receive even less support from them. The very existence of the Village Councils is shaken, and the newer they are, the more shaken they are, causing—according to reports in *Kayhan*—cracks in the ideals of the revolution.[54]

11.3 State Interference in Peasant Matters

Even though the rural population is not permitted to participate in the decisions that affect it most, the state still interferes in farming and human affairs. For example, the state plays a major role, as shown above, in determining land ownership, organizing enterprises, administering the villages, and so on. The extent of its unnecessary interference in economic and other questions that do not concern it has been shown, as have its motives for doing so. Two other examples of unnecessary economic interference by the Islamic state in agriculture will be briefly dealt with below: determining which crops the peasants are forced to plant and what price they have to sell them for.

In its idealized desire to achieve economic self-sufficiency and hence independence from the capitalist world, the Islamic state tries to force the peasants and farmers to plant "strategic crops," especially wheat. The slogan is: "If we plant wheat, we harvest independence."[55] The state uses various methods to push this aim, such as allocating land to peasants only on the condition that they take the "interests of society" into account when choosing crops. Another one is the government's refusal to provide them with the necessities of life if they fail to plant the desired crops.[56] An export ban caused a great stir.[57] The prime minister even called the stubborn planting of nonstrategic crops a political act linked to the conspiracy of the superpowers and their lackeys in the Persian Gulf. He was happy to have thwarted the planting of 1,500ha of cucumbers in Khuzestan, saying that the farmers had intended to put 3bn tomans into their own pockets.[58]

The farmers and peasants, however, turn to the nonstrategic crops because they are more profitable. Planting wheat in Firuz Kuh brings less than 5 percent of the profit a farmer can make if he plants cucumbers.[59] Even though the Islamic regime knows that in such circumstances it is difficult to get the peasants to subordinate themselves to the government's strategic aims, it does practically nothing to make planting strategic crops more attractive by enacting an appropriate pricing policy. "As long as the price of strategic crops is at a low level . . . it is obvious that farmers will in no way be ready to invest their capital in them," argued *Kayhan*—which usually endeavors to play a leading role in approving the state's rigorisms—on August 30, 1984. Despite this insight, it continued its anticapitalist tirades in the same article, cursing the farmers as "damned capitalists" because they had supposedly dealt Khuzestan's agriculture a severe blow by planting summer crops.

The reason for the low wheat price,[60] only abandoned in 1989, is to be found in the political rather than in the economic considerations of the Islamic state. Food has had to be heavily subsidized since the revolution to pacify the increasingly impoverished town dwellers,[61] and the state has passed on the costs to the farmers, who are forced to sell their wheat to the government at a price below that of imported wheat.[62] Thus, a great deal of political pressure must be brought to bear in order to encourage the peasants to plant wheat, resulting in increased interference by the state in the affairs of farmers and peasants. On February 20, 1990, trying to explain the government's lack of a policy of participation, the minister of agriculture said: "We thought the farmers were nobodies." He added: "We wanted to impose everything on them."[63]

Notes

1. DPA, pp. 19, 39, 53, 326, 329f, 332, 359, and 464.
2. See A. R. Khomeini 1982, p. 42; and Montazeri in *Resalat*, January 16, 1988.
3. Khomeini 1982, p. 34.
4. See the articles in *Kayhan* between July 26 and October 16, 1986.
5. *Kayhan*, August 5, 1986.
6. But the Freedom Movement, of which Bazargan is the leader, objects to being viewed as championing capitalism, considering itself a party favoring the distribution of economic power among the three sectors named in Article 44 of the constitution: state, private, cooperative. See Nehzat-e Azadi-ye Iran 1982.
7. Bazargan and the Freedom Movement called for a Democratic Islamic Republic, but they failed to show how they intended to achieve a reconciliation between the Islamist ideology and democracy. Islamist legalism does indeed make such experiments absurd.
8. PP, May 8, 1986, p. 28.
9. According to the organ of the Islamic Student Association at the University of Shiraz in *Resalat*, June 22, 1986.
10. According to Ayatollah Meshgini's greeting to the Second Convention of Village Councils in *Kayhan*, December 21, 1982.
11. Interview with the director of the Social Department at the Ministry of the Interior in *Kayhan*, January 25, 1986.
12. Interview with the director of the Department for Coordination of the Councils at the Ministry of Jahad-e Sazandegi in *Kayhan*, February 9, 1986.
13. *Masa'el-e Keshawarzi* 4 (Autumn 1982), p. 11.
14. Majles-e Shoura-ye Eslami, "Protocols of the Assembly to Work Out the Constitution of Iran," vol. 2, p. 991.
15. *Ibid.*, p. 993.
16. See the newspaper *Khalq-e Mosalman*, September 9, 1979. It later became clear that many of the ulama had meant shour (advice) when, for opportunistic reasons, they used the term shoura (council) shortly after the revolution. Shour excludes the participation by those consulted in the decisionmaking, whereas shoura is an institution whose members have power of decision.
17. E. Hooglund 1982, p. 126f.
18. The Islamic Student Association at the University of Shiraz saw this ten-

dency in the same light and complained that the shouras had been forgotten now that the leftists had been eliminated. See *Resalat,* June 22, 1986.

19. CL 1979/80, pp. 48ff.
20. CL 1982/3, pp. 102ff.
21. *Kayhan,* May 11, 1985.
22. CL 1986/7, pp. 191ff.
23. *Kayhan,* August 2, 1986.
24. *Kayhan,* November 12, 1989. So far I have registered eleven dates set in the period mentioned.
25. See *Kayhan,* May 7, 10, and 13, 1990.
26. *Salam,* January 23, 1993.
27. Mirmord Zehi, representative of the provinces of Baluchistan and Sistan in the Assembly of Experts, takes this position. See Majles-e Shoura-ye Eslami 1985–89, vol. 2, p. 379.
28. See Articles 100 and 102 of the constitution.
29. Majles-e Shoura-ye Eslami 1985–89, vol. 2, p. 1001.
30. The May 1990 amendments restricted even this right to the extent that the municipal councils were only permitted to propose the mayor of their choice to the minister of the interior. He is considered elected if he is confirmed by the minister.
31. PP, July 20, 1982, p. 26, makes it clear that some earlier references to the Quran were meant in this sense.
32. *Resalat,* November 3, 1986, and May 13, 1989.
33. He means the experience of the mullahs in the constitutional revolution but also the significance of shouras for "hypocrites" (People's Mujahidin), who supposedly see the councils as a sort of negation of the Imamat. See *Kayhan,* May 19, 1986.
34. *Kayhan,* June 22, 1986.
35. *Kayhan,* May 14, 1986.
36. *Kayhan,* May 19, 1986.
37. PP, February 25, 1981, p. 20.
38. See Majles-e Shoura-ye Eslami 1985–89, vol. 2, p. 979f; *Kayhan,* February 9 and August 19, 1986; and *Jahad* 89 (1986).
39. See interview with the state secretary for social matters at the Ministry of the Interior in *Kayhan,* May 11, 1985; M. Badi'i in *Kayhan,* October 16, 1986; and the interview with the director of the Department for Coordinating the Village Councils at the Ministry of Jahad-e Sazandegi in *Kayhan,* February 9, 1986, and *Jahad* 89 (1986).
40. According to the Islamic Student Association at the University of Shiraz, which thinks that it is just an excuse to shelve the Law on Local Councils. See *Kayhan,* June 22, 1986.
41. *Masa'el-e Keshawarzi* 4 (1982), p. 14.
42. *Kayhan,* February 9, 1986.
43. *Kayhan,* December 21, 1987.
44. The Department for Coordinating the Village Councils at the Ministry of Jahad-e Sazandegi in *Kayhan,* September 3, 1985. See also Bafekr 1984, pp. 166ff, 174, 181, 198, and 213.
45. They were also intended to attend to the conduct of religious ceremonies and obsequies as well as encouraging the rural population to erect and take care of mosques, premises for passion festivities, and holy tombs. See M. Wusuqi 1987, p. 269.
46. *Kayhan,* November 8, 1982.
47. *Kayhan,* November 21, 1982.

48. The experts we interviewed explained that the council members were not elected but nominated by either Jahad or the Service Centers. At best the villagers put forward some individuals who, after having been vetted, are confirmed by Jahad. See also H. Bafekr 1984, pp. 178ff and 188; and M. Wusuqi 1987, p. 274.

49. See also H. Sabet Qadam 1983, pp. 19–29. She observes that, continuing old customs, the centers themselves decide what the needs of the peasants are and how they can be satisfied.

50. See also F. Rafi' Pur 1985, pp. 309ff.

51. On the initial actions, see *Masa'ele-e Keshawarzi* 1 (Autumn 1981), pp. 67ff; and 4 (Autumn 1982), pp. 11ff.

52. *Kayhan*, January 25, 1986, December 14 and 16, 1987, and January 23, 1988.

53. *Kayhan*, February 9 and August 19, 1986, December 14 and 19, 1987, and December 23, 1988. See the opinion of Kho'iniha, the attorney general in *Kayhan*, June 17, 1986.

54. *Ibid.*

55. *Kayhan*, August 6, 1984.

56. On April 9, 1984, the Central Office for Agriculture in the province of Khorasan announced that farmers who had more than 10ha of nonstrategic crops at the spring sowing would have to reckon with being cut off from supplies of electricity, kerosene, and gas in addition to being denied agricultural services and being prevented from exporting their produce out of the province (*Kayhan*).

57. *Kayhan* reported such cases, e.g. on June 25, July 9, August 30, and September 2, 1984.

58. *Kayhan*, June 20, 1984.

59. P. Kardawani in *Kayhan*, March 27, 1986.

60. See the next chapter on this point.

61. According to *Resalat* (September 19, 1988), food subsidies in 1986/7 came to 150bn rials, almost 70bn more than the state investment for the whole economy that year. According to Rafsanjani, nine-tenths of the cost of bread is subsidized. See *Kayhan*, August 6, 1984.

62. One kilogram of imported wheat cost between 44 and 84 rials in 1984 (depending on the rate of exchange), but the government only paid 40 rials for domestic wheat. See *Kayhan*, August 6, 1984.

63. From his speech at the seminar for ABs, RPCs, and FCs—see *Barzegar*, March 3, 1990.

12

Financial and Technical Measures to Maximize Production

A perusal of the Islamic Republic's documents on agricultural policy shows that it was aware of the financial and technical measures needed to increase production, was familiar with their structures and effects, and generally considered it necessary to apply them. It was also known to what extent they had to be applied in order to achieve certain results. To a certain extent this expertise continues to be available to the Islamists and the ulamas' system of government, despite widespread (forced) resignations and the mass exodus of experts. This expertise surfaced in the drafts of the general and agricultural development plans discussed so far, which also criticized the financial and technical measures to encourage agriculture that were taken (or neglected) both before and after the revolution.[1] But expert knowledge alone has not been enough when it has come to working out and implementing adequate solutions. Ideological, political, structural, and financial obstacles have ensured that probate measures either were too little and too late or were redirected into channels that do not benefit agriculture.

12.1 Financing Agricultural Policy

The criticism of the shah's neglect of agriculture and the subsequent assignment of "first priority" and a "pivotal position" to this sector raised expectations for a redistribution of government investment. Table 12.1 in fact shows a relative increase in government agricultural investment compared with prerevolutionary investment and with spending in other sectors of the economy, but only after 1983/4. At no time after the revolution was agriculture accorded the promised first priority in the allocation of government funds, actually ranking between third (1988/9) and sixth (1982/3 and 1983/4) place.

Table 12.1 Government Fixed Investment by Economic Sectors
(in billions of rials at current prices) (percentages in parentheses)

Year	Agriculture	Water	Electricity	Industry	Oil and Gas	Mines	Traffic	Other
1977/8	42.0	46.0	185.7	116.2	114.9	15.0	102.0	24.5
	(6.2)	(6.8)	(27.7)	(17.3)	(17.1)	(2.2)	(15.2)	(3.6)
1978/9	53.8	42.5	121.2	94.0	NA	20.0	154.1	14.2
	(10.4)	(6.3)	(23.6)	(18.3)	NA	(3.9)	(30.0)	(2.6)
1979/80	55.9	32.8	83.2	71.9	11.2	18.6	74.6	11.4
	(15.5)	(9.1)	(23.1)	(19.9)	(3.1)	(5.2)	(20.7)	(3.2)
1980/1	26.6	38.8	66.6	70.5	26.5	20.7	83.3	12.6
	(8.3)	(12.1)	(20.7)	(21.9)	(6.8)	(6.4)	(5.8)	(3.9)
1981/2	35.3	43.1	75.8	77.2	7.9	24.1	100.1	10.9
	(9.4)	(11.5)	(20.2)	(20.6)	(2.1)	(6.4)	(26.7)	(2.9)
1982/3	48.2	49.7	108.6	118.5	53.0	26.6	114.6	15.5
	(9.1)	(9.3)	(20.3)	(22.2)	(9.9)	(5.0)	(21.4)	(2.9)
1983/4	74.8	76.4	119.1	159.7	89.0	26.5	148.1	22.5
	(10.4)	(10.7)	(16.6)	(23.3)	(12.4)	(3.7)	(20.7)	(3.1)
1984/5	77.8	75.2	111.8	106.1	56.5	21.5	141.6	3.8
	(13.1)	(12.7)	(18.8)	(17.9)	(9.5)	(3.6)	(23.8)	(0.6)
1985/6	53.4	52.5	88.9	89.7	70.8	14.3	118.8	9.8
	(10.7)	(10.6)	(17.9)	(18.1)	(14.2)	(2.9)	(23.9)	(1.7)
1986/7	97.5	58.6	110.4	117.3	192.1	24.2	170.0	10.6
	(12.3)	(8.7)	(14.0)	(14.8)	(24.3)	(3.1)	(21.5)	(1.3)
1987/8[1]	111.3[2]	69.6	45.4	130.6	142.4	18.9	149.0	33.6
	(15.9)	(9.9)	(6.5)	(18.6)	(20.3)	(2.7)	(21.3)	(4.8)
1988/9	84.5	82.3	16.8	147.3	NA	21.1	141.7	7.1
	(16.8)	(16.4)	(3.3)	(29.4)	NA	(4.2)	(22.2)	(1.4)
1987/8 plan	214.8	221.3	194.9	137.0	232.3	69.1	225.8	37.0
	(15.1)	(15.6)	(13.7)	(9.6)	(16.3)	(4.8)	(15.9)	(2.6)
1983–88 plan	755.9	633.6	992.0	758.3	848.2	243.0	940.2	189.9
	(13.4)	(11.2)	(17.6)	(13.4)	(15.0)	(4.3)	(16.6)	(3.3)
1989–94 plan	787.2	787.2	171.2	673.6	NA	289.6	1,197.3	45.2
	(19.6)	(19.6)	(4.2)	(16.8)	NA	(7.2)	(29.9)	(1.1)

Sources: Agriculture Report 1981/2–1986/7; Ettela'at-e Siyasi-Eqtesadi 26; 1983 development plan; 1989–94 development plan (CL 1989/90, p. 853); Bank-e Markazi 1983; Markaz-e Amar 1989.
Notes: 1. Total government expenditure rather than just fixed investments
2. 1987/8 fixed investment in agriculture was 66.4bn rials (Markaz-e Amar 1985)

The picture presented by these nominal increases in government investment changes completely if inflation is taken into account. According to calculations by *Mahname-ye Barresiha-ye Bazargani* (Economic Investigations Monthly), the wholesale price index rose from 56.5 in 1979/80 to 202.1 in 1987/8 (base year: 1982/3).[2] There was a downward trend in government investment at constant 1974 prices, falling from 39.9bn to 32.3bn rials between 1977 and 1984.[3] At a maximum of 400bn rials, government investment in agriculture was lower, both in absolute terms and relative to expenditure in the other sectors of the economy, than desired in the first draft of the 1983 development plan, which earmarked 1,105.7bn rials to attain self-sufficiency between 1983/4 and 1987/8 (p. 121). Comparison of planned and actual expenditure in 1987/8 further illustrates the gap between the plan and reality. In this context it is interesting to note that the fixed government investments provided for in the new five-year plan (1989–94) are only 31bn rials more than envisaged in the 1983 plan, despite the multiple devaluations of the rial.

There was no increase in agricultural activity by the private sector after the revolution. The annual reports by the Ministry of Agriculture repeatedly termed investment "very slight."[4] The reasons for this lack of interest were the insecurity of private property, the large-scale flight of capital, and the comparatively low profitability of agricultural investments.[5] The figures for capital formation in the agrarian sector show how insignificant progress was followed by significant retrogression.

Agriculture ranks from fifth to seventh in terms of capital formation, far behind the other sectors of the economy. In 1987/8 the service sector accounted for 28 percent of gross domestic capital accumulation, construction for as much as 45 percent, and agriculture for a mere 8 percent.

Compared to the year immediately prior to the revolution, there was a nominal increase after the revolution in loans granted by the state Bank for Agriculture to peasants and farmers for agricultural purposes (Table 12.3), a large part again falling victim to inflation. The upward wage drift, which accounted for a growing proportion of the rising production costs, was primarily responsible for negating the effects of increased loans: The wage index for unskilled construction workers rose from 381.5 in 1979 to 1,138.5 in 1985 (base year: 1974). This indicator is largely valid in respect of wage developments in the agrarian sector, too.[6]

Whereas the shah's regime favored giving loans to large-scale projects, loans were scattered broadly in the postrevolutionary period, as both the number and average amount granted make clear. However, a tendency to reduce the spread can be noted. In 1981, 83 percent of loans were for under 500,000 rials, compared to just 45 percent five years later.[7] There was a negative trend in the policy of granting loans to peasant smallholdings, a clear parallel to the Islamic regime's general turning away from the "dispossessed." A new regulation countermanding the Bank for

Table 12.2 Gross Domestic Capital Formation
(at current and constant prices, billions of rials)

	Current Prices			Constant Prices[1]		
	Total	Agrarian	Percent[2]	Total	Agrarian	Percent[2]
1975/6	1,588	77	4.8	875	60	6.8
1976/7	NA	NA	NA	1,181	59	5.0
1977/8	1,784	75	4.2	1,083	47	4.3
1978/9	1,557	57	3.7	885	32	3.6
1979/80	1,253	66	5.3	623	36	5.7
1980/1	1,476	71	4.8	609	31	5.1
1981/2	1,975	86	4.3	562	35	6.2
1982/3	1,887	97	5.1	618	34	5.5
1983/4	2,944	188	6.4	860	62	7.2
1984/5	2,884	136	4.7	770	54	7.0
1985/6	2,537	144	5.7	638	46	7.1
1986/7	2,240	128	5.7	465	31	6.7
1987/8	2,658	218	8.2	445	36	8.1

Source: Markaz-e Amar 1982, 1985, 1988, 1989.
Notes: 1. Constant price base year 1974/5
2. Percent agrarian of total capital accumulation

Agriculture's prerevolutionary practice and waiving collateral to the benefit of the smaller borrower has been having an impact.[8] The official figures are disputed by those concerned. For example, an "exemplary farmer" told *Kayhan* that loans were only given to farmers whose property is entered in the land registry, mainly ones who lived in town (June 9, 1986). Up to half the loans have to be repaid within two years. Loans of over ten years account for at best 2.1 percent of the total,[9] meaning that most loans cannot be used for long-term investments. This conclusion is confirmed both by the decline in the number of loans provided for "supervised projects" and by the fact that borrowers spend up to 44 percent of their loans on "current expenses."[10] The bank grants most loans directly, with the remainder being handled by other organizations that are active in the rural areas, such as the RCs, the Sevener Commissions, and Jahad-e Sazandegi. These last two use their position to impose their authority on the countryside.

As shown in Chapter 7, the Bank for Agriculture grants some of its loans in the form of Islamic contracts. For "interest-free" loans, it charges a 2.5 percent official "administrative fee" (kar mozd); for other Islamic

Table 12.3 Bank of Agriculture Loans to Peasants and Farmers

Year	Total Amount (in billions of rials)	Number (in thousands)	Average (in thousands of rials)	Direct (in billions of rials)	Indirect[1] (in billions of rials)
1977/8	51.7	382	135	26.1	25.6
1978/9	42.1	322	130	25.1	17.0
1979/80	81.7	552	148	43.7	38.0
1980/1	116.3	573	203	67.2	49.1
1981/2	148.4	634	234	94.1	54.2
1982/3	183.7	626	293	124.3	59.3
1983/4	219.9	581	379	145.4	74.5
1984/5	155.7	325	479	108.8	46.8
1985/6	200.0	339	589	117.2	82.8
1986/7	201.9	297	679	117.0	84.8
1987/8	279.0	335	835	200.2	78.8[2]
1988/9	382.0	420	911	235.7	146.3

Sources: Agricultural Report 1985/6 and 1986/7; Statistical Yearbook 1980/1 and 1988/9.
Notes: 1. The bank places indirect credits via the RCs, Sevener Commissions, and Jahad-e Sazandegi
2. Credits placed through the RCs only

contracts the fee is between 6 and 9 percent of the sum granted. The bank deducts a total of 18 percent from its loans at the expense of the borrower, 9 percent or more as tax and insurance for disasters.[11] Even the minister of agriculture criticized this policy, asking: "Why must a farmer pay 17 to 18 percent interest?"[12] Some people maintain that the current state exacts more interest from the farmers than did the shah's regime.[13] Referring to such practices, one member of parliament, Hojjat ol-Eslam Sawouji, noted that the "Islamic transactions of the banks are only Islamic on the surface."[14]

The bank is hampered by a variety of inadequacies and obstacles that severely impair its effectiveness as the state's promoter of private investment and agent of agrarian policy. Twelve points were listed in the agricultural section of the 1983 development plan (p. 40) and others were added in the 1987 self-sufficiency plan (p. 109f). Here is a summary:

1. the lack of laws on agricultural, social, and economic policy to provide a framework for the bank's credit policy

2. inadequate government funds for the bank to satisfy the actual demand for loans
3. insufficient counseling of borrowers to guarantee the use of loans for productive purposes
4. the number of organizations involved in indirect credit deals complicating the bank's credit policy
5. the inadequate number of branches to provide services to outlying villages, as required

In the opinion of Minister Kalantari, these shortcomings are compounded by the bureaucratization of the bank, which binds itself hand and foot with its cumbersome rules and regulations.[15] In 1989 Khadem Adam, an expert, assessed the bank's work in the following words: "The Bank for Agriculture is characterized by a weak balance sheet. It is not in a position to perform its function as a medium for realizing agricultural targets in the form desired."[16]

12.2 Land and Water Use

The Islamic Republic's aim of expanding the area of arable land under cultivation, in particular irrigated land, stems from its awareness of the highly inadequate use it makes of available resources and of the opportunity it has to remedy this shortcoming. This goal is given even greater emphasis by the drive for self-sufficiency. All the Islamic Republic's programs and plans for agrarian policy proclaim this objective above all and attempt to characterize the sinful neglect of resources as a legacy from the shah, even in more recent pronouncements and documents. The specific failings of this legacy are cited as neglect of traditional irrigation methods and plants; inadequate and inconsequent use of dams; gratuitous preference for expensive irrigation projects; failure to prevent land fragmentation; and lack of laws governing equitable distribution of water (DPA 83, p. 4f). The criticism concludes with a list of obstacles that continue to prevent implementation of a successful policy of land and water use in the Islamic Republic. These include lack of knowledge about land and water resources; uncertainty about property rights for land and water; lack of experts and skilled labor; organizational problems; and inadequate funds (p. 33).

Despite these obstacles, the government of the Islamic Republic intends to achieve its goal by a series of measures detailed in the 1983 development plan, such as: repairing old irrigation plants and constructing new ones; covering open canals and waterways; leveling and draining arable regions; consolidating the peasants' fragmented plots of land; and conducting a series of research projects (DPA, pp. 85ff). The plan provides for the government to pay a total of 229.3bn rials for these purposes over the five-year plan.

The same problems, obstacles, and bottlenecks were repeated in the 1987 self-sufficiency plan—sometimes in more detail, sometimes in exactly the same words—and additional points were added (pp. 39ff, 209ff). This plan claimed that between 66 percent and 69 percent of the water for agricultural purposes is lost through technical faults in the irrigation plants (p. 46) and that, at 10t/ha, soil erosion in Iran actually exceeded the 7t/ha lost in Africa (p. 219). The description of the current state of affairs is followed by a presentation of the targets and a list of the measures to achieve them—the same ones as in the 1983 plan.

Table 12.4 Arable Land Area (in thousands of hectares)

Year	Arable	Tilled (percent of arable)	Fallow (percent of arable)	Irrigated (percent of tilled)	Non-irrigated (percent of tilled)
1974/5	16,416	10,461 (64)	5,955 (36)	4,095 (39)	6,366 (61)
1978/9	14,868	9,185 (62)	5,683 (38)	3,825 (42)	5,360 (58)
1982/3	14,777	9,848 (67)	4,929 (33)	3,979 (40)	5,869 (60)
1985/6[1]	18,500	12,186 (66)	6,314 (34)	4,265 (35)	7,921 (65)
1987/8[2]	NA	11,824	NA	6,562 (55)	5,262 (45)
1988/9	16,871	11,507 (68)	5,364 (32)	5,626 (49)	5,881 (51)

Source: Markaz-e Amar 1977a and 1990.
Notes: 1. Data from self-sufficiency plan
2. Targets from 1983 development plan

The figures in Table 12.4 are subject to the familiar reservations about accuracy. Arable land increased by about 450,000ha between 1974/5 and 1988/9. However, the increase is misleading—it includes approximately 500,000ha of wasteland that the Sevener Commissions allocated to peasants. Also, arable land within city limits was counted in the 1988/9 agricultural census but not in 1974/5 and 1982/3. It is safe to assume that this difference in procedure accounts for a considerable proportion of the increase in arable and irrigated land. The 1985/6 data from the self-sufficiency plan cannot be correct—according to the Ministry of Agriculture's annual report for the same year, the area under cultivation was approximately 10m hectares and not over 12m hectares. There is an equally large discrepancy between these two sources concerning the area of nonirrigated land, although both sources agree about the cultivated area under irrigation. The figures for 1987/8 refer to the targets in the 1983 development plan. These targets had not been achieved for irrigated land by 1988/9. The only figure to exceed the target by 1988/9 was nonirrigated cultivated land—but the target called for a *reduction* in comparison to 1980/1, when it accounted for 5,297m hectares.

The other data on the development of land use present a gloomier picture. A significant but undetermined proportion of arable land has been used for nonagricultural purposes in recent years, with reports on the various forms of rededication appearing time and again in the press. Bans and punishments are ineffective because such rededications are advantageous in view of the low profitability of agriculture. The continuing reports about the destruction of arable land caused by incorrect use, among other things, are alarming. According to Kalantari, between 50,000 and 60,000ha of pastures and woods are destroyed and 300,000ha of arable land are transformed into desert each year. (Only 10,000ha of pastures and woods are restored annually.)[17] On another occasion he stated that 500,000ha of irrigated land were lost to production in the first few years after the revolution.[18]

The 1983 development plan aimed to consolidate 170,670ha of fragmented peasant plots by 1987/8 (p. 87). On March 18, 1989, *Kayhan* published a report in which the director of the Qazwin Construction Organization announced the consolidation of 450ha in Qazwin and Takestan and characterized it as the *first* action taken according to the plan (it may actually have been the second—the consolidation of 400ha in Tehran province had been reported some months before).[19] High costs and lack of adequate government funding were given as the reasons for neglecting the plan.[20] Nevertheless, Kalantari did promise that 1m hectares of land would be consolidated during the current (1989–94) five-year plan.[21]

The statements and data coming from the relevant ministries present differing pictures of the increase in irrigation plants and their capacity. The number of diversion cuts started before the revolution had not changed by 1987/8, and four out of nine dams started before the revolution were completed by the same year.[22] The number and capacity of wells, springs, and subterranean channels (qanat) increased several times over from 1976/7 to 1986/7.

Table 12.5 Groundwater Used
            (in thousands of cubic meters)

Year	Deep Wells	Other Wells	Qanats	Springs	Total
1976/7					
Number	16,626	42,546	18,388	8,193	85,753
Quantity	7,470	3,883	7,539	5,450	24,342
1985/6					
Number	45,355	119,068	28,038	20,244	212,705
Quantity	19,115	10,486	9,079	8,127	46,807

Source: Markaz-e Amar 1982 and 1988.

However, the quantity of groundwater used did not increase at the same ratio as the number of plants (1:1.9 versus 1:2.4), although the increase is proportional to the expansion in irrigated land. This progress was largely due to the private initiative of farmers and peasants, funded in part by loans from the Bank for Agriculture. Despite a nominal increase,[23] government investments in land and water use amounted to only 53.3 percent of the 229.3bn rials earmarked to implement the 1983 development plan.[24] A state project to cover the open canals remained largely unfulfilled, with only 1,078 out of 25,983km completed.[25] According to a statement by the minister of agriculture, the inadequate use of dams could not be countered before 1989.[26] In February 1989 the magazine *Jahad* felt obliged to warn against the continued destruction of subterranean canals caused by the uncontrolled drilling of wells,[27] a problem that had been in urgent need of a solution even before the revolution and that the postrevolutionary regime had promised to address.

12.3 Measures to Raise the Yield

Apart from the factors already mentioned, the mechanization of production and the provision of adequate quantities of seed corn, fertilizers, and pesticides contributed to the increased yield. The application of techniques made possible by intensive research and training also helped. Here, too, the Islamic Republic's results have sometimes been positive, sometimes negative, but always well below the targets.

The 1983 development plan commenced with a criticism of the shah's legacy and a list of existing bottlenecks, complaining not only of extensive neglect in research and training but also that certain policies had been copied from abroad and ignored the country's real needs. The bottlenecks were summarized in eighteen points (DPA, p. 38). Obviously, there had been no change since the revolution, and thus there was no need to assess things any differently.

With respect to the mechanization of production, the development plan observed that for technical reasons it was only possible to use an average of 54 percent of the power available to the 100,000 tractors of 65 horsepower (hp) in Iran in 1982, equal to 0.44hp/ha for the 9m hectares of cultivated land—well below the world average (p. 13). It also complained about the inadequate domestic production of machines, the unserviceability of imported machines, the inappropriate distribution of machines, the lack of repair garages for the equipment, and so on. The situation was described as critical or even catastrophic (p. 13f). There was similar criticism regarding the supply of other inputs, such as processed seed corn, pesticides, and fertilizers.

According to the development plan, these bottlenecks were to be removed and the course of mechanization, research, training, and counseling directed by planned steps. "The mechanization process" was to be "controlled with consideration given to questions of employment, managerial organization and local conditions as well as with due regard for all the technical, economic, political and social indicators." This approach was intended to encourage "domestic initiative as well as the creative and innovative power in the production and use of machines and equipment within the country" (p. 51). The use of tractors was to be raised from 0.44 to 0.65hp/ha by 1987 (p. 48). Research, training, and counseling were to be expanded in all relevant agricultural areas in order to improve the conditions necessary for cultivation (pp. 52 and 111ff). The use of artificial fertilizers was to be increased considerably, and more and more processed seed corn was to be produced within the country (pp. 47 and 91ff). The quantitative details of the planning targets are presented in Table 12.7.

The immediate aim of these measures was to increase the yield to the extent shown in Table 12.6 for 1987/8. Comparison of that year's results with those of the self-sufficiency plan's base year on the one hand and those for 1988/9 on the other make it clear that the plan had largely failed to achieve its targets. Table 12.6 nevertheless shows that the yield for some products has grown in comparison to the year immediately prior to the revolution. Output of onions rose in particular, although it should be pointed out that they attained yields of up to 25,000kg/ha in 1974/5 and 30,000kg/ha in 1975/6. Sugar beets yielded 26,000kg/ha from 1974 to 1976, and the cotton yield before the revolution was always higher than in 1978/9 and even exceeded the 1986/7 result in two years.[28] If the yields before the revolution are taken into account over a longer period and compared to the postrevolutionary results, the growth in yields is less

Table 12.6 Yield for Selected Agricultural Products (in kilograms per hectare)

Product	1978/9	1986/7	1987/8[1] irrigated	1987/8[1] nonirrigated	1987/8[1] average	1987/8[2] irrigated	1987/8[2] nonirrigated	1987/8[2] average	1988/9 irrigated	1988/9 nonirrigated	1988/9 average
Wheat	1,016	1,174	2,400	940	NA	1,900	710	NA	1,833	706	1,082
Barley	1,084	1,299	2,290	750	NA	NA	NA	NA	1,970	763	1,233
Rice	3,966	3,925	4,320	0	4,320	3,000	0	3,000	2,814	0	2,814
Cotton	1,525	1,845	2,280	1,490	NA	NA	NA	1,747	NA	NA	NA
Sugar beets	23,714	28,051	28,010	0	28,010	28,020	0	28,020	NA	NA	NA
Potatoes	16,351	16,260	18,110	0	18,110	0	0	16,110	10,555	NA	10,555
Onions	16,323	19,137	19,720	0	19,720	NA	NA	NA	19,518	NA	19,518

Sources: Agriculture Report 1986/7; Bank-e Markazi 1983; Markaz-e Amar 1989; 1983 development plan; 1987 self-sufficiency plan.
Notes: 1. Targets from 1983 development plan
2. Targets from 1987 self-sufficiency plan

significant, further proof that agricultural production in the Islamic Republic has not made a quantum leap.

The reason for the discrepancy between the targets and yields is the equally large gap between the planned and realized supply of inputs and other means of production maximization in agriculture, as made clear in Table 12.7. The procurement and sale of tractors provides an example for the development of mechanization. After an initial threefold increase, tractor sales dropped off to about one-fifth of the 1977/8 level, mainly because of the reduction in dollar revenues from oil but also because of the diversion of funding away from agriculture. Foreign currency earmarked for the state Organization for Agricultural Machines fell from $240m to $18m between 1984/5 and 1986/7.[29] This belt-tightening led the organization not only to restrict its imports of machines but also to reduce domestic production and assembly, which is dependent on supplies of parts from abroad. On July 12, 1988, *Resalat* reported that the only state factory producing agricultural equipment had been forced to close because of the lack of foreign currency. According to the state secretary at the Ministry of Agriculture, Angaji, only 20 of the 1,000 tractors and 30 of the 200 combine harvesters planned for production in Tabris were actually delivered.[30] Domestic tractor production dropped from 19,657 in 1984 to 2,823 in 1987.[31] Interestingly enough, imports rose parallel to the drop in domestic production, though not to the same extent—from 3,641 in 1984/5 to 5,956 two years later[32]—meaning that the available foreign currency was being spent not on increasing domestic production but on importing the required tractors. According to a resolution passed at a meeting of the functionaries responsible for maximizing wheat production, the reason for importing was the poor quality of the domestic product.[33]

The 183,000 tractors claimed by the minister of agriculture in 1989 were only being used at 30 percent of capacity at the time[34] (this figure had been 53 percent in 1982), the lack of foreign currency again being given as the reason for difficulties with imports and the production of spare parts.[35] But there were structural causes, too: At the National Congress to Investigate the Problems of Agricultural Development held at the beginning of March 1989, experts pointed out that machines were being used in Iran's agriculture not because they were necessary but because it was fashionable to use them. What was needed was a comprehensive infrastructure that would enable proper use to be made of the machines.[36] Iran's agriculture had not been mechanized, merely equipped with tractors, according to an agrarian sociologist.[37] This alienation has apparently gained in intensity in the Islamic Republic—the massive use of agricultural machinery in the war was typical of this period, and was mentioned as an indicator of bottlenecks in agriculture in the 1983 development plan (p. 37).

There was rapid growth in the supply of artificial fertilizers to agriculture after the revolution, followed by a decline from 1984 onwards. It

Table 12.7 Sales of Tractors and Other Inputs

Year	Tractors	Fertilizers (thousands of tons)	Pesticides (thousands of tons)	Processed Wheat (tons)	Seed Corn Rice (tons)	Cotton (tons)
1977/8	10,142	772	32	64,000	61	10,620
1978/9	7,482	582	32	59,900	70	11,040
1979/80	12,012	900	27	56,600	54	6,103
1980/1	13,517	1,097	21	84,400	60	6,485
1981/2	14,727	1,312	20	109,000	565	9,000
1982/3	28,940	1,653	30	75,000	1,470	10,994
1983/4	32,918	1,931	45	73,000	NA	11,000
1984/5	23,836	1,679	45	87,000	1,052	NA
1985/6	15,840	1,626	39	89,000	1,740	10,447
1986/7	7,269	1,699	35	124,000	10,560	10,560
1987/8	3,278	1,722	NA	NA	NA	11,300
1987/8[1]	38,156	2,893	NA	394,493	36,409	14,310
1988/9	1,757	1,428	NA	NA	NA	NA

Sources: Agriculture Report 1981/2 to 1986/7; Statistical Yearbook 1981/2, 1984/5, and 1988/9; 1983 development plan.
Note: 1. Target from 1983 development plan

should be borne in mind that the government heavily subsidized them by providing farmers and peasants with these materials at constant prices for several years. But despite increased supplies, the targets set by the 1983 development plan for any particular year were not attained. Table 12.7 illustrates the wide gap between the fertilizers distributed and the demand for them in 1987/8. This state of affairs caused repeated complaints by farmers, the press, and officials at the Ministry of Agriculture about the lack of artificial fertilizers, among other things, and they cited the shortage as proof that talk of the pivotal position of agriculture was not meant seriously.[38] The shortage was pushing black market prices so high that it was more profitable for many farmers to sell the subsidized fertilizer instead of enriching their fields with it.[39] A further characteristic of the period following the revolution was the sharp drop in domestic fertilizer production, which accounted for only 0.2 percent of the total sold in 1984.[40] The cause given was the destruction of the factories during the war.[41]

Regarding processed seed corn, the agriculture report pointed out that, in addition to experiencing shortages, the peasants were unable to use it properly because of a lack of appropriate instruction. As a result, this food could not be fully exploited (1986/7, p. 78).

The self-sufficiency plan described the results of the research work undertaken in the following words: "It must be admitted that what has been done is nothing in comparison to what needs to be done. Iran continues to remain, with respect to the number of researchers and expenditure on research, at the very bottom of the world scale. India has ten times more research personnel than Iran. Even Turkey invests one and a half times more in research than Iran" (p. 229f). At a conference on research held in Tehran in August 1989, a state secretary at the Ministry of Agriculture said that per million inhabitants Iran only had forty researchers, whereas the ratio was 5,000 or 6,000 per million in Europe.[42] The minister of agriculture viewed the "damaging laws that have been enacted for the training of the labor force at higher levels of training" as one cause of this catastrophic state of affairs, warning that "the gates of our research institutes will be closed in the near future. In the past two years we have only been able to send three individuals to study abroad. At the same time we lost dozens of such people at higher levels"—which is why the minister subsequently felt obliged to raise the alarm.[43]

The discrepancy between government investment in research and the amounts earmarked for it in the 1983 development plan provide a further indication of neglect. The following table makes the discrepancy clear:

Table 12.8 Government Investment in Agricultural Research (in millions of rials)

	1983/4	1984/5	1985/6	1986/7
Investment Planned	14,343	13,746	9,165	4,494
Investment Effected	2,436	2,678	4,244	5,943

Sources: Agriculture Report 1981/2 to 1986/7, and 1983 development plan.

Still, the number of research projects rose from 600 to 1,300 between 1981 and 1982, according to a statement by the former minister of agriculture.[44]

The miserable state of affairs in research had its counterpart in training. The disinclination on the part of pupils or students to study agricultural subjects was strikingly obvious. According to a 1988 report in *Resalat*, only 0.07 percent of all secondary pupils were at agricultural colleges (December 25, 1988), and graduates from them accounted for only 2.4 percent of the total from all vocational training colleges. The same year a mere 5.3 percent of students took agricultural courses.[45]

There has been an increase since the revolution in the number of advisers (morrawej) instructing the peasants in the use of more modern techniques,[46] although here, too, the relevant targets were not achieved. The 1983 development plan considered 125,995 "auxiliary advisers" (mo'in) to be needed by 1988. There were in fact 19,000 to 20,000 by then, including the 12,000 "auxiliary advisers" from the Ministry of Jahad.[47] These auxiliary advisers were peasants who took crash courses and "have their eye more on their own interests than on passing their knowledge on to other peasants."[48] An "exemplary farmer" assessed their expertise as being less than that of the farmers they were supposed to advise.[49]

This section ought not to be concluded without a glance at a plan to raise yields. Jahad pushed to be allowed to implement the so-called ears project (tarh-e sanabal), designed to increase productivity on nonirrigated land by using more modern techniques. The agency is very pleased with its success. Average yields on the 1,405,897m hectares so far involved have risen from 976 to 1,487kg/ha. An overall increase of 718,467t in wheat production was registered on this land[50]—an achievement to be proud of in view of the other failures.

12.4 Pricing and Marketing Policy

The pricing and marketing policy of the government in the postrevolutionary era is characterized by guaranteed prices for some products and fixed prices for others. This approach goes hand in hand with the purchasing monopoly of the state agencies, cooperatives, and government processing plants, which control the market by subsidizing and/or rationing certain goods and combatting profiteering and hoarding. The extent to which such practices can promote production can best be seen using examples of individual agricultural products. The ruling Islamists—at least, the experts among them—are aware of the possibilities for stepping up production by means of an appropriate pricing and marketing policy. They criticize the shah's pricing policy because they think it was intended to ensure low prices for urban consumers.

Wheat is the ruling Islamists' favorite product, and promoting its production is seen as the best route to achieving economic independence. Self-sufficiency in wheat is also seen as proof that the Islamist development alternative is workable. The government fixes the price of wheat each year and, in an attempt to corner a purchasing monopoly, buys up whatever the peasants produce in excess of their own needs plus whatever the farmers produce for market. As a result, the price fixed by the government largely determines the producers' inclination to grow wheat. The price is calculated by the experts at the Ministry of Agriculture on the basis of the cost trend and put to the Supreme Economic Council, which then fixes it.

As Table 12.9 shows, the price is normally fixed below the one put forward and always below the wholesale one, which can be obtained whenever the producers or middlemen succeed in circumventing the state on the market. According to the 1983/4 and 1985/6 agricultural reports, the modernized enterprises can still produce at a profit at this fixed price. For peasants, however, the difference between the price proposed and the one approved means a loss to at least the same extent. Minister of Agriculture Kalantari stated that in 1989 the wheat producer suffered a loss of 20 rials/kg. When the price was raised to 75 rials/kg toward the end of November 1988, the loss dropped to 4 rials/kg.[51]

Table 12.9 Wheat Price
           (in rials per kilogram)

Year	Proposal	Approved	Cash	Premium	Wholesale	Difference
1981/2	28	28	28	0	35.5	7.5
1982/3	30	30	30	0	38.1	8.1
1983/4	34	30	32	0	49.4	19.4
1984/5	45	40	30	10	55.0	15.0
1985/6	48	40	30	10	52.8	12.8
1986/7	50	46	40	6	59.4	13.4
1987/8	NA	53	49	4	NA	NA
1988/9	NA	57	49	8	NA	NA
1989/90	NA	105	100	5	NA	NA
1990/1	NA	100	100	0	NA	NA

Sources: Agriculture Report 1981/2 to 1986/7; *Keshawarz* 114 (1989), p. 4; *Kayhan,* January 10, 1990.

As implied in Chapter 11.3, the reasons for keeping the price of wheat low are political, an assertion with which the experts at the Ministry of Agriculture agree.[52] The government subsidizes bread in the towns at a price (18 to 20 rials/kg) far below the price fixed for wheat. The state passes the costs of this subsidy on to the farmers and peasants by keeping the wheat price as low as possible, thereby recovering some of the costs of subsidizing farm inputs such as fertilizers. The difference between the price of bread in the towns and the price fixed for wheat induces the peasants, especially those in villages close to towns, to become customers of the municipal bakeries, which drives up the demand for wheat and allows them to sell more wheat to the state.[53] The low price is partly compensated for by the premiums the peasants receive. These premiums are coveted because they are paid in kind in the form of utensils. The prices of these utensils are fixed by the state and are much lower than those on the free market. Therefore, the peasants can sell their premiums to recoup some of the losses they suffer because of the low price of wheat. But the government has attempted to make the rise in the fixed price more bearable for itself by reducing the premiums. The peasants increasingly complain that premiums are only paid to government favorites (although they are sometimes only promised, not actually paid).[54] *Barzegar,* however, considers the premiums to be the main motive behind producing wheat for the market: "If they were to be abolished nobody would produce wheat any more" (June 4, 1988). The government nonetheless abolished the premiums in 1989. The government believes that it finally overcame its inefficient pricing policy for wheat with the massive increase in the fixed price in 1989/90. To what extent this approach works will depend, among other things, on the development of production costs and input subsidies. The planting of wheat is also encouraged by government assistance and services.[55]

Barley, unlike wheat, can be offered for sale on the market without much government intervention. It is primarily used as animal fodder and as such is in great demand. The market price is much higher than the guaranteed price, which does not even cover the production costs. It costs 10 percent less to grow than wheat but brings the same price on the free market,[56] which is why production is increasing much faster for barley than for wheat (Table 12.6). Here the Islamic state's quest for independence has not had any effect—to the benefit of the producers.

The price of rice is the subject of a struggle that breaks out anew almost every year between those elements in the government favoring the consumer and the influential wholesalers who have lobbyists in the government and among the clergy.[57] The government is unsuccessfully attempting to contain the upsurge in prices by using an inconsistent import policy and by controlling domestic sales.

The retail price of rice in 1989 was 1,450 rials/kg; in 1980 it was 220 rials/kg.[58] The wide gap between the production costs—280 rials/kg—and the wholesale price—440 rials/kg—in 1986[59] ensures that as much land as possible is given over to planting rice (85 percent at the Caspian Sea). The limits are set by natural conditions, which are favorable in only a few areas of Iran. The middlemen are the main beneficiaries of this high profit margin.[60] However, the producers and agricultural workers benefit, too: From 1984 to 1986 the daily wage for rice growers rose from 3,500 rials to 6,000 rials. The price and wage development for rice work to the detriment of other crops (such as vegetable oils) in the rice-growing areas, crops that cannot keep pace.[61]

The planting of crops for vegetable oils is subject to the same extreme and irregular fluctuations as the price dictated for them by the state processing plants. The price was raised by 54 percent in 1981 and kept arbitrarily stable for the next three years, only to be raised by another 50 percent in 1984, and so on. The price increases regularly come late in reaction to the farmers' growing disinclination to produce at a dictated price. The processing plants get a higher price for their by-product (which is used as animal fodder) than the farmers get for their crop, much to the chagrin of the latter. In 1986 the peasant received only 70 rials/kg for his soya; the price of the by-product was 300 rials/kg, and the oil itself sold for 1,500 rials/kg.[62] The farmers' dissatisfaction with the fixed price forces them onto the black market, where they can get a better price for their product. The government attempts to counter this tendency by means of administrative measures.[63]

The same incongruity between the prices of the crop and its by-product can also be observed in the market for sugar beets. The state-owned sugar factories are the purchasers, and once again they can exploit their monopoly position to practically dictate prices.[64] Here, too, the fluctuations in production are a direct result of the government's belated and inappropriate reaction to the rise in production costs and to galloping inflation. Although 400,000t of sugar are imported each year and the domestic industry is not working at full capacity, the government has still not succeeded in increasing production of sugar beets by means of a consistent pricing policy.[65]

In the postrevolutionary era there has been an increase in sales of potatoes as a substitute for a variety of other foodstuffs. The Agriculture Report 1986/7 stated: "Because of the lack of regulations for production and marketing, the wholesale price of this product dropped from almost 200 rials/kg in March 1984 to 100 rials/kg the following year and to 39 rials/kg in March 1986" (p. 156). In autumn 1989 the price rose rapidly to 800 rials/kg.[66] The producers had to bear the cost of the decline in prices, but the influential middlemen,[67] who are strong enough not to be intimidated even by the government's rigorous antiprofiteering, got to pocket the profits of the increase. In spring 1990, when the potato market experienced the same rise in prices as it had the previous year, the government attempted to stabilize the market by imposing the death penalty for racketeering and by importing foreign potatoes—even though the country was supposedly self-sufficient in this respect.

Fruit and summer crops are not among the "strategic" products, and that is why they are not mentioned at all in the annual reports on agriculture. A considerable proportion of the arable land is nevertheless given over to growing these crops. Horticulture and tree nurseries accounted for 1.2m hectares in 1988/9; the same year production of citrus fruit, dates, and wine totaled 2,472,366t (Markaz-e Amar). In 1986, 6.5m tons of summer crops were grown on some 473,000ha.[68] Fruit is one of the few agricultural products the country is able to export. Of the nonstrategic products, pistachios deserve special mention here, as they are the third-largest item in the country's export statistics, after carpets and oil. As the income from summer crops and fruit is many times higher than that from cereals, the farmers are inclined to plant as much land as possible with them despite the government's obstructive measures.

According to a report in *Commercial Investigation Monthly,* at least two million workers were supposed to be employed in growing and processing cotton in Iran. However, after the revolution cultivation suffered an abrupt decline, from which it has not yet recovered. The government's pricing policy, which is far from making cotton-growing attractive for the peasants,[69] is partly to blame for this decline, together with unfavorable weather conditions, the question of land ownership, competition from artificial fibers, increasing production costs, and the higher profits on some other crops. In 1989/90 there was a difference of at least 134 rials/kg between the guaranteed price for cotton and the cost price.[70]

The sharpest criticism of the Islamic government's pricing policy comes, significantly, from the Ministry of Agriculture's experts in their annual report on the agricultural situation. Their 1985/6 report first castigated the government for its failure to encourage the peasants to plant "essential products," then blasted it for having ignored the part that reasonable prices could have played if they had been approved and paid (pp. 198ff). The 1986/7 report stated that the government's agrarian policy was contradictory, inconsistent, and opportunistic. "The government considers prices to be a political instrument for pacifying the consumers. Its measures to control production and prices have been largely unsuccessful" (p. 124). At the National Congress to Investigate the Problems of Agricultural Development, one speaker declared that "the prices for the strategic products are determined as unjustly as possible, devoid of any economic consideration and according to political opportunities."[71]

12.5 Development of Agrarian Production

Despite the negative influence of all the factors dealt with in this chapter, there has been an upward trend in some of the crop production figures since the revolution, especially for cereals, legumes, potatoes, and onions, as Table 12.10 shows. But progress can also be seen in the output of tobacco, tea, citrus fruits, and some other nonessential crops. Cotton production, however, has fallen to such an extent that it can no longer be exported, as it was before the revolution.

The production data are so contradictory that it is difficult to discern the trends. Table 12.10 makes these contradictions clear by comparing the 1982/3 figures from the Ministry of Agriculture and the Central Bank side-by-side with the results of the agricultural census conducted by the Central Statistical Office the same year. The difference between the two sets of

Table 12.10 Crop Production
(in thousands of tons)

Year	Wheat	Barley	Rice	Sugar Beet	Sugar Cane	Cotton Oil	Cotton Plant	Potato	Onion	Legume
1974/5	2,886	751	826	3,749	1,097	648	71	354	136	186
1975/6	5,500	1,400	1,500	4,670	1,100	470	100	225	550	148
1976/7	6,000	1,500	1,600	5,200	800	510	130	370	340	230
1977/8	5,526	1,230	1,400	4,150	1,000	535	105	697	392	187
1978/9	5,526	1,276	1,531	3,652	898	322	126	932	506	203
1979/80	5,946	1,262	1,271	3,814	1,399	322	99	997	515	227
1980/1	5,744	1,265	1,181	3,917	1,307	219	69	1,270	631	225
1981/2	6,610	1,700	1,624	3,231	1,696	275	84	1,540	676	290
1982/3	6,660	1,903	1,605	4,146	1,810	302	123	1,814	965	296
1982/3[1]	4,277	1,499	1,085	3,496	2,212	269	78	833	444	134[2]
1983/4	5,956	2,034	1,216	3,648	2,053	300	188	1,740	736	290
1984/5	6,207	2,293	1,484	3,392	2,126	351	118	1,784	844	303
1985/6	6,630	2,296	1,772	3,924	2,413	324	137	1,725	719	341
1986/7	7,400	2,762	2,049	4,965	2,362	345	127	2,349	809	370
1987/8	7,571	2,719	1,420	4,450	1,420	342	57	2,348	NA	376
1987/8[3]	8,998	2,518	2,244	6,324	4,200	613	288	2,086	1,025	466
1988/9[4]	5,775	2,099	1,227	3,370	1,310	332	NA	815	508	122[5]

Sources: Agricultural censuses 1974/5, 1982/3, and 1988/9; Bank-e Markazi 1983; 1983 development plan; *Kayhan*, November 30, 1989; Markaz-e Amar 1989.
Notes: 1. 1982/3 agricultural census results
2. Without Kurdistan and West Azerbaijan
3. Targets from 1983 development plan
4. 1988/9 agricultural census results
5. Incomplete data

data for wheat production comes to 2,383,000t, or 36 percent of the higher figure. Comparison of the 1987/8 and 1988/9 production data shows a similar difference, one so big that it cannot be explained away by a change in production conditions (such as weather, area under cultivation, etc.).[72]

Two explanations for these contradictions come to mind. First, there are differences in both the methods and sources on which the surveys are based. Some of the figures are based on the agricultural census, which is conducted at irregular intervals, and others are estimates. The former are without doubt more accurate and should thus be trusted more, when available. Results from the 1982/3 and 1988/9 censuses are available and can be compared with the 1974/5 results, as was done to show the development in the area of arable land. It should be noted, however, that 1974/5 was characterized by particularly bad weather conditions and is thus not typical of prerevolutionary developments. It therefore needs to be supplemented by data from subsequent prerevolutionary years, which are based on samples and thus presumably are more accurate than the estimates.

Obviously, the differences in the year-by-year yields for a given crop are caused by varying weather conditions or changes in the area cultivated in a particular year; the latter can be determined and appear in the annual reports on agriculture. These factors do not, however, explain away the differences with respect to the production of a certain crop in a single year.

A second explanation for discrepancies in the data is that bureaucrats manipulate the figures according to the goals being pursued at the time, and factional and personal power struggles and aversions come into play. There is also a fairly widespread dislike of quantifying life, which does not encourage a sense of the need for figures. The figures for the overall development of agrarian production given by two successive ministers of agriculture, Zali and Kalantari, show how far the contradictions between officials can go. In October 1989 the current minister, Kalantari, put the annual increase in production over the past ten years at 2.9 percent;[73] his predecessor spoke of much higher rates—8.9 percent, 10.1 percent, and 5.2 percent, respectively—for the years between 1985 and 1987,[74] with an annual average of 5.6 percent before that.[75] In the opinion of Zanjani, the minister of planning and budget, agrarian production has increased by a total of 5 percent since the revolution.[76] The figures provided by Dr. Zali are so far removed from reality that one parliamentarian suggested giving him a doctorate in propaganda.[77]

The figures for the conspicuously high rates of growth contradict the assessment of agricultural development given by some members of parliament and experts. Hojjat ol-Eslam Dorri Najafabadi, chairman of the Advisory Reconstruction Organization, observed that "with respect to agriculture we have shouted more slogans in the past ten years than achieved performances."[78] One member of parliament criticized the balance of the Ministry of Agriculture under Dr. Zali (August 1984–September 1988) as very weak,[79] and another saw no growth in agriculture: "We have ensured that it has lost all attractiveness in the villages."[80] Such statements were made time and again with varying degrees of vehemence and bias.

According to the 1983 development plan, agriculture was to achieve an annual growth rate of 7 percent in order to attain self-sufficiency in certain products, with farming making the major contribution. The production targets for the individual stages of the five-year plan were set on this assumption. Table 12.10 shows that none of the targets set for any particular year were achieved. As for the production planned for and attained in 1987/8, the enormous difference between the figures for that year and the following year can only be explained one way: The figures for production in 1987/8 must be inaccurate—i.e., the actual numbers must be lower than those in the table. How seriously should the data for cereals for the years between the 1982/3 and 1988/9 censuses be taken? Let it suffice to say that they were not even included in the statistical yearbooks for their respective years,[81] unlike the figures for other products (cotton, sugar beets, etc.), for which the Central Statistical Office does not suspect manipulation. This fact confirms the theory that this arbitrary treatment of production data was confined primarily (or perhaps exclusively) to cereals, specifically wheat, because the success of the Islamic development model was to be measured in terms of self-sufficiency in wheat, as mentioned above.

Comparison of production before and after the revolution produces different impressions depending on the sources used. A comparison of individual crops in 1974/5 with the two postrevolutionary censuses is, with two exceptions (cotton and sugar beets), favorable to the Islamists. However, it is a matter of record that weather conditions in 1974/5 were very bad, so the figures are not a particularly good basis for comparison. Comparison with the data for other years greatly reduces the Islamic state's positive balance: Only in sugar cane, barley, and potatoes does postrevolutionary production exceed that before the revolution. The production of rice is about the same before and after the revolution, and there are no figures for a comparison of legumes. If the uncertain data from other postrevolutionary years is taken into account, the Islamists' performance is much better, especially for cereals. It is only for cotton, sugar beets, and crops for vegetable oils that the Islamic state harvest results are worse.

But the comparison is much worse for the Islamists in per capita terms, as Table 12.11 makes clear. Per capita agricultural production in Iran fell from 106.63kg in 1981 to 98.42kg in 1986, according to an index calculated by A. Mojtahed and H. Esfahani on the basis of the FAO's Production Yearbooks. Cereals dropped from 110.87kg to 105.43kg and total production of plants from 112.21kg to 104.75kg (1989, p. 845). The per capita wheat output dropped by 70kg from 1976/7 to 1988/9, although the crop accounted for over half the arable land under cultivation and the major part of government expenditure. There is still a drop of 28kg between 1976/7

Table 12.11 Per Capita Crop Production[1]
(in kilograms)

	1976/7	1986/7	1988/9
Population (thousands)	33,708	49,445	53,716
Wheat	177.9	149.7	107.5
Barley	44.4	55.8	50.6
Rice	47.4	41.8	22.8
Sugar beets	154.2	100.4	62.7
Cotton	15.1	6.9	6.1
Legumes	6.8	7.4	7.4
Potatoes	10.9	47.5	15.1

Sources: Bank-e Markazi 1983; *Keshawarz* 113 (1984).
Note: 1. Per capita production calculated by author on the basis of data for population in annual tables by Markaz-e Amar

and the unreliable 1986/7 result.[82] The figures are positive only for barley, legumes, and potatoes—i.e., for those crops whose production is determined by market forces and to which the government makes no positive contribution.

The decline in per capita production has to be compensated for by imports in order to ensure the population's food supply. Table 12.12 provides an overview of the increase in imports into the Islamic Republic. It should be noted that the fluctuations do not mirror the rise and fall in annual production but are independent of the level of stocks. The relative decline in imports after 1984 reflects more a result of the drop in government revenue from oil exports.

Resulting shortages of food, among other things, are causing reductions in rations[83] and increases in prices for the goods concerned. According to a report in *Resalat* (May 1, 1990), 5m tons of wheat and 700,000t of rice were imported in 1989/90.

Taken together, the decline in per capita production, the increase in imports, the food shortage, and the population increase have caused many experts and functionaries to paint a bleak picture of the future, a picture that could become reality if relief is not given soon. The minister of economics and finance, Irawani, says the gap between demand and production will increase fivefold within twenty years if present conditions are permitted to continue.[84] According to the state secretary at the Ministry of Agriculture, Iran will have to pay $6bn for food imports in ten years time if one-third of the food needed still has to be imported.[85] A resolution passed

Table 12.12 Food Imports
              (in thousands of tons)

	1977/8	1980/1	1983/4	1985/6	1986/7	1988/9
Wheat	1,197	1,747	3,214	1,908	1,908	5,000
Barley	386	503	427	533	149[1]	NA
Rice	590	402	671	489	465	716
Maize	387	679	830	592	934	1,600[2]
Meat	183	175	228	163	176	202
Olive oil	258	83	519	439	490	NA

Sources: Bank-e Markazi 1983; Agriculture Reports 1983/4 and 1986/7; *Resalat,* May 15, 1990.
Notes: 1. Given as 400 in Mojtahed/Esfahani 1989
2. Includes all fodder

at a Conference on Population Growth held in Tehran in September 1988 warned that the country will have to spend about $5bn in 1996 just on imports of "essential agrarian products."[86] Exports of agricultural produce, though a considerable proportion of Iranian nonoil exports, are still far from being able to earn the revenue needed to pay for food imports. In 1986 the ratio of these exports to imports was 1:3 in terms of value and 1:13 in terms of quantity.[87]

The five-year plan approved at the end of January 1990 is to counteract these trends by ensuring an annual growth of 6.1 percent in production—3.5 percent to compensate for the population increase and 2.5 percent to reduce imports.[88] The prospects for the plan were discussed in Chapter 4, but the outcome remains to be seen.

Notes

1. The resolution passed by the National Congress to Investigate the Problems of Agricultural Development (Tehran, February–March 1989) was an interesting document criticizing previous agricultural policy. The speech by Minister Kalantari was equally interesting. See *Resalat,* March 2, 1989; the Rafsanjani government's program in *Barzegar,* December 3, 1988; and M. Mojtehedzade and M. Najafi 1986.

2. The monthly is published by the Institute of Trade Studies and Investigations. See no. 6 (1989), p. 9; and 1.2 of the previous chapter for price developments.

3. A. Mojtahed and H. Esfahani 1989, p. 857.

4. 1983/4, p. 52; 1984/5, p. 57; and 1985/6, p. 95.

5. Profits of up to 240 percent can be made in the service sector, whereas the

productive sectors of the economy show an average annual profit of 15 percent. *Resalat*, September 24, 1989.

6. The FAO uses this index, presumably because of the lack of better data, to determine wage developments in the agrarian sector. Taken from Mojtahed and Esfahani 1989, p. 850. This tendency in the labor market admittedly only affects peasants who hire on as wage laborers.

7. Agriculture Report 1986/7, p. 87f.

8. As stated in the Agriculture Report 1986/7, p. 89.

9. Agriculture Report 1986/7, p. 94.

10. *Ibid.*, 1985/6, p. 77; and 1986/7, p. 96.

11. According to the chairman of the bank, Tala'i, in *Keshawarz* 118 (1989), p. 56.

12. *Barzegar*, September 9, 1989.

13. *Kayhan*, November 21, 1984.

14. *Resalat*, October 30, 1988.

15. *Barzegar*, September 9, 1989.

16. In *Ettela'at-e Siyasi-Eqtesadi* 25 (1989), pp. 56ff.

17. *Ettela'at*, May 28, 1989. The destruction of the woods has reputedly reached unimaginable proportions. According to the secretary of state at the Ministry of Agriculture, Rasulof, the wooded area has dropped from 21.4m to 10.1m hectares since the revolution (*Resalat*, May 3, 1989). The minister of economics and finance, Irawani, put the annual destruction of farmland and pasture at 1.5m hectares (*Resalat*, March 1, 1989). Kalantari's figure is obviously a gross understatement. The discrepancies in the figures (from Kalantari, Rasulof, and Irawani) must be due to the fact that no exact surveys have been conducted. It would, however, seem that the general tendency in developments is clear.

18. *Resalat*, September 4, 1989. He also stated that each year over 1m hectares of arable land were taken out of use because of erosion, *Ettela'at*, May 20, 1990.

19. *Barzegar*, December 8, 1988.

20. *Ibid.*

21. *Ettela'at*, May 6, 1990.

22. Markaz-e Amar 1982 and 1988.

23. Between 1973 and 1984, government investment for water use fell from 12.3bn to 7.2bn rials at constant prices. See Mojtahed and Esfahani 1989, p. 857.

24. Agriculture Report (various years), DPA and SP.

25. *Hafte Name Otaq-e Bazargani* 8 (1988), p. 53.

26. *Kayhan*, March 4, 1989. The use of surface waters reputedly increased from 18.5bn to 20bn cubic meters.

27. No. 115; pp. 12ff; and no. 116, pp. 10ff.

28. Bank-e Markazi 1983, p. 511.

29. *Barzegar*, December 17, 1988.

30. *Barzegar*, February 25, 1989.

31. Agriculture Report 1986/7, p. 73.

32. *Barzegar*, February 25, 1989; *Resalat*, March 27, 1989.

33. *Keshawarz* 124 (March 1990), p. 9.

34. *Barzegar*, March 11, 1989.

35. *Kayhan*, October 29 and November 7, 1987. There were nine tires every other year for 700 tractors in the district of Ahar (*Kayhan*, July 9, 1984).

36. *Resalat*, March 4, 1989.

37. In a personal interview with Hushang Keshawarz, an adviser to Dr. Izadi in the Bazargan government.

38. According to the minister of agriculture, for example, on October 21, 1987. See also *Barzegar*, December 2, 1989.

39. *Barzegar* (June 4, 1988) reported on this practice by some farmers.
40. Mojtahed and Esfahani 1989, p. 853.
41. Agriculture Report 1981/2, p. 34; 1983/4, p. 35.
42. *Kayhan*, August 27, 1989.
43. *Keshawarz* 110 (January 1989), p. 59.
44. Zali in *Ettela'at*, July 18, 1989.
45. Markaz-e Amar 1988.
46. Sometimes twice as numerous, according to A. Khaza'i in *Jahad* 119 (1989), p. 19. The same article states that the number of technicians, advisers, and experts dropped from 1,800 in 1983 to 1,300 in 1988.
47. *Ibid.*, p. 18f.
48. *Ibid.*
49. *Resalat*, December 1987.
50. These figures are for 1988. See *Jahad* 116 (1989), pp. 46ff.
51. *Kayhan*, February 2, 1989. The price was raised again to 100 rials the same year.
52. Agriculture Report 1986/7, p. 127.
53. *Resalat*, April 15, 1989; *Barzegar*, October 22, 1988; Agriculture Report 1985/6, p. 116.
54. *Barzegar* (February 25, 1989) reported that the government agencies had promised the peasants of Bijar 800,000 rials for 225t of wheat but had not kept their promise.
55. According to Nuri Na'ini 1977, p. 62.
56. Agriculture Report 1986/7, pp. 134ff.
57. Agriculture Report 1985/6, pp. 120ff; 1986/7, pp. 137ff.
58. *Keshawarz* 115 (1989), p. 16, quotes the 1980 wholesale price as 179 rials/kg. The author knows the retail price from his own experience.
59. Agriculture Report 1986/7, p. 138.
60. *Ibid.*, p. 139; and *Keshawarz* 116 (1989), p. 19.
61. *Keshawarz* 116 (1989), pp. 16ff.
62. Agriculture Report 1984/5, p. 96f; 1986/7, p. 150.
63. See *Keshawarz* 118 (1989), pp. 27ff, on the problems of growing crops for vegetable oil.
64. Agriculture Report 1985/6, p. 127.
65. *Ibid.*, 1986/7, pp. 146ff.
66. *Keshawarz* 113 (1989), p. 10.
67. The middlemen unload potatoes and onions onto the market at a price twenty to twenty-five times above cost. They are hoarded in storehouses (presumably state-owned) known to everyone until they realize this extortionate price. *Barzegar*, July 1, 1989.
68. Ministry of Planning and Budget: Statistical Quarterly 6 (1986).
69. *Ibid.*, no. 9 (1990), pp. 26ff.
70. *Resalat*, January 2, 1990.
71. *Barzegar*, March 22, 1989.
72. However, precipitation in 1988/9 was less than the year before in most areas of the country; see Markaz-e Amar 1989. Minister Kalantari gave 1988/9 wheat production as 7m tons in *Resalat*, August 22, 1989.
73. *Kayhan*, October 4, 1989.
74. *Ettela'at*, August 1, 1989.
75. According to the Agriculture Report 1986/7, p. 215. Experts interviewed either agreed with Kalantari or expressed their doubts about the accuracy of such data in general. A third group was of the opinion that the two were referring to different things.

76. *Kayhan*, June 16, 1988. In the opinion of a deputy minister of jahad, the country achieved an annual average growth rate of 2.6 percent in agriculture between 1977/8 and 1989/90. *Ettela'at*, May 20, 1990.

77. He literally said: "If one wanted to give him a doctorate, it would have to be for propaganda." PP, September 11, 1988, p. 22.

78. *Resalat*, March 1, 1988.

79. PP, September 20, 1988, p. 27.

80. *Kayhan*, December 5, 1989.

81. I have the statistical yearbooks from four of the six years in question, including the last two.

82. On this subject, see M. Gorgani 1989.

83. According to *Keshawarz* 114 (1989), p. 8, the annual per capita rations at state prices in 1988/9 were: 3kg of rice, 0.75kg of butter, 1kg of cheese, 5.6kg of eggs, 3.3kg of chicken.

84. *Resalat*, February 1, 1989.

85. *Kayhan*, August 27, 1989. According to Kalantari, $1.9bn was spent for this purpose in 1987/8. See *Resalat*, February 26, 1989.

86. *Ettela'at-e Siyasi-Eqtesadi* 22 (1988), p. 43.

87. From 28.6bn to 92.5bn rials, according to Agriculture Report 1986/7, pp. 233 and 238.

88. According to Kalantari in *Barzegar*, December 16, 1989. See CL 1989/90, p. 885.

13
The Urban-Rural Divide and Rural Depopulation

13.1 Diagnosis and Theory

Given the inadequate development of production, it will prove impossible to achieve another aim of agricultural policy in the Islamic Republic—namely, closing the urban-rural gap. The Islamists seem well aware of the linkage between the level of agricultural production and the rate of rural depopulation. The latter is one of the most hotly disputed issues in discussions about Iranian agricultural policy. All the relevant draft plans and programs have raised the issue and proposed measures to solve it.

The 1979 Izadi program emphasized that Iran was confronted not simply by a "migration" of villagers to the towns during the last years of the shah's reign but rather by the "deplacement" of the rural work force. This trend was the result of the unequal competition staged by the government between agriculture and the urban sector, above all the unproductive construction industry. "The result was nothing less than the substantial collapse of rural society and agricultural production" (p. 2). This state of affairs had to be countered by a series of measures intended to increase production and raise the standard of living of the rural population (pp. 4, 10, and 12f).

The report by the September 1979 seminar on planning dealt with the problem in more detail, discussing various proposals for slowing down rural depopulation by ending the "enduring domination of rural areas by the towns existing in Iran." Both the landlords living in the towns and the government showed scant regard for the rural population and deemed it unworthy of assistance (p. 3/1f). The unusual degree of centralization in decision-making in the shah's regime, the urban orientation of the administration, and the disproportion between the state's construction programs and the needs of the rural population gave a concrete form to this disdain (p. 3/3). Rural depopulation was also caused by the higher level of income, the better job prospects, and the other opportunities for making life easier enjoyed by the townspeople (although the lack of integration in the towns destroyed the social and economic balance here as well) (pp. 10/3f and 1/9f). However, it was impossible to a slow down rural depopulation merely by stepping up state improvement programs or welfare campaigns—these would have to be harmonized with a series of measures to increase production. The whole fabric of rural life and its links with urban life would have to be reformed to slow down rural depopulation, with the state's function reduced to giving assistance. "Villagers and nomads must, as especially productive entities, be in a position to oversee and direct their own productive activities on the basis of their own cultural order. They must also have the right to decide about such matters as concern the work that is to be done to improve their surroundings."

To this end, the report considered it necessary to implement the Law on Local Councils, among other things, as soon as possible and to extend the councils' purview as far as possible in the areas of culture, training, hygiene, work, industry, and agriculture. It was also considered vital to set up small industrial enterprises in the small towns and transform suitable rural areas into settlements capable of absorbing the rural population (pp. 3/7ff). The document did not discuss how to contain rural depopulation, only how to direct it away from the cities and into the small and medium towns. It focused on "conscious integration of the rural migrants into the towns" (p. 10/7), a policy based on the assumption that the rural settlements will not be able to hold on to their excess population in the long run.

In contrast, the 1983 development plan aimed at the "containment of rural depopulation," which was to prevent the peasants and nomads, "who are among the most deprived groups in society and at the same time among the few productive classes in our consumer-oriented society," from moving into the towns (p. 1/13). The lasting poverty of the rural population caused by the shah's regime had forced them to relocate to shantytowns on the outskirts of the cities. Without having made any contribution of their own, these slums enjoyed the benefits of social services and infrastructure paid for by the government's oil revenues. "The policy of providing cheap services in the towns . . . and of financing these services with oil revenue" was "partly responsible for the rural population's invasion of the towns and the unfettered expansion of the latter" (p. 3/10). The draft proposed to reverse this process by redistributing government assistance and services to benefit the rural population (p. 3/15) and giving them the opportunity to raise their income level. This aim could be achieved by expanding industry and other productive activities concomitant to agriculture. "These activities ought, if possible, to complement and not replace agriculture" (p. 1/13). The 1983 development plan was intended to link the objectives of increasing and diversifying production on the one hand and providing rural areas with government assistance and services on the other. There were, in addition, measures for containing any further expansion of the towns, to be implemented within the framework of a "comprehensive settlement policy" intended to create "an ordered and organic mesh" of town and countryside (p. 1/15).

Regardless of whether the individual plans and programs aim to contain rural depopulation or just to redirect it, everyone agrees that this problem cannot be resolved by stepping up rural construction and agrarian production alone. Rather, additional sources of income must be provided for the rural population. Nevertheless, the functionaries at the Ministry of Jahad-e Sazandegi have tried to draw a dividing line between their ideas and those of the staff at the Ministry of Agriculture, referring to their own program as the "paradigm for rural development" (olgu-ye tous'e-ye rusta'i), which is supposedly different from the "paradigm for agricultural growth" (olgu-ye roshd-e keshawarzi).[1] Whereas the latter reputedly only strives to increase production, the former encompasses an integrated development strategy to create an optimal balance between the various sectors of the economy on the one hand and population distribution on the other. In this paradigm, agriculture (in its broadest sense) and rural industry would together be the subject of rural development planning, and the improvement in income thus achieved would lessen the incentives for rural depopulation. In concrete terms, the plan involves increased efforts to provide the rural areas with infrastructure plus cultural and health services. These resources would not be brought to the rural settlements from outside but would be an inevitable consequence of diversifying production within the village.[2]

The expansion of rural industry plays a prominent role in the paradigm favored by Jahad, and miraculous results are expected of it.

> [The] expansion of rural industry . . . makes certain investments in certain projects—like the electricity and water supply systems, road building and telecommunications, the provision of technical services, as well as training in and marketing of the services concerned—necessary. Looked at in this way, the industrialization of part of the rural economy can become the start of significant changes in the rural and national economy. The most salient results of such a development include: employing part of the country's labor force, satisfying part of rural society's needs, containing unofficial rural depopulation, solving the problems arising from the growth of population in the cities, creating a link between industry and agriculture, encouraging the population to individual saving, [and] creating a basis for absorbing small amounts of capital. . . . This list ends with "the intensification of the decentralization policy."[3]

The problem of rural depopulation is given due attention in the new development plan, too. It is addressed in a program for regulating population distribution, which aims at a "containment of the rural depopulation" by means of the now familiar measures found in previous development drafts.[4]

Rural depopulation is discussed just as intensely outside of the authorities and government commissions charged with working out the problem. Reports and analyses are published fairly frequently in newspapers and magazines, and the members of parliament take it up time and again. Numerous seminars and conferences held by the two ministries concerned with agriculture deal with the causes of rural depopulation and ways to solve the problem. The proposals submitted to the government are legion. The suggestion was made once that agriculture should be declared a service to God so that the peasants would not turn their backs on it.[5] Now and then the idea is put forward that rural depopulation should not merely be contained but that the direction of the movement should be changed. The minister of jahad-e sazandegi then typically calls on all the ministries and state organizations to assist him in realizing this goal.[6]

13.2 Practical Measures and Results

Combatting rural depopulation has fallen primarily to the Ministry of Jahad-e Sazandegi. As the organization entrusted from the very start with rural construction, it has taken on more and more agricultural tasks and the responsibility for providing most of the social services to the rural population. By now it is the number-one authority in this field. In an "Insight into the Internal and External Problems of Jahad," written for its tenth anniversary, the agency said its work revolved around two basic axes: first, "efforts to overcome the deprivations in rural areas by means of measures that consist of ensuring hygienic care, carrying out infrastructural work, and improving rural milieus";[7] and second, "efforts toward agricultural self-sufficiency through achievements in the field of farming, animal husbandry, and irrigation projects."[8]

In the ten years since it was set up, Jahad has indeed achieved considerable successes, listing them in the document.

> Ten thousand villages have come to enjoy healthy drinking water and electricity. Over 30,000km of village roads have been built. Extensive efforts have been made to ensure 7bn cubic meters of water to irrigate arable land by constructing dams, canals, irrigation systems, and drainage. Annual wheat production on nonirrigated land has been increased by more than half a million tons. Maize is grown on more than 40,000ha of land. ... The setting up of more than 30,000 village libraries and 40,000 Village Councils and providing 10,000 advisory auxiliaries who are occupied with training and service tasks at the village level [and] elaborating and implementing projects to improve the rural milieus ... in 300 villages are also among Jahad's outstanding and splendid achievements.

This list of Jahad's achievements is not complete—it does not include, for example, its efforts in the field of hygiene and medical care. The Statistical Yearbook 1984/5 lists fifteen different types of work reputedly carried out by Jahad that year, from setting up forty small clinics to providing free treatment for patients in 892,219 cases. Free milk and medicine were distributed to more than three and a half times that number, and almost a million patients were bandaged or injected. The same is true every year. The provision of telephone links, encompassing 1,000 villages by 1984, deserves mention.[9] Only 8,000km of village roads were built before the revolution, according to the minister, but Jahad had constructed 43,000km of village roads by summer 1988.[10] Jahad's funding doubled between 1981 and 1987,[11] but it should be noted that the rural population was obliged to make a large contribution in money and labor toward the success of this improvement work.

Jahad's achievements are supplemented by those of the other ministries. Yet all of these gains have been insufficient to improve the quality of life in the rural regions to the extent that rural depopulation slows, so the problem remains unsolved. It will be helpful here to trace the development of the urban-rural divide in the Islamic Republic.

The first question in this connection is whether the development in agriculture compares favorably with that in other sectors of the economy. As shown in Chapter 12.1, the government gave agriculture and natural resources some degree of preference, albeit inconsistently, in the allocation of its fixed investments, but nowhere near enough to justify all the talk of "priority" or a "pivotal position." There has been a consistent increase in value added for agriculture, independent of government contributions and in contrast to the other economic sectors (Table 13.1).

Table 13.1 Net Value Added by Sector
(in billions of rials at 1974/5 constant prices, and in percent of GDP at factor costs)

Year	Agriculture		Oil		Industry and Mining		Services	
	Value Added	Percent	Value Added	Percent	Value Added	Percent	Value Added	Percent
1977/8	327.3	8.3	1,362.7	34.7	591.6	15.1	1,642.4	41.9
1979/80	356.3	11.1	767.6	24.0	511.9	16.0	1,560.7	48.8
1981/2	404.0	14.9	273.6	10.1	534.5	19.7	1,504.1	55.4
1983/4	429.0	12.3	531.1	15.3	683.1	19.6	1,833.7	52.7
1985/6	526.0	14.9	470.3	13.3	673.5	19.1	1,865.3	52.8
1987/8	562.9	17.5	457.1	14.2	599.3	18.7	1,587.8	49.5

Source: Markaz-e Amar 1985 and 1989.

Although its share of GDP rose, it never exceeded that of industry and mining and remained far below that of the service sector. The increase was less a result of the net value added in the agricultural sector than of a depreciation in value elsewhere, in particular for oil. Above all, agriculture benefited from its comparatively lower dependence on those factors (particularly imported inputs) that have had a negative influence on the economy as a whole and especially on industry.[12]

Comparison of income and consumer costs between urban and rural households further illustrates agriculture's favorable development in net value added. Whereas the nominal income of urban households increased by 290 percent from 1977/8 to 1988/9, that of rural households rose by 540 percent. However, consumer costs climbed much faster for rural households (510 percent) than for urban ones (410 percent). Thus, despite the rural households' faster income development, the urban sector continued to have a much higher income level. The income differential decreased at first but increased again after 1982; although there was a break in this trend in 1987/8, it continued the following year. The gap in consumer expenditures increased until 1985/6, decreased in 1986/7, then increased again (Table 13.2).

Table 13.2 Rural and Urban Income and Consumer Expenditure (in thousands of rials at current prices)

	1977/8	1979/80	1982/3	1985/6	1986/7	1987/8	1988/9
Urban:							
Income	448	514	709	1,037	1,126	1,149	1,339
Consumer Expenditure	438	528	883	1,279	1,312	1,488	1,800
Difference	10	–14	–174	–242	–186	–339	–461
Rural:							
Income	166	213	391	531	568	723	908
Consumer Expenditure	207	288	505	677	761	908	1,058
Difference	–41	–75	–114	–146	–193	–185	–150
Rural/Urban Difference:							
Income	282	301	318	506	558	426	431
Consumer Expenditure	231	240	378	602	551	580	742

Source: Markaz-e Amar, various years.

In his study of postrevolutionary income distribution up to 1984, Sohrab Behdad concluded, "The lot of rural household improved relative to their urban counterparts, and inequalities within urban and rural economy were reduced." But since 1981, rural households had been losing ground. "By 1984, although urban/rural and interurban and interrural inequalities were less than they were in the last prerevolutionary year, they were significantly more than in 1980." The development in the income gap between urban and rural households corresponds to the one between the rich and the poor in the Islamic Republic. "The gap between the very rich and the very poor . . . is as wide as it was before the revolution for urban households, and for the rural population ever wider."[13] The former prime minister confirmed these observations when questioned by a reporter.[14] On March 18, 1989, *Kayhan* quoted an expert who thought that in 1987/8 about 10 percent of the population had to live on a daily per capita income of 60 rials, while 60,000 people earned 3 million or more rials. Zawware'i, a former member of parliament, said in *Resalat* (October 26, 1988) that an elite of the one thousand richest families had formed again after the revolution (October 19, 1988). Hojjat ol-Eslam Mohtashami, the former minister of the interior, stated that the development in the postrevolutionary era has been so much to the disadvantage of the dispossessed that the country needs a new revolution to reverse the process.[15]

It has been impossible to reduce the urban/rural gap in services and improvements to any significant degree, despite the Ministry of Jahad's considerable achievements. The gap in government expenditures increased to the benefit of the towns until 1981, was then subsequently reduced, but has always been greater than the prerevolutionary gap (Table 13.3).

It should be noted that in the last five-year plan under the shah, the government budgeted expenditure—for the same purposes—at a ratio of 50bn to 66.6bn rials in favor of *rural* areas.[16] The new five-year plan to

Table 13.3 **Government Expenditure on Improvement (in millions of rials at current prices)**

	1978/9	1980/1	1981/2	1983/4	1984/5	1985/6	1987/8
Urban	12,548	19,194	22,233	18,303	8,843	17,702	25,696
Rural	12,040	5,804	5,532	8,717	4,797	3,823	7,129
Difference	508	13,390	16,701	9,586	3,846	13,879	18,567
Rural/Urban Ratio	1:1.0	1:3.3	1:4.0	1:2.0	1:1.7	1:4.6	1:3.6

Source: Markaz-e Amar, various years.

1993/4 budgeted for almost 109.9bn rials to be spent on the towns and only 58bn rials in rural areas. But the extent of this difference only becomes worse when it is borne in mind that the private sector spends several times more than the government on such things, but almost exclusively in the towns. Its total investments during the new five-year plan are estimated at 885.0bn rials, with only 16.5bn rials earmarked for the villages.[17] Although other indexes show progress for the rural population with respect to the urban/rural gap, it remains so big that there can be no serious talk of a turn-around, as the following examples illustrate.

There has been very little change regarding the number of schools built or the number of pupils; what change there has been has not always improved the relative lot of the rural population. The number of pupils has increased both in urban and rural areas, but rural areas' share of the overall student population rose only 0.4 percent between 1981 and 1987, from 39.5 to 39.9 percent—and there was a simultaneous reduction in the number of classes, the rural share dropping from 48.5 percent to 46.9 percent.[18] There continues to be a considerable difference in the urban and rural population's level of literacy: 73 percent of the townspeople but only 48.4 percent of the rural population over six years old could read and write in 1986/7, narrowing the gap from 35 (1976/7) to 24.6 percentage points. There continues to be a gap in schooling, although it, too, is narrowing. The proportion of the overall population with schooling that lives in urban areas fell from 72.9 percent to 68.9 percent between 1976/7 and 1986/7, with a corresponding increase for the rural population from 27.1 percent to 37.1 percent. There was equivalent improvement in the level of education, but the higher the level, the wider the gap becomes. In 1986/7 only 6.7 percent of the rural population had a college or university education, though this figure was only 4.3 percent in 1976/7.[19]

Developments in health services for the rural population are in part negative: The urban share increased from 45 percent to 54 percent between 1983 and 1988[20] (the pre-1983 data does not differentiate between urban and rural). The distribution of hospital beds between the province of Tehran and the provinces with a predominantly rural structure shows a slight shift in favor of the latter from 1981 to 1987, but not enough of one to substantially alter the situation. In 1981 the province of Tehran had 15 percent of the total population and 35.7 percent of the beds; in 1987 the figures were 17.6 percent and 33.4 percent, respectively. The province of Lurestan's percentage of the total population remained constant; its share of hospital beds increased only from 0.95 percent to 0.98 percent.[21]

There continues to be a wide gap in housing construction. Despite a radical reduction in construction, the proportion of housing located in rural areas rose from 9.98 percent in 1977/8 to 19.8 percent nine years later. However, the remaining gap widens the more the *quality* of new housing is included in the comparison. Urban accommodations with all modern conveniences accounted for about 98.2 percent of the total of 13,903 units built in 1977/8, increasing by 0.5 percent by 1986/7. Accordingly, the rural share fell from 1.8 percent to 1.3 percent. This discrepancy in standards is already apparent if the housing is supplied with electricity and increases if bath and telephone are provided.[22]

The data on rural development and welfare services must be considered in terms of both quantity and quality. They are full of contradictions, especially in respect of Jahad's achievements. It was stated in 1987 that Jahad had established 40,000 village libraries by the end of the previous year[23]—the total fell to 30,000 a year later.[24] Whereas 75 percent to 90 percent of the rural population had supposedly been supplied with electricity by mid-April 1983 (according to *Jomhuri-ye Eslami,* April 26, 1983), the proportion was reported as only 70 percent six years later.[25] Such claims leave unanswered the question of how progress can be made by electrifying the villages in a country where, in 1989, there was no electricity for up to twelve hours a day in Tehran. As Taleb, an agrarian sociologist, remarked in *Kayhan* (November 14, 1989), "There is no experience which would confirm that peasants who have no bread to eat ask for electricity and tapwater." In a letter to the same newspaper (August 21, 1989), the inhabitants of a village in the Saweh district reported how, with the help of the funds and labor they contributed, Jahad had built a school, a public bath, and a system to supply drinking water in their village. They had been unable to use any of it for years as there was no teacher and no water. Similar complaints were frequently published in the newspapers.

These and other statements, including ones made by functionaries of the Islamic Republic, articulate a widespread conviction that the state has not succeeded in eliminating the urban/rural gap. Ja'afari, a member of parliament, said: "The peasants ask us why we speak of support for the peasantry but in practice distribute most funds for the economy and welfare in the towns." Another member of parliament observed that "although all those in responsible positions talk about peasants, rural population and the dispossessed . . . we see that they are discriminated, this even in the distribution of basic and generally needed food. We see that a difference is made between town and country."[26]

The functionaries at the Ministry of Jahad put the failure of the "improvement of rural milieus" down to the lack of a comprehensive urban and rural development strategy, which would have to be provided with a "paradigm of rural development." "We still do not know," said the director general responsible for such improvement, "whether we should steer toward agriculture or industry and what place they should have. Are we aiming at an import substitution strategy or an export-oriented one or something else? That is our biggest problem, which influences everything, including of course our choice of a strategy for rural development." He gave as additional reasons for the failure: "the lack of the laws that ought to support us and show us the way," the fact that laws are mainly written for the towns, and shortages of personnel and funds.[27] His minister went a step further, charging that "in the past ten years we have not even pondered, defined, and taken cognizance of the term development."[28]

Nor has the Islamic state had any decisive success in expanding its rural industry. Rural crafts, which still accounted for over 1.2m workshops in 1974, lost a lot of ground as a result of the shah's modernization policy. The Organization of Iranian Crafts was founded the same year to revive them, but it was unable to halt the decline. It continued to exist after the revolution and was taken over in 1985 by the Ministry of Jahad-e Sazandegi, which wanted to get rural industry going in its own revolutionary way. Said the minister, "Despite the great significance which rural industry has had in our country, it has not been given much attention."[29] The expansion of rural industry did encounter considerable problems, which Jahad summarized towards the end of 1988 as follows: (1) lack of demand for its products; (2) lack of skilled workers and the wages to interest them in working in it; (3) lack of capital (the peasants do not even have enough money to invest in agriculture); and (4) problems with management and market analysis. However, Jahad considered the main problem to be that the government had not made a decision on the position of rural industry in the national economy and only saw it as a tactical instrument for solving acute problems.[30]

Production nevertheless reputedly increased by 29 percent from 1985/6 to 1987/8 despite a 73 percent reduction in government investments. This increase was helped by the fact that Jahad increased purchases of rural industry's products by 56 percent.[31] The number of workshops reportedly rose by 15,200.[32]

Whether fully implementing all the measures for containing rural depopulation would have the desired effect—and to what extent—is a legitimate question, but it cannot be discussed here. The fact of the matter is that the rural population's migration into the towns continued undiminished after the revolution. The minister of jahad-e sazandegi even spoke of "the rural regions increasingly emptying of people after the revolution." Comparison of the 1976/7 and 1986/7 census results makes the extent of this migration apparent: the urban population increased by 68.5 percent, from 12,924,205 to 26,844,561, whereas the rural population increased by 28.3 percent, from 17,449,000 to 22,394,000.[33] The urban proportion of the total population thus rose from 47.2 percent to 54.2 percent over the same period.

The faster rate of increase in the urban population will continue in the coming years, according to a conference on population problems held by the Ministry of Planning and Budget in September 1989. The conference also concluded that by the year 2002, towns will probably account for some 80 percent of the total population.[34] There is a growing number of towns

(496 in 1986 instead of 252 in 1976), in particular towns with more than 100,000 inhabitants, up from twenty-three in 1976 to forty-two ten years later. This trend indicates that the swelling urban population will concentrate in the cities, namely in and around Tehran and in Mashhad, Isfahan, and other provincial capitals.[35]

The urban population's faster growth can be attributed in part to the migration of the rural population, which accounts for 45 percent of the increase.[36] Despite its much higher birthrate, the rural population is growing much more slowly than the urban population. If it had increased at the same rate as the total population it ought to have been 25.6m. But it was only 22.3m, which means the rural sector lost at least 3.2m people to the towns.

The rural population's migration to the towns has been accompanied by a similar migration of the inhabitants of smaller rural settlements to larger ones. In the period between the 1982/3 and 1988/9 censuses, the proportion of settlements with less than 100 inhabitants fell from 6.4 percent to 4.7 percent and that of hamlets with less than 500 from 43.2 percent to 32.2 percent. One possible unpleasant consequence of this movement is that the estates of the abandoned settlements could be left uncultivated.[37]

Despite the large-scale migration to the towns, the population in the rural areas is increasing in absolute terms. This increase only heightens the pressure for further rural depopulation, as unemployment and underemployment in rural areas continue to be major problems. Officially, rural unemployment was 14.8 percent in 1986. A fully employed peasant only works 150 days a year,[38] and the low income he earns drives him in the direction of the towns. The experts and functionaries in the Islamic Republic seem increasingly to consider rural depopulation inevitable and to have capitulated to a problem that cannot be solved—at least, not the way they want.

Notes

1. See the numerous contributions in *Jahad* on this point—e.g., the series of articles "An Introduction to Rural Development" that began in no. 108 (1988).
2. The minister of jahad summarized these ideas in a speech to the National Congress to Investigate the Problems of Agricultural Development, published in *Jahad* 117 (1989).
3. *Jahad* 109 (1989), p. 10.
4. See *Resalat,* November 28 and 30, 1989, and CL 1368, pp. 853ff.
5. *Kayhan,* March 27, 1984.
6. *Kayhan,* June 16, 1982, May 17, 1984, and August 13, 1984.
7. Jahad's use of the term "improving rural milieus" (behsazi-ye rustaha) signifies a holistic project in which, from a central village outwards, differential measures to improve a complete district village and its associated villages are both worked out and implemented. Such a project also includes elaborating proposals for solving the production problems. See *Jahad* 121 (1989), p. 42.

8. *Jahad* 109 (1989), p. 2.
9. *Kayhan*, June 3, 1984. According to that year's Statistical Yearbook there were 1,675 villages with a "telephone link." According to the 1988/9 edition, 3,220 villages could contact the outside world by telephone.
10. *Ibid.*, September 16, 1988.
11. From 70.1bn to 146bn rials. The doubling was, however, nominal and thus made no allowance for inflation, which increased by a much larger rate in the same period. The figure refers to the funds allocated to the Ministry of Jahad in the government's budget. See Markaz-e Amar 1984 and 1989.
12. See M. Haddad 1987 p. 18.
13. S. Behdad 1989, p. 351f. See also *Kayhan*, September 19, 1987, H. 'Azimi 1987, and Athari 1988, pp. 48ff.
14. *Resalat*, September 5, 1988. He confirmed that since 1984/5 things had changed for the worse for the poorer classes.
15. *Kayhan*, January 25, 1989.
16. Markaz-e Amar 1977.
17. CL 1368, pp. 835ff.
18. Markaz-e Amar 1982 and 1988.
19. *Ibid.*
20. The considerable difference between urban and rural standards should be noted as it does not permit direct comparison.
21. *Ibid.* According to the 1986/7 census there were 1,195 doctors in 103,000 rural settlements—i.e., one doctor for every 18,702 people. The ratio for dentists was 1:72,095 and for chemists 1:112,876. See *Kayhan*, October 21, 1990.
22. *Ibid.*
23. *Kayhan*, February 22, 1987.
24. *Jahad* 109 (1988), p. 2. It must have been obvious to those in charge that it is barely credible to claim that libraries have also been set up in the 5,000 rural settlements with less than 100 inhabitants.
25. *Resalat*, February 12, 1989.
26. PP, November 27, 1988, p. 18.
27. From an interview in *Jahad* 121 (1989), pp. 41ff.
28. *Ibid.*, no. 117 (1989), p. 48.
29. *Resalat*, May 21, 1988.
30. Wezarat-e Jahad-e Sazandegi 1988.
31. *Jahad* 116 (1988), p. 27. This source is the second part of a series of articles about Iranian crafts and their place in the countryside. The first part appeared in no. 114.
32. Wezarat-e Jahad-e Sazandegi 1988, p. 22.
33. Markaz-e Amar 1988. Although the 1987/8 census is based on a different definition of towns (communities with a town hall) than the one in 1976/7 (communities with more than 5,000 inhabitants), this shift does not distort the results in any significant manner.
34. *Ettela'at-e Siyasi-Eqtesadi* 22 (1989), p. 43.
35. A. Arjomand Nia 1989, pp. 59ff; P. Piran 1989, pp. 43ff.
36. A. Arjomand Nia 1989, p. 63.
37. The minister of jahad mentioned this problem, indicating that 2.4m hectares of irrigated and 3.3m hectares of nonirrigated land are close to villages with less than 250 inhabitants that are threatened by rural depopulation. See *Jahad* 117 (1989), p. 46f.
38. See the interview with the sociologist Shadi Talab in *Kayhan*, November 14, 1989, and M. Alizade 1989, pp. 38ff.

legalistic Islamists. We have seen, for example, how self-sufficiency was continually praised not because it could make people's lives easier but because it would demonstrate the "model character of the Islamistic path to development." But even this aim was to be realized by war, propaganda, and playing down the capabilities of the hated "world rulers," as well as by unrealistic projections of the legalistic Islamists' domestic capabilities—in short, by political means devoid of any economic or other support.

The pricing policy of Musawi's government provides yet another example: It sacrificed considerations for increasing production and for improving the peasants' lot to the expectations of the town dwellers in order to safeguard its own political power against the dangers inherent in high prices. Even the development targets were based on considerations and illusions that were politically induced: The few experts in the planning departments were given the task of setting goals that would bear comparison on a global scale, irrespective of the country's capacity to implement them.

The inability of the legalistic Islamist regime to mobilize the human development potential has to do with a characteristic that could be termed antiparticipatory. Despite talking about participation by the masses, the leaders have resolutely rejected any involvement of the people in decisionmaking processes. This thoroughly elitist form of government views the ideal people as dependents whose interests have to be safeguarded by the state but who can provide the muscle-power to carry out the decisions made over their heads. Insofar as it abides by the relevant interpretation of the sharia, it only acknowledges the right of property owners or contracting parties to participate in those aspects of social and economic life that it has not preempted for itself—and not as free owners or contracting parties acting in response to economic considerations or mutual agreements but as subjects of a state that reserves for itself the right to repeal the laws on private property or contracts in the "interests of order." In this sort of state, the democratic interpretation of the shoura order is almost automatically transformed into an autocratic system that turns to elders for advice when decisions have to be made.

This legalism is by no means monolithic. Its inner contradictions must become more apparent and more serious the more it succeeds in driving modernistic Islamists and secularists into the arms of the banned opposition and denying them any opportunity for effective participation in the political decisionmaking process. The more openly these contradictions can be aired, the more they become obstacles on the road to unanimous decisions promoting development. Although the legalistic camp in the postrevolutionary era cannot be split into parties, factions, or other permanent organizations, it is possible to recognize three rough groupings—a radical etatistic one, a conservative-privatist one, and a pragmatic one. Their boundaries are unclear and individuals move back and forth between them, with each camp trying to remove the others from all positions of power. However, as such a consolidation is not practicable because of the balance of power or because of the dangers threatening the system as a whole, they build strongholds within the state apparatus, from where they conduct their policies or try to disrupt their opponents. The ministries, parliament, the Council of Guardians, the Revolutionary Institutions, and so on are just such strongholds.

The parallel organizations that have come into being both within and without the old administrative system can be seen as a result of these divisions within the state apparatus. They are also an indication that the reform of the old machinery of government and its transformation into so-called Revolutionary Institutions has fallen by the wayside, resulting in increased bureaucracy, duplication of work, and mutual obstruction, inter alia. Although these so-called revolutionary organizations had their origins in the desire to replace the old, parasitic bureaucracy with new, popular, and functioning organizations, they were soon transformed into organs for governing, concentrating power, building client networks, or enriching administrators. Jahad-e Sazandegi was transformed into a castle from whence a motley array of occupants sallied forth to plunder the surrounding area, with Village Councils serving as the vanguard. The Ministry of Agriculture took shape as a system of large superintendents' offices where, as the minister said, the development of agriculture is the missing link.[8]

Other serious results of this segmentation of state power have appeared at the legislative level, demonstrating the system's inability to reach a consensus. Laws are passed and then dropped soon after due to pressure from opponents; approval of draft laws is delayed until the original version is watered down beyond recognition; the fate of laws becomes dependent on the shifting balance of power within the state apparatus; laws are approved because the pressure from below does not allow further delay, which might endanger the system as a whole. In order to find a way out of this cul-de-sac, new legislative bodies are created, but this solution only lengthens the chain of communication and kicks the pile of proposals and initiatives awaiting decision upstairs. Draft laws are not approved but are implemented; implementation of laws is refused. There is agreement only on passing and implementing laws that are in the self-serving interests of all the legalist camps, not laws that serve to promote the development of the country. There also can be agreement not to implement laws passed at a time when the legalists did not have the legislature under complete control.

All of the above factors, which are inimical to any form of development, were responsible for the situation confronting the leadership of the Islamic Republic when, in January 1990, it finally adopted the first development plan. That situation was marked by a drop in per capita GNP and gross domestic investment to 1967/8 levels; 49 percent unemployment, including hidden unemployment; 50 percent budget deficit; and a per capita reduction in agricultural production. The country was even further from self-sufficiency than before, despite the fact that the Islamists had declared this goal to be the basis for independence. The administrative reform had brought forth more complications than solutions, and production management was characterized by chaos and confusion. Though the land reform was implemented under pressure from the peasants, it was reduced to the minimal redistribution of landed property and the transfer of state waste-land. The problems of urban-rural inequality and uncontrolled rural depopulation still await solution.

What part has the Islamization of the state played in creating this dilemma? The question needs to be rephrased, as it is quite conceivable that any other authoritarian state leadership would have produced more or less the same result if it had been similarly split into various camps that were incapable of reaching a consensus. In theory at least, Islam could contribute to solving the existing problems if it were to be interpreted in such a way as to provide the framework for a consistent, realistic, and dynamic development concept based on a broad social consensus. Such would have been the case if Islam had been interpreted not as a religion of specific laws but rather as one of undogmatic guidelines and principles that are in keeping with development. Under these conditions, legislation would be left to the people and their democratically elected representatives, who would have the right to make decisions on a majority basis. In short, Islam should acknowledge decisions democratically arrived at by the people as legitimate.

Islam as understood by the legalists, however, is far from meeting this requirement. It is based on the sharia, which (so it is claimed) has answers to every conceivable question (although it hardly does, as has been demonstrated in the course of this work). Many of the practical questions raised are not even mentioned in the sharia, and even the terminology the legislature is obliged to use has to be borrowed from modern, non-Islamic sources. The corresponding institutions are likewise of foreign origin. The directives and forms of contract that are termed "Islamic" provide almost no clues from which any direct solutions to the existing development problems can be expected. They must largely be considered anachronistic, and even where they are close to current practice (e.g., mozare'e) they do not lose this stigma.

Islamic guidelines (mawazin) and rules (qawa'ed) play a central role, especially in discussions about the property question, the shoura order, cooperatives, and the powers of the state. However, they are not clear enough to prevent differences from arising nor to enable unequivocal decisions to be made where such differences exist. They are often controversially interpreted, even to the point of contradiction, and exploited at will to support this or that interest. Seen in this light, Islamic tenets, rather than solving problems, actually aggravate things by allowing contradictory interpretations to be held up as Islamic—i.e., godly—and so both are considered absolute and immutable, which makes it difficult to reach a consensus or compromise. They are only of use where a certain position has proved stronger for other, more worldly reasons, in which case it is useful to portray the position as sanctioned by God. If the advocates of private property were ultimately better able to hold their ground, it was only in part because the relevant Islamic rule supported their position; economic and social structures and social processes, experiences, values, and pressures both within and without Iran were much more significant. But the problem of perceiving a specific position as absolute remains and hinders compromises and adjustments, even if they are necessary for development.

The Islamization of the state cannot be expected to overcome the differences that exist in society, nor was it able to transform the multiplicity of positions into unequivocal positive law. In this sense, the Islam that has been raised to a political ideology reflects the fact that Iranian society is not a whole that is more than the sum of its parts. The Islamization of the state leadership has contributed to preserving its elitist and autocratic character. As God's word is considered to be law, those who see themselves as experts in these matters reign while others are excluded—a flock that is led to pasture in God's name by self-righteous, self-appointed, and self-serving shepherds.

Complications arising from positions based on Islamic directives gave rise early on to the tendency to avoid them where necessary. Initially, the preferred way of legitimatizing things was to fall back on the "principle of necessity" and the secondary decrees, which meant no less than abrogating the primary decrees. This tendency has become all the stronger among the radical legalists as it has become apparent that politicoeconomic and social trends tend to support their conservative and privatist rivals, who are supported by mainstream scholars of the classical Islamic legal tradition. However, even the pragmatists are inclined to make considerable use of the "principle of necessity"; they have been forced to realize that they cannot always base their policies on conservative interpretations of the sources.

This inefficient solution has pushed the legalists to go even further. They increasingly fall back on the "state decrees," whose only semblance of justification is the "interests of order." It is strongly emphasized that these interests are those of the Islamic system of government. The more persistently the state abrogates the primary Islamic decrees, however, the more its Islamic character must suffer. The Council of Guardians' loss of influence parallels the increasing use of the principle of necessity and state decrees. Together with parliament, the Council has been subordinated to the Determination Council, whose guiding principle when solving legislative and other questions is the interests of state order.

There are of course still many Islamic (in the meaning of the legalists) features of the state. Even now it is largely run by the ulama; Islamic moral and penal codes are still applied; the civil code still largely corresponds to the sharia; it honors and celebrates Islamic symbols more than was the case in the prerevolutionary era. But the importance of these indications is diminishing: The ulama are being transformed into state functionaries and bureaucrats; the Islamic moral and penal codes are being circumvented by the state itself; and even after the revolution, Islamic symbols were given new meanings as and when required.

The state that is ruled by the Islamist jurists is thus becoming increasingly independent of religion. This trend is illustrated, apart from in the points mentioned above, by the following considerations. The number of laws with no discernible link to the sharia exceeds by far the number contained in any collection of Islamic decrees, such as Khomeini's "Tahrir al-Wasila." Where the legislature has passed a law, the final version often differs from all the draft positions that were put forward as the "only true Islamic" one. Circumstances are increasingly forcing the ruling Islamists to adopt positions at variance with the ones they declared to be Islamic when they were still struggling to seize power, and it is becoming ever more obvious that the country's actual human and material resources as well as its borders and interests are factors that can no longer be ignored when formulating policy. Life, the need for joy, love of art and pleasure, sexuality, and, not least, productive work and the economy demand to be respected and could pose a threat if the Islamists continue to disregard them. It is imperative to abandon orthodoxy and turn to pragmatism.

The victorious advance of the pragmatic camp, in particular after Khomeini's death, can be put down to the above processes. In the field of agriculture this trend is given expression by resolutions by the Determination Council on the question of landed property; adoption of a development plan that can be considered less illusionary than previous drafts; the passing of a relatively acceptable price policy; and the relaxation of the conditions for transferring land.

It is still too early to hazard a guess about the extent to which the pragmatists will succeed in freeing themselves from the fetters that continue to bind them to their legalist-Islamist home. They are still authoritarian and still cling to the ulamas' monopoly of power. But if they do not break free, they will not be in a position to bring the development potential that is still in the womb of society to fruition.

Notes

1. *Payam-e Enqelab,* May 26, 1984.
2. *Ibid.,* September 17, 1983.

3. *Kayhan,* April 5, 1986.
4. *Ibid.,* April 22, 1986.
5. *Ibid.,* June 12, 1985.
6. Khamene'i in *Resalat,* December 7, 1988.
7. For example, Rafsanjani in *Ettela'at,* February 8, 1989.
8. Kalantari in *Resalat,* June 1, 1989.

Bibliography

Abrahamian, E. *Iran. Between Two Revolutions.* Princeton, 1983.
———. *Radical Islam. The Iranian Mojahedin.* London, 1989.
Adamiyat, F. *Fekr-e azadi wa moqaddame-ye nehzat-e mashrutiyat* (The Idea of Freedom and Prelude to the Constiutional Revolution). Tehran, 1961.
———. *Fekr-e demokrasi-ye ejtema'i dar nehzat mashrutiyat* (The Idea of Social Democracy in the Constitutional Revolution). Tehran, 1976.
——— and H. Nateq. *Afkar-e ejtema'i wa siyasi dar asar-e montasher nashode-ye douran-e qajar* (Social and Political Ideas in the Unpublished Writings of the Qajar Era). Tehran, 1976.
Adib Saberi. *Gelsefid.* Tehran.
Agriculture Report. *See* Farnbush, B. and H. Refahiyat.
Ahmadi, H. *Ketabname-ye keshawarzi ta payan-e sal-e 1349* (Agricultural Bibliography to the End of 1349). Tehran, 1974.
Ahmadi Miyanji, A. *Osul-e malekiyat dar eslam* (Islamic Principles of Property). Qom, 1984.
Afshar, H. *An Assessment of Agricultural Development Policies in Iran.* In Afshar, H. *Iran. A Revolution in Turmoil.* Basingstoke, 1985.
Afshar, I. "Fehrestname-ye ahham-e motun-e keshawarzi dar zeban-e farsi" (List of the Most Important Agricultural Texts in the Persian Language). In *Ayande,* No. 10 (1982), pp. 686–694; No. 11, pp. 710–714.
'Ajami, E. *Sheshdangi* (The Village of Sheshdangi). Tehran, 1973.
———. *Estratezhi-ye sewwom* (The Third Strategy). Shiraz, 1978.
———. "Naqsh-e nezam-e bahrebardari dar touse'e-ye keshawarzi" (The Role of Enterprise Organization in the Growth of Agriculture). In *'Olum-e ejtema'i,* No. 2 (1976), pp. 189–199.
Akhavi, S. *Religion and Politics in Contemporary Iran. Clergy-State Relations in the Pahlavi Period.* Albany, 1980.
Alizade, M. "Estratezhi-ye eshteghal-e keshawarzi" (Employment Strategy in Agriculture). In *Ettela'at-e siyasi-eqtesadi,* No. 27 (1989), pp. 58–60.
'Alimorad, et al. *Gozaresh-e moqadamati-ye mas'ale-ye wagozari-ye zemin, wahedha-ye toulidi-ye mosha' dar sharestan-e fasa* (Preliminary Report on the Problem of Land Transfer and on the Work of the Mosha's in the County Town of Fasa). Tehran, 1984.
Alwandi, M. "Dar bare-ye taqsim-e mahsul bar asas-e 'awamel-e panjgane" (On the Product Distribution on the Basis of the Five Factors). In *Ketab-e Agah* (1982), pp. 401–419.

Amini, A. *Eslahat-e arzi dar jomhuri-ye eslami* (Land Reform in the Islamic Republic). Masters thesis. Tehran, 1986.

Amini, S. *Der Agrarkredit im Iran. Ergebnisse empirischer Untersuchungen in südiranischen Dörfern.* Dissertation. Hohenheim, 1973.

———. "The Origin, Function and Disappearance of Collective Production Units (Harrasehs) in Rural Areas of Iran." In *Zeitschrift für die Landwirtschaft in den Tropen und Südtropen*, vol. 84 (April 1983), pp. 47–61.

Amirahmadi, H. "War Damage and Reconstruction in the Islamic Republic of Iran." In H. Amirahmadi and M. Parvin, *Postrevolutionary Iran.* 1988, pp. 126–152.

Amir al-Momenin Ali ebn-e Abi Taleb. *Nahj al-Balaqa* (Path of Eloquence). Trans. and ann. by H. Feiz ol-Eslam. S A N, Tehran.

Amuzegar, J. *The Dynamics of the Iranian Revolution: The Pahlavis Triumph and Tragedy.* Albany: State University of New York Press, 1991.

Anoushirwani, A. and A. Dana'i. *Barresi-ye eqtesadi wa arzeshyabi-ye fa'aliyat-e sherkat sahami-ye zera'i-ye rawansar* (Economic Study and Assessment of the Work Done by the Farm Corporations). Tehran, 1978.

Anoushirwani, A., et al. *Negareshi bar zera'atha-ye jam'i-ye dasht-e arzu'iye* (A Survey of Collective Field Works in the Arzu'iye Plain). Tehran, 1982.

Anoushirwani, A., et al. *Barresi-ye gruha-ye kar-e zera'i ba'd az enhelal-e sherkat-e sahami-ye zera'i-ye nim bluk-e qa'enat* (Investigation of Agricultural Work Groups after the Liquidation of the Farm Corporations in the Nim Bluk of Qa'enat). Tehran, 1984.

Anoushirwani, A., et al. *Barresi-ye ta'awoniha-ye rusta'i-ye ebqa shode dar ostan-e esfahan* (The Investigation of the Nonliquidated Rural Producer Cooperatives in the Province of Isfahan). Tehran, 1985.

Anushe. "Mobareze-ye hezb-e tudeh-ye Iran dar rah-e eslahat-e arzi" (The Battle of the Tudeh Party of Iran for Land Reform). In Donya (Summer 1961), pp. 26–31.

Arjomand, Nia A. "Naqsh-e shahrha-ye miyane dar nezam-e oskan-e jam'iyat" (The Role of Medium-Sized Towns in the System of Sedemtarization of the Population). In *Ettela'at-e siyasi-eqtesadi*, No. 29 (July 1989), pp. 59–65.

'Araqi, A. *Tashkilat wa edare-ye sherkatha-ye ta'awoni* (Organization and Administration of the Cooperatives). Tehran, 1968.

'Asgari, M. *Qodrat-e 'olama-ye shi'e* (The Power of the Shi'ite Clergy). In *Nouruz* (July–August 1978).

Ashraf, A. "Dehqan, zemin wa enqelab" (Peasantry, Land and Revolution). In *Ketab-e Agah* (1982), pp. 6–49.

———. "State and Agrarian Relations Before and After the Iranian Revolution, 1960–1990." In F. Kazemi and J. Waterbury, *Peasants and Politics in the Modern Middle East.* Miami, 1991.

Ashtiyani, Ayatollah M. B. *Malekiyat wa bahrebardari az zemin az didgah-e eslam* (Property and Use of Land in the View of Islam). Tehran, 1979.

Athari, K. "Tawarrom-e bonyani-t'amiq-e tafawoutha-ye ejtema'i" (Structural Inflation and Deepening of Social Inequality). In *Ettela'at-e siyasi-eqtesadi*, No. 21 (1988), pp. 48–50.

'Azimi, H. "Budje wa touse'e-ye eqtesadi" (Budget and Economic Growth). In *Ettela'at-e siyasi-eqtesadi*, No. 5 (1987), pp. 28–39.

Azkia, M. *The Effect of the Rural Development Program on the Iranian Peasantry Between 1962 and 1978, with Special Reference to Farm Corporations.* Dissertation. Aberdeen University, 1980.

———. *Sherkatha-ye ta'woni-ye rusta'i dar shesh mantaqe* (The Rural Cooperatives in Six Regions). Tehran, 1969.

———. *Sherkat-e sahami-ye zera'i-ye dargazin-Hamedan* (The Dargazin-Hamedan Farm Corporation). Tehran, 1970.

———. "Wahedha-ye kar-e zera'i wa abyari dar fardis" (The Agricultural Work and Irrigation Units in Fadis). In *'Olum-e Ejtema'i* 2 (1976), pp. 180–188.

———. *Jame'e shenasi-ye tous'e wa tous'e nayaftegi-ye rusta'i-ye iran* (The Sociology of Development and Underdevelopment of the Rural Regions of Iran). Tehran, 1986.

———. *Moruri bar moutale'at-e rusta'i dar iran* (An Overview of the Investigations on the Rural Regions of Iran). Tehran.

Bafekr, H., et al. *Barresi-ye masa'el-e marbut be wagozari-ye zemin wa wahedha-ye toulidi-ye mosha' dar mantaqe ye jiroft* (Investigation of the Problems of Land Transfer and of Mosha' Organizations in Jiroft). Tehran, 1982.

———. *Barresi-ye masa'el-e marbut be wagozari-ye zemin wa wahedha-ye toulidi-ye mosha' dar gorgan wa gonbad* (Investigation of the Problems of Land Transfer and of Mosha' Organizations in Gonbad and Gorgan). Tehran, 1984.

Bahar, M. T. *Tarikh-e mokhtasar-e ahzab-e siyasi* (Short History of the Political Parties). 2 vols. Tehran, 1944 and 1984.

Bakhash, Sh. *The Reign of Ayatollahs: Iran and the Islamic Revolution*. London, 1986.

———. "The Politics of Land, Law and Social Justice in Iran." In *Middle East Journal* 34 (1989): 2, pp 186–201.

Bani Sadr, A. *Eqtesad-e Touhidi* (Economics of Unity). 1978.

———. *Naft wa solte ya naqsh-e naft dar touse'e-ye sarmayedari dar zemine-ye jahan wa zaman* (Oil and Rule or the Role of Oil in the Develompent of Capitalism on the Global Scale of the Era). 1976.

———. *Bayaniye-ye jomhuri-ye eslami* (Manifesto of the Islamic Republic). Hannover, 1981.

———. *Kar wa kargar in Islam* (Work and Worker in Islam). In the Persian and English languages. Tehran, 1980.

———. *Khiyanat be Omid* (Betrayal of Hope). 1982.

Bank-e Markazi-ye Jomhuri-ye Eslami-ye Iran (Central Bank of the Islamic Republic of Iran). *Barresi-ye tahawwollat-e eqtesadi-ye keshwar b'ad az enqelab* (Investigation of the Economic Changes after the Revolution). Tehran, 1984.

Bazargan, M. *Shoura-ye eqelab wa doulat-e mouwaqqat* (The Revolutionary Council and the Provisional Goverment). Tehran, 1983.

Behdad, S. "Winners and Losers of the Iranian Revolution. A Study in Income Distribution." In *International Journal of Middle East Studies* 21 (1989): 3, pp. 327–358.

Behn, W. *Power and Reaction in Iran*. A Supplement to the Bibliographies. The Iranian Opposition in Exile. Berlin, 1981.

Bergmann, H. and N. Kahdemadam. *The Impact of Large-Scale Farms on Development in Iran. A Case Study of Certain Aspects of the Iranian Agrarian Reform*. 1975.

Blaustein, P. H. (ed). *Constitutions of the Countries of the World*. New York, 1980.

Central Insurance of Iran. *Decade of the Revolution. Resurrection of a Nation. A Miracle of Leadership 1963–1973*. Tehran, 1974.

Chalibi, Dr. F.J.A. "The Causes and the Implications for OPEC of the Oil Price Decline of 1986." In *OPEC Review* (Spring 1988).

Dawani, A. A. *Nehzat-e Rohaniyun-e Iran* (The Movement of the Iranian Clergy). 10 vols. Tehran.

Dehkhoda, A. A. *Charand wa Parand* (The Gossip). Tehran, 1962.

Dreskornfeld, F. *Agrarstrukturwandel und Agrarreform in Iran*. Saarbrücken, 1976.

Dumont, R. *Some Remarks on Iranian Agriculture*. The National Institute of Agriculture. Paris, 1975.

Ehlers, E. "Die iranische Agrarreform. Voraussetzungen, Ziele und Ergebnisse." In

Elsenhans, H. (ed). *Agrarreform in der Dritten Welt.* Frankfurt, 1979, pp. 433–471.

———. *Iran. A Bibliographic Research Survey.* Munich, 1980.

———. "The Iranian Village: A Socio-economic Microcosm." In Beaumont, P. and McLachlan, K., *Agricultural Development in The Middle East.* 1985.

Elyasian, H. *Shiweha-ye bahrebardari-ye jam'i-ye zera'i wa yekparchegi-ye arazi* (Methods of Collective Agricultural Organization and of Merging Estates). Tehran, 1985.

Esfahani, R. *Eqtesad-e moqayese-i* (Comparative Economics). 4 vols. Tehran, 1978.

Eskandari, M. *Mas'ale-ye arzi, jonbesh-e deqanan, siyasat-e ma* (The Land Question, the Peasant Movement and Our Policy). Tehran: Organization of People's Fada'iyan, 1974.

Etehadiye-ye Anjomanha-ye Eslami-ye Daneshjuyan dar Urupa (Association of Islamic Students in Europe) (ed). *Do maqale dar bare-ye eqtesad eslami* (Two Contributions on the Islamic Economy). 1975.

Etemad Moqaddam, F. *The Effect of Farm Size and Managment System on Agricultural Production.* Dissertation, 1978.

Fada'iyan-e eslam. *Ketab-e rahnama-ye haqayeq* (Book That Shows the Way to the Truth). Tehran, 1950.

Fallah, S. W. "Mashini shodan-e Keshawarzi dar iran" (Mechanization of Agriculture in Iran). In *Ketab-e Agah* (1982), pp. 95–134.

Farahiyan, M. R., et al. *Barresi-ye mohajerat-e zare'in-e rustaha-ye shahrestan-e hamedan wa asarat-e an dar nahwe-ye estefade az arazi* (Investigation of the Migration of Peasants From the Rural Regions of the Country Town Hamedan as well as Their Effect on the Use of the Soil). Tehran, 1978.

Farazmand, A. *The State, Bureaucracy, and Revolution in Modern Iran: Agrarian Reform and Regime Politics.* New York, 1989.

Farnush, B., et al. *Oza'e eqtesad-e keshawarzi-ye keshwar dar sal 1362* (The Situation of Agriculture of the Country in the Year 1362). Tehran, 1984.

———. *Gozaresh-e eqtesad-e keshawarzi-ye keshwar dar sal-e 1365* (Report on the Agriculture of the Country in the Year 1365). Tehran, 1988.

Fatemi, H. *Majmu'e-ye maqalat-e doktor hosein-e fatemi, shahid-e nehzat-e melli-ye iran dar bakhtar-e emruz* (Collected Articles of Dr. Hosein Fatemi, Martyr of the National Iranian Movement in Bakhtar-e Emruz). 1979.

Gahratschehdaghi, C. *Landverteilung in Waramin.* Opladen, 1967.

Gholamasad, D. *Iran. Die Entstehung der Islamischen Revolution.* Hamburg, 1985.

Gil Azar. "Mobarezat-e dehqani dar Iran" (Peasant Movement in Iran). In *Donya* 7 (1980), pp. 74–77.

Gorgani, M. "Jam'iyat wa touse'e-ye eqtesadi" (Population and Economic Growth). In *Keshawarz* 113 (1989), pp. 20–21, 58.

Guruh-e Enqelabiyun-e Marksist-Leninist (Revolutionary group of Marxist-Leninists) (ed). *Darbare-ye sakht-e jame'e-ye Iran* (On the Structure of Iranian Society). 1978.

Haddad, M. *Barresi-ye waz'e mojud dar keshawarzi-ye iran* (Investigation of the Present State in Iranian Agriculture). Tehran, 1986.

Haghayeghi, M. "Agrarian Reform Problem in Post-Revolutionary Iran." In *Middle Eastern Studies* 26:1 (January 1990), pp. 35–51.

Haque, Z. *Landlord and Peasant in Early Islam.* Islamabad, 1977.

Hamidi, A. *Qanun-e madani* (The Civil Law). Tehran.

Hamsi, M. and Ayatollahi, A. *Tarh-e barresi-ye 'elal wa 'awaqeb-e mohajerat rustaiyan dar shahrestan-e shiraz* (Draft for the Investigation of the Causes and Effects of the Migration of Villagers in the Country Town of Shiraz). Tehran, 1978.

Hemmati Baba'i Qh. *Sherkat-e sahami-ye zera'i-ye farah sanandaj* (The Farah-Sanandaj Farm Corporation). Tehran, 1971.
Hojjati, Ashrafi Gh. *Majmu'e-ye qawanin. asasi wa madani* (Constitution and Civil Law). Tehran, 1983.
Hojjati Kermani, A. (ed). *B'esat* (Mission). Secret organ of the students of the religious academy of Qom. Tehran, 1989.
Hooglund, E. *Land and Revolution in Iran, 1960–1980*. Austin, 1982.
Hoseini Kazeruni, M. R. *Taswiri az mas'ale-ye arzi dar iran, qesmat-e awwal, shenakht-e waz'e mojud* (The Image of the Land Question in Iran. First Part. Knowledge of the Given State). Tehran, 1981.
———. *Mohajerat-e makani wa mohajerat-e shoghli. Negareshi be padide-ye mohajert dar dou dahe-ye akhir* (Local and Professional Migration. An Overview of the Phenomena of Migration in the Past Two Decades). Tehran, 1982.
Iranian Research Group. *Iran Yearbook* 1989–90. Bonn.
Izadi, A. M. *Taqsim-e arzi dardi ra dawa nemi konad* (The Land Reform Solves No Problems). Shiraz, 1958.
———. *An Economic Evaluation of Irrigation Water Pricing on Farm Incomes and Cropping Patterns*. Marv Dasht-Plain in Fars, Iran. Ph.D. Dissertation. Oregon State University, 1975.
———. *Nejat (Deliverance)*. Canada, 1983.
Jahad-e Sazandegi. *Awwalin seminar-e barresi-ye masa'el-e rusta'i* (First Seminar on the Investigation of Rural Problems). Tehran, 1983.
J'afari Langerudi, M. *Terminolozhi-ye huquqi* (Lexicon of Jurisprudence). 2nd ed. Tehran, 1984.
Jame'e-ye Sosialistha-ye Irani dar Urupa (League of Iranian Socialists in Europe). "Eslah-e arzi dar iran" (Land Reform in Iran). In *Socialism* 7 (October 1966), pp. 7–23.
Jam'iyatha-ye M'otalefe-ye Eslami (Allied Islamic Leagues). *Asnadi az jam'iyat ha-ye m'otalefe-ye eslami, Jama, Hazb-e melal-e eslami* (Some Documents of the Allied Islamic Leagues and the Party of Islamic Nations). 1974.
Janzen, J. *Landwirtschaftliche Aktiengesellschaften im Iran*. Saarbrücken, 1976.
Johansen, B. *The Islamic Law on Land Tax and Rent:* The Peasants' Loss of Property Rights in the Hanafite Legal Literature of the Mamluk and Ottoman Periods. London, 1988.
Jonbesh-e Mosalmanan-e Mobarez (Movement of Combatant Muslims). *Asnad wa madark-e jonbesh-e mosalmanan-e mobarez* (Documents of the Movement of Combatant Muslims).
Kadiwar, S., et al. *Shenakht-e sherkatha-ye kesht wa san'at wa sazmanha-ye 'omran wa touse'e-ye keshawarzi dar iran* (A Survey of Agri-Businesses and Agricultural Development Organization in Iran). Tehran, 1976.
Katouzian, H. *The Agrarian Question in Iran*. Geneva, 1981.
———. *The Political Economy of Modern Iran. Despotism and Pseudo-Modernism, 1962–1979*. London, 1981.
Keddie, N. R. "Stratification, Social Control, and Capitalism in Iranian Villages: Before and After the Reform." In Keddie, *Collected Essays: Iran. Religion, Politics and Society*. London, 1980, pp. 158–202.
———. "The Iranian Village Before and After Land Reform." In *Journal of Contemporary History* 3 (1968), pp. 69–91.
Kermani, H. M. *Resale dar 'elm-e falahat* (Treatise on the Science of Agriculture). Kerman.
Keshawarz, H., et al. *Sherkat-e sahami-ye zera'i-ye qasr-e shirin* (The Qasr Shirin Farm Corporation). Tehran, 1971.

Ketab-e Agah (Authors' Collective). *Masa'el-e arzi wa dehaqani* (Problems of Land and the Peasantry). Tehran, 1982.

Khadem Adam, N. "Siyasat-e eqtesad-e keshawarzi dar kazh mehwari" (Agricultual Policy at Odd Pivot). In *Ettela'at-e siyasi-eqetsadi* 25 (1989), pp. 54–57.

Khala'atbari, P. "Eslahat-e arzi-ye nou est'emari, eslah-e arzi-ye demokratik" (Neocolonial Land Reform, Democratic Land Reform). In *Donya* (Spring 1965), pp. 56–65.

Khaza'i, A. "Masa'el-e asasi dar toulid wa 'arze-ye bakhsh-e keshawarzi" (Basic Problems of Production and Marketing in the Agricultural Sector). In *Jahad* 115–119 (1989).

Khomeini, A. R. *Welayat-e faqih. Hokumat-e eslami* (The Rule of Jurists). Tehran, 1982.

———. *Mataleb, mozu'at wa rahnamud ha-ye eqtesadi dar bayanat-e hazrat-e ayatollah emam Khomeini* (Economic Viewpoints and Signposts in the Statements of His Excellency Imam Khomeini). Tehran, 1984.

———. *Tahrir al-wasile* (Notes on the Means). 4 vols. Qom, 1988–1990.

———. *Resale-ye nouwin* (The New Treatise). Trans. and ann. A. Biazar Shirazi. Tehran, 1989.

Khosrawi, Kh. *Pazhuheshi dar jam'e-ye rusta'i-ye iran* (Research in Iranian Village Society).

———. *Jam'e shenasi-y rusta-ye iran* (Sociology of the Iranian Village). 3rd ed. Tehran, 1979.

Kiyani Manesh, D. *Sherkat-e sahami-ye zera'i Garmsar*. (The Garmsar Farm Corporation). Tehran, 1970.

Kiyanuri, N. "Eslahat-e arzi dar iran" (Land Reform in Iran). In *Donya* (Spring/Summer 1963), pp. 9–28.

Koleini, A J M b Y. *Gozide-ye Kafi* (A Selection from the Al-Kafi). sel., trans. and ann. M. B. Behbudi. 3 vols. Tehran, 1984.

Kooroshi, J. "Land Tenure Under Shiite Islam." In *Quarterly Journal of International Agriculture* 26 (December 1987): 4, pp. 391–397.

———. "Eine kritische Betrachtung der Entwicklung der iranischen Landwirtschaft seit Bestehen der Islamischen Republik. In *Orient* 28 (1987), pp. 229–243.

Lahsaeizadeh, A. *The Effect of the 1962 Iranian Land Reform on Rural Social Class Structure*. Dissertation. Michigan State University, 1984.

Lambton, Ann K. S. *Landlord and Peasant in Persia*. London, 1953.

———. *The Persian Land Reform 1962–1966*. Oxford, 1969.

Looney, R. E. *Economic Origins of the Iranian Revolution*. New York, 1982.

Lotze, H. J. *Dollar in der Krise*. Berlin, 1987.

Madani, S. J. *Huguq-e asai dar jomhuri-ye eslami-ye iran* (Basic Laws in the Islamic Republic of Iran). 4 vols. Tehran, 1986–1988.

Mahdawi, H. "Molahezati dar bare-ye masa'el-e arzi dar iran" (Reflections on the Agrarian Problems of Iran). In *Ketab-e Agah* (Authors' Collective), pp. 167–190. Tehran, 1983.

Maher, F. *Naqdi bar "ahdaf-e kammi-ye tous'e-ye keshawarz dar doure-ye 1362–1371"* (A Criticism of the Quantitative Objectives for Agriculture in the Period 1983/4–1992/3). Tehran, 1983.

Majd, M. G. "The Oil Boom and Agricultural Development: A Reconsideration of Agricultural Policy in Iran." In *Journal of Energy and Development* 15: 1, pp. 125–140.

Majles-e Shoura-ye Eslami (Islamic Council Assembly). *Negahi be majles-e shoura-ye eslami* (A Look at the Islamic Council Assembly). 2 vols. Tehran, 1982–83.

———. *Ashna'i ba majles-e shoura-ye eslami* (A Guide to the Islamic Consultative Assembly). 4 vols. Tehran, 1981–84.

———. *Karname-ye majles-e shoura-ye eslami* (Balance of Work of the Islamic Consultative Assembly). 3 vols. 1985–87.

———. *Fehrest-e mouzuʻi-ye dastur-e jalasat-e mozakerate-e majles-e shoura-ye eslami* (List of the Subjects Debated in the Sessions of the Islamic Council Assembly). 2 vols. Tehran, 1986 and 1990.

———. *Surat-e mashruh-e mozakerat-e majles-e barresi-ye qanun-e asasi-ye jomhuri-ye eslami* (Protocols of the Assembly to Work out the Constitution of the Islamic Republic of Iran). 4 vols. Tehran, 1985–89.

———. *Mashruh-e mouzakerat e majles-e shoura-ye eslami-ye iran* (Parliamentary Protocols, or PP). Tehran.

Malek, H. *Sonnat wa sanʻat. Gozaresh az dezful* (Tradition and Industry). Report from Dezful. Tehran, 1978.

———. *Gozaresh dar bare-ye nabesamani ha-ye keshawarzi-ye mamlekat wa emkanat-e moqabele ba anha* (Report on the Chaos in the Agriculture of the Countries and on the Possibilities of Combating It). Tehran, 1979.

Malekaniyan, A. *Pazhuheshi dar nezam-e zemindari. Malekiyatha, Nezame-e bahrebardari, shiwe-ye toulid-e keshawarzi dar iran* (Research on the Land Property System: Landed Property, Organizational System and Agrarian Production in Iran). Tehran, 1986.

Markaz-e Amar-e Iran (Iranian Center for Statistics). *Natayej-e Sarshoumari-ye keshawarzi. Marhale-ye awwal 1352* (Results of the Agricultural Census. First phase). Tehran, 1976.

———. *Salname-ye amari 1355* (Statistical Yearbook 1976/7). Tehran, 1977.

———. *Natayej-e amargiri-ye keshawarzi-Marhale-ye douwoum sarshomari-ye keshawarzi 2533* (Results of the Agricultural Survey, Second Phase of the Agricultural Census 1974/5). Tehran, 1977a.

———. *Salname-ye amari 1360* (1981/2). Tehran, 1982.

———. *Iran dar aʼineh-ye amar* (Iran in the Mirror of Statistics). Tehran, 1983.

———. *Salname-ye amari 1362* (1983/4). Tehran, 1984.

———. *Salname-ye amari 1363* (1984/5.) Tehran, 1985.

———. *Iran dar aʼineh-ye amar*. Tehran, 1985a.

———. *Hazineh wa daramad-e khanewarha-ye rustaʼi. 1363* (Revenue and Expenditure in Rural Households, 1984/5). Tehran, 1985b.

———. *Natayej-e amargiri-ye keshawarzi-ye rustaʼi* (Results of the Surveys in the Rural Agriculture). Tehran, 1985.

———. *Iran dar aʼineh-ye amar*. Tehran, 1986.

———. *Salname-ye amari 1366* (1987/8). Tehran, 1988.

———. *Iran dar aʼineh-ye amar*. Tehran, 1989.

———. *Sarshoumari-ye ʻomum-ye keshawarzi bar asas-e 2.5% khanwarha-ye bahre bardar-e rustaʼi* (Agricultural Census on the Basis of 2.5% of the Peasant Household). 2nd ed. Tehran, 1989a.

Masʻud. "Arzyabi-ye barkhi az jawaneb-e roushd-e eqtesadi-ye iran pas az kudeta" (Evaluation of Some Aspects of Iran's Agricultural Develompent After the Putsch). In *Donya* (Autumn 1966), pp. 8–23.

Maʻsumi, K. "Shouraha-ye rustaʼi ra daryabid" (Save the Rural Councils). In *Masaʼel-e keshawarzi* 1 (Autumn 1980), pp. 67–71.

McLachlan, K. "Food Supply and Agricultural Self-sufficiency in Contemporary Iran." In *Bulletin of the School of Oriental and African Studies,* vol. XLIX, Part I. 1986. pp. 148–162.

———. *The Neglected Garden: The Politics and Ecology of Agriculture in Iran*. London, 1988.

Mehner, H. "Die iranische Agrarwirtschaft—Ihre Struktur und gegenwärtige Produktion." In *Orient* 1 (1978), pp. 34–52.

Meshgini, A. *Zemin wa anche dar an ast* (Land and What It Contains). Tehran, 1980.
Modaressi Tabataba'i, H. *Zemin dar feqh-e eslami* (Land in Islamic Law). 2 vols. Tehran, 1983–84.
Mohammadi, M. *Dar bare-ye mas'ale-ye arzi dar iran wa shiwe-ye hall-e demokratik-e an* (On the Land Quesion and the Democratic Methods for Its Solution). 1973.
Mohaqqeq, Helli. *Sharay'e al-eslam* (Islamic Legal Regulations). 4 vols. Tehran, 1983–85.
Mohsen, S., and M. Reza'i. *Matn-e kamel-e defa'iyat dou tan az sazman-e mojahedin-e khalq-e iran dar dadgah-e nezami* (Complete Text of the Defense Speeches of Two Members of the Organization of the People's Mujahidin of Iran). Confederation of Iranian Students, 1973.
Mojtahed, A., and H. Esfahani. "Agriculture Policy and Performance in Iran: The Postrevolutionary Experience." In *World Development* 17 (June 1989): 6, pp. 839–860.
Mojtehedzade, M., and M. Najafi. *Taswiri az moshkelat wa tangnaha wa bon bastha-ye bakhsh-e keshwarzi* (A Picture of the Problems, Bottlenecks and Blind Alleys in the Agricultural Sector). Tehran, 1986.
Mosaddeq, M. *Khaterat wa t'alomat-e Mosaddeq* (Memoirs and Suffering of Mosaddeq). 2nd ed. Tehran: Iraj Afshar, 1986.
Motahhari, M. *Nazari be nezame eqtesadi-ye eslam* (Overview of the Islamic Economic Order). Tehran, 1989.
Moumeni, B. *Sima-ye rustaha-ye iran* (The Face of the Iranian Villages). Tehran, 1978.
———. *Mas'ale-ye arzi wa jang-e tabqati dar iran* (Land Question and the Class Struggle in Iran). Tehran, 1980.
Najmabadi, A. *Land Reform and Social Change in Iran.* Salt Lake City, 1987.
Nattagh, N. *Agriculture and Regional Development in Iran 1962–1978.* Cambridge, 1986.
Nehzat-e Azadi-ye Iran (The Freedom Movement of Iran). *Shesh name-ye sar goshade* (Six Open Letters). Tehran, 1983.
———. *Asnad-e nahzat-e mouqawemat-e melli* (Documents of the National Resistance Movement). Vols. 2 and 5. Tehran, 1984.
———. *Asnad-e nahzat-e azadi-ye iran* (Documents of the Freedom Movement of Iran). Vols. 1 and 2, 1982; vol. 3, 1984a.
———. *Rishe-ye geraniha* (Cause of the Inflation). Tehran, 1987.
———. *Enhelal-e wezarat-e keshawarzi eshtebahi bozorg* (Dissolving of the Ministry of Agriculture—A Great Mistake). Tehran, 1987a.
Nik A'in, A. "Hezb-e tudeh dar defa'az manaf'e-e tabqati-ye dehaqanan-e zahmat kesh wa be khater-e hall-e bonyadi-ye mas'ale-ye arzi" (Tudeh Party in the Struggle for the Class Interests of the Working Peasantry and for a Basic Solution to the Land Question). In *Donya* 5 (special edition). 1976.
Nik Kholq, A. A. *Sherkat-e sahami-ye zera'i-ye samaskande* (The Samaskande Farm Corporation). Tehran, 1970.
Nuri-Na'ini, M. S. *Kara'i-ye keshawarzi-ye dehqani-ye iran* (Efficiency of Iran's Peasant Agriculture). Tehran, 1977.
Nouruzi, M., et al. *Arzeshyabi-ye fa'aliyatha-ye sherkat-e t'awoni-ye toulid rusta'i marun* (Balance of Activities of the Marun Rural Production Cooperative). Tehran, 1977.
Pahlawi, M. R. (Shah). *Enqelab-e sefid* (The White Revolution). Tehran, 1966.
Parsa, B. *Tarhi dar bare-ye eslahat-e arzi* (A Draft for the Land Reform). Tehran, 1978.

Peyman, H. *Malekiyat, kar wa sarmaye az didgah-e eslam* (Property, Labor and Capital From the Standpoint of Islam). 1978.
Piran, P. "Touse'e-ye borunza wa shahr dar mored-e iran" (Externally Oriented Development and Urban Life. Case Study) In *Ettela'-e siyasi-eqtesadi* 31 (1989), pp. 43–46.
Planck, U. "Der Teilbau im Iran." In *Zeitschrift für Ausländische Landwirtschaft* 1 (1962), pp. 47–81.
———. *Iranische Dörfer nach der Landreform*. Opladen, 1974.
———. "Die Rolle der Landwirtschaft in der neuen iranischen Wirtschaftspolitik." In G. Esters and J. Langkau, *Iran in der Krise. Weichenstellungen für die Zukunft*, pp. 161–182. Bonn, 1980.
Pur Karim, H. "Jomhuri-e eslami-ye iran wa siyasat-e keshawarzi" (The Islamic Republic of Iran and the Agrarian Policy). In *Masa'el-e Keshawarzi* 2 (1981), pp. 23–62.
Qahreman, B. "Dou yaddasht dar bare-ye keshawarzi-ye tejari-ye iran" (Two Notices on Commercial Agriculture in Iran). In *Ketab-e Agah* (op. cit.) 1982, pp. 135–154.
Raf'ati, H. *Mohajerat wa m'aishat dar rustaha-ye hariraz, shahkandi, qara nabas dar ostan-e hamedan* (Migration and Livelihood in the Villages of Hariraz, Shahkandi and Qara Nabas in the Province of Hamedan). Tehran, 1977.
Rafi'i, M. *Anjoman, Organ-e anjoman-e ayalati-ye Azarbaijan* (Anjoman Organ of the Azerbaijan Provincial Council). Tehran, 1983.
Rafi' Pur, F. *Das "Extension and Development corps" in Iran*. Saarbrücken, 1974.
———. *Jame'e-ye rusta-i wa niyazha-ye an* (Rural Society and Its Requirements). Tehran, 1985.
Rawanbakhash, M. *Gozareshi az marakez-e khadamat-e keshawarzi, rusta'i wa 'ashayeri-ye dasht-e moghan* (Report on the Agricultural, Rural and Nomadic Service Centers in the Moghan Plain). Tehran, 1983.
Rawasani, Sch. *Sowjetrepublik Gilan. Die Sozialistische Bewe gung im Iran seit Ende des 19. jahrhunderts bis 1922*. Berlin, 1973.
Razzaqi, E. *Eqtesad-e iran* (Iran's Economy). Tehran, 1988.
Refahiyat, H., et al. *Tahqiq piramun-e oza'-e eqtesad-e keshawarzi-ye keshwar dar sal-e 1363* (Agricultural Report 1984/5). Tehran 1986.
———. *Gozaresh eqtesad-e keshawarzi-ye iran dar sal-e 1364* (Agricultural Report 1985/6). Tehran, 1987.
Riyahi, F. *Kholase-ye mozakerat wa natayej-e ma hasal az seminar-e barresi-ye 'elal-e mohajerat-e rusta'iyan be shahr dar daneshgah-e bu 'ali sina* (Report on the Debates and Results of the Seminar to Investigate the Causes of Migration by the Rural Population to the Towns Held at Bu Ali Sina). University of Hamedan, 1976.
Rohani, S. H. *Nehzat-e emam khomeini* (Movement of Imam Khomeini). 2 vols. Tehran, 1985.
Rostami, T., and Alwandi, M. *Mohajerat-e fasli rusta'iyan wa t'asir-e an bar toulid-e zera'i mantaqe-ye dasht-e esfahan* (Seasonal Migration by the Rural Population and Its Influence on Agrarian Production in the Isfahan Plain). Tehran, 1980.
Sabet Qadam, Haqiqi. Interview with the magazine *Ettela'at-e siyasi-eqtesadi* 14 (1987), pp. 62–64; 15 (1987), pp. 50–56.
———. *Tahlili bar marakezi ke taht nam-e markez-e khadamat-e keshawarzi, rusta'i wa 'ashayeri tashkil shodehand* (An Analysis of the Centers Set Up Under the Name Centers for Agricultural, Rural and Nomadic Services). Tehran, 1983.
Sadr, M. B. *Eqtesad-e ma* (Our Economy). 2 vols. Tehran, 1969.

Sa'edlu H. *Ta'in-e mizan-e had aqall-e wos'at-e bahrebardari baray-e yek wahed-e zera'i* (Determining the Minimal Size of Enterprise for an Agrarian Production Unit). Tehran, 1974.

———. *Masa'el-e keshawarzi-ye iran* (Problems of Iranian Agriculture). 2nd ed. Tehran, 1978.

Safari, H. *Yek barresi-ye enteqadi az waz'-e konuni-ye eqtesad-e iran* (A Critical Examination of the Present State of the Iranian Economy). 1977.

Safi Nezhad, J., et al. *Sherkat-e sahami-ye zera'i-ye niwan nar-golpaygan* (The Niwan Nar-Golpaygan Farm Corporation). Tehran, 1971.

———. *Bone* (Bone Producer Cooperative). Tehran, 1972.

———. *Ta'woniha-ye toulid zera'i-ye sonnati dar iran* (Traditional Agrarian Producer Cooperatives in Iran). In *'Olum-e ejtema'i* 2 (1976), pp. 165–179.

———. *Nezamha-ye abyari-ye sonnati dar iran* (Traditional Irrigation Systems in Iran). Tehran, 1980.

Safizadeh, F. *Agrarian Change, Migration and Impact of the Islamic Revolution in a Village Community in Azerbaijan, Iran.* Ph.D. Dissertation. Harvard University, 1986.

Sahabi, 'E. *Bahsi dar bare-ye jang wa solh wa bazsazi dar enqelab-e eslami-ye iran* (Thoughts on War, Peace and Reconstruction in the Islamic Revolution of Iran). Tehran, 1988.

Saidi, K. "Landwirtschaftliche Aktiengesellschaften als Instrument der landwirtschaftlichen Entsicklung im Iran." In *Zeitschrift für Ausländische Landwirtschaft* 12 (1973), pp. 286–297.

Sanjabi, K. *Essai sur l'economie rurale et le regime agraire de la perse.* Paris, 1934.

———. *Omidha wa naomidiha. khaterat-e siyasi-ye doktor karim-e sanjabi* (Hope and Hopelessness: Memoirs of Dr. Karim Sanjabi). London, 1989.

Sarmadi, Mohtasham. *Barzegar* (July 20, 1984).

Sazman-e Barname wa Budje (Organization of Planning and Budget). *Gozaresh-e ejra-ye barname-ye haft sale-ye douwom* (Implementation Report of the Second Construction Plan). Tehran, 1964.

———. *Gozaresh-e 'amalkard-e barname-ye sewom 1341–1346* (Implementation Report of the Third Construction Plan). Tehran.

———. *Barname-ye Chaharom-e 'omrani-ye keshwar 1347–1351* (Fourth Construction Plan of the Country 1968/9–1972/3).

———. *Barname-ye panjom-e 'omrani-ye keshwar 1352–1356. Kholase-ye tajdid-e nazar shode* (The Fifth Construction Plan of the Country 1973/4–1977/8. Synopsis of the Revised Edition). Tehran, 1973.

———. *Gozaresh be senminar: "bar resi masa'el-e eqtesadi-ye iran* (Report to a Seminar on the Investigation of Iran's Economic Problems) (RS). Tehran, 1979.

———. *Peywast-e layeh-ye barname-awwal-e touse'e-ye eqtesadi, ejtema'i, farhangi-ye jomhuri-ye eslami-ye iran 1362–1366* (Appendix to the Legislative Proposal on the First Economic, Social and Cultural Construction Plan of the Islamic Republic of Iran 1983/4–1987/8). Vol. 1, 1983.

———. *Negareshi bar baraward-e khesarat-e eqtesadi-ye jang-e tahmili-ye 'eraq 'elayh-e iran ta esfand-e 1362* (Short Look at the Estimate of the Economic Damage Caused by Iraq's War Against Iran Until February/March 1984). Tehran, 1985.

Sazman-e Cherikha-ye Fada'i-ye Khalq (Organization of People's Fedaiin). *Dar bare-ye eslahat-e arzi wa natayej-e mostaqqim-e an* (On the Land Reform and Its Direct Consequences). 1973.

———. *Barresi-ye sherkatha-ye sahami-ye zera'i* (Investigation of the Farm Corporations). 1973a.

———. *Barresi-ye sakht-e eqtesadi-ye rustaha-ye fars* (Investigation of the Economic Structure of the Villages in the Province of Fars). 1974.
———. *Barresi-ye sakht-e eqtesadi-ye rustha-ye kerman* (Investigation of the Economic Structure of the Villages in the Province of Kerman). 1974.
Sazman-e Enqelabi-ye Hezb-e Tudeh-ye Iran (Revolutionary Organization of the Tudeh Party of Iran). *Piruz bad rah-e mohasere-ye shahrha az tariq-e dehat* (Long Live the Way of Encircling the Towns Form the Villages). 1969.
Sazman-e Markazi-ye Ta'awon (Central Organization for Cooperatives), *Malekiyat-e amlak-e mazru'i wa ta'awon* (Ownership of the Fields and the Cooperatives). Tehran, 1969.
———. *Marahel-e tatawwor-e qawanin wa moqararat-e ta'woni dar iran* (Phase of Development in the Laws and Regulations Concerning Cooperatives in Iran). Tehran, 1971.
Sazman-e Mojahedin-e Khalq-e Iran (Organization of People's Mujahidin of Iran). *Rusta wa enqelab-e sefid* (Rural Regions and the White Revolution). 1972.
———. *Eqtesad be zeban-e sade* (The Economy in Simple Language). 1972.
———. *Seh Gozaresh. Sherkat-e sahami-ye zera'i-ye ariamehr* (Three Reports. The Aryamahr Farm Corporation). 1974.
Schirazi, A. "Iranische Landreform unter der Perspektive oppositioneller Gruppen." In *Mardom Nameh* 2 (1976), pp. 41–54.
———. *Genesis der sozio-ökonomischen Unterentwicklung des Iran*. Berlin, 1977.
———. "Gesellschaftspolitisches Vorstellungen im schiitischen Islam." In *Religion und Politik im Iran*. Frankfurt: Jahrbuch für Geschichte und Gesellschaft des Mittleren Ostens, 1981, pp. 163–177.
———. *The Problem of the Land Reform in the Islamic Republic of Iran*. Complications and Consequences of an Islamic Reform Policy, Berlin, 1987.
———. *Texte zur Agrargesetzgebung in der Islamischen Republik Iran*. Translated, annotated and commented by A. Schirazi, Berlin, 1988.
Schokatfard, F. D. "Sozio-ökonomische Auswirkungen der landwirtschaftlichen Aktiengesellschaften im Iran." In *Zeitschrift für Ausländische Landwirtschaft* 2 (1972), pp. 120–137.
Schmucker, W. *Untersuchungen zu einigen wichtigen bodenrechtlichen Konsequenzen der Islamischen Eroberungsbewegung*. Bonn, 1972.
Sedaqat, Nezhad N. "Arzyabi-ye barnameha wa siyasatha-ye dami-ye keshwar" (Investigation of the Programs and Policies of the Country Effecting Stockbreeding). In *Ettela'at-e siyasi-eqtesadi* 11 (1987), pp. 58–62.
Setad-e Markazi-ye Hey'at ha-ye Haft Nafare (Central Office of the Sevener Commissions). *'Amalkard-e hey'atha-ye haft nafare-ye wagozari-ye zemin* (Report on Land Allocation by the Sevener Commissions). Tehran, 1984.
Soudagar, M. *Barresi-ye eslahat-e arzi 1340–1350* (Investigation of the Land Reform 1961/2–1971/2). Tehran, 1979.
Statistical Yearbooks. See Markaz-e Amar-e Iran.
Taheri, T. *Mas'ale-ye mohajerat-e rusta'i dar iran* (The Problem of Rural Depopulation in Iran). Tehran, 1981.
Talebof, A. *Masalek ol-Mohsenin* (Charitable Ways). Tehran: B. Moumeni, 1967.
———. *Ketab-e Ahmad* (The Book of Ahmad). Tehran: B. Moumeni, 1967.
Taleqani, M. *Eslam wa malekiyat* (Islam and Property). Tehran, 1954.
Tawanayan Fard, H. *Jame'e shenasi-ye eqtesadi az didgah-e 'ali shari'ati* (Economic Sociology in the View of Ali Shari'ati). Tehran, 1983.
———. *Eqtesad-e siyasi-ye touhidi* (Political Economy of Unity). Tehran.
Tehrani, A. *Eqtesad-e eslami* (Islamic Economy). Tehran, 1974.
Tusi, Sh. M. H. *Al-nahaya fi al-mojarrad al-feqh wa al-fatawi* (Conclusion on

Abstracts of the Science of Islamic Law and Fatawa). Edited by: Sabzewari, M. B., Tehran, 1955.
Vesel, J. "Negahi ejmali be resaleha-ye qadimi-ye keshawarzi-ye farsi" (A Short Survey of Old Persian Tracts on Agriculture). In *Nashr-e Danesh*, Mehr/Aban, 1989, pp. 510–515.
Wezarat-e Barname wa Budje (Ministry of Planning and Budget). *Faslname-ye amari* (Statistical Quarterly) 6 (1986).
Wezarat-e Dadgostari (Ministry of Justice). *Majmu'e-ye qawanin* (Lawbooks).
Wezarat-e Ershad-e Eslami (Ministry of Islamic Leadership). *Karname ye doulat-e jomhuri-ye eslami* (Activity Report of the Government of the Islamic Republic of Iran). Tehran, 1985.
Wezarat-e Jahad-e Sazandegi (Ministry of Holy War for Construction). *Naqsh-e Sanay'-e rusta'i dar ijad-e eshteghal* (The Role of Rural Crafts by Creating Employment). Tehran, 1988.
Wezarat-e Keshawarzi wa 'Omran-e Rusta'i (Ministry of Agriculture and Rural Construction). *Touse'e-ye keshawarzi-ye iran* (Growth of the Iranian Agriculture). Part 2. Tehran, 1977.
———. *Khotut-e asli-ye hadafha, siyasatha wa sazman-e keshawarzi dar iran* (The Guidelines and Objectives in Iranian Agricultural Policy and Organization) [Izadi's Program—IP]. Tehran, 1979.
———. *Barname-ye panjsale-ye touse'e-ye keshawarzi* (Five-year Plan for Development of Agriculture). Vol. 1, 1983.
———. *Barresi-ye mehwar budan-e keshawarzi ya olawiyyat be bakhsh-e keshawarzi* (Investigation of the Pivotal Position of the Agriculture or the Priority of Agriculture). Tehran, 1983.
———. *Barname-ye afzayesh-e toulid-e mahsulat-e keshawarzi 1366–1375* (Plan for Increasing Agrarian Production 1987/8–1996/7) [Self-sufficiency plan—SP]. Tehran, 1987.
Wusuqi, M. *Jame'e shenasi-ye rusta'i* (Rural Sociology). Tehran, 1988.
Yawari, A. R. *Moqaddame-i bar shenakht-e keshawarzi-ye sonnati-ye iran* (An Introduction to Knowledge of the Traditional Iranian Agriculture). Tehran, 1980.
Yazdi, E. "Eqtesad-e eslami" (Islamic Economy). In *Maktab-e mobarez* 2 (1967), pp. 20–34; 5 (1969), pp. 29–40.
Yeganeh, C. *Agrarian Structure Under Adaptation, Reform and Revolution: The Case of Iran in a Comparative Historical Perspective*. Dissertation, 1986.
Zali, A. *Nokati Chand dar moured-e keshawarzi mehwar-e touse'e-ye eqtesadi dar jomhuri-ye eslami-ye iran* (Notes on the Question of Agriculture as the Axis of Economic Development in the Islamic Republic of Iran) [letter to Khomeini]. Tehran, 1984.
Zabih, S. *The Communist Movement in Iran*. Berkeley, 1966.
Zahedi Mazanderani, M. J. *Keshat wa san'at-e moghan tawali cherkin bar peykar-e dasht* (The Moghan Agribusiness. A Festering Tumor on the Body of the Moghan Plain). Tehran, 1984.
———. *Wahedha-ye "keshawarzi—san'ati." Naqd-e tarh-e wagonzari-ye kesht wa san'atha* ("Agribusiness": A Criticism of the Transfer of the Agribusinesses). Tehran, 1986.
Zamani, M. *Eslam wa tamaddon-e jadid* (Islam and the New Civilization). Tehran, 1969.

Index

Administration: agricultural, 135–164; decentralization of, 114; duplication of responsibility, 136, 141, 149, 152–153; Islamization of, 135; reform, 135–164
Advisory Reconstruction Organization, 295
Afzali, Hojjat ol-Eslam, 190
Agribusiness, 15, 19–20, 174, 250–252; overcapitalization of, 9, 20; reform of, 34; success rate, 20
Agricultural Cooperatives, 243
Agricultural Councils, 138, 139, 175, 177, 180
Agricultural Organizations, 138
Agriculture, 1; administrative reform, 135–164; allocation of funds to, 23; counselors for, 138; crisis in prerevolutionary regime, 7–25; current Islamist thinking, 53–64; decentralization in, 125; development crisis in, 73–83; domestic demand, 7; in economic policy, 95–100; effect of land reform on, 61; five year plans, 104; inadequate production in, 7–8; investment in, 23, 105; lack of information on, 63; legislation, 2–3; management problems, 233–255; maximizing production, 275–298; mechanization, 181; mechanization of, 17, 63, 126, 283, 284, 286; modernization of, 32, 54; neglect by prerevolutionary regime, 8–10; operational organization of, 14–21; by ownership, 13*tab*; planning, 103–131; as policy axis, 95–100, 110; policy of Rafsanjani government, 3; postwar planning, 127–131; production, 8; self-sufficiency in, 62–63, 87–92; share of gross domestic product, 23, 95, 111; size of holdings, 12*tab,* 246–247; in social policy, 95–100; standard of living in, 113; state intervention in, 109, 182; state investment in, 126, 276*tab*; theories of, 31–64; in traditional literature, 48–50; war damage, 81; and war priority, 97–98
Ali, 49
Amoli, Ayatollah, 82, 318
Animal husbandry, 14, 17, 115, 150, 152, 155, 164, 177, 192
Ardebili, Ayatollah, 202, 206, 219, 264
Army of Counseling and Construction, 22
Army of Health, 22
Army of Knowledge, 22, 54
Association for the Support of Peasants, 42
Association of Iranian Economists, 97
Association of Islamic Students Abroad, 63, 64*n*9
Autarky, 87, 88, 89
Authoritarianism, 21, 76
Azerbaijan, 228

Bahonar, Hojjat ol-Eslam, 107
Balance-of-payments, 96
Baluchistan, 164, 170, 266
Bani Sadr, A., 50, 51, 52, 59, 60, 64, 68*n*99, 88, 107, 108, 263
Bank for Agriculture, 32, 193, 236, 240, 241, 244, 277, 278, 283; loans, 279*tab*
Banki, M. T., 107
Banking: Islamization of, 236; nationalization of, 43, 115; and politico-financial oligarchy, 105; system inadequacy, 14
Bank of America, 20
Barley, 90, 123, 246, 251, 296; imports, 298*tab*; per capita production, 297*tab*;

337

pricing, 291; production, 294*tab*; yield, 285*tab*
Bazargan government, 2; agricultural policy, 88, 95, 317; development planning in, 105–116; land reform in, 171–175
Bedashti, Allah, 209
Behbahani, Ayatollah J'afar, 53
Beheshti, Ayatollah, 91, 139, 159, 176, 178, 196*n33*, 202, 208, 217, 220
Bill Annulling Ownership of Derelict Municipal Land, 223
Bill on the Authority for the Determination of Wasteland and Annulling Land Registers Concerned, 224
Borqe'i, Ayatollah, 68*n105*
Boyer Ahmadi, 76*tab*
Brujerdi, Ayatollah, 53
Budget: balancing, 80; defense, 99, 129; deficits, 79, 320; planning, 120–122; state, 78, 106, 111, 120–122; war costs, 81
Bureaucracy, 320; excessive, 154; size, 105
Bushehr, 76*tab*, 188

Capital: flight, 277; foreign, 57, 128, 251; formation, 23, 277, 278*tab*; goods, 74, 89; lawful, 229*n34*; monopoly, 43; repatriation, 20
Capitalism, 43, 51, 60, 105
Center for Rural and Agricultural Research, 91
Center for Rural and Agricultural Surveys, 32
Centers for Agricultural, Rural and Nomadic Services. *See* Service Centers
Centers for Agriculture and Rural Improvement, 138
Centers for Improving Productive and Constructive Services, 245
Central Bank, 32, 80
Central Office for Rural and Agricultural Research, 239
Central Office for the Transfer of Land, 188
Central Organization of Rural Cooperatives, 16, 32, 244, 246
Centre for Rural and Agricultural Research, 114
Cereals, 88, 293; exports, 7; imports of, 7; production, 8
Chahar Mahal Bakhtiyari, 249
Commission for Plan Studies, 88
Communism, 35, 37, 39–44, 51, 57, 66*n33*, 132*n35*, 177, 202, 209; suppression by shah, 40; as urban phenomena, 40
Confederation of Iranian Students, 43, 44
Conference of Provincial Governors, 148
Confiscation, 211
Conflict: ethnic, 170; land, 175
Constituent Assembly of Experts, 266
Constitution, 3, 157; Article 3, 87, 135; Article 43, 87; Article 44, 103, 104, 210, 236, 237, 245, 271*n6*; Article 49, 133*n77*, 201, 210–213; Article 100, 263; guarantee of participation, 261; revisions, 130
Constitutional Revolution, 36
Construction, 137; counselors for, 138; housing, 116, 310; planning for, 128; prerevolutionary, 106, 120; rural, 98, 106, 152; urban, 106
Consumerism, 110, 116
Consumption: patterns, 74, 126; per capita, 23
Contracts, 45; annulling, 225; ejare, 45–46; Islamic, 278; ja'ale, 46; lease, 181, 187, 225, 227; mosaqat, 45; mozarebe, 46, 129; mozare'e, 45, 52; sharecropping, 235
Cooperatives: mosha', 238–246; producer, 237; rural, 245–246; and sharia, 236–238
Cooperatives of Wheat Farmers, 245
Corn, 88, 90, 251; imports, 298*tab*; self-sufficiency in, 126
Corporations, multinational, 20
Corruption, 20
Cost-of-living index, 79
Cotton, 88, 251, 284, 287*tab*, 293, 296; per capita production, 297*tab*; production, 294*tab*; yield, 285*tab*
Council of Guardians, 3, 69*n106*, 99, 122, 151, 156, 177, 180, 183, 186, 191, 204, 211, 215, 216, 217, 218, 255*n1*, 322
Council of Ministers, 88, 107, 124, 130, 139, 152, 157, 227; and development plan, 97, 124; factions in, 127; and Ministry of Jahad-e Sazandegi, 148; refusal of self-sufficiency plan, 127
Council of United Muslims, 55
Council to Determine the Interests of the Order, 191
Counterrevolution, 150, 175, 203–204
County Town Council, 141
Crafts, traditional, 17, 25, 111, 155, 164, 312
Credit system, 14

Crops: essential, 109; nonstrategic, 271, 274n56; regionalization of, 109; strategic, 241, 271, 292; summer, 241, 255, 271, 292
Currency: earnings, 79, 80, 119; foreign, 74, 79, 80, 96, 113, 119, 286

Decisionmaking, 54; lack of machinery for, 115; of legalist faction, 21 participation in, 261; state level, 2
Decrees: rulership, 219, 220, 221; secondary, 184, 322; state, 122, 322. *See also* Edicts
Democracy, 38, 76
Democratic Party of Azerbaijan, 41
Democratic Party of Kurdistan, 189
Determination Council, 191, 194, 215, 221, 239, 322, 323
Development: autocentric, 34; contradictory objectives, 114–115; economic, 78; effect of war with Iraq, 80–82; import substitution, 74; investment in, 98; Islamic policies, 73–83; planning criticism, 114–116; plans, 90, 91, 97, 105–131; policy, 103; postwar, 98–99; private sector investment in, 110; spiritual aspects, 149; state expenditures, 78–79; state investment in, 121
Distribution systems, 51
District Village Council, 137, 141, 268, 270
Dow Chemicals, 20
Draft Bill on the Limits and Nature of the Cooperative Sector in the Islamic Republic, 237

Ears project, 289
East Azerbaijan, 171
Economic Council, 107
Economic Pointers of the Right Reverend Imam Khomeini, 60
The Economy in Simple Language, 60
Edicts: primary, 216, 217; secondary, 216, 217, 231n82, 231n97. *See also* Decrees
al-Edris, Ebn, 207
Education, 131, 152; level, 310; rural, 114, 137. *See also* Schools
Ejare, 45–46
Electoral law, 53–54
Electricity, 113, 159, 274n56, 305, 306, 311; state investment in, 276tab
Employment, 32, 75; in agriculture, 126
Energy, 106; supply shortfall, 74
Enfal, 48, 51, 207, 222

Environment: protection of, 96, 111; saving, 138
Erosion, 299n18
Esfahani, Reza, 52, 109, 175–176, 196n27, 206, 207, 209, 235, 255n8
Exchange: earnings, 96, 98; rates, 74, 78, 80
Experts: foreign, 57, 114; lack of, 143, 144, 147, 154, 280; in planning, 107; purges of, 147, 317; qualifications, 144, 154
Exports: agricultural, 79, 90, 116, 119, 298; cereals, 7; earnings through, 96; fruit, 292; increased, 111; industrial, 79, 96; of national resources, 89; oil, 2, 7, 62, 74, 77tab, 77–80, 105, 130, 134n83; uncompetitive, 74
Extension Corps, 139

Fada'iyan-e Eslam, 58
Fahim, Hojjat ol-Eslam, 208
Farm Corporations, 15, 17, 18, 21, 32, 143, 145, 178, 243, 248; dissolution of, 249, 258n91; rehabilitation of, 258n98; replacement of, 137
Fars, 169, 171, 188, 199n117
Fatwas, 3, 45, 66n50, 197n39, 219
FCs. *See* Farm Corporations
Fertilizer, 100, 113, 119, 145, 241, 283, 284, 286, 287, 287tab
Feudalism, 55, 56, 57, 60, 65n21, 175, 179, 187, 196n27, 228, 247, 270; abolition, 36, 37, 39, 41
"First Economic, Social and Cultural Development Plan of the Islamic Republic of Iran," 107
First National City Bank, 20
Fishing industry, 152, 155, 192
Foundation Authority, 55
Foundation for Disabled War Veterans, 164
Foundation for the Dispossessed, 161, 163, 164, 174, 180, 247, 251
Freedom Movement, 56, 57, 165n34, 271n6

Ghafuri, Ayatollah, 264
Gigantism, 76
Gilan, 169, 207
Gilani, Ayatollah, 202
Golpaygani, Ayatollah, 177, 197n39, 209
Gonbad, 189, 190
Gorgan, 188, 189, 190
Government. *See* State
Gross domestic product, 78, 80, 81, 95, 111, 308

340   Index

Gross national product, 74; per capita, 320
Growth: agricultural, 301n76; annual, 131; economic, 75; population, 7, 11, 23, 75, 78, 91, 114, 126, 131, 193, 297, 305, 313; rates, 8

Habbati groups, 254
Hadith, 206
Hamab groups, 254
Hamedan, 169, 188
Harandi, Hojjat ol-Eslam, 162, 178, 192, 194, 197n39, 198n67, 198n72, 199n117, 200n131, 208, 210–211, 216, 219, 235, 241
Hawaiian Agronomics, 20
Helli, Mohaqqeq, 207
Hezbollah, 136, 146
Hoarding, 46, 133n77, 206, 289, 300n67
Holy Foundation of Imam Reza, 227, 228, 235
Holy War for Construction. *See* Ministry of Jahad-e Sazandegi
Hormozgan, 188
Hostages, 129
House of Justice, 22
House of Rural Culture, 22
Housing, 17, 106, 110, 116, 310, 311

Imam's Relief Committee, 161, 163–164, 247
Imperialism, 57, 92, 104, 129; dependency on, 88; independence from, 88–90
Import: substitution, 74, 311
Imports, 274n62, 286; agricultural, 105; cereal, 7; dependence on, 87, 108; food, 96, 98, 298tab; foreign products, 59; increases in, 8, 59, 297; manufactured, 89; raw materials, 74; restrictions, 107, 129; unnecessary, 87–88
Income: additional sources of, 25; and consumer costs, 308, 308tab; distribution, 24, 75, 309; in Farm Corporations, 18; farmers, 113; gap, 309; national, 79; from oil exports, 77–80; peasant, 17, 110; per capita, 17, 78, 309; rises in, 107; rural, 25; rural-urban gap, 92, 113; tax on, 106
Industrialization, 7, 96
Industry: construction, 74; rural, 43, 152, 155, 305, 312; share of gross domestic product, 111; state investment in, 276tab
Inflation, 74, 78, 79, 82, 105, 107, 117, 128, 277

Infrastructure, 19, 139, 246, 306; inadequate, 74; industrial, 97; investment in, 117; rural, 24; social, 76tab
Instances of Emulation, 209
Institute for Social Research and Studies, 33
Insurance, 238, 279; for agricultural produce, 126; medical, 158; social, 32
Interest, 16, 20; rates, 16, 241, 257n51
Investment, 106, 278; agricultural, 23, 105, 109, 200n131, 288tab; in development, 98, 125; encouragement of, 110; in exports, 59; fixed, 276tab; gross domestic, 320; increased, 120; in infrastructure, 117; in mechanization, 9; organization of, 117; private, 20, 109, 125, 127, 193; in research, 288; restructuring, 106; in self-sufficiency, 125; state, 116, 121, 125, 276tab, 288tab; wartime diversion of, 97; for water, 9, 299n23
Investment and People's Participation Centers, 193
Iranian Central Bank, 78
Iran Party, 38, 65n21
Irawani, Minister, 297, 299n17
Irrigation, 114, 130, 152, 254, 281, 282, 306; increasing, 91; neglect of traditional systems, 9; subsidization of costs, 20; traditional, 280
Isadi, Minister, 137
Isfahan, 169, 243, 244, 255
Islamic: Councils, 266; economy, 50–53, 58, 59, 63, 315; justice, 210; radicals, 267; Societies, 135, 136; Student Association, 267, 271n18, 273n40; tax, 202
Islamic law, 66n50, 230n72; agriculture in literature of, 45–48; cooperatives in, 237; debates on land reform, 200n145; expertise in, 217; and foundation estates, 226; on land ownership, 47, 48, 172, 208; potential for problem solving, 3; rule of avoidance, 198n66; sharecropping in, 21, 37, 45; wasteland in, 221–225
Islamic Republic: administrative reform, 130; constitution, 3, 87, 103, 104, 133n7, 135, 157, 236, 245, 263, 271n6; cooperative system, 236–238; development crisis in, 73–83; factions in, 2, 107, 128, 129, 130, 316; five year plans, 88, 90, 91, 103, 116–117; justification for establishment, 1; legalist group, 2; monopoly of power in, 130; opposition to, 82; planning in, 106; purges in, 146, 147; relations with

West, 128–129; suppression of opposition, 317, 318; war policy, 2
Islamism, liberal, 317
Islamist: opposition to shah, 34–36; overemphasis on ideology, 63, 64; radicals, 171, 179; thinking on agricultural problems, 53–64
Izadi, Minister, 64, 64n9, 88, 90, 96, 100n1, 108, 109, 113, 131n14, 139, 142, 173, 175, 233, 248, 250, 261

Jangali movement, 37, 40
Jennati, Ayatollah, 177, 217
Jurists. *See* Legalist faction

Kalantari, Minister, 147, 155, 193, 234, 280, 282, 290, 295
Kamare'i, Ayatollah, 68n105
Kani, Ayatollah, 107
Kanz rule, 206
Kashani, Ayatollah, 216, 217
Kerman, 169, 171, 188, 227, 270
Kermani, Hojjat ol-Eslam, 231n139
Kermanshah, 197n46
Khalkhali, Hojjat ol-Eslam, 202, 207, 267
Khamene'i, President, 89, 92, 98, 99, 127, 130, 221, 318
Khaz'ali, Ayatollah, 267
Kho'iniha, Hojjat ol-Eslam, 179, 188, 212, 213, 225
Khomeini, Ayatollah, 47, 91, 142, 159, 160, 164, 177, 178, 183, 185, 186, 187, 189, 190, 202–203, 206, 209, 217, 219, 221, 223, 227, 238, 262, 317, 323; agricultural policies, 89; in budget planning, 122; and confiscation of property, 174; death of, 130; on land reform, 60–63; and Ministry of Jahad-e Sazandegi, 148; on planning, 103; and planning reconstruction, 129; thinking on agriculture, 96, 99; in war with Iraq, 120
Khorasan, 137, 249, 274n56
Khou'i, Ayatollah, 230n51
Khounsari, Ayatollah, 68n99, 230n51
Khuzestan, 169, 189, 207, 244, 251, 271
Kurdistan, 76tab, 185, 187, 188, 189, 199n117, 254, 259n125, 264
Kurds, 169, 170, 171

Labor: constriction of, 20; export of, 119; hired, 12, 13tab, 18; lack of skilled, 280, 312; productive, 49; rural, 20; wage, 19

Land: anwa, 48, 51; buying and selling, 45, 52; communal, 51; confiscation, 188, 201–205, 211; crown, 56, 65n31; destruction of, 282, 299n17; division, 14; enfal, 48, 51, 207, 222; Foundation, 225–228; fragmentation, 15, 17, 252, 280; inheritance, 182–183; irrigated, 9; occupation of, 14, 169; ownership, 58, 92, 139, 143–146, 162, 205–210; ownership problems, 14; private ownership, 47, 58, 92, 109; reclamation, 152; restrictions on, 109, 185, 205–210, 216; seizure, 69n118; sequestration, 188, 201–205, 211, 252; shareholding, 17, 18; smallholding dissolution, 15; speculation, 225; squats, 174, 178, 179, 180, 185, 186, 187, 188–191, 199n113, 199n117, 200n145, 211, 215, 216, 227, 252; taken in war, 48; tax, 46; tenure, 11, 26n23, 169–195, 211, 234; transfer of, 219–220, 235, 323; use, 155, 280–283; usufructuary rights, 11, 13, 14, 15, 26n23, 51, 52, 68n105; utilization projects, 125; waqf, 207; wasteland, 47, 48, 52, 58, 68n105, 108, 172, 178, 180, 182, 210; yield on nonirrigated land, 25n15
Land reform, 7, 32, 108, 163, 169–195; in Bazargan government, 171–175; benefits, 12; communism and, 40–42; conservative concept, 55–56; criticisms of, 53; disputes on, 175–183, 201–228; effect on agriculture, 61; exemptions to, 21; legality of, 210–213; in Mossadeq government, 38; peasant landholding in, 13; in prerevolutionary regime, 10–14, 39; radical, 175–180, 205, 207; research on, 33; resistance to, 177–178; and self-sufficiency, 92, 182; Sevener Commissions in, 161–162; and social structure, 43, 44; socioeconomic consequences, 60; spontaneous action phase, 169–171; and standard of living, 24; and state intervention, 60; White Revolution in, 21
Law on Local Councils, 263, 264, 265–266, 268, 270, 273n40, 304
Law on the Establishment of Village Councils, 264
Law on the Method of Implementing Article 49 of the Constitution of the Islamic Republic, 211, 212
Law on the National Organization of the Islamic Councils, 265

Laws, inheritance, 47
League of Socialists in Iran, 38–39, 64n8, 69n108
Leases, 47
Legalist faction, 319, 321, 323; absolute power of, 3; decisionmaking, 2; legitimacy of, 3; pan-Islamism in, 317; qualifications, 135
Legumes, 91, 293, 296; per capita production, 297tab; production, 294tab; self-sufficiency in, 126
Liberalism, 51, 76
Limits and Type of Productive Activity in the Private Sector, 92
Loans, 32, 47, 150, 277, 278, 279, 279tab; interest-free, 58, 109, 173, 278; interest on, 16; long-term, 16, 18, 20, 40; to Rural Cooperatives, 15; seasonal, 15–16; short-term, 16; soft, 19
Lurestan, 76tab, 169, 310

Mahallati, Hojjat ol-Eslam, 216
Maher, Farhad, 91, 114
"Major Trends in the Economic, Social and Cultural Development of the Islamic Republic of Iran," 107
Maleki, Khalil, 38
Manhattan Bank, 20
Manifesto of the Islamic Republic (Bani Sadr), 58
Mao Tse-tung, 43, 44
Mar'ashi, Ayatollah, 209
Market: control, 289; international, 82; peasant production for, 12; private money, 16; supply, 25n5; supply reduction, 7
Martyrs' Foundation, 161, 164, 247
Marxism, 51
Mashad program, 40
Mashhad, 199n117
Mazanderan, 188, 208
Mechanization, 13, 17, 21, 26n33, 63, 126, 181, 283, 284, 286; effect on employment, 18; investment in, 9
Media: on cooperatives, 237; and land reform, 184, 188
Medical care, 75, 106, 306, 307, 310
Meshgini, Ayatollah, 176, 177, 178, 202, 206, 209, 211, 217, 220–221, 225
Migration: rural, 23–25, 62, 108, 113, 182, 303–313; and standard of living, 24
Mining, 74; state investment in, 276tab
Ministry of Agriculture, 32, 69n106, 108, 110, 127, 247, 286, 305, 320; competition with Ministry of Jahad-e Sazandegi, 143–144, 145–146; failure of reform in, 136–146; proposed merger with Ministry of Jahad-e Sazandegi, 152–155; relocation to villages, 137; responsibilities taken over by Jahad, 149–155
Ministry of Cooperatives, 17
Ministry of Education and Training, 149
Ministry of Heavy Industry, 132n39, 263
Ministry of Jahad-e Sazandegi, 90, 108, 110, 131, 136, 141, 175, 268, 270, 289, 305, 320; bureaucratization of, 155–158; commercialization of services, 158; competition with Ministry of Agriculture, 143–144, 145–146; criticisms of, 125, 151; development of, 147–161; expansion of authority, 149–155; proposed merger with Ministry of Agriculture, 152–155; as Revolutionary Organization, 147–149; and rural depopulation, 306–313; service in war with Iraq, 158–161
Ministry of Justice, 162, 190, 203, 204, 267
Ministry of Planning and Budget, 81, 99, 121, 153. *See also* Organization of Planning and Budget
Ministry of the Interior, 162, 186, 265
Ministry of Transport, 149
Ministry of Water and Energy, 113, 155, 251
Miyanji, Hojjat ol-Eslam, 208
Modernization, 10, 32, 54, 255; in prerevolutionary regime, 17
Mohtashami, Hojjat ol-Eslam, 309
Mokhabere, 52
Moneylending, 12, 40
Montazeri, Ayatollah, 89, 92, 117, 176, 177, 178, 185, 187, 192, 206, 216, 217, 219, 220, 231n111
Mosaddeq, Mohammad, 37–38, 56, 65n18, 69n108
Mosaqat, 45
Mosha', 46, 109, 110, 194, 236–246, 256n32, 256n44; criticism of, 240–241; dissolution of, 241
Mosharekat, 261–272
Movement of Islamic Combatants, 55
Mozarebe, 129
Mozare'e, 45, 52, 236
Muhammad, 47, 49, 238, 264
Multinational companies, 59, 62

Index   343

Musawi, Prime Minister, 89, 92, 104, 107, 116, 120, 128–129, 153, 155, 158–159, 191, 219, 244, 318, 319; and Islamization, 135–136; and private sector, 119; thinking on agriculture, 99

Nabawi, Minister, 97, 263
Nahj al-Balagha, 48, 49, 50
Najafabadi, Hojjat ol-Eslam, 122, 295
National Agricultural Bank, 37
National Congress of Rural and Agricultural Cooperatives, 244, 245
National Congress to Investigate Problems of Agricultural Development, 155, 234, 286, 293, 298n1
National Front, 38, 39, 41, 131n14, 316
Nationalization, 61, 65n25; of banks, 43, 115; commercial, 158; of estates, 39, 62, 193, 247; of land and water, 39, 43; oil industry, 38; of wasteland, 223
National Resistance Movement, 56
"New Economic Policy," 118–120
Noninterest-Bearing Bank Transactions Act, 235

Obligation Plan, 124
Office for Production Enterprises, 259n115
Office for Revolutionary Projects, 131n8
Oil: boom, 24; dependence on, 74, 90, 106; exports, 2, 7, 62, 74, 77tab, 77–80, 105, 130, 134n83; monoculture, 90; nationalization of, 38; price fluctuation, 2, 77–80; price instability, 73; prices, 96, 111; production, 77; revenues, 8, 98, 105, 117, 118, 130, 318; state investment in, 276tab
Onions, 91, 284, 293; middlemen, 300n67; production, 294tab; yield, 285tab
OPB. See Organization of Planning and Budget
Opposition groups, 34–36; secular, 36
Organization: control of agricultural, 125; of enterprises, 45; large-scale, 243; Western forms, 153
Organization for Agricultural Machines, 286
Organization of Foundations, 226, 227, 228
Organization of Iranian Crafts, 312
Organization of Municipal Property, 231n139
Organization of People's Fada'iyan, 43, 44
Organization of Planning and Budget, 32, 90, 91, 96, 103, 105, 106, 115, 137, 143

Otla rule, 206
Overgrazing, 114–115

Pahlavi, Shah, 2, 204; abdication, 41; agrarian policy, 31–64; failure to reform agriculture, 7, 95, 97; opposition to, 34–36
Panel for the Reform of Consumer Patterns, 119
Panel of Responsibles, 157
Parliamentary Commission for Agriculture, 122, 199n107
Parliamentary Commission for the Institutions of the Revolution, 157
Parliamentary Justice Commission, 203
Parliamentary Planning Commission, 104, 128
Participation, 261–272; shouras in, 263–268
Particularism, 76, 83n13
Partnerships, 47, 237, 238
Party of God, 146, 154
Peasants: agricultural initiatives, 21; banishment, 20, 62; in decisionmaking, 137; income, 23, 110; khoshneshins, 26n23; landowning, 11, 13; leadership, 170; mistrust of government, 23; motivation of, 117; occupation of land, 14, 175, 195n5; per capita income, 17; political power of, 60; provision of services to, 137; radicalization of, 60; and redistribution of land, 169; relations with landlords, 45, 54; relations with shah, 12; relocation, 20; revolt of, 36; and Rural Cooperatives, 16; sale of state land to, 36; standard of living, 63; state interference with, 271–272; as subjects of the state, 22; traditional relations to land and water, 14; wealth among, 60
People's Fada'iyan, 60
People's Mojahidin, 60, 107, 268, 273n33
Pesticides, 100, 113, 241, 283, 287tab
Peyman, H., 50, 52
Policy: agricultural, 2–3, 31–64, 87–92, 275–280; antiparticipatory character of, 21–23; development, 103; economic, 95–100, 118–120; financing, 275–280; foreign trade, 117; marketing, 289–293; objectives, 87–92; opposition thinking, 34–36; pricing, 10, 16, 271, 289–293, 323; social, 95–100
Population: decimation, 15; gaining trust of, 125, 146; growth, 7, 11, 23, 75, 78, 91, 111, 114, 126, 131, 193, 297, 305, 313;

imbalanced structure, 75; participation in decisionmaking, 261–272; preference for agriculture, 96, 126; rural, 8
Potatoes, 91, 292, 293, 296; middlemen, 300n67; per capita production, 297tab; production, 294tab; self-sufficiency in, 126; yield, 285tab
Poultry breeding, 152, 164, 192, 243, 246
Poverty, 11, 58, 182; rural, 173
Premiums, 291
Prices: agrarian, 24; fixed, 289, 290, 292; guaranteed, 289; increases in, 297; industrial products, 24; market, 291; minimum, 20; oil, 2, 73, 77–80, 84n19, 96, 98, 111; policy, 20; wheat, 26n23
Principle of necessity, 187, 214, 216, 220; time limit, 215
Principle of property, 208, 209
Principle of rule, 220
Production, 106; agrarian development, 293–298; agricultural, 8; cereals, 8; collectives, 139; cooperatives, 17; costs, 114, 277, 292; diversification, 106; domestic, 87, 286; Farm Corporations' effect on, 18–19; foreign expectations, 59; inadequacy of, 7–8; increased, 110, 113, 120, 126; industrial, 119, 132n39; maximizing, 275–298; mechanization, 283, 284; modern means, 15; oil, 77; per capita, 296, 297tab; state intervention in, 125; utilization of capacity, 107, 120; wartime, 119
Productive Enterprises, 250
Products: foreign, 55; per capita domestic, 78
Profiteering, 129, 133n77, 289
Property: confiscation of, 174, 181, 188, 201–205, 211; disputes, 174; government attitude on, 106; in Islamic law, 51, 62; joint, 240; landed, 51, 52, 55, 58, 62, 68n105, 185, 198n67, 205–210, 212, 213, 229n22, 323; private, 52, 115, 126, 173; restrictions on, 195n13, 208; rights, 47, 48, 52, 176, 185, 205, 220, 280; sanctity of, 186; sequestration, 211, 252. *See also* Land
Property of Refugees, Disposition of Assets bill, 203
Proposed Legislation on the Establishment of Rural People's Banks, 109
Provincial Councils, 141, 157

Qadam, Sabet, 143, 144, 145

Qomi, Ayatollah, 177, 229n23
Questions of Land Ownership, 250
Quran, 48, 49, 50, 53, 68n97, 131n7, 159, 207, 214, 222, 264, 266, 267; schools, 150

Rabbani, Ayatollah, 197n39
Radicalism, 39
Rafsanjani, President, 80, 85n53, 107, 127, 130, 139, 159, 177, 183, 186, 207, 219, 229n34, 255n16, 318; agricultural policy, 3; and foreign capital, 128; thinking on agriculture, 96
Ramezani, Hojjat ol-Eslam, 212, 213
Rationing, 297
Razawi, Hojjat ol-Eslam, 206, 267
RCs. *See* Rural Cooperatives
Reconstruction, 98–99, 117, 128, 129
Reform: agrarian, 21; agricultural administration, 135–164; of agricultural organization, 233–255; land, 10–14, 169–195; social, 38; tax, 106
Regime, prerevolutionary: agricultural crisis in, 7–25; agricultural policy in, 31–64, 95; criticisms of, 1, 87, 105, 108, 110, 173, 175, 283; land reform in, 10–14, 232n137; legacies to Islamic Republic, 73–76; suppression of communism, 40; theories of agriculture in, 31–64
Reja'i, President, 139
Requirements of rule, 220
Revolution, 60; export of, 89, 130, 318; political, 58; social, 57
Revolutionary Committees, 171, 175
Revolutionary Council, 109, 139, 162, 171, 172, 173, 174, 175, 176, 177, 178, 217, 220, 225, 235, 245, 249
Revolutionary Group of Marxist-Leninists, 66n44
Revolutionary Guards, 171, 175, 207
Revolutionary Institutions, 136, 139, 150, 153, 163, 164, 166n34, 171, 185, 190, 203, 209, 247, 252, 320; Ministry of Jahad-e Sazandegi as, 149, 155–158
Revolutionary Organization of the Tudeh Party, 43, 44
Revolutionary Organization of Workers in Iranian Kurdistan
Revolutionary Organizations: Ministry of Jahad-e Sazandegi as, 147–149
Revolutionary Tribunal, 202
Rice, 88, 123, 131, 287tab, 296, 297;

Index   345

imports, 298*tab*; per capita production, 297*tab*; pricing, 291; production, 294*tab*; self-sufficiency in, 126; yield, 285*tab*
Rights: acquired, 226; inheritance, 204; property, 47, 48, 52, 176, 185, 205, 220, 280; usufructuary, 11, 13, 14, 15, 26*n23*, 40, 51, 52, 68*n105*, 193, 205, 206, 222, 249, 252; water, 40
Rohani, Ayatollah, 177, 209
RPC, *See* Rural Producer Cooperatives
Rule of the dispossessed, 267
Rulership decree, 219, 220, 221
"Rules of Procedure and the Systems of Implementation in the Agricultural Sector," 114
Rural: banks, 109; construction, 106, 152; decisionmaking, 145; depopulation, 23–25, 34, 125, 303–313; education, 114, 137; improvement, 155; industry, 152, 155, 305; migration, 23–25, 62, 108, 113, 182; poverty, 173
Rural Cooperatives, 15, 16; government credit to, 26*n44*; lack of funding, 15
Rural Poles, 15
Rural Producer Cooperatives, 15, 19, 251; dissolution, 242–243, 247–250, 258*n91*; rehabilitation of, 258*n98*
Rushdie, Salman, 129

Sa'adi, General, 160
Sadduqi, Ayatollah, 202
al-Sadeq, Ja'far, 49
Sadr, M. B., 50, 51
Sahabi, Yadollah, 56
Salamati, Minister, 96, 109, 110, 113, 139, 142, 145, 154, 179, 198*n74*, 199*n107*
Sari, 190
Satanic Verses (Rushdie), 129
Saweh, 199*n117*
Sawouji, Hojjat ol-Eslam, 279
Schools, 58, 75, 106, 310; construction of, 149; Quran, 150
Sector, construction: role of migration in, 24
Sector, industrial, 74
Sector, private, 92, 119, 310; economic limits, 106; effect of war on, 119–120; government concessions to, 129; investment, 125, 127; investment in development, 110; in Islamic Republic, 115; limits on, 197*n63*; restrictions on, 116, 237, 262; role in postwar economy, 129
Sector, service, 74, 308; decrease in, 111; profits in, 298*n5*; utilization of capacity, 107
Self-help, 132*n29*; production groups, 245
Self-sufficiency, 7, 132*n29*, 271, 280, 281, 282, 288, 296, 319, 321; as aim of agricultural policy, 62–63, 87–92, 113; critics of, 96; dependency factors, 126; implementation deadlines, 124*tab*; and land reform, 92, 182; organizational structure, 126; planning, 122–127; prospects for, 90–92; references to Islam in, 126; regime's belief in, 91; unrealistic targets, 114, 118; used to legitimize other projects, 92
Sequestration of land, 188, 201–205, 211, 252
Service Centers, 115, 136–139, 153, 242, 245, 248, 249, 251, 268, 270; criticism of, 136, 143, 144, 145–146; evaluations of, 143; preferential treatment in, 145; relations with Village Councils, 145
Sevener Commissions, 161–163, 176, 177, 178, 179, 182, 184, 190, 191, 194, 199*n124*, 250, 268; and foundation estates, 226; land transfers, 194*tab*; and legality of land tenure, 211; and mosha', 239, 256*n41*, 257*n50*; responsibilities, 162; and transfer of land, 189; and wasteland, 224, 281–282. *See also* Edicts
Sharecropping, 11, 18, 21, 37, 45, 47, 52, 66*n52*, 181, 187, 208, 225, 226, 244, 255*n5*, 255*n12*; rehabilitation of, 234–236
Shari'atmadari, Ayatollah, 55
Shell Oil, 20
Sherkat, 237
Shirazi, Ayatollah, 177, 209
Shortages: domestic, 79; food, 297
Shoura, 157, 263–268
Sistan, 164, 170, 266
Slums, 23, 25, 62
Social: equality, 13, 59; infrastructure, 76*tab*; insurance, 32; position, 12; reform, 38; revolution, 57; security, 110, 137; services, 24, 117; tension, 12, 19; welfare, 116
Social Democratic Party, 37, 40
Socialism, 51, 267
Society of Iranian Clerics, 54
Soviet Union, 41
Special Group for Planning Studies, 108

Special Parliamentary Commission for Planning, 120
Squatting, 174, 178, 179, 180, 185, 186, 187, 188–191, 199n113, 199n117, 200n145, 211, 215, 216, 227, 252
Standard of living: in agriculture, 113; and migration, 24; of peasants, 63; rural, 23
State: authoritarianism in, 21; budget, 106, 111, 120–122; decisionmaking of, 2; decrees, 122, 184, 219, 322; disregard for tradition, 8, 10; expansion of authority of, 8; funding of agriculture, 8–9, 23–24; interference in rural areas, 21; intervention in agriculture, 182, 196n21; investment, 116, 125, 276tab, 288tab; investment in agriculture, 126; loans to Rural Cooperatives, 15; opposition groups in, 35; power segmentation, 320; price policy, 16; principle of nonintervention, 139; support for Farm Corporations, 18
State Budget Acts, 81
State intervention: in agriculture, 99, 109, 182, 196n21; economic, 316; in land reform, 60; in peasant matters, 271–272; in private law, 210; in production, 125; in village life, 16, 60
Stock exchange, 129
Subsidization, 289, 290; of agricultural products, 287; of Farm Corporations, 18; of Rural Producer Cooperatives, 19; for urban population, 10, 272
Sugar, 88, 123, 251, 284, 296; imports of, 7; per capita production, 297tab; production, 294tab; yield, 285tab
Supreme Council of Justice, 189, 202, 205, 212, 213
Supreme Court of Inquiry, 203, 212, 213
Supreme Defense Council, 81
Supreme Economic Council, 237, 289
Survey of Feudalism and the Efforts of the Sevener Commissions, 179

Tabrizi, Hojjat ol-Eslam, 202, 217
Taleqani, Ayatollah, 50, 52, 55, 56, 58, 264
Taslit rule, 47
Tawwakolli, Minister, 80
Tax, 279; bases, 79; exemptions, 18, 20; increases, 79; land, 46; poor, 46, 54, 109, 173, 229n24; reduction, 36; reform, 106; religious, 180, 202, 206, 208, 221; revenues, 116; on self-employed, 74, 79

Technology, 138; dependence in, 97; inappropriate use of, 9, 20; provision of, 97
Tehrani, Ali, 50, 55, 88, 206, 235
Tenancy, 45
Textiles, 246
Third Force, 38, 39, 64n8
Tithes, 46, 47, 54, 206, 229n24; abolition of, 7
Trade: embargo by U.S., 82; foreign, 74, 89, 117, 129; international, 128; in Islamic law, 46; retail, 129
Tradition: in animal husbandry, 115; disregard for, 8, 9, 10, 17, 25, 143
Tudeh Party, 36, 41, 42, 43, 44, 65n30, 132n35
Tufan Organization, 43, 44
Turkmen, 170, 240, 264
Tusi, Sheikh, 207
Tuyul system, 37, 65n15

Ulama, 51, 54, 55, 323; bureaucracy of, 323; as landowners, 55; and land reform, 212; monopoly on power, 107, 265; position on reforms, 55
Unemployment, 18, 58, 75, 96, 106, 110, 119, 245, 255n12, 313; hidden, 75
Union of Peasants, 41
United Nations Resolution 598, 80, 120, 127
United States: influence of, 54; protection of shah, 57; trade embargo, 82
Urban construction, 106
Urbanization, 8; slums in, 23, 25, 62
Urban-rural division, 23–25, 105, 303–313
Usury, 47, 202, 210

Village Councils, 114, 137, 139, 141, 143, 150, 163, 178, 186, 268–271, 306, 320; relations with Service Centers, 145
Villages: depopulation of, 125; destruction of, 20, 24, 82; social functions, 18; social position in, 12; traditional structure, 11, 17, 18, 24

Wa'ezi, Hojjat ol-Eslam, 208, 267
Waqf, 207
War with Iraq, 2, 73, 80–82; armistice, 120, 160; effect on development planning, 119–120; effect on oil industry, 78, 82; priority over agriculture, 97–98; reconstruction program, 81, 85n49, 98–99, 117, 128, 129
Wasteland, 54, 68n105, 172, 178, 180, 210,

281–282; distribution of, 222; in Islamic law, 221–225; misappropriation of, 202; in mosha's, 240, 241; nationalization of, 223; private, 223; reclamation, 47, 48, 52, 58, 108, 182

Water, 58, 95; distribution, 280; drinking, 306; hamab groups, 254; investment for, 299n23; management, 106; projects, 125; rights, 40; sources, 91; state investment in, 9, 276tab; traditional installations, 62; use, 155, 280–283

West Azerbaijan, 254

Wheat, 88, 91, 109, 123, 130, 152, 245, 246, 251, 271, 287tab; imports, 274n62, 298tab; per capita production, 297tab; pricing, 26n23, 289, 290tab, 291; production, 294tab, 295; yield, 285tab

White Revolution, 21, 53, 56, 68n99, 69n119

Yad rule, 209, 230n57
Yazd, 169, 255
Yazdi, Ayatollah, 185, 208, 231n80, 267
Yield, agricultural: mechanization in, 10; methods of raising, 283–289; from nonirrigated land, 25n15; raising, 123

Zabolis, 170
Zali, Minister, 90, 95, 99, 139, 146, 153, 295
Zangane, Minister, 152, 153
Zanjan, 188
Zanjani, Minister, 81, 295
Zarar rule, 206, 209

About the Book and Author

Schirazi uses agricultural policy to demonstrate the complications and consequences resulting from the Islamization of development policy in Iran.

Refuting claims by Iran's religious leaders that their interpretation of Islam provides the best possible solution for development problems, not only in Iran, but throughout the world, the author concludes from his research that the conception of Islam as an ideological basis for development policy must change radically if it is to make any contribution to solving the problems that it faces.

Asghar Schirazi is research associate in the Department of Political Science, Middle East Studies Section, at the Free University of Berlin. His research focuses on the sociology of development.